Jose Nava

The epistemological orientation of educational research

Jose Nava

The epistemological orientation of educational research

The philosophy, theory, methodology, technique and instruments for conducting research in the educational sciences

ScienciaScripts

Imprint

Any brand names and product names mentioned in this book are subject to trademark, brand or patent protection and are trademarks or registered trademarks of their respective holders. The use of brand names, product names, common names, trade names, product descriptions etc. even without a particular marking in this work is in no way to be construed to mean that such names may be regarded as unrestricted in respect of trademark and brand protection legislation and could thus be used by anyone.

Cover image: www.ingimage.com

This book is a translation from the original published under ISBN 978-3-659-01752-0.

Publisher:
Sciencia Scripts
is a trademark of
Dodo Books Indian Ocean Ltd. and OmniScriptum S.R.L publishing group

120 High Road, East Finchley, London, N2 9ED, United Kingdom
Str. Armeneasca 28/1, office 1, Chisinau MD-2012, Republic of Moldova, Europe
Printed at: see last page
ISBN: 978-620-8-32430-8

Contents:

The epistemological orientation of educational research

Philosophical assumptions, theoretical foundations,
methodological procedures, technical strategies and
instruments for conducting research in the
educational
sciences.

DR. JOSÉ NAVA BEDOLLA

PRESENTATION

The title of this work explains, in a summarised way, its content. The work reconstructs a fundamentally problematic idea in the development of any enquiry carried out in the educational sciences: the *epistemological orientation* of the research.

This book is aimed at bachelor's, master's and doctoral students in general and, in particular, at anyone interested in research training in the field of educational sciences.

The *epistemological orientation* of the research carried out in the educational sciences is related to certain more common ideas that are observed in any research process: the theoretical framework and the methodological framework or, if preferred, the theoretical-methodological framework.

The category "*epistemological orientation*" does not exclude the above ideas. On the contrary, it recovers them in a broader concept, which includes - in addition to the *theoretical* and *methodological* - the *philosophical*, *technical* and *instrumental* levels of any knowledge process; that is to say, an epistemological orientation is composed of five elements: philosophical, theoretical, methodological, technical and instrumental.

The concept of "*epistemological orientation*" is constructed on the basis that knowledge is a problem, because in all educational research, understood as a process, there is a relationship between two different entities that belong to different worlds, that is, to realities that are not at all similar: the researcher (the cognising subject) and the research (the object to be known).

The spheres of the researcher and his object of research are the *psychological* (the soul) and the *ontological* (the concrete or abstract reality), respectively; therefore, such a *relationship* is not possible in essence, that is, a real contact between the *main elements of knowledge* (subject and object) is not achieved, because they belong to different epistemological planes; therefore, the *relationship of knowledge* can only be established from the qualities that the cognising subject has to relate to the object to be known: his *reason* and his *senses*.

The knowledge relationship between the cognising subject and the object to be known is established in the *logical sphere*; it is only language, a discourse that the cognising subject elaborates, based on his perceptions (sensations) and reasoning (thoughts) about the object. Such a discourse is constructed on the basis of the way the educational researcher solves each and every one of the following *problems of knowledge*: possibility (dogmatism, scepticism, subjectivism, relativism, pragmatism, criticism), origin (rationalism, empiricism, intellectualism, apriorism), essence (*pre-metaphysical solution* - objectivism, subjectivism, dialectics - , *metaphysical solution* - realism, idealism, phenomenalism - , *theological solution* - dualism and theism, monism and pantheism -), classification (rational knowledge, intuitive knowledge) and concepts and criteria of truth (transcendent and immanent). These philosophical problems of knowledge, the educational researcher can solve them from reason, from the senses or from both qualities of the cognising subject and, in doing so, he falls - whether he knows it or not - into a certain philosophical assumption of the above mentioned, solving each and every one of the philosophical problems of knowledge also indicated.

Each *problem of knowledge* (possibility, origin, essence, classification, and concepts and criteria of truth) can be solved by the researcher from any of the different *philosophical assumptions* mentioned (those in brackets after each problem of knowledge), depending on his epistemological and ontological interests, but above all, depending on whether he has derived them from reason, from the senses, or from both qualities of the cognising subject.

The *philosophical* level of an epistemological orientation is the first link in the gnoseological chain, where every researcher must locate his object of study; because this step is decisive for choosing the *theoretical* foundations with which the cognising subject will problematise the reality he is investigating.

The next level on which the researcher must place himself, after the *philosophical* one, is the *theoretical* one. Depending on the *philosophical assumptions* from which the educational researcher solves each and every one of the five main philosophical problems of knowledge, he/she will have the need to choose one or some of the *general theories of knowledge* (mathematics, mechanicism, organicism, chaos, conflict, complexity), *particular to the social sciences* (positivism, functionalism, structuralism, historicism, Marxism) and *specific to the educational sciences* (behaviourism, psychoanalysis, humanism, cognitivism, psychogenetics, sociocultural), in order to problematise their objects of study.

The third level is *methodological*. Depending on the *theories* with which the researcher has problematised the educational reality, he/she must choose a *methodological procedure* or *intellectual operation* (addition, subtraction, multiplication, division, analysis, synthesis, synthesis, indication, deduction, classification, comparison, definition) to construct new knowledge about the educational phenomenon under study.

The fourth level of an epistemological orientation is the *technical* level. Based on the *method* or *methods* that the educational researcher has used to generate new knowledge, he/she will need to choose one or more *technical strategies* to learn about the educational reality that he/she intends to investigate. Only four *techniques* are known to know the reality: observation, experimentation, survey and documentary.

Fifth and lastly, the topic of the *instruments* to collect information on the object of study is developed. Depending on the *technique* used to learn about reality, the *instrument* or *instruments* used to collect empirical or theoretical data will be chosen. The *observation instrument* is the register, which can be quantitative or qualitative; the documentary instrument is the *work sheet*; the survey instruments are the *questionnaire* and the *interview*, quantitative or qualitative; and, finally, the *experiment* is carried out with the materials required.

Therefore, an idea of *perspective, paradigm* or *epistemological orientation* is proposed, understood as a stance taken by the educational researcher with respect to each and every one of the five problems of knowledge mentioned above.

Five *epistemological elements* or *levels* that are present in any research process are suggested: philosophical, theoretical, methodological, technical and instrumental. It is clear that these elements or epistemological levels are mutually determined, in a descending manner, in every educational research process. Thus, the *theoretical foundations*, with which the objects of study are problematised, depend on the *philosophical assumptions*, from which reality is observed; the *methodological procedures*, with which new knowledge is generated, have their origin in the theoretical foundations; the *technical strategies*, with which reality is known, are derived from the methodological procedures; and finally, the *instruments*, with which the information is collected, are derived from the technical strategies.

Three *epistemological orientations* are characterised: objectivist, subjectivist and dialectical; as a result of the researcher's stance on the problem of knowledge, when choosing one or other of the different proposals that refer to the philosophical assumptions, theoretical foundations, methodological procedures, technical strategies and instruments, in order to carry out his work.

It is concluded that, because the different proposals contained in each and every one of the levels or elements mentioned above constitute a position on the problem of knowledge, it is not possible to define a single epistemological orientation for carrying out research in the educational sciences; everything will depend on the object of study and the epistemological and ontological inclinations of the researcher.

It is possible to conclude, among other things already mentioned, that the work that is now in the hands of any reader interested in the subject, tries to become a manual to train and educate in, by and for research in the field of educational sciences. At the same time as this work, we are preparing a proposal for a research project that will make it possible, in the not too distant future, to establish the theory-practice relationship of research carried out in the field of educational sciences.

CHAPTER 1

THE DEFINITION OF EPISTEMOLOGICAL ORIENTATION.
Elements for its construction

1. THE DEFINITION OF EPISTEMOLOGICAL ORIENTATION. Elements for its construction.

The *epistemological orientation* of educational research can be placed in the field of *epistemology*, a branch of philosophy which, among other things, deals with the problem of knowledge, i.e. answering questions such as: is it possible to know, what is the source and basis of our knowledge, how does the relationship between the subject and the object of knowledge take place, how many types of knowledge exist, what are the criteria for determining whether knowledge is true or not, what are the criteria for determining whether knowledge is true or not, what are the criteria for determining whether knowledge is true or not, and what are the criteria for determining whether knowledge is true or not.

For this reason, it is necessary, first of all, to analyse the concept of *epistemology* in order to be able to speak of an *epistemological orientation* of the research carried out in the educational sciences.

1.1 EPISTEMOLOGY, UNDERSTOOD AS THE THEORY OF SCIENCE OR KNOWLEDGE OF KNOWLEDGE (META-SCIENCE).

Also called *theory of knowledge* and, less frequently, *gnoseology* (Ortiz, 2003:152), *epistemology* is understood - etymologically - by Dagoberto D. Runes (1998:114-117) as a branch of philosophy that studies the origin, structure, methods and validity of knowledge (from the Greek *episteme*, knowledge; and *logos*, theory).

Literally, *epistemology* is understood as a discourse (logos) on science (*episteme*) (Miguélez, 1997:7). The concept designates a *general theory of knowledge*.

The Anglo-Saxon and French traditions understand *epistemology* as *philosophy of science* and as *epistemology, theory of knowledge* or *gnoseology*, respectively.

Piaget, according to Rolando García (2000: 25) understands *epistemology* (from psychology), as a theory of scientific knowledge, in order to base the study of genetic epistemology, as the study of the mechanisms of the development of scientific knowledge. In this way, Piaget intends to give a scientific character (understood as scientific method) to the new science that, according to him, he was characterising (genetic epistemology).

The need to define epistemological orientations makes it necessary to understand *epistemology* simply as an idea about science, about knowledge, about its problems and limits, about its constructions, etc.; that is to say, it implies philosophical, theoretical, methodological, technical and instrumental levels.

For the purposes of this paper, *epistemology* is understood as a branch of philosophy which, whatever it is called (philosophy of science, general theory of science, etc.) deals with the philosophical (possibility, origin, essence, classification, criteria of truth, etc.), theoretical, methodological, technical and instrumental problems of knowledge, its scope and limitations. It is, following Miguélez, a discourse on science; science understood as the construction of knowledge.

In this study, knowledge in general is analysed. If science is understood as knowledge, then so-called scientific knowledge is only one of the four possibilities of human fulfilment; the other three are philosophy, religion and art. In this research the knowledge of knowledge in science and education is analysed.

1.1.1   *The etymological origin of the definition of "epistemology".*

The idea, "epistemology", comes from the Greek *episteme* meaning "knowledge" and *logos* meaning "treatise", "theory" or "study".

Etymologically, epistemology means "the study of knowledge". *Epistemology* is concerned with knowledge and the knowledge related to it, the types of knowledge, its sources and the relationship between the subject who knows and the object to be known. Epistemology is also concerned with the degree of certainty that each individual establishes in his or her idea of the object of knowledge (Gutiérrez, 2007:8).

1.1.2   *The dynamics of the idea of "epistemology".*

The term *epistemology* began to become widespread at the end of the 19th century, replacing the older term *theory of knowledge* and, later, *gnoseology*. However, it is somewhat ambiguous, so that it is not always used in the same sense. When attributed a traditional meaning, it refers to the critical study of the conditions and possibility of knowledge in general, concerned with answering questions such as what can we know, or how do we know that what we believe about the world is true? In this case its object of study coincides with that of the *theory of knowledge*. But recently it has been attributed the function of dealing with all cognitive processes, including that of science (Gutiérrez, 2007:9).

For Blanché (1973) *epistemology* is a theory of science. Epistemology is a reflection on science. *Epistemology* is a meta-science. Meta-science is understood as the union between the scientific and the philosophical (we will return to this in the section on the relationship between philosophy and theory).

Blanché (1973: 8) states that "*...meta-science is the study that follows a science and deals with it, taking it in turn as its object and asking at a higher level about its principles, foundations, structures, conditions of validity, etc...". Epistemology, which is a reflection on science, with this title becomes part of meta-science....*".

Blanché (1973: 13) also states that "*... the relationship of epistemology with the theory of knowledge is that between the species and the genus, epistemology being limited to a single form of knowledge: scientific knowledge...*".

Blanché is right when he says that *epistemology* is a meta-science, i.e. knowledge of knowledge; but one disagrees with him when he says that epistemology only deals with scientific knowledge. In reality *epistemology* should be considered as knowledge of knowledge in general. *Epistemology* is knowledge of scientific, religious, artistic and philosophical knowledge; as we will try to prove throughout the present study. With the proviso that the present investigation is directed, in a preponderant way, to the investigation that is carried out from the educational sciences.

1.1.3   *The current discussion on the definition of "epistemology".*

The difficulty in categorising - establishing the specific determinations of the elements that make up the object, i.e. imputing or establishing its properties - of the term *epistemology* is due to the fact that it has been given as many meanings as scholars have been interested in understanding it. In Anglo-Saxon influenced countries *epistemology* is *philosophy of science* or *logic of science*; in the French tradition a distinction is made between the generic reflection on science, *philosophy of science*, and the historical and critical study of knowledge, its principles, methods and results. *Epistemology*, for us, is theory of knowledge (Gutiérrez, 2007:10).

Given that it is difficult to establish an exact, specific and commonly accepted definition of what we should understand by *epistemology* due to the complexity of the definition; for the purposes of this research, epistemology is proposed generically as *the knowledge of knowledge* (Gutiérrez, 2007:11). That is, as a branch of philosophy that deals with the problem of knowledge.

Knowledge, as the object of study of *epistemology*, refers us to problems such as the concept, characteristics, functions, purposes, classifications, possibilities, etc., of knowledge.

Knowledge, as will be seen below, is defined on the basis of different philosophical assumptions. Depending on how the cognising subject solves each and every one of the five main philosophical problems of knowledge. For *epistemology* is a branch of philosophy that deals with the problem of knowledge, in general.

Epistemology, or knowledge of knowledge, has the determining function of helping us to solve the problems of knowledge: its possibility, origin, essence, classification and concepts and criteria of truth; its theoretical foundations, methodological procedures, technical strategies and instruments; among others.

1.2 EPISTEMOLOGICAL ORIENTATIONS AND EDUCATIONAL SCIENCES.

In order to clarify the issue of the conception of an epistemological orientation of educational research, including its philosophical assumptions, theoretical foundations, methodological procedures, technical strategies and instruments for conducting research in the field of educational sciences, it is necessary to divide this sub-chapter into two sections: educational sciences and epistemological orientations.

1.2.1 *Educational sciences*.

In a logical sense, "to define" means to set limits, i.e. to express what an object is without adding to it or taking away from it. In this case we are dealing with two concepts: "science" and "education" and/or their respective plurals. Thus, the first question would be: is there one or several sciences of education?

On the unity or plurality of the science of education (or of the sciences of education) there are different opinions: some defend the existence of a single science of education represented by Pedagogy; others, in addition to considering Pedagogy as the "general science of education", admit the existence of other sciences which, however, do not become independent of the first; A third group considers the existence of a set of sciences of education independent of each other, with the common denominator of considering education as a formal object of study, but from different perspectives; and finally, there are those who give the label "sciences of education" to any science directly or indirectly related to education, even if they do not have it as their own object of study.

The personal position in this respect is in line with that of the curricula of the Masters in Educational Research and the Doctorate in Educational Sciences of the Instituto Superior de Ciencias de la Educación del Estado de México (ISCEEM), which considers the existence of a group of sciences that have education as a common object of study, but each one of them looks at it from a specific perspective, considering the multi-referential nature of the educational phenomenon.

Without pretending to carry out an epistemological analysis in this respect, for the moment, it is necessary to clarify that any definition, of any object of study, is established from a certain worldview, with the support of some theory, following certain paths or steps, using a technique and by means of suitable instruments.

Nominally, by "science", it is intended to mean "knowledge" and by "education", "directing, guiding, indoctrinating", etc. In this sense, "educational sciences" could be understood as "all those activities that direct, guide or lead us towards knowledge"; a very poor definition, in explanatory terms, so, dispensing with it, we will try to elaborate another one that is more realistic; that lists the most typical properties of the object; that describes its essential attributes; that is clear; that is brief but complete, that is to say, exact; and that applies to everything and only to what is defined.

This is only possible logically, but not epistemologically. The concepts of science and education vary according to the philosophical, theoretical, methodological, technical and instrumental position of the cognising subject; thus "science" has been taken to mean "a body of true knowledge", "a body of probably true knowledge that develops historically", "a body of knowledge that is probably true, fallible and incomplete", "a body of hypotheses that are put forward as a test", etc. Similarly, by "education" can be understood "the procedure by which the dominant classes prepare in the mentality and conduct of children the fundamental conditions of their own existence", or "the action exercised by the adult generations on those who are not yet mature for social life, which aims to arouse and develop in the child a certain number of physical, intellectual and moral states required of him by the political society as a whole and the special environment to which he is particularly subjected", etc. The conceptual difference between Marxism and positivism is to be noted.

A first approach to the concept of "educational sciences" from a descriptive, rather than explanatory, approach could be the following:

A set of disciplines which, from different philosophical, theoretical, methodological, technical and instrumental perspectives, make education their object of study. These perspectives or paradigms can also be called epistemological orientations, which is the case of the present study and whose conception is developed in the following lines.

1.2.2 *Epistemological orientations*.

The sciences that take education as a common object of study, approaching it from different *perspectives*, raise the problem of agreeing on what we should understand by different scientific *perspectives* - what are these different *perspectives* of the sciences?

A *perspective* is understood in terms of looking closely. It is the determination of the inclusiveness of what can have reality for an organism. The *point of view* from which an individual considers other existing things (Runes, 1998:287).

The connotation of a research *perspective* is similar to that of a *paradigm*. A research *paradigm* refers to the "...beliefs, values, techniques, etc., shared by members of a given *scientific community*." (Kuhn, 1999: 269). In that sense, *paradigms*, to paraphrase Kuhn, are the universally recognised scientific achievements that, over a period of time, provide models of problems and solutions to a scientific community. That is to say, some accepted examples of scientific practice provide models from which traditions consistent with scientific research emerge; a kind of synthesis of scientific development that attracts the majority of practitioners of the next generation, with the old ones disappearing (Kuhn, 1999: 269317).

Paradigm means model and *scientific paradigm* characterises, rather than defining, the conceptual and methodological framework in which the problems of scientific research are posed and, successively, solved, constituting a more or less coherent whole through which the researcher relates to his study objectives. For Kuhn, this task makes up the so-called "normal science", in which the theoretical, scientific and philosophical bases of the *paradigm* are not questioned, being often implicit in the language used by the scientific community as a common disciplinary matrix (Khun, 1999:280).

The idea of a research *paradigm* is related to that of a *scientific community*: *"A paradigm is what the members of a scientific community share and, conversely, a scientific community consists of people who share a paradigm...".* Kuhn (1999: 271). The ideas of *perspective* or *paradigm* are equated with that of *epistemological orientation*. The meaning of these refers to the philosophical assumptions, theoretical foundations, methodological procedures, technical strategies and instruments that members of a given *scientific community* or *research tradition* use in conducting their research.

Interpreting Kunn and Runes, the members of a *scientific community*, depending on the research *paradigm* to which they adhere and in consideration of the research *perspective* from which they construct their objects of study, share certain philosophical assumptions, to observe reality, in this case, educational reality; certain theoretical foundations, to problematise the objects of study of education; diverse methodological procedures, to generate new educational knowledge; some technical strategies, to know the pedagogical phenomenon; and certain instruments, to collect data, etc.In other words, certain programmes or ways of conducting research to construct their objects of study, which are transmitted to the researchers who join the community in order to learn the *perspective* or *paradigm* shared by the members of the scientific *community*. The scientific *community* guides the research training process and this research training process will be adapted - philosophically, theoretically, methodologically, technically and instrumentally - to the *paradigm* or research *perspective* from which the scientific *community* constructs its objects of study.

The research *paradigm*, the *perspective* (philosophical, theoretical, methodological, technical and instrumental) to which a *scientific community* adheres in order to carry out research, provides the *research model* for the community and commits it professionally in terms of the problems to be addressed for scientific analysis and in terms of the rules for considering them as admissible and their legitimate solution. Scientific activity is based on commitments and agreements between the members of the *scientific community* on the *paradigm* or *perspective* from which they must construct their objects of study, at first; at a second moment, this agreement or commitment commits the members of the community to the type of problems that must be investigated from this perspective; and, at a third moment, they must also agree on the rules for their admission or rejection and even the guidelines on the basis of which the solutions given to the problems will be admitted.

The ideas of *perspective* and *paradigm*, in the above sense, are related to the concepts coined by Lakatos (2001) and Laudan (1986): research *programmes* and research *traditions*, respectively. However, for the purposes of establishing agreement on definitions, three significant dimensions must be distinguished: first, Kuhn clearly establishes that the concept *"paradigm"* designates the theoretical, scientific and philosophical bases that, based on the beliefs, values and techniques shared by the members of a *scientific community* to carry out research, serve as assumptions, foundations, etc. for the construction of the objects of study; it refers to the *epistemological* problem. Second, it also refers to the *scientific community* as the group of researchers who share that paradigm. Third, the assumptions and foundations used by the group of researchers refer to a very original *way* of doing research. Lakatos, on the other hand, is more concerned with the *way* scientific research is conducted, with its *research programmes*; and Laudan is more interested in specifying research *traditions*, i.e., the name to be given to the different groups that conduct research from different *perspectives*; that is, the second significant dimension, scientific *communities*, like Kuhn, or research *traditions*, understood as "....*sets of general assumptions about the entities and processes of a domain of study, and about the appropriate methods to be used to investigate the problems and construct the theories of that domain*" (Laudan, 1986:116).

In this sense, the problem increases: what are the *perspectives, paradigms*, from which educational research can be carried out, what are the scientific *communities* or research *traditions* that construct their objects of study from these perspectives, paradigms, and what are the *programmes* or *ways* of producing knowledge that, based on the perspectives or paradigms, are used by the scientific communities or research traditions to generate new knowledge?

This paper will attempt to define the concept, state the elements, establish the characteristics, describe the functions, determine the aims and propose a classification of *epistemological orientations*; also called, by the aforementioned authors, perspectives or research paradigms. The analysis of the scientific communities or research traditions and their programmes or modes of knowledge production, which depend on the epistemological orientation from which they construct their objects of study, will be left for future work.

When Kuhn refers to *paradigms* or *research perspectives* as the conceptual and methodological frameworks from which scientific research can be carried out; or as the theoretical, scientific and philosophical bases from which it is possible for different *scientific communities* (called by Laudan *research traditions*) to construct their objects of study, in accordance with certain common beliefs, values and techniques; It is possible to infer that he refers, although he does not specify them properly, to several *epistemological levels or dimensions* that can be considered to carry out research; such as the philosophical assumptions, from which reality can be analysed; the theoretical foundations, with which the objects of study can be problematised; the methodological procedures, with which new knowledge can be generated; the technical strategies, to learn about reality; and the instruments, to gather the information needed to carry out the research work.

To characterise these *perspectives* or research *paradigms*, I think it is more appropriate to use the term *epistemological orientations*, because they guide, i.e. direct or direct *scientific communities* to a certain form or *way* of doing research; they also impose, or place the burden, obligation, etc., and instruct research traditions, or scientific communities, on certain philosophical assumptions, from which they must start in order to analyse reality; certain theoretical foundations, which they need to consider in order to problematise the objects of research, and instruct research *traditions*, or scientific *communities*, on certain *philosophical* assumptions, from which they must start to analyse reality; certain *theoretical* foundations, which they need to consider to problematise the objects of study; various *methodological* procedures, which they must follow to generate new knowledge; some *technical* strategies, which are necessary to know the phenomena; and certain *instruments*, which are required to collect the information with which the objects of study will be constructed.

These *horizons* (as it is also possible to consider them) or *epistemological orientations* inform, inform, inform, inform about the *ways* or *forms* of producing knowledge.

Epistemological orientations instruct, teach, doctrine, communicate, etc., ideas, knowledge or epistemological doctrine; they make known *ways* or *modes* of conducting research and inform scientific *traditions* or *communities* about how research can, and should, be conducted.

They are *epistemological orientations* because they refer to the knowledge of knowledge (Gutiérrez, 1997); that is, to the problems of knowing. *Epistemology* has also been called "*theory of knowledge*" and, less frequently, "*gnoseology*". Regardless of the name assigned to *epistemology*, in this study, and in order to characterise *the orientations*

epistemological, it is understood as already stated: knowledge of knowledge, meta-science.

Epistemological orientations are stances on the problems of knowledge, i.e. on the way in which the five problems of knowledge (philosophical, theoretical, methodological, technical and instrumental) can be solved: the philosophical assumptions with which the problems of knowledge are solved (possibility, origin, essence, classification and criteria of truth; the *theoretical* foundations, to problematise the objects of study; the *methodological* procedures, to generate new knowledge; the *technical* strategies to learn about reality; and the *instruments*, to collect information about the objects of study. These are, practically speaking, *perspectives* or *paradigms* for locating, knowing and acting on reality, in the Kuhnian sense.

In the field of education, the *epistemological orientation* of pedagogical research refers to the *philosophical assumptions*, from which it is possible to start to solve the five philosophical problems of knowledge (possibility, origin, essences, classification and concept and criteria of truth); the *theoretical foundations*, from which phenomena can be problematised; the *methodological procedures*, which can be used to generate new knowledge; the *technical strategies*, which can be used to learn about reality; and the *instruments*, which serve to collect the information we need to analyse.

In order to study the *philosophical assumptions* of any perspective, paradigm or epistemological orientation, from which reality can be analysed, depending on the quality with which the cognising subject solves each and every one of the five main problems of knowledge (with reason, with the senses or with both), we rely mainly on the brilliant work of Hessen (2011). This German author analyses the five main philosophical problems of knowledge: its possibility, origin, essence, types and criteria of truth. The problem of the *possibility of knowledge* can be solved differently from six different philosophical assumptions (dogmatism, scepticism, relativism, subjectivism, pragmatism and criticism). The problem of the *origin of knowledge* can be solved, also differently, by four different philosophical assumptions (rationalism, empiricism, apriorism and intellectualism). In the problem about the *essence of knowledge* three possible solutions are posed: *pre-metaphysical* (which can be solved by three different philosophical hypotheses: objectivism, subjectivism and dialectics), *metaphysical* (which can be solved by three different philosophical criteria: realism, idealism and phenomenalism) and *theological* (which can be solved by two different philosophical estimations: dualism and theism and monism and pantheism). The problem about the *types of knowledge* can be solved from three different philosophical conjectures: rational knowledge, intuitive knowledge and mixed knowledge. And, finally, the problem about the *truth criteria* of knowledge can be solved from four different philosophical presuppositions: transcendent or immanent concepts of truth and transcendent or immanent criteria of truth.

In order to analyse the *theoretical foundations* with which educational reality can be problematised, we based ourselves mainly on the great achievements of Gabriel Gutierrez Pantoja (1984), Alan F. Chalmers (1999) and CONALTE (1993), respectively, from which it was possible to classify *the theoretical foundations* that allow any reality in the field of educational sciences to be problematised into three large groups: general theories of knowledge (mathematics, mechanism, mechanicism, organicism, chaos, conflict, complexity, etc.), particular theories of social sciences (positivism, functionalism, structuralism, Marxism, systems theory, historicism, phenomenology, hermeneutics, etc.) and specific theories of educational sciences (positivism, functionalism, structuralism, Marxism, systems theory, historicism, phenomenology, hermeneutics, etc.) and theories of educational sciences.), particular to the social sciences (positivism, functionalism, structuralism, Marxism, systems theory, historicism, phenomenology, hermeneutics, etc.) and specific to the educational sciences (behaviourism, psychoanalysis, humanism, cognitivism, psychogenetics, sociocultural, etc.).

To explain the *methodological procedures* or intellectual operations, with which the cognising subject can generate new knowledge about reality, we base ourselves mainly on the logic of Copi (2000), who, together with other specialists in Logic, allowed us to classify the main intellectual operations or methodological procedures that the cognising subject can carry out to generate new knowledge about his object of study into: addition, subtraction, multiplication, division, analysis, synthesis, induction, deduction, abduction, definition, classification, comparison, etc.

In order to understand the *technical strategies* with which the cognising subject can learn about reality, we base ourselves on the proposal of Dieterich (2003), who analyses each and every one of the technical strategies for learning about reality, which are: observation, experimentation, survey and documentation.

The *instruments* used to collect information can be classified, according to Hernández (2000), as follows: register, items, questionnaire, survey and worksheet, among others.

A first approximation to the *definition* of the concept of *epistemological orientation* can be stated as follows: an *epistemological orientation* consists of the philosophical assumptions from which the cognising subject solves each and every one of the five main philosophical problems of knowledge, the theoretical foundations with which the objects of study are problematised, the methodological procedures or intellectual operations to generate knowledge, the technical strategies to know reality and the instruments to collect data, of any research process. The five levels of knowledge (philosophical, theoretical, methodological, technical and instrumental) can be resolved with the senses, with reason or with both qualities of the cognising subject.

The difference between the philosophical assumptions, theoretical foundations, methodological procedures, technical strategies and instruments of epistemological orientations is one of degree; of epistemological level.

1.3 SUMMARY OF THE CHAPTER.

Epistemology is a theory of science, of knowledge; because science means knowledge. *Epistemology* is not science, it is not scientific knowledge; it is meta-science, because it is knowledge of knowledge, it is theory of science. *Episteme* means knowledge, but it does not refer to the knowledge of reality, but to the knowledge of how reality is known, it is a theory (knowledge too) about how that reality is known. It is one thing to know phenomena (scientific knowledge) and another thing to know how phenomena are known (knowledge of knowledge). The former is science, the latter meta-science.

To do epistemology, researchers stand on science and ask not what reality is (scientific knowledge) but how reality is known (knowledge of scientific knowledge). Epistemologists (if you want to call us that) are interested in knowing how reality is known.

In the field of education, for example, we *epistemologists* are not interested in Durkheim's (2000: 74) definition of education as "... *the action exercised by the adult generations on those who are not yet mature for social life - and whose purpose is to arouse and develop in the child a certain number of physical, intellectual and moral states which are required of him by political society as a whole and by the special environment to which he is particularly destined*". Nor is it of interest to us that Ponce (1998: 224) has defined it, in a different way, as ".*the procedure by which the dominant classes prepare in the mentality and conduct of children the fundamental conditions of their own existence".*

Epistemologists are interested in knowing, among other things, from where both authors solved the five main philosophical problems of knowledge (possibility, origin, essence, classification and criteria of truth), in order to suppose what they supposed convenient about the definition of the concept of education; with which theories (general theories of knowledge, particular theories of social sciences and specific theories of educational sciences) they problematised the concept of education, in order to estimate what they estimated; which were the intellectual operations or methodological procedures (methods) with which they assumed what they assumed; with which technical strategies they conjectured what they conjectured and, finally, which instruments they used to gather information on their object of study.

Each and every one of the five *epistemological* problems mentioned, the educational researcher solves them, whether he knows it or not, from reason, from the senses or from both qualities of the cognising subject.

In conclusion, epistemologists are interested in knowing whether the aforementioned authors constructed the concept of education from reason, from the senses or from both qualities of the cognising subject.

An *epistemological orientation* refers to the stance the researcher takes on the five problems of knowledge (philosophical, theoretical, methodological, technical and instrumental).

The educational researcher, when constructing knowledge, places himself (whether he knows it or not) on a higher plane than science, that is, on a meta-scientific plane; because, even if he ignores it, the exploration, description, explanation, interpretation and understanding of the educational phenomenon that he carries out depends on whether he solves each and every one of the philosophical, theoretical, methodological, technical and instrumental problems of knowledge with reason, with the senses or with both qualities of the cognising subject.

It can be concluded that the relationship between the *educational sciences* and *epistemological orientations* consists in the fact that all knowledge that is constructed in the *educational sciences* will depend, irremediably, on whether the educational researcher solves each and every one of the five main problems of knowledge (philosophical, theoretical, methodological, technical and instrumental) with his reason, with his senses or with both qualities of the cognising subject. Philosophy determines theory, theory influences methodology, methodology is the cause of technique and technique influences the instrument. If the educational researcher "looks" with his reason, he constructs certain knowledge, if he looks with his senses, he constructs a knowledge totally contrary to the one he elaborated with his mind, and if he looks with both qualities of the cognising subject, he knows reality in a conciliatory way between both extremes.

CHAPTER 2

ELEMENTS OF AN EPISTEMOLOGICAL ORIENTATION.
Knowledge as a process.
II. ELEMENTS OF AN EPISTEMOLOGICAL ORIENTATION.
Knowledge understood as a process.

From the definition of "epistemological orientation", it can be inferred that its elements are: the *philosophical* assumptions, from which the researcher can solve each and every one of the five philosophical problems of knowledge (possibility, origin, essence, classification and concept and criterion of truth); the *theoretical* foundations, with which the objects of study can be problematised; the *methodological* procedures or intellectual operations, with which new knowledge can be generated; the *technical* strategies, to know the reality; and the *instruments*, to collect the information. Before analysing the above elements, it is necessary to clarify some ideas about the problems of knowledge.

If *knowledge* is understood as a problem that can be solved from different *philosophical* assumptions, *theoretical* foundations, *methodological* procedures, *technical* strategies and *instruments*, depending on the stance of the researcher with respect to *the senses* and *reason* of the cognising subject, then the *epistemological orientation* will also be understood as that stance that the researcher assumes with respect to the five great *problems* of *knowledge*: philosophical, theoretical, methodological, technical and instrumental.

The elements of an epistemological orientation (philosophy, theory, methodology, technique and instrument) are also analysed, in this subchapter, as five major problems of knowledge, understood as a process: philosophical, theoretical, methodological, technical and instrumental.

2.1 THE PROBLEMS OF KNOWLEDGE.

If we agree that an *epistemological orientation* is composed of five elements or levels: philosophy, theory, methodology, technique and instrument; then the *problems of knowledge* are also five: philosophical, theoretical, methodological, technical and instrumental.

In this subchapter only the five major *problems of knowledge* are mentioned, which will be further developed in chapter two. In this subchapter the five *elements* of an *epistemological orientation* are treated as *problems of knowledge* in general.

As already mentioned, there are five problems of knowledge: philosophical, theoretical, methodological, technical and instrumental. Let us begin by briefly analysing each of them.

2.1.1 *The philosophical problems of knowledge*.

Knowledge can be understood as a *process* in which a cognising *subject is related* to an *object* to be known. This means that the *essential elements of any knowledge process* are the cognising *subject*, the *object* to be known and the *relationship* that must be established between them for knowledge to occur.

Before the *relation of knowledge* is established, both elements, the *subject* and the *object*, are only *entities*; beings that exist independently of each other. Both are in the ontological sphere, in reality, which can be concrete or abstract.

The *object of knowledge* arises insofar as a subject fixes his attention on any entity (material or immaterial) with the intention of knowing it and, in turn, the *cognising subject*, from the simple entity that he was, before relating to the object in order to know it, is transformed into a cognising subject by fixing his attention on an object in order to know it; "....*knowledge is an act, spontaneous as to its origin, immanent as to its termination, by which a man intentionally makes himself present to some region of being...*" (Verneaux, 2011:103-104).

The *problem* arises when the *subject* seeks to establish the *relation* of knowledge with the *object*, because both (the cognising subject and the object to be known) are in different, distinct and even contrary *worlds*: the cognising subject is the human soul, its psyche, its thought, its reason, its mind, etc.; and, therefore, it is in the *psychological sphere*. On the other hand, the object to be known is reality (which can be material or immaterial), it belongs to the ontological sphere. Hessen (2011: 15) states that "*.knowledge presents itself as a relation between these two members* - he means the subject and the object - *which remain eternally separated from each other*". Already the fact that Hessen affirms the separation between subject and object of knowledge, says a lot about the epistemological orientation from which he is elaborating knowledge about his object of study: the knowledge of knowledge. This will be dealt with later.

The fact that they are in different *spheres* means that the *relation* of knowledge between the cognising *subject* and the *object* to be known is not *essential*, i.e. they merge, literally, for a true relation of knowledge to exist. For this reason the relationship is, in essence, impossible. When the cognising subject (the human soul) attempts to break through the barrier of the object to be known (the concrete or abstract reality) in order to apprehend literally the object to be known, it collides, also literally, with a barrier imposed on it by reality. They are different worlds, planes or spheres in which the subject and the object exist; and, for this reason, they cannot be merged; it is like wanting to mix water and oil.

For example, let us suppose that the entity, a certain JOHN, fixes his attention on another entity, a tree, with a view to apprehending it, to knowing it. From that moment on, the entity JOHN becomes the cognising subject and the entity tree becomes the object to be known. At the moment in which

the cognising subject JOHN (who is in the psychological sphere, since human beings know with the soul, reason, mind, or whatever you call that abstract "thing" with which we think) tries to penetrate the ontological sphere of the object to be known, the tree (which is a concrete entity) collides with the bark of the tree (assuming he wants to begin by knowing the trunk). No matter how many attempts the cognising subject JOHN makes to put his head inside the trunk of the object to be known, the tree, he will only get a dent in it and tremendous headaches (it is logical that if the entity JOHN wants to know the tree in essence, he will have to literally put himself inside the tree, to merge and become one with the tree, atom with atom, molecule with molecule. As this is impossible, the problem of knowledge arises; "... *the spirit cannot go out of itself to coincide with things... a thing cannot enter the spirit...*" (Verneaux, 2011: 77). Neither the cognising consciousness can go out of itself to penetrate the sphere of the object; nor can the object enter the mind. Knowledge of reality, in essence, is impossible; it seems that human beings were not born to know reality, perhaps, we only come to this world with the necessary tools to survive in it; not to know it in essence.

We are of the opinion, in this research, that we can only assume what reality is, depending on whether we analyse it with the senses, with reason or with both qualities of the cognising subject.

If one wants to know immaterial entities, such as the concept of "education", the problem becomes more acute. At least, in the case of material entities such as the "tree", if they cannot be known in essence, human beings can agree to describe them; if we cannot know what they are, we can know what they are like, their characteristics (shape, extension, colour, texture), functioning, purpose, classification, etc. On the other hand, immaterial entities (such as the concept of education), because they are abstract entities, which cannot be appreciated with the senses, it is more difficult to agree on their definitions, characteristics, functions, purposes, classifications, etc. That is why there are so many definitions of the concept of "education".

The knowledge relationship between the researcher and his object of study is problematic, because a real contact (relationship) between the cognising *subject* and the *object* to be known is impossible; because they belong to different worlds, spheres or planes.

Hessen (2009: 16) says that "*Seen from the subject, this apprehension presents itself as an exit of the subject out of its own sphere, an invasion into the sphere of the object and a capture of the object's properties. The object is not, however, dragged into the sphere of the subject, but remains transcendent to it...*". It is impossible for the cognising subject (the human soul) to penetrate the sphere of the object to be known (the concrete or abstract reality). That is why the *relation* of knowledge can only take place in the *logical* world, in the *logical* sphere. Everything that a subject can say about a certain object will not be the reality of the object, what it is, but only a discourse about it, it will be a language about the object, a discourse elaborated by a subject that does not necessarily coincide with the discourse elaborated by another subject. All human beings feel and think differently. This is one of the reasons why cognising subjects will have to agree on what is to be understood by a given object of knowledge.

How does the logical relation of knowledge between a cognising subject and an object to be known come about?

It can be observed that the *cognising subject* has only two attributes to establish the *logical relation* of knowledge with the object to be known: his *senses* (eyes, sight, touch, hearing and smell) and his *reason*. It can be affirmed that human beings only have our senses and our reason to *relate* to *reality* and that it is the only thing at hand to know things, both material and spiritual.

For Verneaux (2011: 72) "... *the object and the subject are definable only by their mutual relationship which is knowledge. What is an object, a thing, a being? What is a subject, a consciousness, a spirit? That in whom or to whom an object appears...*". Reality (concrete or abstract) transcends the researcher, i.e. it is outside him, in another world.

Since human beings have only their senses and reason to know, the first question that comes to mind is: what is the source of knowledge, where does it come from, where does it originate, where does it come from, where is it, where is it?

To solve the philosophical problems of knowledge, the cognising subject has no choice but to stick to the attributes he has as an entity (senses and reason) and to *suppose*, but never be sure of it, that knowledge originates in reason (rationalism), in the senses (empiricism), in both: senses and reason, but first in the senses and then in reason (intellectualism) or, in both, but first in reason and then in the senses (apriorism). These are the only four possibilities, mathematically speaking, available to the subject to "give an opinion" on the origin of knowledge. Because there are only two attributes for knowing reality: reason and the senses.

It is understood that the philosophical problems of knowledge, in their essence, have no solution; the only thing left for the cognising subject to do is to suppose that they are solved from reason, from the senses or from both qualities of the cognising subject.

The problem about the origin of knowledge that has just been posed is related to four other great problems of knowledge: its possibility, essence, classification and concepts and criteria of truth); which will have to be solved by supposing from these four possibilities: reason (rationalism), senses (empiricism), senses and reason (intellectualism), reason and senses (apriorism).

A first approach to the philosophical problem can be stated as follows: the main philosophical problems of knowledge are five: is it possible to know (the problem about the possibility of knowledge), what is the source of knowledge (the problem about the origin of knowledge), who determines whom in a knowledge relation: the object to the subject, the subject to the object, or do both determine each other? (the problem about the essence of knowledge), how many kinds of knowledge are there (the problem about the classification of knowledge), and what is the truth criterion for accepting or rejecting knowledge (the problem about the concepts and truth criteria of knowledge).

The five *philosophical problems of knowledge* mentioned can be solved, as has been asserted throughout this study, from different philosophical assumptions that depend on the stance that the researcher assumes with respect to his reason and his senses. In the subchapter corresponding to the philosophical assumptions from which the philosophical problems of knowledge can be solved, they will be dealt with more extensively. In this subchapter only the following are indicated.

2.1.2 *Theoretical problems of knowledge*.

Epistemological orientations are composed, as already observed, of philosophical assumptions, to analyse reality; theoretical foundations, to problematise the objects of study; methodological procedures, to generate new knowledge; technical strategies, to learn about the phenomena; and instruments, to gather the information to be technically analysed.

Therefore, the problems of knowledge are: the philosophical assumptions, to analyse reality; the theoretical foundations, to problematise the objects of study; the methodological procedures, to generate new knowledge; the technical strategies, to know the phenomena; and the instruments, to collect the information to be technically analysed.

The second level, in a descending manner, where other problems of knowledge are located, is the *theoretical* level. Once the researcher has located his object of study in each and every one of the philosophical assumptions from which he is going to solve each and every one of the five philosophical problems of knowledge, using his reason, his senses or both qualities, he needs to determine which *theories* he will use to problematise the studied reality; that is, to choose the *theories* with which he will construct his object of study.

This means that the researcher, in addition to philosophical training to solve the five great philosophical problems of knowledge, requires *theoretical knowledge* that allows him to problematise his object of study.

In this work we propose a classification of *theories*, which is somewhat arbitrary due to the needs of the research being carried out, considering the way in which the cognising subject resolves each and every one of the philosophical problems of knowledge: from reason, from the senses or from both qualities of the researcher; and the extent of the exploration, description, explanation, interpretation and understanding of reality, in a top-down manner, of the theory. Theories can be classified as follows: *general theories of knowledge*: mathematicism, mechanicism, organicism, chaos, conflict and complexity; *particular theories of the social sciences*: positivism, functionalism, structuralism, systems theory, Marxism, hermeneutics and phenomenology; and *specific theories of the educational sciences*: behaviourism, psychoanalysis, humanism, cognitivism, genetic theory (Piaget), and socio-cultural theory.

The researcher's knowledge of these *theories* will allow him/her to have a mastery of authors and ideas, general, particular and specific about educational phenomena, for the construction of his/her object of study.

The level of *theory*, in an epistemological orientation, is placed second (after philosophy) because *theory* depends on philosophy. In this study we will try to show, in the respective subchapter, that any discourse (theory) elaborated by a cognising subject about any object to be known (concrete or abstract) depends on the assumptions from which the researcher solves each and every one of the philosophical problems of knowledge; that is, on what the researcher philosophically assumes about the reality he is investigating. Such an estimation may originate in the reason of the researcher; in his senses; in both, privileging the senses over reason; or, in both, privileging reason over the senses.

The educational researcher, depending on the assumptions from which he/she has solved the philosophical problems of knowledge (reason, meanings or both), will need to choose certain general *theories* of knowledge, particular to the social sciences and specific to the educational sciences, in order to construct his/her object of study from the educational sciences.

The three levels of *theory* mentioned (general, particular and specific) should be congruent, in epistemological terms, with the assumptions from which the educational researcher previously solved the five great philosophical problems of knowledge: its reason, its meanings or both qualities.

Epistemological congruence between the philosophical and theoretical level, in a gnoseological orientation, means something like the following: if to construct the idea of education assumes from reason (rationalism); the general theories of knowledge that relate, epistemologically, to reason are mathematicism, mechanicism and organicism; I should not use another general theory of knowledge (as, for example, chaos theory) because it would be incongruent, in epistemological terms, with the rationalist philosophical assumption from where the problem about the origin of knowledge was solved. All this will be discussed further in the subchapter on the theoretical foundations of an epistemological orientation.

2.1.3 *The methodological problems of knowledge.*

As already mentioned, the way in which the researcher solves the philosophical and theoretical problems of knowledge must be congruent in epistemological terms. For philosophy is the mother of theory. Theory depends on philosophy.

In the case of *methodology*, the third problem of knowledge understood as a process that the researcher has to solve in the construction of his object of study, the same thing happens. The theories (general theories of knowledge, particular theories of social sciences and specific theories of educational sciences), which the researcher chooses to problematise his object of study, must be congruent, in epistemological terms, with the *method* (methodological procedure or intellectual operation) or *methods* that the cognitive subject intends to use to generate new knowledge.

The epistemological congruence between theory and *method* can be understood as something similar to the following: if the educational researcher solved the philosophical problems of knowledge assuming from reason and the theories (general knowledge, particular social sciences and specific educational sciences) he chose to problematise his object of study were, respectively, organicism, positivism and behaviourism; the method to be used, for the generation of new knowledge in his research work, should be, preferably, deduction. If you use induction it would be incongruent, in epistemological terms, the method with the theory.

In the course of this study, it will be shown that only the following methodological procedures or intellectual operations (research methods) are known to generate new knowledge: addition, subtraction, multiplication, division, analysis, synthesis, induction, deduction, classification, comparison and definition. In the respective subchapter, the idea of method will be discussed in more detail.

2.1.4 *The technical problems of knowledge.*

As already mentioned, the way in which the researcher solves the philosophical, theoretical and methodological problems of knowledge must be congruent in epistemological terms. For theory depends on philosophy, and methodology is derived from theory.

In the case of the *technique* that the educational researcher chooses to know the reality, the fourth problem of knowledge understood as a process that the cognising subject has to solve in the construction of his object of study, the same thing happens: the method (methodological procedure or intellectual operation) or methods that the cognising subject intends to use to generate new knowledge, must be congruent, in epistemological terms, with the *technique* to know the reality that is used.

Epistemological congruence between method and *technique* can be understood as something similar to the following: if the educational researcher solved the philosophical problems of knowledge by assuming from reason; the theories (general of knowledge, particular of social sciences and specific of educational sciences) he chose to problematise his object of study were, respectively, organicism, positivism and behaviourism; and the method he used, for the generation of new knowledge in his research work, was deduction; the *technique* to be chosen, to "know" reality, should be any of the following: observation, experimentation, survey and documentary. These *techniques* should, if epistemological congruence is desired, be used only to test the rationalist hypothesis (deduction) that was constructed, i.e. in its quantitative sense. If these *techniques* (in their qualitative sense) are used to interpret and understand the studied reality, to describe it, rather than to explain it, it would be incongruent, in epistemological terms, the technical strategy that was used to "know" reality with the method that was intended to be used to generate the new knowledge.

Throughout this study we will try to show that only the following *technical* strategies are known to know reality: observation, experimentation, survey and documentary. In the respective subchapter, the technical strategies that any researcher can use to "know" any reality will be analysed in more detail.

2.1.5 *Instrumental problems of knowledge.*

The last problem of knowledge, understood as a process, is the instrumental one.

As already mentioned, the way in which the researcher solves the philosophical, theoretical, methodological and technical problems of knowledge must be congruent in epistemological terms. For theory depends on philosophy, methodology is derived from theory and technique is derived from method.

In the case of the *instruments* that the researcher can use to recover the information needed in the construction of his object of study, the fifth problem of knowledge understood as a process that the cognising subject has to solve in the construction of reality, the same thing happens: the instrument that the cognising subject intends to use to collect the information he needs must be congruent, in epistemological terms, with the *technique* for knowing the reality that is used.

The epistemological congruence between the technique for "knowing" reality and the *instruments* for retrieving the necessary information can be understood as something similar to the following: if the educational researcher solved the philosophical problems of knowledge assuming from reason; the theories (general of knowledge, particular of social sciences and specific of educational sciences) he chose to problematise his object of study were, respectively, organicism, positivism and behaviourism; the method he used, for the generation of new knowledge in his research work, was deduction; and the *technique* chosen, to "know" reality, was any of the following: observation, experimentation, survey and documentary. If these *techniques* were, if there was epistemological congruence, used only to verify the rationalist hypothesis (deduction) that was constructed, that is, in its quantitative meaning; then, the instruments that should be used to recover the information should be, if epistemological congruence is desired, the following: the register (derived from the observation technique), the items (derived from the experimental technique), the questionnaire and the interview (derived from the survey technique) and the work sheet (derived from the documentary technique) All these instruments should be used by the researcher in their quantitative meaning, if such *instruments* (in their qualitative meaning) are used to gather qualitative data, it would be incongruent, in epistemological terms, the instrument that was used to recover the information with the technical strategy with which it was intended to know the reality.

Throughout this study we will try to show that only the following instruments are known to retrieve the necessary information about the object of study: the register (derived from the technical strategy to know the reality called: *observation*), the elements (experimentation), the questionnaire and the interview (derived from the technical strategy to know the reality called: *survey*) and the work sheet (derived from the technical strategy to know the reality called: documentary). In the respective sub-chapter, the instruments that any researcher can use to collect the necessary information about his or her object of study will be analysed more extensively.

Up to this point we have presented the five epistemological problems of knowledge (philosophical, theoretical, methodological, technical and instrumental), and now we will analyse the first and main problem of them. We consider this problem to be the cause of all the other problems of knowledge: the philosophical problem.

2.2 THE ASSUMPTIONS FROM WHICH PHILOSOPHICAL PROBLEMS OF KNOWLEDGE CAN BE SOLVED.

The difference between *science* and *philosophy* is the same as that between *philosophical assumptions* (first element) and *theoretical foundations* (second element) of epistemological orientations; *science* (theory) arises from *philosophy* (assumptions), just as *theoretical* foundations arise from *philosophical* assumptions.

In order to analyse educational phenomena, the researcher uses, consciously or unconsciously, certain philosophical *assumptions*.

Philosophical assumptions are just that, estimations, presumptions, conjectures, attributions, concessions, presuppositions, etc., about how to solve the great philosophical problems of knowledge (its possibility, its origin, its essence, its classification and its concepts and criteria of truth), from reason; from the senses; from both, privileging reason over the senses; or from both, privileging the senses over reason.

In the following, the *philosophical assumptions* that any researcher can use to analyse any reality (concrete or abstract) will be discussed in more detail.

2.2.1 *The definition of "philosophical assumption".*

An *assumption* is that which must be *assumed* beforehand if a desired result is to be achieved, it is a postulate. It is something that is logically necessary, implied, *assumed*. It is causally necessary, condition or result. From the Latin suppositicius, *put in place of*; it is an epistemological expression for any object that is *supposed* by the spirit without actually occurring in experience (Runes, 1998:304 and 357). Instead of the certainty that would enable us to solve the main philosophical problems of knowledge (possibility, origin, essence, classification and concepts and criteria of truth); since the definitive solution of these questions is impossible, for the reasons already discussed in previous sub-chapters; we can only *"suppose"* that the above-mentioned questions are solved, in a certain way, from reason; from the senses; from reason and the senses, with the exception that we first think and then we feel; or from the senses and reason, with the difference that we first feel and then we think.

Philosophical assumptions are taken for granted in order to *theorise* about reality. *Theories* are derived from them. They are like the 'lenses' through which we observe phenomena.

We suppose, estimate, presume, conjecture, attribute, concede, presuppose, etc., that the philosophical problems of knowledge can be solved from reason; from the senses; from both, privileging the senses over reason; or from both, privileging reason over the senses: We suppose because we do not know, with certainty, the reality of things. It seems that we do not know things in essence because we do not come with the equipment that allows us to do so.

2.2.2 The *characteristics of philosophical assumptions*.

The main characteristic of a philosophical *assumption*, from its etymological definition, is that it is only a term, an idea, which is placed in the place of another idea, another term.

The fact that reality, in itself, the thing in itself, is unknowable to us, we can only '*suppose*', using our senses and our reason, that it is a certain way. Instead of certainty, we place ourselves in the assumption of certainty.

Assumption replaces the certainty of knowledge. We are not certain of reality, we only assume it in a certain way.

From a philosophical assumption, we analyse reality in one way; from its opposite, in a different way. From a philosophical assumption, we can prove that God exists; from its opposite, we can deny it. What is really true is that we are not born with the necessary qualities that would allow us to know whether we can really know God or not. We can only *assume* that we know him in a certain way.

The *theoretical foundations* are one level below the *philosophical assumptions* because they are derived from them.

The "lenses" (philosophical level) we put on to observe reality, the philosophical *assumptions* from which we observe reality, will determine the explorations, descriptions, explanations, interpretations and understandings we elaborate about phenomena (theoretical level). Philosophy determines theory. Philosophy is reduced to assumptions from which the main philosophical problems of knowledge are to be solved. Therefore, theory is limited to mere opinions about reality.

2.2.3 *The role of philosophical assumptions*.

The important question in this respect would be: what is the need satisfied by an assumption that is used to solve a philosophical problem of knowledge?

Answer: replace the certainty that one would have with the solution of the philosophical problems of knowledge with an opinion on how these problems could be solved.

To do *science* is to create knowledge and to *philosophise* is to reflect on the problems of knowledge. In order to create knowledge, it is necessary to reflect on the problems of knowledge. This reflection is based on *philosophical assumptions* that serve as a starting point for analysing reality.

To *philosophise* is to think about reality in a certain way; to consider certain *assumption*(s) that answer questions about the *problems of knowledge* in different ways.

If the above is true, it is necessary to know the diversity of *assumptions* from which reality can be observed; because the theories that are elaborated about reality will depend on these assumptions; that is, on the "lenses" that the researcher puts on to "look" at the phenomena.

Philosophy is to *science* what *philosophical assumptions* are to *theoretical foundations*, in the terms set out throughout this study.

The *philosophical assumptions of the epistemological orientations* constitute different "lenses" through which reality can be observed, i.e. they answer questions about the *problem of knowledge*. They constitute a stance on the problems of knowledge.

2.2.4 *The purpose of philosophical assumptions*.

If philosophical *assumptions* are estimates about the different solutions that can be proposed to the problem of knowledge, and they function by estimating that questions concerning the difficulties of knowledge can be solved in one way or another, then the *purpose* of a philosophical *assumption* can only be to replace certainty by a mere possibility of a solution to a philosophical problem of knowledge.

2.2.5 *The classification of philosophical assumptions*.

Hessen (2011: 19-20) describes the phenomenon of knowledge from "...*five main problems*...", paraphrasing him, these problems are the following: the possibility of human knowledge, the origin of human knowledge, the essence of human knowledge, the forms of human knowledge and the concepts and criteria of truth of human knowledge. In every *knowledge relationship* there is a cognising subject and an object to be known. In this relationship the researcher is confronted with problems such as the following: can the subject really apprehend the object, is reason or experience the source and basis of human knowledge, does the object determine the subject or does the subject determine the object or do both determine each other, besides rational knowledge can there be intuitive knowledge, what is the criterion that tells us whether knowledge is true or not, and so forth.

I should clarify that the present research is mainly based on the work of Hessen (2011), only with regard to the first element of an *epistemological orientation*: the *philosophical assumptions* from which the five problems of knowledge can be solved. The aforementioned author masterfully clarifies that the five *problems of knowledge* described have been tried to be *solved* in different ways throughout the history of knowledge. In this paper we are of the opinion that these problems have not been solved because they are unsolvable.

These *solutions*, which have been elaborated to answer the five main *problems of knowledge* mentioned by the author, are called *epistemological positions*. Throughout his main work (*Theory of knowledge*), the author describes the different *epistemological positions* that have been developed to answer the questions about the different problems of knowledge, criticises them and takes a position on them.

It is also necessary to clarify that the differences between the commented author and the position of the present research are the following:

FIRST: John Hessen calls *epistemological positions* the *solutions* that, throughout history, have been implemented to *solve* the five main *problems of knowledge* described. This is partly agreed and partly not, because *episteme* means: knowledge, and *position*: situation, state or disposition of one entity with respect to another; therefore, an *epistemological position* is the *situation, state* or *disposition* that a researcher takes with respect to a *problem of knowledge*. So far we agree, however, this title is too big for the question, because the *problems of knowledge* are not reduced to the five mentioned by the author, even though they are the most important in the *philosophical* plane. There are other *problems of knowledge* which the author does not consider and which in this study are called theoretical foundations, methodological procedures, technical strategies and instruments of knowledge. John Hessen stays with the *philosophical problem of knowledge* and forgets the other *problems* mentioned. The importance of calling *epistemological positions* the solutions that have been constructed to answer *the different problems of knowledge* lies in the fact that *these situations, dispositions* or *states of* the subject with respect to the problem of knowledge already constitute a great advance on the *philosophical* level. What Hessen calls *epistemological positions* are, in reality, *philosophical assumptions* for solving the problems of knowledge.

SECOND: For the purposes of this study, an *epistemological orientation* is a researcher's *stance* on the following *levels of knowledge*: philosophical, theoretical, methodological, technical and instrumental. Hessen only deals with the first one and calls it *epistemological position*, reducing the *problem of knowledge* to only one of its levels: the *philosophical*.

THIRD: After Hessen's phenomenological description of the five main *philosophical problems* of knowledge, starting from what he calls *epistemological positions* (and which in this study are called *assumptions* from which the different *philosophical problems of knowledge* can be solved, for the reasons already mentioned), he criticises certain *assumptions* and takes sides with respect to others; He does not recognise that these are mere *assumptions*, since human beings are not born to know the truth of things and, due to the limitations of our reason and our senses, we can only give opinions, at the philosophical level, with respect to the five problems of knowledge mentioned above.

Problems about the possibility, origin, essence, forms and criteria of truth of human knowledge, among others, are solved by scientific communities or research traditions in different ways: from the senses, from reason or from both qualities of the cognising subject, depending on the perspective, paradigm or epistemological orientation of the programme or mode of knowledge production to which they ascribe.

It can be affirmed that no *philosophical assumption* is better or superior than another or others; everything will depend on the epistemological and ontological interests of the researcher. It should also be stated that researchers do not always start from the same *philosophical assumption* to solve any problem of knowledge; the *philosophical assumption* chosen may depend on the space in which the researcher is located, the time in which he lives, the circumstances surrounding him, and his interests, both epistemological and ontological.

The analysis of each and every one of the assumptions from which each and every one of the five philosophical problems of knowledge mentioned above can be solved will be carried out in the following order: concept, characteristics, function, purpose, classification, authors and works.

2.2.5.1 *The philosophical assumptions from which the problem of the possibility of knowledge can be solved.*

Scientific communities or research traditions, depending on the perspective, paradigm or epistemological orientation of the programme or mode of knowledge production they adhere to, solve the problem of the *possibility of knowledge-in* the construction of their objects of study-from *the following philosophical assumptions:* dogmatism, scepticism, subjectivism, relativism, pragmatism or criticality. The epistemological orientation and, therefore, the philosophical assumption(s) from which such research traditions or scientific communities explore, describe, explain, interpret, understand, etc., reality, will depend on the way they solve each of the five main philosophical problems of knowledge: with reason, with the senses, or with both qualities of the cognising subject.

2.2.5.1.1 Assuming it is possible to know.

Dogma implies a fixed doctrine. Dogmatism is a philosophical assumption from which the problem of the possibility of knowledge can be solved by affirming, from reason, that the subject, the cognising consciousness, apprehends its object.

The problem of the *possibility of knowledge*, in which the cognising subject wonders whether he can really apprehend the *object*, whether it is possible to know reality, can be solved *by assuming*, using reason, that the subject really apprehends the object, that the knowledge of phenomena is not a problem, that the contact between the cognising subject and the object to be known is possible and real; because one does not see or does not want to see, paraphrasing Hessen (2011: 21-22) knowledge as a relationship (subject-object), which the human being establishes from his spirit and, therefore, the cognising subject thinks that the objects of knowledge are given to him absolutely.

When an educational researcher wants reality not to move, for phenomena to remain the same, eternally immobile, fixed, he must elaborate his discourses neglecting the subject that knows and judges and concentrating all his attention on the object.

The *function of* the *dogmatic philosophical assumption*, the need that can be satisfied *by assuming* that reality behaves in such a way, is to indoctrinate other subjects to conform to the established order. It works very well in the four possibilities of realisation of the human spirit: philosophy, science, religion and art.

Examples: in philosophy, the Platonic "ought to be" permeated the entire modern era; in science, the "scientific method" served to justify the Platonic worldview of modernity; in religion, Catholic indoctrination reconciled the interests of the different social classes at the time; and, in art, we still talk about Da Vinci's great inventions, although nobody knows exactly what they consisted of, because he was only an "icon" imposed by European cultural colonisation on the rest of the world. To observe an object of knowledge in this way means that one is under the *assumption* or belief that it exists, in itself, independently of whether or not there is a subject who can know it.

The *dogmatic philosophical assumption* implies a fixed doctrine for the knowing and judging subject. It consists of a philosophical assumption from which the cognising subject believes that the problem of knowledge does not exist; he takes for granted the possibility and the reality of real contact between himself and his object of knowledge; the subject *assumes* that he truly apprehends his object, that reality can be discovered; he has absolute confidence in human reason.

When a researcher starts from *dogmatic philosophical assumptions* to observe reality, he will use authoritative arguments to justify his theories, for example, appealing to the faith that it is possible to know about philosophical, religious, scientific, artistic, etc. matters.

The epistemological and, consequently, ontological problem, derived from *assuming* from *dogmatism*, consists in the fact that the researcher is not interested in the cognising subject (which is himself, transformed from entity into subject, due to the fact that he has fixed his senses and his reason in another entity, pretending to know it), but only in the object (the reality he pretends to know). He neglects that knowledge is an endless process, in which two entities are related (the cognising subject and the object to be known) which belong to different spheres (psychological and ontological, respectively) and which can only be related in the logical sphere, in language, by means of the word, of argument, of discourse. That is why the researcher believes, wants to believe, or even *believes* that the objects of knowledge are given to him, absolutely and not merely by the intermediary function of knowledge, by the relation he establishes with the object, through his senses and his spirit. The investigator *presumes* that the objects of knowledge of perception (the concrete objects that are perceived by the senses) and the objects of knowledge of thought (the abstract objects that are best perceived by consciousness) are given to him in the same way directly from his corporeality, as if the object (reality) could penetrate the sphere of the subject (the soul).

For example: in ethical science, (ideal) values are thought to exist independently of the subject who thinks them. The fact that values (entities of reason) presuppose a valuing consciousness is not considered by researchers who place themselves in a dogmatic assumption, nor is it considered that the objects to be known (both real and ideal) imply a cognising consciousness. The cognising subject is overlooked.

From a dogmatic assumption it is presumed, or one wants to estimate, that the object does not move; that reality remains still, always, eternally. The use of this philosophical assumption makes it possible to elaborate discourses (knowledge) that favour the maintenance of the established order, the status quo.

It can be presumed from a radical *dogmatism*, thinking that knowledge of any phenomenon is possible in an absolute way; or from a moderate *dogmatism*, accepting that it is possible to know certain objects of study and not others; because each object of study is known in a different way. Material (concrete) objects are best known with the senses and immaterial (abstract) objects with reason.

For example, in religion, to know the gods it is better to approach them from a rational philosophical assumption than from an empiricist one, because God is an idea, for which we do not possess empirical evidence, on which we all agree.

If the researcher desires, suspects, estimates, presumes, conjectures, attributes, concedes, presupposes, supposes, cares and wants to start from a *dogmatic* hypothesis in order to know facts, phenomena, events, things, reality; this may be due to several reasons: firstly, he may be a naive cognising subject who has not realised that knowledge is a problem, because it implies a relation between him and the object, mediated by discourse; secondly, even knowing the previous problem, he has an interest in reality, the object of knowledge, the phenomenon under study, remaining immobile, always fixed, in eternal stillness (if we think about it, this is the philosophical aspect of the matter).

2.2.5.1.2 Estimating that it is not possible to know.

Scepticism means to ponder, to examine, to doubt. From this *philosophical assumption* knowledge can be denied. The possibility of a real contact between subject and object can be dismissed. *It assumes*

that the subject cannot apprehend the object. It can be affirmed that knowledge, in the sense of a real apprehension of the object by the subject, is impossible. It can be concluded that we should not pronounce any judgement, but refrain from judgement.

It is understood that *supposing* is synonymous with *hypothesising*, because the cognising subject will never be absolutely sure that the knowledge that is elaborated about the objects (phenomena, events, facts) is the true and only one; forever and ever; by virtue of the fact that reality is continuously moving and never stops; the changes in the objects of knowledge are constantly happening, leading the subjects who pretend to know them to the abyss of uncertainty, insecurity and melancholy. It is possible that there will never be certainty about the veracity of knowledge, in the terms set out in the lines cited above.

From *sceptical philosophical assumptions*, as opposed to *dogmatic philosophical hypotheses*, the researcher can *consider* the denial of the *possibility* of a real contact between the cognising subject and the object to be known, *suspect* that it is impossible to know in essence. It can be *presumed* that the subject cannot really apprehend the object. It is possible to *conjecture* that knowledge is a problem because no real contact between the subject and the object is possible; therefore, the subject is recommended to refrain from judging, definitively.

When a researcher chooses this *philosophical assumption*, he does not see the object to be known. It may be because he does not want to consider it, or even because it is not convenient for him to consider it. His reason and his senses are fixed exclusively on the cognising subject. It may be because he has an interest in knowing reality in this way, in order to be able to deny a phenomenon that does not suit him. *It* therefore *assumes* that the only beings (entities) with the capacity to know are human beings, that these subjects are unique and that none of them is equal to any other. Consequently, he deduces that each and every human being, the cognising subjects, thinks and feels differently,

when we seek to know the same fact, phenomenon or event. From this *assumption*, the researcher (cognising subject) applies his soul and his perceptions only to the subjective aspects of human knowledge (passions, emotions, feelings, interests, ambitions, complexes). The researcher is able to *presuppose* that all knowledge is based on the subject's senses (we all feel differently) and that this influences his reason (we all think differently). Using this *sceptical philosophical assumption*, the circumstances (of mode, time and place) surrounding the cognising subjects are also considered: the time in which one lives, the place in which one lives, the culture of the people, traditions, beliefs, customs, myths, creeds, fears, etc.

Paraphrasing Hessen (2011: 22-25), it is possible to consider several levels of *scepticism* that the researcher may consider when confronted with the knowledge of his object: it is possible to assume that human beings will never be able to find certain answers to the phenomena and mysteries of nature and the universe. It is *possible to estimate* that nothing exists, and that if something existed, it could not be known, and that if something could be known, it could not be transmitted from one man to another.

If *radical* or *absolute scepticism* is *assumed*, it can be said that there is no real contact between the cognising subject and the object to be known, due to the problem of knowledge; that it is impossible for the cognising consciousness (soul) to apprehend its object (reality), because both are in different spheres or worlds; that there is no knowledge, because it is impossible for the cognising subject (reason and senses) to penetrate the sphere of the object to be known (concrete or abstract reality); that all subjects think and feel differently, so that, of two contradictory judgements, the one is therefore as exactly true as the other.

If one *considers*, from an *average* or *academic scepticism*, it is possible to affirm that rigorous (universally valid and logically necessary) knowledge is impossible. We are never certain that our

judgements (affirmative or negative) agree with reality. We can never say, then, that this or that proposition is true; but we can say that it seems to be true, that it is probable. There is a possibility of arriving at a probable opinion.

From a *metaphysical scepticism*, it is possible to *suppose* that it is possible to change a previous methodology for generating new knowledge (Aristotelian deduction), because it is deficient; and to change it for a more efficient one (induction) (Hume, 1992:IX-X).

We can suppose, from a *metaphysical scepticism*, that there is an order in phenomena, in the sense that facts are governed by certain laws of inherence and causality; but, the certainty we have regarding the falsity or truth of that order cannot be intuited or demonstrated. The knowledge of reality is not denied; it is recognised that an order prevails in nature. The idea of uniformity, of order in nature, comes from a probable expectation or belief, from a suppositional argument, not from rational evidence. One has only possibilities about causes and effects, not ontological certainty (Hume, 1992: XLII-XLIII). With Hume, science is no longer true, demonstrable, verifiable knowledge (which can be asserted from a dogmatic assumption); science is now probably true, unverifiable knowledge (from a sceptical assumption). Reality is not still (dogmatism) it is moving (scepticism); we are not absolutely sure of the explanations that are elaborated about reality.

From a *philosophical sceptical assumption*, we must stick to the positively given, to the immediate facts of experience and not seriously consider any metaphysical speculation; "... *any proposition which cannot be strictly reduced to the mere statement of a fact, particular or general, can have no real or intelligible meaning...*" (Comte, 1997: 70). Positivism assumes, from *metaphysical scepticism*, that the only true knowledge is that which we can verify through observation and experimentation. Comte comes to this conclusion because he solves the problem of the possibility of knowledge by using his senses, rather than his reason.

From a *methodical scepticism* it is possible to overthrow the philosophical, scientific, religious and artistic authoritarianism of a whole (feudal) era; and to start again a practice of personal meditation (modernity). Sceptical philosophical assumptions allow us to understand that an investigation of human reason must precede knowledge of the world. Before starting an investigation, the cognising subject must consider from which philosophical assumptions he will start to observe reality; and, for this, he will have to start by considering an education for investigation, which will allow him to know the different philosophical assumptions from which the different problems of knowledge can be solved. If man wants to investigate the truth, he must first examine his own intellect, his reason (Descartes, 1981: VIII). Descartes is considered, by some scholars of epistemology, as the father of modern rationalism, however, his work is mentioned in this part of the study so that it is understood that there are several levels of scepticism.

The *methodical sceptic doubts* in order to know. Doubt from a *methodical scepticism* carries the intention of discovering the truth; even if it is partial. The Cartesian principle "*I think, therefore I am*", allows us to have some certainty about human existence. In fact, this principle constitutes a rationalist demonstration of the existence of the human soul (Descartes, 1981: XIII-XIV). In this introduction to Descartes' "Discourse on Method", written by Francisco Larroyo, it is stated that the author did not obtain this knowledge by means of a syllogism, but by means of an immediate intuition. This is something we do not agree with, because Descartes obtained the aforementioned principle, as well as the other one that says "I doubt, therefore I think", by applying the laws of Aristotelian formal logic; deductive logic, which is the rigorous method followed from a *rationalist philosophical assumption*, to generate new knowledge from reason.

The *sceptical philosophical assumption works* by doubting, pondering, examining all our immediate certainties, in order to know phenomena in a more real way.

Regarding the *aim* of anyone who uses a *sceptical philosophical assumption* to observe reality, it is possible to affirm that one thinks, or wants to think, because it may suit the interests of the subject who elaborates the sceptical discourse, that reality is in constant movement, movement being understood as change.

2.2.5.1.3 Presuming that it is not possible to establish a universal truth.

It can be affirmed, from a *subjectivist philosophical assumption*, that there is a truth, but that it has a validity limited to each subject. It can be said that there is no universally valid, absolute, eternal and immutable truth for all subjects, in general. Each subject elaborates his own truth, based on what he feels and thinks. This means, among other things, that all people are subjects who feel (senses) and think (reason) differently. All judgements are valid only for the subjects who formulate them. Therefore, there are no universally valid judgements. Protagoras claimed that man is the measure of all things (Hessen, 2011: 25 - 27). This statement has an individualistic sense, it can be justified that every human being can construct his own reality. Protagoras comes to this conclusion because he is solving the problem about the possibility of knowledge with the senses, rather than with reason.

The researcher can argue, placing himself on a *subjectivist philosophical assumption*, that each individual human being is a unique and unrepeatable entity; the result of millions of light years of cosmic evolution and that, in this sense, according to Schpenhauer (1997: 19) "*There is no other truth more certain, more independent and less in need of proof than that everything that can be known, that is, the entire universe, is only an object for a subject, the perception of the perceiver; in a word: representation...".* Each human being represents the world differently, depending on his senses and reason; on his material and spiritual evolution; on the time and place in which he lives; on the culture in which he recreates himself; on his emotions, feelings, prejudices, ambitions, fears; on the myths, traditions, customs, beliefs of the society in which he lives.

It can be affirmed that the *function of* the *subjectivist philosophical assumption,* the necessity it fulfils, is precisely: the liberation of the individual human being. Nietzsche (1976: 41) puts it more or less as follows: *"Independence is the privilege of the strong, of the small minority who have the courage to assert themselves...".* Nietzsche is interested in the realisation of the human being, "beyond good and evil". He uses extreme *subjectivist philosophical assumptions.*

When a human being wishes to impose his or her will on others, he or she can use the *subjectivist philosophical assumption,* elaborating discourses that serve that end: the realisation of the individual human being.

2.2.5.1.4   Conjecturing that truth is relative.

Following Hessen 2011: 25-27), from a *relativistic philosophical assumption* it can be stated that there are only truths in relation to a given humanity. Truth depends on the circumstances of time, place and the way of life of human beings. On the basis of relativistic philosophical assumptions, it can be asserted that truth, in itself, does not exist, that it is a cultural elaboration and, therefore, the validity of truth is a decision of the group that elaborates it.

In Kuhn (1999: 319) *".scientific knowledge, like language, is either intrinsically the common property of a group, or it is nothing at all...";* science is relative, both in its development and in its criteria of truth. Kuhn comes to this conclusion because he is solving the problem about the possibility of knowledge from his senses, rather than with his reason.

When an educational researcher uses *relativistic philosophical assumptions* to construct an object of study, he or she *considers* that reality is moving, that the contact between the subject and the object of knowledge is not possible in a definitive way for two reasons: first, because the subject (soul) and the object (reality) are in different worlds and, second, because reality is not still, it is constantly changing. Therefore, knowledge is a never-ending process.

In this sense it is philosophically assumed: is reality one reality or are there several realities, does reality move or does it remain still?

2.2.5.1.5   Attributing that what is true is what is useful.

From a pragmatic philosophical conjecture, according to Hessen (2011: 27-29), the educational researcher can abandon the idea of truth, in the sense of the concordance between thought and being, and concede that what is true is what is useful, valuable, what serves the subject to survive. It can be considered that human beings, as individuals, are practical, action-oriented; that we are only interested in our own security and well-being. It is also possible to conjecture that intelligence was given to human beings, individually, to orient themselves in reality, not to know it. It is possible to presuppose that human knowledge is only important for its usefulness. Truth can be attributed to the congruence of thoughts with practical ends, which are useful and helpful for the realisation of the human being.

For James (1975: 156-158), truth means "...*adequacy with reality...true ideas are those which we can assimilate, make valid, corroborate, and verify; false ideas are those which we cannot...*". To possess true thoughts means, for James, to have instruments of action, which tell us which realities can be useful or harmful. Truth is provisional, group truth, discourse must adapt to reality to be useful, true. James takes this view because he is solving the problem of the possibility of knowledge from his senses, rather than from his reason.

If this is as it is said, in the religious field, for example, a person would not be concerned with the problem of the existence of God in order to accept a certain religion, but rather that it would provide him with some utility, for example, that his family, by practising it, would be fulfilled morally, socially, economically, etc. For Frederick Nietzsche (1976: 88), "*From the senses comes every manifestation of certainty, every good conscience, every evidence of truth*". So truth is changeable, relative; because the senses do not provide us with stable knowledge. Nietzsche affirms the above from his senses, rather than from his reason.

We consider Hessen's assertion to be correct, in the sense that James and the other *pragmatists* mentioned avoid the debate on the objectivity or subjectivity-relativity of truth, with respect to the problem of the possibility of knowledge, that is, whether or not it is possible to know; but we also believe that, when analysing it in terms of utility, they take a sceptical, subjectivist and relativist stance on it.

2.2.5.1.6   Granted that it is possible to know, but not in essence.

Following Hessen (2011: 29-30), schools of thought that start from *critical philosophical assumptions* are of the opinion that it is indeed possible to know (dogmatism) but not in essence, so that one should analyse the claims of others and not accept anything without reflecting, pondering, analysing the judgements of others (scepticism); because human beings feel and think differently from other human beings (subjectivism); because judgements change in time, space and circumstances (relativism); and because the knowledge we approve as true must be useful to us in the realisation of our objectives, in the achievement of our purposes, both individually and in our relations with other human beings (pragmatism).

This *philosophical assumption* allows educational researchers to hope for certainty. Because *criticism* is a *philosophical presupposition* from which it is possible to establish a mediation between the radical extremes (dogmatism and scepticism) in order, on the basis of *subjectivist, relativist and pragmatic* philosophical assumptions, to try to clarify the *problem* of the *possibility of knowledge*, in terms of dialogue between one and the other, in order to reach an agreement on what is to be understood by true knowledge.

Kant (1996: 6), the founder of the *critical philosophical assumption*, characterised the epoch in which he lived as follows: "...*our age is the age of criticism, to which everything has to submit. Religion, because of its sanctity, and legislation because of its majesty, generally want to avoid it. But then they arouse justified suspicions against themselves and cannot aspire to a sincere respect, which reason grants only to those who have been able to sustain free and public scrutiny*".

Kant called his *conjecture* of teaching to philosophise from *philosophical assumptions* that mediate between the dogmatic and the sceptical "*critique*". His endeavour was to teach how to philosophise, to think for oneself; not to transmit the principles of a ready-made philosophy. "*Criticism*" means just appreciation, one might say the Aristotelian middle ground. Above all, it is an appreciation of man's potential as a creator and sustainer of culture. The task of *criticism* is both negative and positive. It is a criticism of human reason, it reveals its limitations, but at the same time, or within these limitations, it guarantees its possible and creative work.

Kant is *critical*, in terms of *philosophical assumptions*, when he promotes a dialogue between *dogma* (faith) and *scepticism* (doubt) and establishes an agreement between the two. To think, in philosophy, science, religion and art, let us assume, although one can never be completely certain, that one can know (dogmatism), but not in essence (scepticism), because all human beings are unique and unrepeatable and we reason and feel differently.

(subjectivism), ideas are subjective creations that are transformed in time, space and circumstances (relativism) and all knowledge must have some practical utility for human beings (pragmatism).

From a *critical philosophical assumption*, possibilities are given to achieve one of the great ideals of education: to train critical, analytical and reflective students. The materialisation of one of Kantian maxims: "dare to think for yourself".

In Kant (1994: 25) it is said that "*laziness and cowardice are the cause why so great a part of men continue at ease in their state of pupilage...they are also the cause why it becomes so easy for others to set themselves up as tutors...*". To dare to think for oneself means to free oneself from the great evils that afflict humanity: ignorance, fanaticism and ambition. The first leads to the second and the second to the third.

That is why Kant (1994: 25) understood enlightenment as the possibility of "*.man's liberation from his guilty incapacity.*" This incapacity is understood as "*.the impossibility of making use of his intelligence without the guidance of another...*" (Kant 1994: 25). It is a culpable incapacity because "*...its cause lies not in the lack of intelligence but in the lack of decision and courage to make use of it by himself without the guidance of another...*" (Kant 1994: 25). (Kant, 1994: 25) That is why Kant (1994: 25) said: "*... Sapere aude! Have the courage to make use of your own reason!...*". Kant concludes the above because he is solving the problem about the possibility of knowing with his reason and with his senses, only that he first uses reason and then the senses.

By way of conclusion, and after this overview of the *philosophical assumptions* from which the *problem* of the *possibility of knowledge* can be solved, it is personally considered that, of all the *philosophical assumptions* discussed, from which the *problem* of the *possibility of knowledge can* be solved, none of those analysed (dogmatism, scepticism, subjectivism, relativism, pragmatism and criticism) is better than the others. The *assumption*(s) that an educational researcher chooses, in order to analyse phenomena, will depend on the object of study and the epistemological and ontological interests of the researcher. What is important to note is that the philosophical assumption chosen, whether the researcher knows it or ignores it, will have implications on theories, on the types of theories to be used to problematise the object of study, to construct it.

Moreover, every researcher who constructs an object of study, whether he knows it or not, does so on the basis of one or several *philosophical assumptions*, in this case, *about the possibility of knowledge.* Because every discourse is constructed from certain philosophical assumptions, irremediably; because the cognising subject is using his reason, his senses or both of his qualities to solve the problem about the possibility of knowing.

The question that every researcher should ask himself/herself, before attempting to begin with the knowledge of any of the phenomena of education, is this: can the fact, phenomenon, educational event that I want to know about be explained, can it be explored, described, interpreted or understood? If the above is possible, from which *philosophical assumption* should it be approached? That will depend on whether you use your reason, your senses or both qualities to answer the question posed.

2.2.5.2 *The philosophical assumptions from which the problem of the origin of knowledge can be solved.*

Understanding the *philosophical problem* of the *origin of knowledge* is fundamental for interpreting the other four *philosophical difficulties of knowledge* (possibility, essence, classification and criteria of truth of knowledge). This without forgetting that the other *four types of knowledge problems* remain to be clarified: its *theoretical* foundations, to problematise reality; the *methodological* procedures, to generate new knowledge; the *technical* strategies, to know reality; and the *instruments*, to recover the information needed to analyse phenomena; in accordance with the concept of *epistemological orientation* of research carried out from the educational sciences, the general idea that guides the present research work.

It has already been mentioned (supra, 2.1.1) that, in accordance with the *critical* stance taken in this research, it is impossible for the cognising subject (soul) to penetrate the sphere of the object to be known (reality: material and spiritual), it seems that we human beings were not born to know reality as it is, in essence. If we educational researchers can only count on our reason and our senses to "know" educational reality, we have, at first, mathematically speaking, only two *possibilities* to establish contact with reality: reason and the senses. We can *assume*, but never be definitely sure, that *knowledge originates* in *reason* (then we would be rationalists) or that *knowledge originates* in the *senses* (and we would be empiricists). Educational researchers, in a second stage, have two other *possibilities* of approaching the objects of study, derived from the two previous *possibilities*: we can *assume* that knowledge originates both in reason and in the senses, but that our senses participate first and then our reason (and we would be intellectualists); or that reason participates first and then the senses (and we would be apriorists). Each of these four *assumptions* has a great representative and founder: Plato, Lucke, Aristotle and Kant, respectively.

It is important to note that we are only talking about "assumptions", not *truths. We believe that even the very idea of truth is a rationalist invention,* as we will try to show in the course of this research.

It can be stated that scientific communities or research traditions (to which we educational researchers adhere), depending on the perspective, paradigm or epistemological orientation of the research programme or mode of knowledge production to which they adhere, construct knowledge using *philosophical assumptions* such as rationalism, empiricism, intellectualism or apriorism;

depending on whether they solve the philosophical problem of the origin of knowledge from reason, from the senses or from both qualities of the cognising subject.

Being a little more daring, we propose that all researchers, whether or not they are aware of the fact, fall into any of the aforementioned *assumptions*, when they try to know the educational reality. And that the same happens when taking a *position* on the other four *problems of knowledge* (possibility, essence, types and criteria of truth).

In this section we will try to analyse the concept, characteristics, function, purpose, classification, authors and works of the mentioned *philosophical assumptions*; which every educational researcher can use, sometimes with ignorance of the fact, when elaborating explanations about the educational reality. It is considered that the *only four assumptions* that human beings can consider to solve the *philosophical problem* about the *origin of knowledge*, none is better than the other. The philosophical assumption(s) chosen to give an opinion on any reality will depend, as already mentioned, on the epistemological and ontological interests of the researcher and the object of study he/she intends to construct.

2.2.5.2.1 Assuming that knowledge springs from reason.

Rationalism is a *philosophical assumption* from which an educational researcher can construct knowledge by solving the problem of the *origin of knowledge*, *conceding* that all our *knowledge* comes from the *reason*, mind, brain, intelligence of human beings.

The question that immediately arises is: if *human knowledge* has its original *source* in *reason*, who put it there, or how did knowledge reach the human *soul*? The answer will be constructed from the following observations:

From a *rationalist point of view*, one can be *of the opinion*, but never be completely sure, that a knowledge can only be true when it is logically necessary and universally valid. When can a certain knowledge be considered valid for all human beings, one *assumes* that it is true when the whole human race agrees that this knowledge is true. When can a judgement be said to be logically necessary, one *assumes* that it is also true when reason judges that a thing, phenomenon, event or fact must be so and that it cannot be otherwise or in any other way, that it must always and everywhere be so.

For example: the propositions "the whole is greater than the part" and "all bodies are large" are examples of logically necessary and universally valid judgements; because they are judgements that are born of the *soul*, propositions that proceed from the *reasonings* of the *brain*. Judgments founded on *thought*, judgments originating from *reason*, from the soul, possess a logical necessity and universal validity. All knowledge, to be true, from a *rationalist* conjecture, must originate in thought, come from the mind; the human soul is the true source from which judgements emerge, the brain is the container of human knowledge.

It is clear that the above judgements are logical propositions, that human thought is *ordering* reality. These judgements are similar to the following: two plus two equals four (symbolically: $2 + 2 = 4$), which is a mathematical judgement. So then, the judgements of the sciences Logic and Mathematics are propositions, knowledge generated in reason. *They are supposed to* be in the mind and it is necessary to take them out of the mind (going back to the question that is guiding this exposition).

Mathematical thinking is conceptual and deductive. Reason can only create concepts, judgements, reasoning. But why create ideas, judgements, reasoning, it is *supposed* to establish certain orders in reality. *Reason* wants to establish order in reality. In Geometrical science, all knowledge is derived (by deduction) from some supreme concepts and axioms (supposedly universally valid and logically necessary laws). Thought works absolutely independently of all experience, coming from the senses, following only its own laws (postulates, axioms, concepts). All judgements formulated from geometry are supposedly distinguished by the characteristic notes of logical necessity and universal validity. It is *reason* bringing order to reality.

Plato observed that any judgement claiming to be true must be governed by the two characteristics already mentioned: logical necessity and universal validity. According to Plato, reality, which can impact the senses and provide experiences to the soul, is continually transforming, constantly changing, moving, shifting (relativism) and therefore cannot provide the soul with certain knowledge about itself. The senses can deceive us, they can hardly provide the soul with true knowledge about reality.

Plato was of the opinion that the senses, by providing the soul with only sensations, lead it to elaborate pure *opinions* about reality. What he failed to say is that *reason* too can only produce mere *opinions*; because to say - for example - that two plus two are four, constitutes a judgement that one *reason* is proposing to other *reasons*, as a convention, in order to agree with them, on certain aspects of reality.

Plato thought that in addition to the sensible world, which only provides the soul with mere sensations through the senses, there must necessarily exist another, suprasensible world, from which reason, the

cognising consciousness must "draw out" its contents (Hessen, 2011: 31-35).

The philosophical debate on the *origin of knowledge* can only be solved, as with the other philosophical problems of knowledge, *by supposing*; either from *reason* or from *experience*; or from both, privileging one or the other, in order of appearance. There are only four known possibilities (mathematically speaking) to solve this problem, since the cognising subject has only two attributes to relate to the objects to be known: his *reason* and his *senses*; but, as each subject feels and thinks differently from the others, this is the fundamental problem: which subjects should we listen to and which others should we ignore when they pretend to draw their knowledge, *supposedly* valid for all and logically necessary? Are they not mere *assumptions* that in certain times, spaces and circumstances have been elaborated to put order in a certain reality?

Plato, perhaps unknowingly, was also *assuming* that the origin of knowledge was to be found in *reason*. Possibly, in that very sense, he wanted to estimate that; or perhaps his personal interests demanded this stance and it was in his interest to philosophise (reflect) on reality in this way. It should not be forgotten that Plato belonged to the wealthy class of classical Greece and it was in his interest to maintain the status quo, the social inequalities of the time in which he lived. It should not be forgotten that philosophical assumptions, in the sense in which they are being exposed in the present research, are neither good nor bad, in themselves, nor are any of them better than the others, to solve the philosophical problems of knowledge; that everything will depend on subjective or group interests, both at the epistemological and ontological levels.

It is known that Plato was an Athenian disciple of Socrates, and that he founded the Academy, one of the most famous schools of philosophy of the time. It should not be forgotten that, in order to belong to this institution, a knowledge of mathematics was required; because it was *assumed* that, in order to be able to start studying philosophy, this prior training was necessary. To paraphrase Gaarder (2001), this is suggested by the sign posted at the entrance to this intellectual centre, which read: "No one enters here if he does not know geometry". Geometry is a mathematical and therefore rational science; it is *assumed* or, it is necessary to *assume*, that its judgements come from the soul, independently of the senses. But on closer inspection, the axioms and postulates of geometry are really only "conventions" that allow a certain part of humanity to agree on how to act in nature and society. The limitations we have on mathematical knowledge prevent us from making a deeper analysis in this respect. We will only add that the mathematical sciences are neither false nor true, in themselves; but that they require the assumption of the truth and falsity of their judgements, in order to establish conventional knowledge.

Plato (A, 2001: 145-196), in the dialogue "*Protagoras or of the Sophists*", (one of the 14 books he wrote) develops the issue of whether or not it is possible to teach virtue. In this book Plato *assumes* that virtue is objective and, therefore, that it is possible to teach it, since virtue exists in itself, independently of the subjects. If any subject has it, it is possible that he can transmit it to others; teach others to be virtuous. From a *rationalist philosophical assumption* it can be *conceded* that the human soul is naturally good and that, by means of questions and answers (dialogue), the teacher can help his pupils to discover their virtues in the depths of their souls; because the human soul comes to this world loaded with all the knowledge necessary for its worldly realisation.

Plato (A 2001, 287-321), in the dialogue "*Menon or of virtue*", which is related to the dialogue "*Protagoras or of the Sophists*", develops the theme of the nature of virtue and the possibility of teaching it. Plato begins by saying that the soul is full of ideas, as if in potency, as if dormant; that they can be extracted from the soul, as mentioned above, by means of dialogue. From the *rationalist assumption* that Plato uses to solve the *problem* of *the origin of knowledge*, it is possible to *argue* that "apprehending" is the same as "remembering"; because the soul comes to this world with all the knowledge necessary to function in it, only that at birth it was forgotten, because the body took over all its attention for the sake of survival; the soul remained a slave of the body, subject to satisfy its needs; and it only has "memories" of what it already knew, on the occasion of the sensations it experiences through the senses. He also addresses the issue of the degrees of knowledge, with its extremes: truth and falsehood. For Plato true knowledge is that which is generated from one of the methodological procedures or intellectual operations, which the human soul is capable of performing, to generate new knowledge, called definition; (rationalism). In definition, as will be observed in the subchapter 2.3, limits are set between what a thing is and what it is not; as these limits imply putting order into things, it is reason that imposes them. Whose reason? Answer: the reason of a subject or group of subjects, if we assume that there is no universal reason.

Plato (A, 2001: 415-492), in the dialogue "*Theaetetes or of science*", discusses knowledge on the *assumption* that it is a product of human *reason* alone (rationalism). According to him, the immaterial and invisible essence of things can only be grasped by means of reason, but all true knowledge must be capable of being demonstrated in facts, in experience. Knowledge goes from the rational to experience in a rigorously *deductive* way. *Deduction* is another of the intellectual operations or *methodological* procedures, with which new knowledge can be generated from *rationalist philosophical assumptions*.

Plato (A, 145-196), in the dialogue "*Protagoras or of the Sophists*", recognises, despite being the father of the *rationalist assumption* to solve the *philosophical problem* of *the origin of knowledge*, that knowledge is a progressive task (relativism) which, step by step, advances its conclusions. According to Plato, the road to knowledge leads from the multiplicity of things to the unity of truth. Real, for Plato, is that which has the power to be an effect or to produce an effect.

Plato (B, 2001: 1-246), in the dialogue "*The Republic or the Just*", specifically in the seventh book (nowadays, chapter VII, because previously the chapters of a work were called books) develops the myth of the cave, where it is explained that individual things (being) are only copies of ideas (ought to be). Using an objectivist assumption to solve the problem of the essence of knowledge, with respect to the pre-metaphysical solution to it (the subject-object relation), he is of the opinion that, in a relation of knowledge, the object determines the subject. It is first the ought to be and then the being. The being must conform to the ought to be. One can think that, from Plato onwards, the dominant philosophical assumption for solving the philosophical problem of the essence of knowledge, as far as its theological solution is concerned, is dualism. Plato initiated the division of reality into two opposing poles: being and ought to be. The philosophers before Plato spoke only of being; the question to be answered was: what is reality made of (materialism)? From Plato onwards, the question would be: what were we made for (ought to be)? Plato himself affirms, in the aforementioned book, that we were made to do good (ought to be).

Plato (2001 B: 247-300), in the dialogue "Phaedrus or of love", constructs his educational theory. In the Academy he teaches that "to apprehend" is "to remember". He deals mainly with the problem of the soul, spirit, reason, which is characterised as self-activity. The soul is the noblest thing in man. The soul suffers, imprisoned by the passions of the body, the longing to return to the realm of absolute ideas (idealism), where true love, truth, justice and all the virtues can be appreciated in their fullest expression.

In the "Symposio" (Plato 2001 A: 493-540) the theme of the human soul, reason, mind, intelligence (dogmatism), prisoner of the body, trying to escape from this world of sensible facts, longing for an eternal, perfect, immutable, beautiful existence (rationalism), is addressed.

For Plato, the world of ideas is the true abode of the soul, the eternally true, the always beautiful and the enduringly good (idealism, ought to be). He thought that there must be a reality behind the world of the senses and called this reality the world of ideas. Here we find the eternal and immutable model images behind the various phenomena we encounter in nature. We call this concept Plato's theory of ideas (Gaarder, 2001: 94-111).

Plato reached the above-mentioned conclusions because he solved each and every major philosophical problem of knowledge from reason.

Zeno of Cicius (342-270 BC), the founder of *Stoicism*, so called because, according to Gaarder (2001), he stood on the portico of Athens (*stoa*), together with Roman representatives such as Seneca and the emperor Marcus Aurelius, also assumed that the origin of knowledge was to be found in reason. They cultivated deductive logic, and their worldview was purely *rational*. The human ideal of the Stoic is the wise man who is governed exclusively by *reason*, giving no place to the impulses of the passions (empiricism), which are judged to be evil (dualism). *Reason* must bring man into harmony with his own nature and with the nature of the cosmos. It is thanks to reason that the virtues (ought to be) and thus happiness are acquired.

The stoic is impassive, trying to balance reason and passion. The stoic has to renounce pleasures and endure his own pains and hardships. This is the origin of the well-known expression: "I bear pain in a stoic attitude". Seneca famously said: "If you agree willingly, fate will carry you; if not, it will drag you by force".

Stoicism has, positively, the ideal of duty (idealism), renunciation and universal brotherhood; because of this it was a doctrine appreciated by the early Christians. The Stoics, like Plato, or rather following his teachings, solved each and every one of the five main problems of knowledge on the basis of rational assumptions.

Plotinus is the most famous neoplatonic author (he also assumes that the source of knowledge is in reason). He wrote "*The Enneads*" (a work divided into six treatises, each of nine books). For Plotinus, the principle of everything is the One, a kind of God from whom all things emanate, but completely transcendent to the world and to man (dualism). Nothing can be affirmed about it, it is unknowable and inexpressible. By emanation from the One, three kinds of entities arise, in successive cascades of lower value. These are: intelligence (or nous), soul and matter. The intelligence contains the ideas (according to Plato) and, from it, the soul. The intelligible world is composed of this triad, the one, the intelligence and the soul (rationalism). On a lower level is matter, the ultimate result of divine emanation and the root of all evils (empiricism). Man must climb this ladder until he identifies himself with God (objectivism). His life will thus consist in detachment from matter and in the assimilation of soul, intelligence and the one, through mystical contemplation (idealism). Ecstasy is the final stage, where man is depersonalised and completely united with God (Gutiérrez, 1997: 65 - 69). Plotinus was a follower of Plato, so he starts from the same philosophical assumptions as Plato.

According to Hessen (2011: 33-35), a distinction must be made between several types of *rationalism*: logical, transcendent, theological, immanent and ontological. According to *logical rationalism*, the contents of experience (on an empiricist assumption) do not give the thinking subject any point of support for his conceptual activity. The idea of consciousness in general is distinct from concrete, individual consciousness. It is something purely logical, an abstraction, and means nothing else than the set of supreme assumptions or principles of knowledge.

Thought is the only source of knowledge (if we assume rationally). The content of human knowledge is deduced (deduction is the method by which we pretend to generate new knowledge from the rationalist imaginary -assumption-) from those supreme principles by a rigorously logical deductive way. All true knowledge possesses logical necessity and universal validity. It is mainly applied to mathematical knowledge.

It is necessary to assume that mathematical knowledge is logically necessary and universally valid, so that human beings, living together in a group, can agree on how to achieve their daily goals: two plus two must be four. Otherwise, it would be impossible to live together.

Logical rationalism is dogmatic, it believes it can penetrate the metaphysical (ontological) sphere by the path of purely conceptual (rational) thought. It derives from formal principles (ought to be) material propositions (being); it deduces (rational method, par excellence, to generate new knowledge), from mere concepts (idealism), knowledge. It pretends that it can be derived (deduction) from the concept of God (rationalism), his existence (empiricism). It imagines that, from the concept of substance, the essence of the soul can be inferred (deduction).

For *transcendental rationalism*, the realm of ideas (objectivism) is in relation to empirical reality (empiricism) in the first place. Ideas (objectivism) are the models of empirical things (empiricism). The realm of ideas (objectivism) is, secondly, in relation to cognising consciousness (rationalism). Not only things (empiricism), but also the concepts (idealism) by means of which we know things (empiricism) are copies of ideas (idealism), they come from the world of ideas (idealism). For example: *anamnesis* is a concept, created by Plato, which can be understood in the sense that all knowledge (subject-object relationship) is a reminiscence (recollection). According to Plato, the soul has contemplated ideas in a pre-earthly existence (innate knowledge) and remembers them on the occasion of sensible perception (born knowledge).

According to *theological rationalism*, it has already been established that, according to Plotinus, the rational part of our soul is continually nourished and enlightened from above. God is supposed to be the cause and end of all human knowledge.

For Augustine all knowledge, all knowledge, in the proper and rigorous sense, comes from human reason or from divine illumination (rationalism). The question was whether one had to believe in Christian miracles or whether it was also possible to approach Christian truths through reason. Truth is not to be sought outside man, but within him. It is not the senses that provide it (from the empiricist imaginary), but the activity of the rational spirit (from the rationalist imaginary). Truth is eternal and immutable (objectivism), therefore it does not come from things (empiricism), which are mutable (subjectivism). Truth is God himself, and his ideas are moulds of these material and imperfect things (Plato). So far what can be affirmed about theological rationalism, in obvious space and time of the investigation.

According to *immanent rationalism*, and following Descartes, there are certain ideas which constitute human reason, called, therefore, innate, inborn ideas, and which not only provide the basis of true knowledge, but also of the wisdom of life as a whole.

It is assumed, pretended, imagined, even if one is never really sure, that religious thought, logical principles, the concept of substance and cause, of extension and number, are planted by God in our reason and come with us at birth (from a rationalist assumption).

According to Descartes (1981. XVI), from the thought of God, from the logical principles, from the concepts of substance and cause, of extension and number which, by the fact of having been sown by God in our reason, come with us at birth, we can derive self-evident conceptual principles, such as the theorems of geometry. Innate concepts (with which we are born, according to the rationalist assumption) are the possible foundations of scientific knowledge of the universe, unlike the contents of sensible experience (criticising the empiricist assumption), whose concepts are never free from confusion.

Descartes, besides the innate, inborn ideas (from a rationalist assumption), observes two other kinds of ideas: the adventitious ones, provoked by external reality; and the fictitious ones, created by the imagination. The innate, inborn (rationalist) ideas are, however, the only ones that constitute the true foundations of knowledge (rationalism).

If the cognising subject has only his reason and his senses to know reality, it can be *assumed* (from reason) that he comes to this world with all the knowledge to survive in it (innate ideas). External reality provokes sensations in him and, on the occasion of these sensations, he remembers the knowledge he already knew (adventitious ideas). When reason (which is born with all the knowledge of reality) is at rest, the imagination plays its part and, piecing together the jigsaw of innate and adventitious ideas (being and ought to be), creates irrational ideas about reality. For example: Sometimes we dream (imagination) that we live with people who have already died and, at the same time, with people who are still alive, in different spaces, times and circumstances.

For Descartes, mathematics is the example of knowledge in which two important conditions of rational knowledge (innate ideas) can be observed: mathematical principles are clear in themselves and with distinct contents.

However, it must be said that mathematics is conventional.

According to *ontological rationalism*, we know things by immediately contemplating the absolute in its creative activity.

Leibniz (rationalist) shows, contrary to Locke (empiricist), that there are innate truths and necessary truths, or truths of reason, as well as natural truths, or truths of fact, which come from experience. The former, therefore, are elaborated by the spirit without the aid of empirical observation, as is the case with the truths of arithmetic and geometry. The latter are acquired through the senses (empiricism).

Assuming from rationalism that the source of knowledge is in reason, this innate knowledge is not, therefore, knowledge of permanent actuality. They are not imprinted in the mind to be taken up. They exist in the mind only virtually (apriorism), as dispositions, i.e. as preformations. The intellect has to struggle and strive to obtain them. Experience helps, yes, to provoke and confirm them, but it is not the very source of their validity.

Nor is the fact that many people accept innate ideas a sign of objective proof. The certainty of innate knowledge, says Leibniz, above all subjectivism, is not founded on generalised opinion (empiricism). Their foundation lies in the logical principle of non-contradiction (immanent criterion of truth).

Innate (rationalist) notions do not only belong to the knowledge of the pure sciences (logic and mathematics). There are also practical notions of full validity. This is the basis of (rationalist) ethics as a proven knowledge of human behaviour. Moral science (the rationalist), like arithmetic, is innate; for it too depends on proofs provided by inner light. And since the proofs leap before our eyes, it is no wonder that men are not aware of all that they possess in themselves and do not always read quickly enough the outlines of the natural law, which God, according to St. Paul, has written in the heart (Leibniz, 1991: 56-57).

By way of conclusion, the educational researcher can use the rationalist philosophical assumption by accepting that the origin, source and basis of knowledge is in reason, in thought. In this way he would be solving the philosophical problem about the origin of knowledge from his reason.

What theoretical consequences can be drawn from the assumption of rationalism? It is assumed, or is meant to be assumed, that knowledge must be logically necessary and universally valid, because our reason judges that it must be so and that it cannot be otherwise, that it must be so always and everywhere, in order to be true.

Why seek the truth?

The question can be answered in the sense that eternal, immutable, universal truth allows us to bring order to reality. To have the certainty that judgements are always and everywhere true.

And what is the point of trying to bring order to reality?

To maintain the status quo. To preserve the established order.

The rationalist philosophical assumption goes hand in hand with its dogmatic cousin. Assuming that knowledge can be known also implies assuming that there is an order to knowledge. It is a matter, in both cases, of reality not moving, perhaps because it suits certain interests. This is where we see the philosophical sense of the assumption: that reality does not move.

Rationalism, like dogmatism, both epistemological and ontological, is of great help to those who wish to maintain the established order.

2.2.5.2.2 Believing that knowledge originates in the senses.

Another *philosophical assumption*, from which the *problem* of the *origin of knowledge* can be solved, contrary to *rationalism*, consists in the *assumption* that all human *knowledge* comes from the *experience* provided by our *senses*: empiricism.

It is important to note that, when this philosophical assumption is used to solve the problem of the *source of knowledge*, in order to know reality, the cognising subject uses his *senses* in preference to his reason. It has already been said that the cognising subject relies only on his reason and his *senses* to establish the relationship with the objects he wants to know. In the case of the *empiricist assumption*, it is the *senses* that are *supposed* to make it possible to know the phenomena. Some philosophers say that the senses are "the windows of the soul".

The educational researcher, as already mentioned, can choose between *assuming* that knowledge originates in *reason* (rationalism), in *experience* (empiricism), in both, privileging *experience* over *reason* (intellectualism), or, in both, preferring *reason* over *experience* (apriorism). The assumption he chooses will determine the theory with which he problematises his object of study. Everything will depend on the epistemological and ontological interests of the cognising subject. The assumption the researcher chooses to relate to reality will also depend on the characteristics of his object of study. When dealing with concepts, such as education, it is better to use rationalist rather than *empiricist* assumptions; but if the object of study is tangible phenomena, such as student behaviour, *empiricist* assumptions work better to establish the knowledge relationship.

Empiricism is a philosophical assumption from which it can be *estimated* that the human soul comes into this world totally empty (contrary to *rationalism*, from which it can be *assumed* that the human soul comes with all the knowledge of reality) and that it is filled with knowledge, throughout life, thanks to the *experiences* that the senses provide it with. In this way, students learn best by providing them with experiences, experiences, etc.

The first to use the *empiricist* assumption to try to explore, describe, explain, interpret, understand reality, perhaps without realising the epistemological and ontological consequences that this would entail, was Democritus, the builder of the theory of the atom. On the problem of the origin of knowledge, Democritus, according to Hessen (2011: 35-38), takes the *view* from an *empiricist* philosophical assumption that when we grasp something with our senses (empiricism) it is due to the movements of atoms in empty space. This means that if there are only atoms moving in empty space, reality is in constant motion and change (relativism).

Relativism is another philosophical assumption from which another problem of knowledge can be solved: the possibility of knowledge. The truth of knowledge, according to this philosophical assumption, is in constant change, depending on place, time and the circumstances of the subjects who construct it.

According to Democritus, when we see the moon, it is because the atoms of the moon reach our eyes (the objects of reality provoke sensations in the senses of the subject). He imagines that the soul is made up of atoms of the soul, round and smooth. He assumes that, at the death of the person, the soul atoms disperse everywhere, they leave the body. They can then enter another body in the process of creation. The *theoretical* consequences of establishing the relation of knowledge with the objects of study from the empiricist assumption, in this case, lead the subject to the opinion that the human being does not have an immortal soul. It can be concluded that the soul is connected to the brain and we cannot have any kind of consciousness when the brain has disintegrated.

To paraphrase Gaarder (2001:50-56), quoting Democritus, atoms, although very many and very different from each other, are all eternal, unalterable and indivisible. There are only atoms with quantitative properties. Everything qualitative is aggregated by the senses. We know that we cognising subjects think and feel differently. Then the empiricist philosophical assumption is related to another assumption that can be used to solve another problem of knowledge: *subjectivism*, from which the problem about the *possibility of knowledge* can be solved. So if we solve the problem of the *possibility of knowledge* from a *subjectivist* assumption, affirming that it is possible to know but that each subject elaborates his own truth, because he feels and thinks differently from other subjects, we are also *assuming* that it is only our experiences (empiricism) that allow us to know reality; and that each subject knows phenomena in a different way.

The word atom means indivisible. It was important for Democritus to be able to say that what everything is made of could not be divided into smaller parts. If that had been the case, they could not have been used as building bricks. For the atoms could have been filed and split into smaller and smaller parts. Nature would have begun to float in an ever more liquid paste. Moreover, the bricks of nature had to be eternal, for nothing can come out of nothing, fixed and solid, but they could not be identical with each other. The only things that exist are atoms and empty space. When a body dies and disintegrates, the atoms disperse and can be used again in another body. For atoms move in space, but because they have inputs and outputs they fit together to form the things we see. If we accept at the outset that nothing can arise from nothing and that nothing disappears, then nature must necessarily be made up of tiny bricks that come together and separate again. Democritus agreed with Heraclitus that all nature flows (relativism). Forms come and go (relativism). But, behind all that flows are some eternal and unchanging things that do not flow: atoms.

If it is accepted that from nothing, nothing can arise, then the law of physics that states that matter is neither created nor destroyed, but only transformed, makes some sense. From this philosophical assumption it can be stated that matter, like ideas, is in constant flux, in constant change.

From an *empiricist* assumption, experience (everything we perceive through the senses) is the only source of human knowledge, the origin of all knowledge. The cognising consciousness (subject) draws its contents (object) from experience. The human spirit is by nature empty, the soul is a blank slate, the spirit is a sheet of paper on which experience writes. The soul experiences only sensations (experiences). Ideas are copies of impressions, derived from sensations. All our concepts are derived from experience. He starts from concrete facts. Justifies his position by referring to the evolution of human thought and knowledge. The child begins by obtaining concrete perceptions. On the basis of these perceptions he gradually comes to form general representations and concepts. These arise organically from experience. Its advocates come from the natural sciences. It is above all a matter of verifying the facts exactly, by means of careful observation. Experience can be internal, self-perception, or external, sense perception (sensualism). That is why the *Sophists* thought in this way. Also the *Stoics* - as will be seen later - and the *Epicureans* were of the same opinion (Hessen, 2011: 35-38).

From an *empiricist* assumption, facts are ascertained by observation and experimentation. Therefore, the aim of those who use this assumption, in order to determine the origin of knowledge, is to conform to the facts, to what can be verified with the senses.

Some empiricist authors are the Sophists, the Stoics, the Epicureans, John Locke (founder of the assumption), David Hume, Condillac, John Stuart Mill, etc.

Epicurus (341-270 B.C.) based on a *materialistic* worldview, with roots in Democritus, founded the scientific community of the *hedonists*, who proposed pleasure (in Greek: *Edoné*) as the supreme value, to which all other values should be subordinated. The rule of practical conduct is therefore: to seek the maximum pleasure, with the minimum of pain. All knowledge is sensual (empirical).

Paraphrasing Gaarder (2001: 76-80), Epicurus insists on the theme of ethics. Virtue is nothing but a means subordinated to pleasure (sensual experiences). And this is where we find the greatest opposition with *Stoicism*, which, from a *rationalist* philosophical assumption (regarding the problem of the origin of knowledge) and a *dogmatic one* (regarding the problem of the possibility of knowledge), proposes virtue as an end, and not as a means. From a *rationalist* philosophical *assumption*, virtue is an end in itself; from its opposite, it is a means subordinated to pleasure. Contrary philosophical *assumptions* allow the elaboration of contradictory *theories*.

Lucretius developed Aristippus' ethics of pleasure and combined it with Democritus' atomic theory. The principle was: live in secret, live for the moment. *"Stranger, here you will be well, here pleasure is the first good. Death does not concern us, for as long as we exist, death is not present, and when death comes we no longer exist. The four healing herbs are: the gods are to be feared, death is nothing to worry about, the good is easy to achieve and the terrible is easy to bear"* (Gaarder, 2001: 66).

John Locke is considered the founder of the *empiricist* philosophical assumption. He derives knowledge about reality from what our senses tell us (subjectivism), from our sensations, from what we can experience, verify. Lucke assumes that we have no innate idea about the world, God, eternity, substance. Lucke considers that it is necessary to analyse all human ideas in order to see if they can be proved by authentic experiences (scepticism). Where do human beings get their concepts from, can we trust what our senses tell us? All our thoughts and concepts are only reflections of what we have seen and heard (subjectivism). Before we grasp something with our senses, consciousness is like a tabula rasa or blank slate. Before we grasp something with our senses, consciousness is as empty and devoid of content as the blackboard before the teacher enters the classroom. But then we begin to grasp simple ideas with the senses, simple ideas of the senses that are elaborated through thought, reasoning. Faith and doubt are ideas of sense reflection. We sense (subjectivism) and we reflect. All we receive through the senses are simple impressions, but little by little we put these sensations together to form concepts (Locke, 1994: 47-74).

All the material of our knowledge about the world enters through the senses (realism). Knowledge that cannot be derived from simple sensations (subjectivism) is false knowledge and must be rejected. The world is really as we perceive it (naive realism). The senses have primary and secondary qualities. The former are the extent of things (weight, shape, movement, number), we can be sure that the senses reproduce the true qualities of things, sweet, sour, green, red, cold, hot, etc.; the latter (colour, smell, taste, sound) are sensations, they do not reflect the true qualities that are inherent in the things themselves; they only reflect the influence of external reality on our senses, our tastes. The primary qualities are in the things themselves. Secondary qualities may vary from one animal to another and from one person to another, according to the constitution of one's senses (subjectivism) (Locke, 1994: 139- 161).

As far as external reality (realism) is concerned, Locke agreed with Descartes that this reality has certain qualities which human beings can grasp with their reason. The soul is a white paper which experience gradually covers with the strokes of writing. We have absolutely no content in consciousness before we acquire our experiences through the senses (subjectivism). There are two types of experience: internal (reflection) and external (sensation). The contents of experience are ideas or representations, either simple or complex. Primary and secondary sensible qualities. Thought does not add a new element, but merely joins together the various data of experience. Although all the contents of knowledge are derived from experience, their logical value is by no means limited to experience. There are truths independent of experience (those of mathematics, for example) (Locke, 1994: 175176).

David Hume (1992) is another thinker who assumes that we only know by experiencing sensations (empiricism).

To paraphrase David Hume (1992: 5-8), in order to know, we must start from the everyday world (from experience). According to him, man has two different kinds of perceptions: impressions and ideas. The former consist of the immediate perception of external life; the latter are the memories of impressions. Both can be simple or compound.

Impressions are the sensations that we have when we see, hear, touch, etc. Ideas are of two kinds: sensations and reflections. All ideas come from impressions.

The only sure method of philosophising, according to Hume, is experience and observation. His *critical empiricism* leads him to the problem of the genesis of ideas. The entire contents of consciousness, or perceptions, are of two kinds: impressions and ideas. The former are properly sensations (hearing, seeing, feeling, desiring, rejecting, etc.);

the latter, representations, albeit weakened, of the former. In turn, impressions are subdivided into two groups: those of sensation and those of reflection. Here is an impression that makes one feel hot or cold, thirsty or hungry through the senses. The consciousness then produces a copy of it, a copy which usually remains after the sensation has vanished. This copy is called an idea, and the impression from which it comes is called the impression of sensation. When such an idea, accompanied by pleasure or pain, later appears in the soul, new impressions of desire or aversion, joy or fear, etc., may arise. These latter impressions are impressions of reflection. The productive aptitude of the mind does not extend beyond the capacity to bind, shape or rework the contents supplied by perception. The work of the understanding lies in somehow combining these materials, how? The linking of representations together takes place in three ways called principles. The principles of association or resemblance, contiguity in time or space, and cause and effect. All ideas come, in their initial appearance, from simple impressions; they have their correspondence in composite impressions and represent these in consciousness. In other words: ideas, as weakened representations, are copies of impressions. Even those ideas which at first sight seem so distant from experience, have their origin in experience. The idea of God itself does not escape this psychogenetic law. The understanding conceives it in so far as it associates, through its imagination, the limitless with the ideas of wisdom and goodness, empirically obtained in the beginning. There are ideas that are the product of memory and ideas that are the product of imagination. Furthermore, there are simple perceptions and ideas and complex perceptions and ideas. The latter are formed according to the aforementioned principles of association, just as by virtue of these principles simple ideas can be distinguished from complex ones. Complex ideas are of three kinds: relations, modes and substances. The notions of mode and substance are merely collections (collections) of representations, assembled by the imagination, under certain names evoked by memory. They come, strictly speaking, from impressions of reflection.

Think, for example, of the substantial being mentioned in the idea of gold, or the way beauty exists in various women. On the other hand, relations can be grouped into seven categories: likeness, identity, space and time, quantity (number), quality (degree), contrariety and cause and effect. Hume concludes his reflections with the subject of abstract or general ideas, arguing in favour of the theory that such ideas are, at bottom, particular ideas linked to a certain name which gives them a wider significance and makes them evoke individual ideas similar to them (nominalism). With regard to the ideas of space and time, and against Newton's doctrine of the function of infinity in conceiving them, Hume, linking himself to the *empiricism* of Locke and Berkeley, supports the thought that such ideas are generated in the observation of a finite number of facts. The representation of space comes from the ordering of perceived objects; that of time, from the succession of impressions of all kinds. The capacity of the spirit is limited. The notion of infinite divisibility is illusory. Space and time are not something that exists factually side by side with observed things, as traditional philosophy assumes. They are something different; they are ways of perceiving of the subject, and, indeed, space is the way of perceiving co-existence, and time the way of perceiving the succession of impressions. The mind usually sees in them certain real ideas, but they are only abstractions, and to abstractions nothing corresponds in reality. As abstractions they exist only in the words (names) by which they are conventionally designated. Thus Hume explains the origin of the belief in such abstractions by way of *nominalism*. That is, by the work of the imagination, associated with the power of language, man invents the substantial existence of space and time. But this is only one of the frequent cases of metaphysical illusion. The human faculty itself even invents the ideas of existence in general and of external existence in particular.

When looking for the causal relationship between facts, knowledge remains within the realm of probability. The necessity of the succession of one fact (cause) with respect to another (effect) cannot be given by mere reasoning. Past experience is the answer. The observation of the linking of certain facts brings with it the habit of associating them with each other as contiguous and successive. The perception of one necessarily determines the production of the other. The habitual linking of facts impels the mind to pass from one to the other by internal necessity. The intensity of impressions spreads over the ideas associated with it. From this comes belief, namely, the acceptable expectation of the order and connection of ideas representing facts. Hume indicates that in order to judge of the cause-effect relation (logic of causality) one must submit to the following eight rules: rule of contiguity of causes and effects, rule of priority of causes over effects, rule of necessary nexus of causes and effects, rule of constancy of causes and effects, rule of community or coherence of causes and effects, rule of differentiation of causes and effects, rule of variations of degree of causes and effects, and rule of completeness of causes (Hume, 1992: 5-8).

Condillac is another empiricist who only accepts knowledge when it comes from the senses. According to Condillac (sensualist) there is only one source of knowledge, sensation. The soul has originally only one faculty, that of experiencing sensations.

So far we can see the two opposing philosophical *assumptions* from which it is possible to elaborate contradictory explanations of the same reality: *rationalism* and *empiricism*. It all depends on where the researcher places himself in relation to reason and the senses. If reason is privileged, one falls into the first assumption; if it is the senses from which the cognising subject starts, one falls into the second. If it is accepted that the cognising subject has only his reason and senses to relate to reality, it can be concluded that he has, in mathematical terms, only four philosophical *assumptions* to analyse it: *rationalism* (reason), *empiricism* (experience), *intellectualism* (both reason and experience, but starting with the senses and ending with reason), or *apriorism* (both reason and experience, but starting with reason and ending with the senses). It can be seen that the latter two reconcile the radical positions of the first two.

2.2.5.2.3 Presuming that the source of knowledge is in both reason and the senses, but that we feel first and then we think.

According to Hessen (2011: 38-40) *intellectualism* is a philosophical assumption that means "reading within". For this philosophical assumption the source and basis of knowledge is both thought (reason) and experience (senses), i.e. it mediates between empiricism and rationalism. Cognitive consciousness reads in experience, draws its concepts from experience (empiricism). In addition to the intuitive sensible representations (empiricism) there are the concepts, contents of consciousness, not intuitive (rationalism); but in genetic relation to them, because they are obtained from the contents.

Aristotle (384-322 BC) places the Platonic world of ideas (rationalism) within empirical reality (empiricism). Ideas are the essential (rationalism) forms of things. Experience (empiricism) is the basis of all knowledge. Through the senses we obtain perceptual images of concrete objects. In these sensible images is contained the general essence, the idea of the thing; which is extracted by the real or agent understanding and is then received by the possible or passive understanding; thus knowledge is realised (Hessen, 2011: 38 - 40); that is, it mediates between empiricism and rationalism, privileging the former.

Aristotle, according to Gaarder (2001: 20) was a meticulous man who wanted to bring order to the concepts of human beings. Philosopher and scientist, he was interested in the processes of nature. In addition to the intelligence that Plato used (rationalism), he also used the senses (empiricism). Plato was a poet, Aristotle an encyclopaedic systematiser who founded and ordered the various sciences. Aristotle put order into concepts and founded Logic as a science. Aristotle was not an Athenian, Plato was 61 years old when Aristotle arrived at the Academy. Aristotle, the son of a physician, was most concerned with living nature; he can be regarded as Europe's first (empiricist) biologist (Gaarder, 2001: 126-147).

Intellectualism can solve the problem of the origin of knowledge by supposing, from reason and the senses (but estimating first the senses and then reason), that both thought (rationalism) and the senses (empiricism) are the source and basis of knowledge; but that first we feel and then we think. This applies very well in Natural Sciences, because those sciences work with concrete objects (such as nature); but not in Mathematics and Logic, which work with concepts.

The need that intellectualism satisfies is to reflect (rationalism) on perceptions (empiricism).

One of the greatest followers of Aristotle in the Middle Ages was St. Thomas Aquinas (1225-1274): A great *intellectualist*, in terms of philosophical assumptions; According to him, we begin by receiving from concrete things sensible images, sensible species (empiricism). The *intelectus agens* (reason) extracts from them general essential images, the species *intelligibilis* (sensations). The *intelectus posibillis* (reason) receives these in itself and thus judges about things (rationalism).

We do not acquire the ideas of real things, but through contact with reality (empiricism). They are existential truths of fact, which we only grasp through reflection on sensible data. On the other hand, the first principles, for example: "the whole is greater than each of its parts", we could know them, even if we had no experience, simply by analysing the terms of the subject and the predicate (rationalism). Basically, first principles tell us the essences of things, and the essential relations, which are the very structure of nature.

Whereas the data acquired by the senses (empiricism) give us to know, analysed (rationalism), the existential reality of things.

What would be more important in Thomistic doctrine, first essential principles (rationalism), or existential experience (empiricism)? Both aspects. Without experience, we could not know reality; without reason, we could not know it in essence, but only contingently. Therefore, necessarily, all knowledge has to start from the senses, and has to be realised (or applied) by means of conclusions, which are a conjugation of these first principles with experiential reality. These are, of course, the fundamental sciences, such as mathematics, philosophy, etc., which lend the principles to the others. For it is obvious that the positive sciences must of necessity start from observation and experiment. For example, the notion of the triangle, and the relations of its angles, is not experimental. As a fundamental principle, it would be true even if no perfect triangle existed in the world. And applying the laws of Logic (i.e. the very structure of human thought), error in such cases would be impossible. On the other hand, it is not so in its application to particular cases, where observation must necessarily be introduced, as would be the case in the triangulation drawn imaginary to measure by trigonometry the distance from the earth to the moon.

It is necessary to start from the fact of existence first (empiricism), and only then, in a second step, to search for what the object in question essentially is (rationalism).

Our reason, applied to experience, orders it, regulates it, for practical purposes, rather than for purposes of essential knowledge. It is reason putting order into passion: first we feel and then we think. It seems that reason and the senses were given to the subject, rather than to know the essence of things, in order to survive on this earthly plane.

Man does not know everything by reasoning alone (rationalism). In fact, even in everyday, purely human experience (empiricism), our knowledge goes far beyond our reasoning. For example, it is not possible to reduce to logical terms the certainty we have about the love of a friend. If we have it, it is because he has revealed his inner self to us, by means of some signs that I am willing to accept (De Aquino, 1991: XXV-XXXV).

Thomas Aquinas was an *intellectualist*, in terms of the philosophical assumptions from which he starts to solve the problem of the origin of religious knowledge (reason and the senses, privileging the latter over the former); that is, he first locates himself in reality (empiricism), in order to be able to analyse it (rationalism).

2.2.5.2.4 Conjecturing that the basis of knowledge lies in both reason and the senses, but that we think first and then we feel.

Paraphrasing Hessen (2011: 40-41), if we assume from *apriorism* both experience (empiricism) and thought (rationalism) are considered; that is, both reason and the senses, as the sources of knowledge, just like *intellectualism*, only that, while from this philosophical assumption priority is given to experience (empiricism), from the former it is given to the mind (rationalism). Our knowledge presents elements a priori (before experience) and independent of experience. They are not contents (knowledge) but forms of knowledge (methods). These forms (procedures) receive their content from experience (senses). Concepts (rationalism) without intuitions (empiricism) are empty, intuitions (empiricism) without concepts (rationalism) are blind. The a priori factor does not come from experience, but from thought, from reason. In a certain sense, reason imprints the a priori forms of empirical matter and thus constitutes the objects of knowledge. Thought does not behave receptively and passively in the face of experience, but spontaneously and actively. In *apriorism* we assume that the philosophical problem about the origin of knowledge can be solved, as in intellectualism, from both qualities of the cognising subject: reason and the senses. The difference in the way in which both assumptions solve this problem is that in apriorism reason is considered first, and then the senses, as the origin of knowledge.

From the *apriorist* assumption it can be conjectured that people come into this world "programmed" to know only certain things (e.g. the characteristics, functions, purposes, causes, consequences, classifications, etc., of phenomena); but that other things (such as the essences of the realities we experience) are forbidden to us.

Kant is of the opinion, in agreement with Hessen, that the matter of knowledge (sensations) comes from experience (empiricism), and the form (ideas) from thought (rationalism). It is conceded that with matter the sensations are signified. Our thought (reason) is considered to order the contents of sensations by means of the forms of intuition (empiricism) and thought (rationalism). The forms of intuition (empiricism) are hypothesised to be space and time. It is presupposed that cognising consciousness (reason) begins by introducing order into the tumult of sensations (empiria), ordering them in space and time, in juxtaposition and succession. It is argued that the cognising subject then introduces a new connection between the contents of perception with the help of thought forms. This connection, it is argued, is determined by the laws of thought, by the a priori forms and functions of consciousness. This is *intellectualism-empiricism*. It derives concepts from experience: *apriorism-rationalism*. It prefers the rational factor, not to experience, but to reason.

According to Gaarder (2001), Immanuel Kant (1724-1804), a student at Berkeley, was the first professor of philosophy at a university. Gaarder argues that Kant's philosophical concern was to see what we can know about the world, whether it is exactly as we perceive it (empiricism), or whether it is as it presents itself to our reason (rationalism).

In this respect, according to Gaarder (2001: 388-413), Kant assumes that the law of cause-effect (categories) itself is part of human reason. The causal law (rationalism) always rules absolutely because both perception (empiricism) and reason (rationalism) play an important role when we perceive the world. He believes that there are also important conditions in our reason for how we grasp the world around us. He argues that there are certain conditions in the human mind that contribute to determining our concept of the world. There are certain dispositions in our reason and these dispositions mark our perceptions (apriorism). He is of the opinion that what we see we perceive first and foremost as a phenomenon in time and space.

Kant, perhaps without realising that he was only supposing about reality from both qualities of the cognising subject (reason and the senses), in the terms set out in the previous paragraphs, invented the apriorist assumption in an attempt to solve the problem of the origin of knowledge.

By way of conclusion, and after this overview of the *philosophical assumptions* from which the *problem* of the *origin of knowledge* can be solved, we consider that, as with the problem of the possibility of knowledge, of all the *philosophical assumptions* discussed, from which the *problem* of the *origin of knowledge* can be solved, none of those analysed (rationalism, empiricism, intellectualism and apriorism) is better than the others. The *assumption*(s) that an educational researcher chooses to analyse phenomena will depend on the object of study and the epistemological and ontological interests of the researcher. What is important to note is that the philosophical assumption chosen, whether the researcher knows it or ignores it, will have implications on theories, on the types of theories to be used to problematise the object of study, to construct it.

It is good to remember a maxim of quantum theory: "in the beginning everything is possibility, but when one of the possibilities is chosen, it becomes experience and has consequences on the subjects". For the way in which the philosophical problem of knowledge is solved, respectively (using reason, the senses or both), will determine what is assumed about reality.

What is more, every researcher who constructs an object of study, whether he knows it or not, does so on the basis of one or more *philosophical assumptions*, in this case, *about the origin of knowledge*. Because all discourse is constructed from certain philosophical assumptions, irremediably.

The question that every researcher should ask himself, before attempting to begin with the knowledge of any of the phenomena of education, is this: where does the knowledge of the object of study that I intend to address originate from, what is the source, where is it born, where does it come from, how does it originate, from reason, from experience, or from both? The construction of the discourse on the object of study will depend on the choice made regarding the assumptions from which the origin of knowledge can be legitimised. And this choice will be made, whether the educational researcher knows it or not, by solving this problem with reason, with the senses or with both qualities of the cognising subject.

In this sense, the educational researcher should ask a second question: from which *philosophical assumption* should I approach the object of study? There are four options: rationalism, empiricism, intellectualism and apriorism. And the choice of any of these options will depend on the way in which the problem of knowledge under study is solved.

2.2.5.3 *The epistemological relationship between the philosophical assumptions from which the problem of the possibility of knowledge can be solved and the philosophical assumptions from which the problem of the origin of knowledge can be solved.*

The philosophical assumptions from which the problem of the origin of knowledge can be solved (rationalism, empiricism, intellectualism and apriorism) can be compared with the philosophical assumptions from which the problem of the possibility of knowledge can be solved.

A rationalist (origin of knowledge) is also a dogmatist (possibility of knowledge). Whoever assumes that it is possible to know, imagines that truth exists, may think that it lies in the depths of the soul (Plato) and that the subject can obtain it by discovery. What already exists can be discovered. For a rationalist (origin of knowledge) the same as for a dogmatist (possibility of knowledge) reality does not move, that is why he thinks that true knowledge exists. The subjects imagine, on both assumptions, that reality always remains fixed, eternally immobile. From both assumptions they seek to bring order to reality, to establish finished knowledge. This is due, as already mentioned, to the fact that the problem of the origin of knowledge from reason is being solved.

An empiricist (origin of knowledge) is also a sceptic, subjectivist and relativist (possibility of knowledge). From both assumptions one can try to overthrow the established order. They imagine that the subject never finishes knowing objects (scepticism); that reality moves, that each subject feels and thinks differently (subjectivism) and that, therefore, there is no universal, eternal, immutable truth; that truth changes in time, space and circumstances (relativism). By virtue of the fact that the soul comes into this world blank, without any knowledge, all knowledge must be acquired by experience (empiricism). This is because the problem of the origin of knowledge from the senses is being solved.

An intellectualist and/or apriorist (origin of knowledge) is also a critic (possibility of knowledge). From both assumptions, one can think that it is possible to know (dogmatism), but not in essence (scepticism), because each subject feels and thinks differently (subjectivism), because truth changes in time, space and circumstances (relativism) and because all knowledge must be useful to the one who formulates it (pragmatism). This is because the problem of the origin of knowledge from reason and the senses is being solved. If it is first reason and then the senses, the assumption from which one starts to know will be apriorism; if one starts from the senses to know and then finishes with reason, one is assuming from Aristotelian intellectualism.

Here, what is truly philosophical, if one can speak of a truth, is to suppose that, at the origin of knowledge, reality remains still (dogmatism and rationalism) or moves (scepticism and empiricism).

Next, the most important problem of knowledge will be addressed: the subject-object relationship. Gutiérrez Pantoja (2005) in his book: *Methodology of the social sciences I*, specifically in chapter III, argues that method depends on the way in which the cognising subject is linked to its object of knowledge. The title of the aforementioned chapter is entitled "*Alternatives for linking thought and reality*", which can be interpreted as: the different *assumptions* from which the cognising *subject* can *relate* to the *object* to be known, in order to try to explore it, explain it, interpret it, understand it, etc. Depending on the form in which it solves each of the five main problems of knowledge.

Once again, as with the two previous problems of knowledge (the *possibility* and *origin* of knowledge), we see that the cognising subject only has his *senses* and his *reason* to "know" the object of knowledge, to *relate* to it. Since it is impossible to know whether he knows with his reason or with his senses, in terms of what has already been clarified, it is necessary to assume from one or the other, or from both, privileging one or the other. What is certain is that the theory depends on the assumption, that is to say, if the cognising subject is located in reason, the relation with his object of study will be established in a totally different way to the fact of starting from the senses.

The problem of the essence of knowledge is important because it seeks to clarify the way in which the relation of knowledge is established between the cognising subject and the object to be known. It is about the alternative links between thought and reality, according to Gutiérrez (2005).

2.2.5.4 *The philosophical assumptions from which the problem of the essence of knowledge can be solved.*

Scientific communities or research traditions, depending on the perspective, paradigm or epistemological orientation of the research programme or mode of knowledge production to which they adhere, construct their objects of study in a pre-metaphysical (objective, subjective or dialectical), metaphysical (realist, idealist or phenomenalist) and theological (dualist and theistic or monist and pantheistic) way, depending on how they solve the problem of the essence of knowledge: With reason, with the senses or with both qualities of the cognising subject.

Following Hessen (2011: 15-20), the main elements of knowledge are the subject, which is located in the psychological sphere; the image, which is located in the logical sphere; and the object, which is located in the ontological sphere. The main problem of gnoseology, theory of science, epistemology, theory of knowledge or philosophy of science, consists in determining the relation of the subject to the object; that is, who determines whom; the object to the subject (objectivism), the subject to the object (subjectivism) or whether the two determine each other reciprocally and indefinitely (dialogical).

To answer questions such as the above Hessen (2011: 4460) proposes three solutions: *pre-metaphysical*, in which he only considers objectivism and subjectivism (we include in this study, in addition to the two assumptions proposed by Hesse, dialectics; because this assumption tries to establish a mediation between the two previous ones); *metaphysical*, such as realism, idealism and phenomenalism; and *theological*, such as monism and pantheism and dualism and theism.

2.2.5.4.1 Solving the problem of the essence of knowledge from the philosophical assumptions of the pre-metaphysical solution.

The *pre-metaphysical solutions* tell us nothing about the ontological character of the subject and the object; they refer only to the relation of knowledge between the two; that is, to the epistemological problem, the problem of knowledge.

In this section we will try to solve the problem of the subject-object relation in pre-metaphysical terms, that is, considering only the relation of knowledge between the subject and the object, without referring to reality, but only to the relation between thought and reality, to the relation of knowledge between the subject and the object.

Interesting things happen in this relationship, from an epistemological point of view:

2.2.5.4.1.1 Assuming that the object determines the subject.

From an *objectivist* philosophical assumption it can be considered that the object to be known determines the cognising subject. Objects can be thought of as something given, something that presents a totally defined structure; a structure that is reconstructed by the cognising consciousness.

That the object determines the subject is to be interpreted in the sense that there is universally valid and logically necessary knowledge, which the cognising subject only has to internalise and repeat in order to regulate his daily activities, concerning the different possibilities of realisation of the human spirit on this earthly plane: art, science, religion and philosophy.

For example: in religion it is assumed, or wanted to be assumed, that there is only one true God: Jehovah, in the case of the followers of Christianity.

To be determined, by the object, as a subject, means, practically, to be dogmatised. It works like brainwashing. The soldier, who gives his life for the Fatherland, is determined, as a subject, by the object, that is, by the institution, by the idea that another rationality instituted and established in his conscience.

Assuming from objectivism goes very well with giving an opinion on reality from *dogmatism* (an assumption to solve the problem of the possibility of knowledge) and *rationalism* (an assumption to solve the problem of the origin of knowledge). The three assumptions mentioned above, although they solve different problems of knowledge, do so from the standpoint of reason.

In a logical (discursive, language) relation of knowledge, one can assume, but never be certain, that the object to be known (which is in the ontological sphere) determines the cognising subject (which is in the psychological sphere). If objects are thought to be something given, something totally definite, forever and ever, it does not require discussion, it is only memorised. For example: $2 + 2 = 4$. The whole is greater than the part. In *deductive* mathematics and *deductive* logic we work with *rationalistic dogmas*. The truth is that these *rational dogmas objectively* determine the subjects because it is necessary for them to establish order in their relations with others. It can be a question of commercial relations, labour relations, etc.

Nothing is said about the ontological character of the subject and the object; it refers only to the relation of knowledge between a cognising subject and an object to be known.

From this philosophical assumption it is thought, or can be conjectured, that the cognising subject takes upon himself the properties of the object to be known, that he reproduces them, literally speaking. Example: it can be thought that there is a unique and universally valid concept of education, regardless of what different subjects may think about the same idea. It is assumed that this concept must be discovered by reason and that, once this has been done, all subjects must be taught the same idea, without any change, in order to bring order to educational reality. Objects are thought of as something given, something that presents a structure that is reconstructed by the cognising consciousness.

It is Plato's realm of ideas or essences. For Plato (dogmatist, rationalist and objectivist) ideas are objective. They form a substantive order. The sensible world has the suprasensible world in front of it. And just as we discover the objects of the former, in the sensible intuition, in perception, so we discover the objects of the latter, in a non-sensible intuition, the intuition of ideas (Hessen, 2011: 44-46). Thinking about reality in this way gives the subject security. It can be assumed that God exists, that there is true justice, universal morality, etc. Order will always be sought by reason, with a view to regulating passion and giving security to other souls. That is why the *objectivist* assumption gets along very well with its "cousins", the *dogmatic* and *rationalist* philosophical assumptions.

Plato (from *dogmatic*, *rationalist* and *objectivist* philosophical assumptions) attributes a metaphysical reality to essences (*objectivism*). He defines ideas as suprasensible realities, as metaphysical entities (Gaarder, 2001: 94-114).

The *objectivist* philosophical assumption can be used to elaborate discourses (logical relation) on objects (abstract or concrete) with pretensions of truth, making the subjects to whom the message is addressed believe that the world of ideas (*dogmatism*, *rationalism*) has its own existence and that reality (*scepticism*, *empiricism*) is a mere reflection of it.

To be religiously objectified means to assume that gods exist whether one thinks about them or not. To be philosophically objectified means to think that reality exists independently of cognising subjects. To be scientifically objectified means to think that knowledge exists independently of the mind. To be objectified artistically, means to think that art exists independently of the subjects who can appreciate it.

Before we continue, let us remember a popular saying: nothing is true or a lie, everything is the colour of the glass you look through!

2.2.5.4.1.2 Believing that the subject determines the object.

From a *subjectivist* philosophical assumption it can be considered that the cognising *subject* determines the object to be known. Nothing is said about the ontological character of subject and object; it refers only to the knowledge relationship between a cognising *subject* and an object to be known. If a researcher starts from this assumption to construct his object of study, what he is really doing is to place the world of ideas, the set of principles of knowledge, in the subject. He tries to ground human knowledge in the subject (Hessen, 2011: 46-47).

Assuming that the *subject* determines the object, in a knowledge relationship, leads the educational researcher to try to base knowledge on the *cognising subject*. It is assumed that the *cognising subject* determines the object to be known. The world of ideas, the set of principles of knowledge, is placed in the *cognising subject*. The researcher's attention remains on the *subject* who knows and judges, without taking into account the object to be known.

That the *cognising subject* determines the object to be known means that discourse is not neutral, that science is self-interested. Every cognising subject, whether he knows it or not, constructs his knowledge on the basis of his emotions, passions, feelings, ambitions, prejudices, etc. All these subjective qualities contaminate discourse. In political science, for example, it can be observed that the knowledge that is constructed about the economic, political and social reality of a country like Mexico varies, depending on the partisan affiliation of the researchers. That is why the discourses of the National Action Party (PAN) are not compatible with the discourses of the Party of the Democratic Revolution (PRD). The former solves the philosophical problem of the essence of knowledge from reason, the latter from the senses.

One of the important *functions* of the *subjectivist philosophical assumption* is to try to convince others that what one feels and thinks about reality (on the basis of emotions, feelings, passions and ambitions, personal and subjective) can be generalised to the human race as a whole. In this way it is possible to objectify others in a particular idea which, by that fact, becomes general.

It can be inferred from what has been said that the subjectivist philosophical assumption can be used to transform reality to the liking of the researcher and the group he or she represents, and if not, at least a proposal is elaborated with such ends in mind.

Many thinkers assumed, at the time of elaborating their knowledge about reality, that the cognising subject determines the object to be known. Most likely, this happened without the researcher's knowledge.

A clear example in this respect is provided by Schopenhauer (1997: 216), according to him *"...the will is not only free, but omnipotent; it creates not only its own conduct, but its own world; and just as it determines itself in its actions and shapes its mute, both are the knowledge that the will has of itself and not something else; and in so doing it determines the other two things, for outside of it nothing exists; and man's conduct and the world itself are will; only on that assumption is it truly autonomous"*. The world is what the will of the subject represents. Reality is a representation of the will. The cognising subject determines the object to be known. The entity is as the investigator wants to represent it. Neutral, essential knowledge is not possible. All knowledge is of the nature of the subject who formulates it. All knowledge is contaminated by the emotions, feelings, passions, emotions and ambitions of the subject. Shopenhauer solved the pre-metaphysical problem of the essence of knowledge from the senses.

The *subjectivist philosophical assumption* (from which the problem about the *possibility* of knowledge can be solved) is related to the *subjectivist philosophical assumption* (from which the problem about the *origin* of knowledge can be solved). Because both solve their respective philosophical problem from the senses.

I consider it necessary to clarify the situation of the two *subjectivist philosophical assumptions*: the first belongs to the *ontological* sphere, the second to the *epistemological* sphere. From the first one one can solve the problem of the *possibility* of knowledge (ontological sphere), from the second one can solve the problem of the *essence* of knowledge (epistemological sphere), i.e. the way in which the relation of knowledge between the two elements of knowledge is given. The first one refers to *reality* (it can be assumed that each subject constructs his own reality, each subject elaborates his knowledge), the second one refers to the *relation* of knowledge (it is assumed that, in a relation of knowledge, the *cognising subject* determines the object to be known; that is, the passions, emotions, feelings and ambitions of the *cognising subject* contaminate the discourse he elaborates on reality). The most important similarity between the two assumptions is that they both solve their respective problem of knowledge from the senses.

The *subjectivist philosophical assumption* is also related to the *empiricist philosophical assumption*, from which the problem of the *origin* of knowledge can be solved *by assuming* that knowledge is acquired through *experiences*. If we assume that knowledge is the product of the experiences of the subject and if all subjects are unrepeatable, unique and different from other subjects, then the world is what each subject represents of it, in the way Schopenhauer understands it.

2.2.5.4.1.3 Presuming that the object and the subject are mutually determined.

From a *dialectical philosophical assumption*, reality can be analysed by considering the two extremes of the pre-metaphysical solution: Objectivism and Subjectivism.

Why dialectic, because it affirms that, in a relation of knowledge, the cognising subject and the object to be known mutually determine each other; that is, both the subject determines the object and the object determines the subject, in an infinite *dialectical* relation. This can be interpreted in the sense that we never finish knowing reality.

We never know the essence, but at least we know better and better. That is to say, if we do not have the truth about the essence of any phenomenon, we can at least have the best explanation at the moment.

It can be assumed, but never known for certain, that in a (logical) knowledge relationship, the educational researcher and his object of study are in a *dialogue* that never ends and that, therefore, the cognising subject gradually approaches the understanding of his object of study.

In the dialectical philosophical assumption, the pre-metaphysical problem about the essence of knowledge is solved from both qualities of the cognising subject: reason and the senses.

An important feature of the *dialectical philosophical assumption* can be inferred: it is conciliatory of the other two extremes (objectivism and subjectivism).

Therefore, the *dialectical philosophical assumption* can be used to construct knowledge that benefits both subjects (people) and objects (institutions).

But the ultimate aim of the *dialectical philosophical assumption* is the reconciliation of opposites, both epistemologically and ontologically, in search of a better world.

Examples of thinkers who constructed their objects of study in this way are Aristotle (in antiquity) and Beauchot (today). The former, when constructing his ethics; the latter, when elaborating his epistemology. The former, on the *ontological* level, the latter, on the *epistemological* level:

To paraphrase Aristotle (1999), the virtue of courage is a middle ground between two vicious extremes: cowardice and recklessness. Between the coward (subjectivist) and the reckless (objectivist), one finds

the courageous (dialectician) who, like the coward, feels fear in the face of imminent danger; but, like the daredevil, he masters his fear and seeks the best way to resolve the dangerous situation.

Beauchot (1995:20), possibly based on the Aristotelian theory of the middle ground, establishes that in the face of the extremes of equivocism (subjectivism) and univocism (objectivism), an analogical (dialectical) model of interpretation is presented, where equality (objectivism) and diversity (subjectivism) are combined, privileging the subject over the object; by virtue of the fact that, to become what is wanted (objective), we must start from what we are (subjective).

Solving the problem about the essence of knowledge in a pre-metaphysical way, assuming philosophically from dialectics, in order to construct objects of study, is related to the *critical* (from which the problem about the possibility of knowledge can be solved), *intellectualist* and *apriorist* philosophical assumptions (from which the problem about the origin of knowledge can be solved).

From the four philosophical assumptions (criticism, intellectualism, apriorism and dialectics) the respective problems of knowledge (possibility, origin and essence) can be solved by trying to reconcile the opposing extremes (dogmatism-scepticism, rationalism-empiricism and objectivism-subjectivism).

Up to this point, with regard to the problem of the *essence* of knowledge, we have dealt with the *assumptions* corresponding to the *pre-metaphysical solution*; that is, the *assumptions* from which the problem of the relation of knowledge that is established between the cognising subject and the object to be known can be, but need not necessarily be, solved: the objectivist, subjectivist and dialectical *philosophical assumptions*. The question guiding the analysis was: *who determines whom in a knowledge relation: the object to the subject, the subject to the object or both determine each other?*

It is important to clarify our position, just as we elucidated on the other two philosophical problems of knowledge discussed above: the possibility and origin of knowledge.

It is not possible to establish, for certain, which of the aforementioned *philosophical assumptions* (objectivism, subjectivism and dialectics) is better (or better) or worse (or worse) for solving the problem of the *essence of knowledge*. What can be stated is that which philosophical assumption is chosen to solve the problem about the essence of knowledge depends on the researcher and his object of study and, moreover, will have important theoretical consequences; as will be seen in subchapter 2.2.

Once the relation of knowledge has been analysed, the next section will deal with the second solution to the problem of the essence of knowledge: the metaphysical solution.

Why metaphysics, because now we will place ourselves outside or above reality and ask ourselves whether reality exists without the intervention of the subject (realism), whether it is a subjective construction (idealism), or whether it exists independently of the subjects, but, moreover, each subject knows it differently, that is to say, as a phenomenon (phenomenalism).

2.2.5.4.2 Solving the problem of the essence of knowledge from the philosophical assumptions of the metaphysical solution:

The *metaphysical solutions* (realism, idealism and phenomenalism) consider the ontological character of the object, i.e. they refer to the existence of the subject and the object.

The problem about the existence of the subject and the object can be solved from three assumptions: realism, idealism and phenomenalism; which depend on the way in which the cognising subject solves the problems about the essence of knowledge: with reason, with the senses or with both qualities of the educational researcher.

2.2.5.4.2.1 Assuming that the object exists independently of the subject.

The educational researcher can solve the problem of the existence or non-existence of his object of study by assuming that the metaphysical solution to the problem of the essence of knowledge can be established from *realism*. If it is philosophically assumed from *realism*, it can be argued that, in addition to ideal objects, there are real objects, independent of thought (realism) (Hessen, 2011: 47-51). This is because the metaphysical problem about the existence or non-existence of reality is being solved from the senses.

When a researcher relates to a reality, he can solve the problem about the existence of his object of study from a *realist philosophical assumption* (which frames a metaphysical solution to the problem about the essence of knowledge), stating that his object of study exists, independently of his consciousness.

One of the fundamental theses on which the researcher who constructs his object of study from the philosophical realist assumption relies is that real objects are presumed to exist which act on the senses of the different subjects by provoking perceptions in them. This is because the metaphysical philosophical problem of the essence of knowledge is being solved, as has been insisted, from the senses.

Important thinkers, ancient and modern, built their knowledge on realist philosophical assumptions: Democritus, Aristotle, Galileo, Locke, Gaarder, etc.

Following Gaarder (2001: 120), Democritus assumes that there are only atoms with quantitative properties (realism). He is of the opinion that everything qualitative (idealism) is an addition of our senses (realism).

Aristotle assumes that perceived properties (empiricism) also apply to things (realism), independently of the cognising consciousness (idealism). What is in the soul (reason) of the human being are mere reflections of the objects of nature (senses). There is nothing in the mind (spirit) that has not previously been in the senses (empiricism) (intellectualism) (Hessen, 2011: 47-51).

Galileo conjectures that matter (realism) has only spatio-temporal and quantitative properties, while all other properties must be considered subjective (idealism).

John Locke (1994: 16) divides sensible qualities into primary: those that we perceive by means of the senses, such as size, form, movement, space, number; he assigns them an objective character, they are properties of things (realism). And secondary: those which we perceive only by means of one sense; such as colours, sounds, smells, tastes, softness, hardness, etc.; he assigns them a subjective character (idealism), they exist merely in our consciousness, although objective elements corresponding to them must be supposed in things. The understanding, like the eye, judging objects only by its own sight, can only be pleased with what it discovers and less sorry for what escapes it, since it is unknown to it.

Gaarder (2001: 126-147) assumes that we subjects have an innate ability to sort all our sensations into different groups and classes. This is how concepts arise. Our intelligence (reason) is totally empty before we feel anything (senses). Forms are the qualities of things. Reality is composed of a series of individual things that constitute a set of matter and form. Matter is the material of which a thing is made and form is the specific qualities of the thing. Every change is a transformation of matter from possibility to reality. There is always a possibility of achieving a certain form. All things (realism) in nature have an inherent possibility of realising or concluding a certain form (idealism). There are no innate ideas (rationalism).

All the above-mentioned thinkers solved the metaphysical problem of the essence of knowledge from the senses.

Following Hessen (2011: 47-51), the fundamental thesis of *realism* is that there are objects (realism) independent of consciousness (idealism). In order to arrive at this result, he starts from an elementary difference between perceptions (sensations) and representations (ideas). Perceptions (experiences) are objects (reality) that can be perceived (experiences) by several subjects (idealism) and the contents of representations (sensations) are only perceptible for the subject who possesses them (idealism). There is thus an independence of perceptions (realism) from the will (idealism). We can evoke, modify and make representations (ideas) disappear at will; on the other hand, the coming and going, the content and vividness, of perceptions (sensations) are independent of our will (realism). Perceptions (sensations) are caused by objects that exist independently of the perceiving subject (realism), i.e. they exist in reality. There is an independence of the objects of perception (experiences, sensations) from our perceptions (ideas). The objects of perception continue to exist (realism), even if we have withdrawn our senses from their influence and as a consequence no longer perceive them. In perception we encounter objects that exist outside of us (transcendents), which possess a real being (realism). Reality cannot be proved, only experienced and lived. There are real objects that act on the various subjects, provoking perceptions in them. It is a *volitional realism* in which it is the experiences of the will that give us the certainty of the existence of objects outside the consciousness. Things (experiences) resist our volitions and desires (ideas), and in these resistances we experience the reality of things (realism).

Assumptions from *realism* to solve the problem of the essence of knowledge by means of the metaphysical solution are related to the philosophical assumptions that can be used to solve the problems of possibility (scepticism, subjectivism, relativism and pragmatism) and the origin of knowledge (empiricism).

In all the above-mentioned assumptions, the respective problems of knowledge are solved by focusing on one of the three elements of knowledge: the cognising subject and, as a consequence, the metaphysical problem of the essence of knowledge was solved from the senses.

It is necessary to remember the impossibility of knowing the essence of reality. We can only assume from the subject (soul), or the object (reality) and establish a logical relationship with the object of study.

In the present case, the subject is the centre of the knowledge relation. The object remains excluded.

The main theoretical consequences of choosing this assumption (realism) are that the discourse to be elaborated (the theory) will be sceptical, subjectivist (ontologically speaking), relativistic, pragmatic, empirical, subjectivist (in epistemological terms), and realist; as will be seen in subchapter 2.2, corresponding to the theoretical foundations.

2.2.5.4.2.2   Believing that without a subject there is no object.

From the *idealistic philosophical assumption*, the educational researcher can solve the metaphysical problem of the essence of knowledge, as far as the existence of reality is concerned, by affirming that without a subject there is no object; that is, it is assumed that if there is no subject that can account for the existence of reality, reality simply does not exist; and thus it is concluded that reality is ideal, because it is a construction of the mind of the cognising subject (subjective idealism).

According to Hessen (2011: 51-54), unlike those who assume from *realism* that reality exists independently of whether there is a subject who can know it or not, those who think about reality from *idealism* consider that all objects possess an ideal, mental being. This means that those who account for the existence of entities are the subjects who fix their attention on certain realities and, due to this act, are transformed from entities into cognising subjects; and the entities on which the subjects have fixed their reason and their senses, in turn, are transformed from entities into objects to be known. Both terms of the relation of knowledge pass from the ontological sphere (reality) to the epistemological sphere (knowledge of reality).

In *metaphysical* terms, those who assume that reality has spiritual forces, ideal powers, etc., as its background, have the conviction that reality (the object) is constructed by the subject. Epistemologically, subjectively or psychologically, there are no real things, independent of consciousness. The alleged real objects are only objects of consciousness, ideal objects.

It is assumed that there are no real things independent of consciousness. It can be argued that all reality is enclosed in the consciousness of the subject, because it is ideal. It can be argued that things are nothing more than contents of the consciousness. The being of things is thought to consist in their being perceived by cognising subjects, in their being contents of consciousness. It is said that as soon as things cease to be perceived by us, they also cease to exist. It is conjectured that objects do not possess a being independent of our consciousness. It is asserted that our consciousness, with its various contents, is the only real thing.

In idealism, the metaphysical problem of the essence of knowledge is solved by reason.

Some authors who construct knowledge about reality on the assumption that it is ideal are. Plato, Berkeley, Avemarius, Schuppe, Herman Cohen, Fichte, Schelling, Hegel, and Hessen, among others.

Plato assumes that everything we can touch and feel in nature (realism) flows, i.e. changes, moves. Absolutely everything that belongs to the world of the senses (realism) is made of matter that wears out over time. Everything is made of an eternal and immutable mould (idealism). The eternal and immutable are the spiritual or abstract moulds, in whose image everything is modelled. He called these moulds ideas (Gaarder, 2001:126-147). Plato assumes that true reality is to be found on a metaphysical plane, beyond this world, in the objective world of ideas. This kind of idealism can be called objective.

Berkeley assumes that the being of things consists in their being perceived by subjects (subjective idealism). It is an epistemological (because it arises from a relation of knowledge between the subject and the object), *subjective* or psychological *idealism*, preferably working with visual and tactile sensations; material things. The soul has an independent existence. Sensible perceptions are independent of our desires and volitions. It is assumed that there is nothing but sensation and all being is immanent to consciousness.

The aforementioned authors solve the metaphysical problem of the essence of knowledge from the standpoint of reason.

If the being of things consists in their being perceived by us, then the concepts of cognising *subject* and *object* to be known arise from a *relation* of knowledge: a given entity (the human being) fixes its senses and reason on another entity (material or immaterial) in order to know it and, in this way, becomes a cognising subject, since it is relating to another entity for the purpose of knowing it; in turn, the entity (material or immaterial) that is the reason for the relation of knowledge that the subject intends to carry out, becomes an object to be known, by the mere fact that another entity (the human being) has fixed its senses and reason on it in order to establish a relation of knowledge.

What should we assume: that reality exists independently of thought or that it is constructed by the subject, based on sensations (subjective idealism) or that it exists in the world of ideas (objective idealism)?

It seems that we will never know, perhaps we were not born to know what reality is, but only to survive in it, based on its conceptualisation.

It can be assumed, at the same time, that reality exists independently of thought and that, at the same time, it is a construction of the subject. Kantian phenomenalism offers us this opportunity.

2.2.5.4.2.3 Presuming that the object exists independently of the subject, but that the subject only perceives the object as a "phenomenon".

From a *phenomenalist* philosophical assumption it can be affirmed - from both qualities of the cognising subject: reason and senses - that we do not know things as they are, but as they appear to us. Phenomenon means appearance. It is conceded that our knowledge of reality is reduced to pure appearances, which are obtained differently by each cognising subject, because each and every human being feels and thinks differently.

The educational researcher can solve the metaphysical problem about the essence of knowledge (about the existence of reality) by assuming that reality (both material and immaterial) exists independently of thought (realism) but, nevertheless, each subject knows it differently (subjective idealism), because he feels and thinks differently from others. If this is so, we do not perceive reality as it is, but as it presents itself to our limited reason and deficient senses.

Paraphrasing Hessen (2011: 54-56), from a *phenomenalist* philosophical assumption, it can be assumed that cognising subjects do not know things (material or immaterial reality) as they are, in themselves, but as they appear to us. From this philosophical assumption the phenomenon, the appearance, is considered. Researchers can only know that there are real things (realism), but we cannot know their essence. From *phenomenalism* it is assumed that human beings can only know that things are (realism), but not what they are. As has been argued throughout this study.

An important feature of this philosophical assumption is that it agrees with *realism* in admitting real things; but it also agrees with *idealism* in limiting knowledge to consciousness, to the world of appearance; from which immediately follows the unknowability of things in themselves. It is assumed, according to *critical realism*, that things are not constituted as we perceive them. Secondary qualities: smells, colours, tastes, etc., do not belong to the things themselves, but arise only in our consciousness (subjective idealism).

In phenomenalism, the metaphysical problem about the essence of reality is solved from both qualities of the cognising subject: reason and the senses. First we work with reason and then with the senses.

Kant is the founder of *phenomenalism*. Gaarder (2001: 388-413) supposes that Kant (also founder of apriorism) agrees with Hume (empiricist) that we cannot know anything certain about the world itself, about what reality itself is; that we can only know what the thing (reality) is like for me, that is, for each and every human being, in particular (ontological subjectivism). It is argued that there are two different aspects of reality, the thing in itself (the essence of reality) and the thing for me (the phenomenon, as reality presents itself to the limitation of my reason and senses). It is opined that we can never know how things are in themselves (the essence of reality), that we can only know how things appear to us (the appearance of reality, due to our limited senses and our deficient reason). Nevertheless, it can be conjectured that before every experience (empiricism) we can say something about how things are perceived by men's reason (apriorism). It can be conjectured that before going out in the morning we cannot know anything about what we will see or perceive during the day (empiricism), but we can know that whatever we see or experience we will perceive as an event in time and space (apriorism). Moreover, we can be sure that causal law governs, simply because we carry it with us as a part of our consciousness (apriorism). Of the two things that contribute to how people perceive the world, one is the external conditions (sensations), of which we can know nothing until we perceive them (empiricism), which we may call the material of knowledge; the second is the internal conditions of the human being himself (rationalism), i.e., that we perceive everything as events in time and space and also as processes that follow an unbreakable causal law, which we may call the form of knowledge (apriorism).

To paraphrase Hessen (2011: 56-58), the philosophical assumption of *idealism* fails to demonstrate that the position of the philosophical assumption *of realism* is contradictory and thus impossible. Nor does the philosophical assumption of *realism* succeed in defeating its adversary; its reasons are not logically convincing, but only probable.

Assuming, from *phenomenalism*, it can be argued that reality exists, independent of thought (realism), but that thought only perceives reality as appearance (idealism).

What to think of the existence and cognizability of objects, can we know the existence and essence of things or the thing for itself and in itself, can we affirm anything about the subjective and objective properties of objects or must we be content with being able to know the existence, but not the essence of things in the sense of *phenomenalism*?

Hessen believes to solve the problem of the existence of real objects by assuming an immediate self-certainty of the self, based on the processes of will established by Maine de Biran; and the problem of the cognizability of real objects, based on Kantian thought, on the understanding that sensations represent pure chaos, and that all order proceeds from consciousness. Thinking is supposed to mean ordering.

In Kant there are no made objects of knowledge, but the objects of knowledge are produced by our consciousness. Cognising consciousness itself creates the objective order of things. Knowledge is an active, reproductive function.

It can be concluded that none of the aforementioned philosophical assumptions: realism, idealism and phenomenalism, solves, in a definitive way, the metaphysical problem about the essence of knowledge, as far as its metaphysical solution is concerned; that is, the problem of the existence and essence of reality. The educational researcher will have to be satisfied with *assuming*, from any of the three philosophical assumptions mentioned, such a solution, in order to construct his object of study. This will depend on his or her interests as a researcher and on the very object of study he or she intends to construct.

So far we have broken down the philosophical assumptions that the educational researcher can use to solve the problem of the *essence of knowledge*: the *pre-metaphysical solution* (through three philosophical assumptions: objectivism, subjectivism and dialectics), which refers to the relation of knowledge between the subject and the object, in the sense of giving an answer to the following question: who determines whom in a relation of knowledge: the object to the subject (objectivism), the subject to the object (subjectivism) or both determine each other (dialectics)? and the *metaphysical solution* (through three philosophical assumptions: realism, idealism and phenomenalism), which refers to the existence of reality (realism), to its knowledge (idealism) and to both (phenomenalism); that is, to the ontological, epistemological and logical planes. A third solution is missing: the theological one. It is so called because it applies very well to religion; but it also applies to science, art and philosophy. Let us see what it consists of.

2.2.5.4.3   Solving the problem of the essence of knowledge from the philosophical assumptions of the theological solution.

From the philosophical assumptions of the *theological solution* (dualism and theism and monism and pantheism) to the problem of the *essence of knowledge*, the educational researcher can argue about reality in two ways: assuming that reality is *dual* or assuming that reality is *unique*. In the first case the *dualistic* (duo

= two) and *theistic* (Teos = God) assumption is being used, in the second case the *monistic* (monos = one) and *pantheistic* (Pan = All; Teos = God) assumption is being used.

2.2.5.4.3.1 Assuming that reality is dual.

From a *dualistic* and *theistic philosophical assumption*, the educational researcher can solve the problem of the essence of knowledge by arguing, from this theological solution, that thought and being, good and evil, subject and object, consciousness and reality, ideality and reality, the ideal realm and the real real realm, are contrary and definitely separate.

Some important features of the *dualistic* and *theistic* philosophical assumption are the following:

- It separates the subject from the object.
- It maintains the essential metaphysical diversity of thought and being, consciousness and reality (Hessen, 2011: 59-60).
- He solves the theological problem of the essence of knowledge from the senses using dualistic philosophical assumptions.

One need that can satisfy this philosophical assumption in the educational researcher is to divide reality into two opposing, contradictory and irreconcilable poles.

To what end would the educational researcher seek to rely on this philosophical assumption, dividing reality in two in the construction of his or her object of study? Possible answer: to maintain the epistemological and ontological inequality of reality, changing everything so that nothing changes. To justify processes of exclusion of undesirable people; to pass (those who get "good" grades) and fail (those who get "bad" grades); to reward the "good" and punish the "bad"; etc.

From this philosophical assumption, it can happen that, in religion, the "good" go to "heaven" and the "bad" go to "hell". In science, some people "know"; others "ignore" knowledge. In art, there are people with "talent" and people without "talent". In philosophy, there is an ontological and epistemological inequality of reality.

Some important authors, who built their knowledge from the *dualistic and theistic philosophical assumption*, perhaps ignoring the theoretical and practical consequences of it, are, within Christian theism: Plato, Aristotle, Plotinus, St. Augustine and St. Thomas Aquinas. In the Modern Age: Descartes and Leibniz.

Plato (B, 2001: XII) assumed (perhaps without being fully aware that he was only conjecturing) that the human being is divided into two parts. Plato believed that one of these two parts (the body) flows, changes, transforms etc.; because it is linked to the senses. Plato conjectured that the senses are linked to the body and are therefore unreliable, because all human beings feel things differently.

The other part of the human being, Plato presumed, was the soul. Plato conceded that the soul was immortal and immaterial. Therefore, for Plato, the soul was the house, the abode, the dwelling, the temple of reason; because it is immaterial. The material can transform, change form; the immaterial is the eternal, the immutable, the perfect. That is why Plato suspects that the soul can see the world of ideas.

Plato pits two worlds: the empirical world, where things are constantly changing, against the supra-empirical (rational) world, where the entities that constitute it are the ideas. Ideas, as such, are perfect, immutable, eternal (dogmatism). Plato assumes that it is thanks to ideas that knowledge is possible, and therefore teaching and learning. Plato is of the opinion that a thing is known when it is ordered and qualified by a general concept (rationalism). An entity is supposed to be known when it is ordered by the word that defines it, for example: Protagoras; and it is qualified in some way, for example: man. *Protagoras is a man.* Here the idea in question is the idea of man. Thanks to ideas, science and, consequently, the learning of virtue is possible (objectivism).

Aristotle (1993: XLV-XLVI) assumed that every object consists of matter (realism) and form (idealism). Aristotle considered form to be the essence of every object, capable of being known by the concept (rationalism). Aristotle presumed that form is what makes the thing what it is. Aristotle conjectured that essences are within things.

The fundamental difference between Aristotle and Plato is that for Plato there are not two worlds, as Plato supposed: the world of ideas and the world of things. Aristotle conceded that there is only one world, consisting of matter and form, things and ideas.

Descartes (1981: 55-90) assumes that God is an infinite substance and that the spirit and the body are two finite substances (dualism and theism). Descartes considers that the spirit is thinking (consciousness) and that the attribute of the body is extension, for without it no body is possible. Descartes understands by modes or accidents those properties of substances which presuppose the existence of attributes. Feeling, willing, longing, imagining, judging, are "modes of thought" (i.e. modifications of consciousness), figure, position, movements (of space) are, on the contrary, modes of extension.

It seems that the traditions, customs and beliefs of Mexicans (in philosophy, science, religion and art), myths, rites, in short, the whole culture, are based on this philosophical assumption. I believe that this is because we are the heirs of Western culture, which came to Mexico and all of Latin America, to stay, through the Spanish conquest.

The practical consequences are obvious: we seem to see "in black and white", assuming that we are separate and live in eternal conflict with others and with ourselves.

Notwithstanding the above observation, we must not forget that this is only a philosophical assumption: are we really separate entities?

Another philosophical assumption, from which the problem of the essence of knowledge can be solved on the basis of a theological solution, is *monism* and *pantheism.*

2.2.5.4.3.2 . Believing that reality is unique.

Monism and *pantheism* is a philosophical assumption from which it is possible to affirm that reality is unique, that it is one, a whole.

Paraphrasing Hessen (12011: 58-59), from the *monistic* and *pantheistic* philosophical assumption, the problem of the essence of knowledge is solved, from a theological solution, starting from the absolute, the last principle of reality, the immanent absolute. Thinking that subject and object are absorbed in a unity, thought and being, consciousness and things. Conjecturing that they are two aspects of the same reality. Saying that the empirical sees a duality, that metaphysical knowledge sees a unity, that, in doing so, it arrives at the essence (Hessen, 1999: 49-50).

Hessen fails to show how, assuming that reality is a whole, one arrives at the essence. Because, precisely, he is only supposing. The proofs he offers to support his assertion consist of a kind of historical overview of how some authors have constructed knowledge on the basis of the *monistic* and *pantheistic* assumption; among them, we can mention - in antiquity - Heraclitus, the Stoics, Marcus Tullius Cicero, Seneca, Silesius - in modern times - Baruch Spinoza, Schelling, among others.

Hessen mentions that, for Heraclitus, both good and evil have a necessary place in the whole, and that if there were not a constant interplay between opposites the world would cease to exist. Hessen states that, for Heraclitus, God is day and night, winter and summer, war and peace, hunger and satiety. Hessen says that, according to Heraclitus, God shows himself precisely in this contradictory and constantly changing nature. Hessen argues that, for Heraclitus, God must be a kind of universal reason that directs everything that happens in nature; that in the midst of all these changes and contradictions that occur in reality, in nature (empiria), Heraclitus saw a unity, a whole; and that this something, which was the basis of everything, Heraclitus called God or logos (reason).

Hessen suggests that the Stoics, like Heraclitus, believed that all human beings were part of the same universal reason or logos (rationalism). Hessen assumes that they thought that each human being is like a miniature world, like a microcosm which, in turn, is a reflection of the macrocosm. Hessen concludes that, for the Stoics, there is only one nature.

Thus, an important feature of *monism* and *pantheism* is that it allows the researcher to assume that we (entities) are all one, that we are all God.

Cicero (1993: IX - XXIII), tries to prove that God exists, supposing a universal and eternal order in the world (rationalism). Cicero thought, like the Stoics, that there is a universal and provident reason that pervades all beings and manifestations of the cosmos, forever and ever. In the field of science, Cicero believes that there is Natural Law (independent of subjects), based on human reason and universal reason. For Cicero, Law, which is one, unique, eternal and immutable, springs from human nature itself. Cicero presumes that the nature of man is the origin and substance of law. For Cicero, there are not several rights, but only one: Natural Law; the set of eternal, immutable rules that flow from the very nature of man. Cicero conjectures that it is not man's will that makes something just or unjust, honest or clumsy, good or bad, but man's rational nature. For Cicero, this nature dictates what is bad or good, just or unjust, and men cannot change it. Cicero presupposes that the foundation of law is natural law, eternal, immutable and universal; that from this law comes the value of positive individual and social law. Cicero conjectures that positive law is natural law determined and sanctioned by human will, but ultimately natural. For Cicero, law is nothing more than human equality determined by the will of the legislator for the common good.

It can be argued, based on Cicero's saying, that to assume from reason that there is an eternal, universal and immutable order is also to assume that there is only one reality for all (monism and pantheism).

Seneca (1989: IX-XXXVIII), assumed that all natural processes, such as illness and death, follow the unbreakable laws of nature (rationalism); that human beings have to reconcile themselves with their destiny; that nothing happens by chance; that everything happens by necessity and, therefore, it is of little use to complain when destiny knocks at the door; that mourning is of no use, because we are born to die; and that death follows birth.

It can be argued that Seneca assumes from reason because his soul seeks the security that comes from bringing order to things. If everything is determined there is no need to worry about reflecting on reality, we just have to follow the pre-established rules of the game. One reality for all, always and forever, but what would that reality be? Seneca's would be to endure hardship, fatally, to the last breath.

Spinoza (1990: 7-35), assumes that there are no created or uncreated substances; he considers that God, as a transcendent being, has not created the world out of nothing; he presumes that the world is an immanent reality in him; he conjectures that all the beings of which the world consists are in the world and God in them; and he concedes that, for the same reason, God is the substance in which everything rests.

Spinoza assumes that God and the world have always existed and that they constitute a radical unity; he considers that God is the cause of all beings and that he lives together with them; he presumes that nothing can exist outside God; he conjectures that God is always within the world; he attributes that everything that exists, exists in God, and that nothing can exist or be conceived without God; he concludes, like Aristotle, that God is nature.

If the above is true, there can be no personal God, as in Christianity. If God is nature, every man is a living manifestation of the divine. Religion, man's religious act of coming into contact with his creator, takes the form of a bond with himself. Spinoza assumes that substance (God, Nature) has two attributes: thought and extension, the material world and the ideal world or world of consciousness. He regards both attributes as one thing in the universal substance, which is God or nature.

It can be assumed that all living beings are one being, that we are all one and that we are all God.

Spinoza presumes that man's life is conditioned by the laws of nature. Therefore, he concludes that human beings must free themselves from their feelings and affections, in order to find peace and be happy. Spinoza attributes that all that exists is nature, that God is the world, and that everything that exists comes from that substance. Spinoza concedes that human beings know two of the forms or qualities of God's appearance, attributes of God: thought and extension (Descartes); God or nature appears as thought, or as extended nature; that everything in the world, or in nature, is thought (idea) or extension (matter); the two attributes of God. Spinoza presupposes that God or the laws of nature are the internal cause of everything that happens; that God directs the world by the laws of nature; that He is the internal cause of everything that happens; that everything that happens in nature happens necessarily (determinism).

So, in the same sense that Aristotle assumed, it can also be argued that God is that balance that exists in nature, between predator and prey.

Spinoza assumes that everything necessarily happens (dogmatism). Therefore he concludes that we (human beings) must not allow ourselves to be

We only live as free beings when we can freely develop all our possibilities. Spinoza believes that only a being who is fully the cause of himself can act in total freedom; that only God or nature can be so free and non-casual in their activity. Spinoza attributes to the passions (ambition, desire, etc.) the cause that prevents human beings from achieving true happiness and harmony.

It can be concluded that human beings must be more rational than emotional in order to find harmony between ourselves and others.

Spinoza concedes that if we human beings recognise that everything happens out of necessity, we can achieve an intuitive recognition of nature as such; that we can come to a harmonious coexistence with the other parts of reality, because we are all one.

So the absolute (as Schelling rightly mentioned) is the unity of nature and spirit, of object and subject.

Assuming that we (beings) are all one, that we are all part of the same God and that this God is the natural balance between thought and extension, that substance of which everything is made, would provide the basis for promoting a more rational society.

2.2.5.4.3.3 Presuming that reality is multiple.

Leibniz (1991: 389-400), assumes that in the whole (reality) there is a pre-established harmony. He believes that the connection and order of the parts of the universe rest on a harmony originally established by God. He presumes that in that harmony rests also the concordance of thought and being, of subject and object.

It is only assuming a total harmony where the parts of reality are interrelated in an order originally promoted by God.

Leibniz argues in favour of a dynamical theory of the universe. Leibniz assumes that substances are, in essence, force. Therefore, there are neither two substances as in Descartes (dualism), nor one as in Spinoza (monism). The number of substances is infinite (*metaphysical pluralism*). The metaphysical structure of each substance is a monad. This term (from the Greek *monas*) means unity. Monads are the indivisible elements of things. An act of creation produces them. The monad is not subject to any external action; nor does it itself work on anything external.

If substances were forces, and if the number of these force-substances (monads) were infinite; then an infinite world of possibilities for the realisation of human beings opens up around the four forms of realisation of the spirit: philosophy, religion, science and art.

Recall a maxim of quantum theory: in the beginning, everything is possibility; but when a decision is made, it becomes experience. This principle warns us to be careful when making a decision regarding any spiritual activity.

So far this corresponds to the theological solution of the problem of the essence of knowledge.

Some conclusions on the problem of the *essence* of knowledge:

The problem of the *essence* of knowledge, i.e. to really know what it is to know, is unsolvable, because human beings, it seems, were not born to know the essence of reality (in this case, not just any reality: artistic, scientific, religious), philosophical). Here the problem is duplicated, because it is not a question of knowing whether we know reality (science) but whether we know how reality is known (meta-science). The problem is not metaphysical (science) but pre-metaphysical (meta-science). The problem is placed on a higher plane: it is about the knowledge of knowledge. The essence of the problem of the essence of knowledge, i.e. what knowledge is in itself, we are not allowed to know. We can only *suppose*, from three different solutions (pre-metaphysical, metaphysical and theological), how it is known, but not what it would be to actually know the phenomena. To know the essence of the relation of knowledge between subject and object is impossible.

A) In the *pre-metaphysical* solution there are three competing philosophical assumptions from which the problem of the relation between the subject and the object of knowledge can be solved: objectivism, subjectivism and dialectics. It must be remembered that the cognising subject has only his senses and his reason to relate to his object of knowledge. It can be assumed that the problem of the relationship between the subject and his object of knowledge can be solved by locating it in reason (objectivism), in the senses (subjectivism) or in both (dialectics).

A1) If we locate the problem from the point of view of *reason* (objectivism) we can only *assume* that the object determines the subject. To draw an analogy, the objective is the instituted, the artistic, religious, scientific and philosophical institutions.

A2) If we locate the problem from the *senses* (subjectivism), as in the objectivist philosophical assumption, we can only *assume* that the subject determines the object.

A3) If we locate the problem from both qualities of the cognising subject (reason and the senses), as in the objectivist and subjectivist philosophical assumptions, we can only *assume* that both elements of knowledge determine each other.

Notwithstanding the above, the educational researcher can be certain of two important phenomena:

First: when constructing your object of study, you must be able to locate the theory, with which you are grounding your research, in the problem of how the subject-object relationship of knowledge is established; that is, which of the two elements of the knowledge relationship determines whom, or whether the two determine each other; and determine what is the philosophical assumption from which the discourse with which you are problematising reality was constructed.

Second: He must be able to discriminate, among the different assumptions, which aim to solve the problem of the subject-object relationship of knowledge, which is the best one to construct his own object of study.

A) In the *metaphysical* solution there are three competing philosophical assumptions from which the problem of the essence and existence of reality can be solved: realism, idealism and phenomenalism. It can be assumed that the problem of the essence and existence of reality can be solved from the senses (realism), from reason (idealism) or from both (phenomenalism).

A1) If we locate the problem of the essence and existence of reality from the standpoint of *reason* (idealism) we can only *assume* that reality is constructed by the cognising subject.

A2) If we locate the problem of the essence and existence of reality from the *senses* (realism), as in the idealist philosophical assumption, we can only *suppose* that reality is a construction of the cognising subject.

A3) If we locate the problem from both qualities of the cognising subject (reason and the senses), as in the idealist and realist philosophical assumptions, we can only *assume* that reality exists and that it is only known to the subject as a phenomenon.

Nevertheless, as in the pre-metaphysical solution to the problem of the essence of knowledge, the educational researcher can be certain of two important phenomena:

First: when constructing your object of study, you must be able to locate the theory, with which you are basing your research, in the problem about the essence and existence of reality, and determine what is the philosophical assumption from which the discourse with which you are problematising reality was constructed.

Second: He must be able to discriminate, among the different assumptions, from which a problem about the essence and existence of reality can be solved, which is the best one to construct his own object of study.

A) In the *theological* solution there are three competing philosophical assumptions from which the problem of the unity, dualism or pluralism of reality can be solved. It can be assumed that the problem of monism, dualism or pluralism of reality can be solved from the senses (dualism), from reason (monism) or by placing oneself in both (pluralism).

A1) If we locate the problem of unity, duality or plurality of reality from the standpoint of *reason* (monism) we can only *assume* that reality is unique.

A2) If we locate the problem of the unity, duality or plurality of reality from the *senses* (dualism), as in the monistic philosophical assumption, we can only *assume* that reality is dual.

A3) If we locate the problem of the unity, duality or plurality of reality from both qualities of the cognising subject (reason and the senses), as in the monist and dualist philosophical assumptions, we can only *assume* that reality is plural.

Nevertheless, as in the metaphysical solution to the problem of knowledge, the educational researcher can be certain of two important phenomena:

First: when constructing your object of study, you must be able to locate the theory, with which you are grounding your research, in the problem about the unity, duality or plurality of reality, and determine what is the philosophical assumption from which the discourse with which you are problematising reality was constructed.

Second: He must be able to discriminate, among the different assumptions, from which a problem about the unity, duality or plurality of reality can be solved, which is the best one to construct his own object of study.

2.2.5.5 *The epistemological relationship between the philosophical assumptions from which the problem of the origin of knowledge can be solved and the philosophical assumptions from which the problem of the essence of knowledge can be solved.*

The philosophical assumptions from which the problem of the *essence* of knowledge can be solved (pre-metaphysical, metaphysical and theological) can be compared with the philosophical assumptions from which the problem of the *origin* of knowledge can be solved.

First, the philosophical assumptions from which the problem of the *essence* of knowledge can be solved in a *pre-metaphysical* way (objectivism, subjectivism and dialectics) will be compared with the philosophical assumptions from which the problem of the *origin of* knowledge can be solved (rationalism, empiricism, intellectualism and apriorism).

A *rationalist* (origin of knowledge) is also an *objectivist* (pre-metaphysical solution to the problem of the essence of knowledge). Whoever assumes that the origin of knowledge is in reason, imagines that truth exists, may think that it lies in the depths of the soul (Plato) and that the subject can obtain it by discovery. What already exists can be discovered. For a *rationalist* (origin of knowledge) as well as for an *objectivist* (pre-metaphysical solution to the problem of the essence of knowledge) the object determines the subject. The cognising subjects imagine, on both assumptions, that knowledge exists independently of the subjects.

An *empiricist* (origin of knowledge) is also a *subjectivist* (pre-metaphysical solution to the problem of the essence of knowledge). On both assumptions the subject determines the object. Both imagine that the passions, emotions, feelings, ambitions, traumas, life history and life project etc. of the cognising subject contaminate the object of knowledge and that it is therefore impossible to assume (objectively) neutral knowledge. All knowledge depends on the ontological and epistemological interests of the subject who formulates it.

An *intellectualist* and/or *apriorist* (origin of knowledge) is also *dialectical* (pre-metaphysical solution to the problem of the essence of knowledge). From both assumptions, one can think that, in a relation of knowledge, the cognising subject and the object to be known mutually determine each other, in an endless relation that is established through the dialogue between the two elements of knowledge. From both philosophical assumptions, it can be estimated that we never finish knowing reality. It has already been said that the only difference between intellectualism and apriorism is that in intellectualism it can be assumed that we first feel (empiricism) and then think (rationalism); in apriorism, on the other hand, it is assumed that we first think (rationalism) and then feel (empiricism).

Here, what is truly philosophical, if one can speak of a relation of knowledge, is to suppose that there are two worlds separate from each other: that of ideas (objectivism), which are eternal, immutable, perfect, good, beautiful, etc.; and the real (subjectivism), which is finite, changing, imperfect, bad, ugly, etc., (rationalism and objectivism) or moving (empiricism and subjectivism),and the real (subjectivism), which is finite, changing, imperfect, bad, ugly, etc., (rationalism and objectivism) or moving (empiricism and subjectivism); or a mixture of the two (dialectics).

Secondly, the philosophical assumptions from which the problem of the *essence* of knowledge can be solved *metaphysically* (realism, idealism and phenomenalism) will be compared with the philosophical assumptions from which the problem of the *origin of* knowledge can be solved (rationalism, empiricism, intellectualism and apriorism).

A *rationalist* (origin of knowledge) is also an *objective idealist* (metaphysical solution to the problem of the essence of knowledge). Whoever assumes that the origin of knowledge is in reason, imagines that truth exists, may think that it lies in the depths of the soul (Plato) and that the subject can obtain it by discovery. What already exists can be discovered. For a *rationalist* (origin of knowledge) as well as for an *objective idealist* (metaphysical solution to the problem of the essence of knowledge), without a subject there is no object. Subjects imagine, on both assumptions, that reality is discovered by the subject. That without a cognising subject who discovers reality there can be no object, but that, nevertheless, reality exists whether or not there is a subject who can know it.

An *empiricist* (origin of knowledge) is also a *realist*. On both assumptions reality exists independently of the subject who may or may not know it. Both imagine that there are real things, independent of cognising consciousness. Perceptions are independent of representations. It is assumed that there are real objects that act on the senses of the different subjects, provoking perceptions in them; and that, nevertheless, each subject represents reality differently.

An *intellectualist* and/or *apriorist* (origin of knowledge) is also a *phenomenologist* (metaphysical solution to the problem of the essence of knowledge). From both assumptions it can be thought that, in a relation of knowledge, the cognising subject does not know things as they are, but as they appear to him (phenomenon, appearance). From both philosophical assumptions it can be considered that there are real things (realism) but that the knowledge of reality is limited to consciousness (idealism), to the world of appearance, from which the unknowability of the thing in itself immediately results.

Here, what is truly philosophical, if one can speak of reality at all, is the assumption that reality exists in itself (realism), is a construct of cognising consciousness (idealism), or a mixture of both assumptions (phenomenalism).

Thirdly, the philosophical assumptions from which the problem of the *essence* of knowledge can be solved *theologically* (dualism and theism and monism and pantheism) will be compared with the philosophical assumptions from which the problem of the *origin of* knowledge can be solved (rationalism, empiricism, intellectualism and apriorism).

A *rationalist* (origin of knowledge) is also a *dualist* and *theist* (theological solution to the problem of the essence of knowledge). Whoever assumes that the origin of knowledge is in reason, imagines that thought and being, good and evil, subject and object, consciousness and reality, ideality and reality, the ideal and the real realm, are contrary and definitely separate. What already exists can be discovered. For a *rationalist* (origin of knowledge) the same as for a *dualist* and *theist* (theological solution to the problem of the essence of knowledge). The subjects imagine, on both assumptions, that reality is divided into two opposing, contradictory and irreconcilable poles. There is an epistemological and ontological inequality between subject and object.

An *empiricist* (origin of knowledge) is also *dualistic and theistic*. On both assumptions reality is divided into two opposing, contradictory and irreconcilable poles. Both imagine that good and evil exist, in themselves, independently of the cognising subjects. Thought and being, good and evil, subject and object, consciousness and reality, ideality and reality, the ideal and the real realm, are assumed to be contrary and definitely separate.

An *intellectualist* and/or *apriorist* (origin of knowledge) is also a *monist* and *pantheist* (theological solution to the problem of the essence of knowledge). From both assumptions it can be thought that reality is one, a whole. From both philosophical assumptions it can be considered that subject and object, thought and being, consciousness and things, are two aspects of the same reality. Substance has two attributes: thought and extension, the material world and the ideal or consciousness world. Both attributes are one in the universal substance (Spinoza). Here, what is truly philosophical, if one can speak of reality, is to suppose that reality is one, that there are two contradictory realities, or that there are multiple realities.

To suppose that the elements of the knowledge relation (subject and object) are separate or united; to estimate that reality exists, by itself or that it is a construction of consciousness; and to presume that reality is only one or that there are two or more realities; have very important theoretical consequences, which will be analysed in the chapter corresponding to theoretical foundations.

So far what has been said about the problem of the essence of knowledge. The fourth important problem of knowledge will now be dealt with: its classification.

2.2.5.6 *The philosophical assumptions from which the problem of the classification of knowledge can be solved.*

Scientific communities or research traditions, depending on the perspective, paradigm or epistemological orientation of the research programme or mode of knowledge production to which they adhere, construct their objects of study *rationally*, *intuitively* or *in a mixed manner*, depending on how they solve problems about the classification of knowledge: from reason, from the senses or from both qualities of the cognising subject.

To paraphrase Hessen (2011: 60-73) to know means to spiritually apprehend an object. Hessen assumes that this apprehension can be mediated, discursive (*rational* knowledge) or immediate, intuitive (*intuitive* knowledge). We are of the opinion that, in addition to the two forms of knowledge mentioned, we can speak of two other types of knowledge: *mixed* knowledge (rational-intuitive) where both reason and the senses are considered as sources of knowledge, but the former is privileged over the latter; and *mixed* knowledge (intuitive-rational) where both the senses and reason are considered as sources of knowledge, but the former is privileged over the latter. For Hessen, the question is: in addition to rational knowledge, can there be intuitive knowledge? The question we ask is: besides rational knowledge, can there be others: such as intuitive and mixed knowledge (which reconciles rational knowledge and intuitive knowledge)?

In order to answer the question of the possibility of *intuitive* knowledge, assuming that *rational* knowledge exists, we will first try to explain the origin of the problem of the *classification of knowledge.*

Following the same procedure that has been carried out to analyse the other three *philosophical problems of knowledge*

(possibility, origin and essence), we must place ourselves in the relation of knowledge. That is to say, to understand the definition of knowledge as a process, not as a result.

In the phenomenon of knowledge, understood as a process, three elements are involved, as already mentioned: the cognising subject, which is located in the psychological sphere (it is the human soul), the object to be known, established in the ontological sphere (it is reality, concrete or abstract); and the relation of knowledge, which can only occur in the logical sphere (it is a discourse on reality), due to the impossibility of the subject to penetrate the sphere of the object. It is known that the subject cannot apprehend the object in an essential way because both elements of the relation of knowledge are in different "worlds", they belong to different realities: the knowing subject is the human soul; the object to be known is reality, which can be concrete, like a tree, or abstract, like the concept "education".

The logical (discursive) relationship, which the cognising subject intends to establish with the object to be known, can only be carried out by using the only two qualities that every person has to connect with his object of study: reason and his senses. In mathematical terms, the cognising subject has only four possibilities to relate to reality: he can use reason; make use of the senses; or use both, privileging reason over the senses; or, the senses over reason.

If the cognising subject uses only his reason to relate to his object of study, then only *rational* knowledge is possible. If the educational researcher only uses his senses to connect with reality, then only *intuitive* knowledge is possible. If the researcher uses both, then *mixed* knowledge is possible: *rational-intuitive* or *intuitive-rational*, depending on whether it is reason or the senses that predominate in the relationship with the phenomenon under investigation.

The four forms of knowledge mentioned above will be developed in the following.

2.2.5.6.1 Assuming that knowledge is rational.

In accordance with what was stated in previous paragraphs, the species into which knowledge can be divided, following John Hessen (2011: 60-73), are two: *rational* (when the researcher uses reason to solve the problem of classifying knowledge) and *intuitive* (when he uses his senses). We, as already mentioned, add a third and a fourth form of knowledge, considering both reason and the senses (*mixed*). *Rational* knowledge is suspected to rest on the fact that man is exclusively or preponderantly a theoretical being, whose main function is thought. *Intuitive* knowledge is assumed to be based on man being emotional and volitional. It is now time to examine and confront the reasons on which both assumptions are based in order to make such assertions, following the authors already discussed.

If the cognising subject is situated on the basis of his reason in order to know, i.e. in order to solve the problem of the classification of knowledge, it is possible for him to "suppose" that the only true knowledge is *rational* knowledge. Because this kind of knowledge claims to be universally valid and logically necessary. We have already seen that the judgements of logic and mathematics claim to have these characteristics.

The main *characteristic* of *rational* knowledge is its immediacy, i.e. between the research question and the answer to it, there is a methodological procedure, an intellectual (rational) operation is involved.

That is why the definition of *rational* knowledge is stated as the spiritual apprehension of an object, as mediate, discursive knowledge. It is rational because reason is involved. Because the cognising subject, as already mentioned, solves the problem of the classification of knowledge with his reason.

Rational knowledge is discursive because it is mediated. The educational researcher has to elaborate a discourse to explore, describe, explain, interpret, understand, etc., reality. To do so, he/she uses certain intellectual operations such as addition, subtraction, multiplication, division, analysis, synthesis, induction, deduction, comparison, classification, definition, etc. It could be said that intuition, as a type of knowledge, does not, by the same token, fall within *rational* knowledge.

An example of *rationally* obtained knowledge would be the following:

QUESTION	METHODOLOGICAL PROCEDURE OR INTELLECTUAL OPERATION	RESPONSE
How much is two plus two?	SUMA 2+2	4

Subchapter 2.3 (intellectual operations, or methodological procedures, to generate new knowledge) will expand on this analysis.

In rational knowledge, the problem of the classification of knowledge is solved by reason.

Among the rationalist authors, who built cono

In the case of the assumption that there can only be *rational* knowledge, Plato, Fichte, St. Augustine, Descartes, etc., can be mentioned in preference.

It has already been analysed that Plato assumes that the origin of knowledge, the source of ideas, is to be found in reason. Plato accepts only *rational* knowledge, because this knowledge is the product of a function of the intellect (a deduction, for example), of a theoretical (methodological procedure), intellectual activity (an intellectual operation, such as those already mentioned). Plato assumes that true knowledge can only be obtained by the mediation that reason establishes between the question and the answer to an investigative problem.

Fichte (1994: XI-XXXVI) assumes that one can only speak of a purely rational (spiritual, intellectual) knowledge. The absolute self knows itself and its actions rationally.

In the three problems of knowledge discussed in sections 2.2.5.1 (the possibility of knowledge), 2.2.5.2 (the origin of knowledge) and 2.2.5.3 (the essence of knowledge) one can observe philosophical assumptions akin to the assumption that only *rational* knowledge can exist.

The *dogmatic* philosophical assumption, from which the problem of the possibility of knowledge can be solved by affirming that real contact between subject and object is possible, is perfectly related to the conjecture that there is only rational knowledge. In both cases one has full confidence in human reason, one has faith that reason alone can provide us with true knowledge.

The *rationalist* philosophical assumption, from which the problem of the origin of knowledge can be solved by asserting that the only source and basis of human knowledge is reason, is perfectly related to the assumption that only *rational* knowledge can exist. In both cases it can be asserted that if the source of human knowledge is reason, then only *rational* knowledge is possible.

The *objectivist* philosophical assumption, from which the problem about the essence of knowledge can be solved in a pre-metaphysical way (stating that, in a relation of knowledge, it is the object to be known that determines the cognising subject), is perfectly related to the estimation that only *rational* knowledge can exist. In both cases it can be asserted that, if there is an objective world of ideas (objects to be known) that is determining the knowledge that cognising subjects can obtain, then educational researchers need only use their reason to find that knowledge; for it can only be obtained, according to Plato, by rational means.

The *idealistic* philosophical assumption, from which the problem of the essence of knowledge can be solved metaphysically (by asserting that reality is based on spiritual forces, subjective or logical ideal entities), is perfectly related to the estimation that only *rational* knowledge can exist. In both cases it can be asserted that if reality (the object to be known) does not exist in and of itself (realism), but is only a construct of the cognising subjects (subjective idealism), then only knowledge of a rational kind is possible.

Finally, the *monistic and pantheistic* philosophical assumption, from which the problem of the essence of knowledge can be solved theologically (by affirming that reality is one), is perfectly related to the estimation that only *rational* knowledge can exist. In both cases it can be affirmed that, if reality is one, then only rational knowledge is possible; because only from reason can one speak of unity.

So much for the assumption that there can only be *rational* knowledge. The assumption that there can only be *intuitive* knowledge will now be discussed.

2.2.5.6.1 Believing that knowledge is intuitive.

To paraphrase Hessen (2011: 60-73), *intuitive knowledge* means knowing by seeing (sensations). In it it is assumed that the cognising subject immediately apprehends the object to be known; as is especially the case in vision (sensations). It is presumed that we immediately apprehend everything given in internal (thoughts) or external (the sensations provided by our senses) experience. It is estimated that we immediately perceive the red or green that we see (senses), the pain or joy that we experience (memories of sensations).

Intuitive knowledge is a philosophical assumption from which we can claim that there is a kind of immediate knowledge. It is presumed that we know by "seeing". It is estimated that we immediately apprehend everything given in internal (thoughts) and external (sensations) experience.

An important feature of the assumption that only *intuitive* knowledge can be given is that this kind of knowledge is empirical, it involves the senses. It is our nature as living, feeling beings.

Material reality is supposed to be known, first, through the senses. It can be conjectured that these are the sensations or feelings we experience when material entities affect our senses.

We can assume that the existence of material things is known through the senses. If we consider that the origin of knowledge lies in the senses (empiricism), then we can presume that only *intuitive* knowledge can be given.

In intuitive knowledge, the problem about the classification of knowledge is solved from the senses.

In the intuitive philosophical assumption, the problem about the classification of knowledge is solved from the senses.

Some authors who have studied in depth the assumption that there is only *intuitive* knowledge are: Schopenhauer, August Messer, etc.

Schopenhauer (1997: IX-XXV) assumes that reality is as the cognising subject represents it, according to his will. The educational researcher, on the basis of his preferences, represents the reality he wants to investigate.

Auguste Messer (1999: XVIII-XIX), assumes that there is only *intuitive* knowledge. He considers that value judgements arise from the senses. This concerns both aesthetic values and ethical values. He assumes that these values can only be known by means of *intuition*. He also concedes that the cognising subject lives and intuits immediately, the existence of the self and its freedom. He conjectures that truth can be defined as the concordance of our ideas with reality. It is a transcendent definition of truth, as will be seen in section 2.2.5.8, corresponding to the problem of the concepts and criteria of truth of knowledge.

The commented authors solve the problem of the classification of knowledge from the senses.

As was done in the analysis of the assumption that only rational knowledge can exist, philosophical assumptions akin to the assumption that only *intuitive* knowledge can exist can be observed in the three problems of knowledge discussed in sections 2.2.5.1 (the possibility of knowledge), 2.2.5.2 (the origin of knowledge) and 2.2.5.4 (the essence of knowledge).

The *sceptical, subjectivist, relativist* and *pragmatist* philosophical assumptions, from which the problem of the possibility of knowledge from the senses can be solved, affirming that no real contact between the subject and the object is possible, are perfectly related to the conjecture that only *intuitive* knowledge exists. In both cases the cognising subject is located in the senses, he supposes from sensations and, by understanding that each and every human being thinks and feels differently, he can conclude that it is not possible to know in essence, because each cognising subject can think and feel his object of study differently, because truth is transformed in time, space and circumstances and because, in addition, all knowledge must serve the practical ends of man and, these ends, cannot necessarily be, neither universally valid, nor logically necessary.

The *empiricist* philosophical assumption, from which the problem of the origin of knowledge can be solved by affirming that the only source and basis of human knowledge is in the senses, in the experiences of the senses, is perfectly related to the assumption that only *intuitive* knowledge can exist. In both cases it can be asserted that if the source of human knowledge is in the senses (empiricism), then only *intuitive* knowledge is possible.

The *subjectivist* philosophical assumption, from which the pre-metaphysical problem about the essence of knowledge can be solved (claiming that, in a knowledge relation, the cognising subject determines the object to be known), is perfectly related to the estimation that only *intuitive* knowledge can exist. In both cases it can be asserted that, if it is the passions, emotions, feelings, ambitions, prejudices, etc., of the subject that determine the knowledge of the object to be known, then educational researchers only have to use their senses to construct such knowledge; for such knowledge can only be elaborated, according to John Locke, from the sensations of the senses.

The philosophical *realist* assumption, from which the metaphysical problem about the essence of knowledge can be solved (asserting that reality exists, independently of a cognising subject fixing his reason and senses on it for the purpose of knowing it), is perfectly related to the estimation that only *intuitive* knowledge can exist. In both cases it can be affirmed that, if reality (the object to be known) exists in itself and for itself

(realism), regardless of whether a cognising subject relates to it (realism), then only intuitive knowledge is possible.

Finally, the *dualistic and theistic* philosophical assumption, from which the theological problem about the essence of knowledge can be solved (affirming that reality is dual), is perfectly related to the estimation that only *intuitive* knowledge can exist. In both cases it can be affirmed that, if reality is dual, then only intuitive knowledge is possible; because only from the senses can one speak of duality.

In each and every one of the aforementioned assumptions, the cognising subject solves each and every one of the respective philosophical problems of knowledge posed by the senses.

So far what has been said about the assumption that there can only be *intuitive* knowledge. The assumption that there can only be *mixed (rational-intuitive)* knowledge will now be discussed. Based on the Kantian idea that we think first and then we feel.

2.2.5.6.2 Presuming that knowledge is mixed (rational-intuitive <aprioristic>).

It is possible to suppose that there can be a kind of knowledge that can be both *rational* and *intuitive* (mixed, aprioristic). For it can be considered that there are two types of apprehension: the spiritual (*rational* knowledge) and the sensible (*intuitive* knowledge). Authors such as Pascal put alongside knowledge through the intellect, a knowledge through the heart, *rational, emotional.*

In the rational-intuitive philosophical assumption, the problem about the classification of knowledge is solved from both qualities of the cognising subject: reason and the senses; but first reason works and then the senses.

As was done in the discussion of the assumption that only *intuitive* knowledge can exist, philosophical assumptions akin to the assumption that only *mixed* (rational-intuitive) knowledge can exist can be observed in the three problems of knowledge discussed in sections 2.2.5.1 (the possibility of knowledge), 2.2.5.2 (the origin of knowledge) and 2.2.5.4 (the essence of knowledge).

The *critical* philosophical assumption, from which the problem of the possibility of knowledge can be solved by affirming that it is possible to know (dogmatism), but not in essence (scepticism), because each cognising subject feels and thinks differently from others (subjectivism), because truth changes in time, space and circumstances (relativism) and because, furthermore, all knowledge must be useful for the practical life of the subjects who elaborate it; they are perfectly related to the conjecture that only a *mixed* type of knowledge exists (rational-intuitive). In both cases the cognising subject is located first, in reason, and then, in the senses; it assumes from both qualities of the subject; and, by understanding that it is possible to know (dogmatism), but not in essence (scepticism), because each cognising subject feels and thinks differently from others (subjectivism), because truth changes in time, space and circumstances (relativism) and because, in addition, all knowledge must be useful for the practical life of the subjects who elaborate it; can conclude that knowledge can be neither solely rational, solely intuitive, but a mixture of both (mixed), with the proviso that we first reason (rational) and then feel (intuitive).

The *apriorist* philosophical assumption, from which the problem of the origin of knowledge can be solved by affirming that the source and basis of human knowledge is both in reason and in the senses, is perfectly related to the assumption that only *mixed* (rational-intuitive) knowledge can exist. In both cases it can be asserted that if the source of human knowledge is both in reason (rationalism) and in the senses (empiricism), with the proviso that we think first and then we feel, then only one kind of knowledge is possible, *mixed* (rational-intuitive) knowledge.

The *dialectical* philosophical assumption, from which the pre-metaphysical problem about the essence of knowledge can be solved (stating that, in a knowledge relation, both the cognising subject and the object to be known determine each other reciprocally and endlessly), is perfectly related to the estimation that only a *mixed* (rational-intuitive) type of knowledge can exist. In both cases it can be stated that, if the two aspects of the knowledge relation (the cognising subject and the object to be known) are determined reciprocally and endlessly, then educational researchers have to use both their senses and their reason to construct such knowledge; because such knowledge can only be elaborated, according to Aristotle and Kant, on the basis of sense sensations and thought.

The *phenomenological* philosophical assumption, from which the metaphysical problem about the essence of knowledge can be solved (affirming that reality exists, but that the cognising subject only perceives it as a phenomenon), is perfectly related to the estimation that only a *mixed* (rational-intuitive) type of knowledge can exist. In both cases it can be asserted that, if reality (the object to be known) exists in and of itself (realism), but that each cognising subject perceives it differently, because he feels and thinks differently from others (idealism), then only mixed (rational-intuitive) knowledge is possible.

Finally, the *monistic and pantheistic* philosophical assumption, from which the theological problem about the essence of knowledge can be solved (affirming that reality is unique), is perfectly related to the estimation that only *mixed* (rational-intuitive) knowledge can exist. In both cases it can be affirmed that, if reality is unique, then only *mixed* (rational-intuitive) knowledge is possible; because reason and the senses are absorbed by the total reality, which is unique; and only in this way can one speak of unity.

In each and every one of the philosophical assumptions addressed, the cognising subject solves each and every one of the respective problems of knowledge posed from both qualities: reason and the senses; with the proviso that reason works first and then the senses.

So far what has been said about the assumption that there can only be *mixed* (rational-intuitive) knowledge. The assumption that there can be only one kind of knowledge will be discussed next: mixed (rational-intuitive) knowledge, based on the Aristotelian idea that we first feel and then we think.

2.2.5.6.3 Conjecturing that knowledge is mixed (rational-intuitive<intellectualist>).

It is possible to suppose that there must be a type of knowledge that can be both *intuitive* and *rational* (mixed, intellectual). Because it can be estimated that there are two types of apprehension: the sensible (*intuitive* knowledge) and the intellectual (*rational* knowledge). David Hume (empiricist) assumes that reason is the organ of theoretical and *rational* knowledge and faith (*intuitive* and emotive apprehension and assent) is the organ of practical and irrational knowledge. He is of the opinion that faith is more an act of the affective part of our nature than of its thinking part. He suggests that it is through faith that certainty of the reality of the external world is achieved.

We can assume that there are two types of *intuition*: sensitive and intellectual. For example: When we compare two colours (red and green), we say: "red and green are different". This is an immediate spiritual intuition.

On the intuitive-rational philosophical assumption, the problem about the classification of knowledge is solved from both qualities of the researcher: the senses and the reason; but first the senses work and then the reason. As was done in the analysis of the assumption that only *mixed* (rational-intuitive) knowledge can exist, in the three problems of knowledge discussed in sections 2.2.5.1 (the possibility of knowledge), 2.2.5.2 (the origin of knowledge) and 2.2.5.3 (the essence of knowledge) one can observe philosophical assumptions akin to the assumption that only *mixed* (intuitive-rational) knowledge can exist.

The *critical* philosophical assumption, from which the problem of the possibility of knowledge can be solved by affirming that it is possible to know (dogmatism), but not in essence (scepticism), because each cognising subject feels and thinks differently from others (subjectivism), because truth changes in time, space and circumstances (relativism) and because, furthermore, all knowledge must be useful for the practical life of the subjects who elaborate it; they are perfectly related to the conjecture that there is only *mixed* (intuitive-rational) knowledge. In both cases the cognising subject is located first, in the senses, and then, in reason; it assumes from both qualities of the subject; and, by understanding that it is possible to know (dogmatism), but not in essence (scepticism), because each cognising subject feels and thinks differently from others (subjectivism), because truth changes in time, space and circumstances (relativism) and because, furthermore, all knowledge must be useful for the practical life of the subjects who elaborate it; can conclude that knowledge can be neither solely intuitive nor solely rational, but a mixture of both (mixed), with the proviso that we first feel (intuitive) and then think (rational).

The *intellectualist* philosophical assumption, from which the problem of the origin of knowledge can be solved by affirming that the source and basis of human knowledge is both in the senses and in reason (in that order of appearance), is perfectly related to the assumption that there can only be a *mixed* type of knowledge (intuitive-rational). In both cases it can be asserted that if the source of human knowledge is both in the senses (empiricism) and in reason (rationalism), with the proviso that we first feel (empiricism) and then think (rationalism), then only one kind of knowledge is possible, *mixed* (intuitive-rational) knowledge.

The *dialectical* philosophical assumption, from which the pre-metaphysical problem about the essence of knowledge can be solved (stating that, in a knowledge relation, both the cognising subject and the object to be known determine each other reciprocally and endlessly), is perfectly related to the estimation that only a *mixed* (rational-intuitive) type of knowledge can exist. In both cases it can be stated that, if the two aspects of the knowledge relation (the cognising subject and the object to be known) are determined reciprocally and endlessly, then educational researchers have to use both their senses and their reason to construct such knowledge; because such knowledge can only be elaborated, according to Aristotle and Kant, on the basis of sense sensations and thought.

The *phenomenological* philosophical assumption, from which the metaphysical problem about the essence of knowledge can be solved (affirming that reality exists, but that the cognising subject only perceives it as a phenomenon), is perfectly related to the estimation that only a *mixed* (rational-intuitive) type of knowledge can exist. In both cases it can be asserted that, if reality (the object to be known) exists in and of itself (realism), but that each cognising subject perceives it differently, because he feels and thinks differently from others (idealism), then only mixed (rational-intuitive) knowledge is possible.

Finally, the *monistic and pantheistic* philosophical assumption, from which the theological problem about the essence of knowledge can be solved (affirming that reality is unique), is perfectly related to the estimation that only *mixed* (rational-intuitive) knowledge can exist. In both cases it can be affirmed that, if reality is unique, then only *mixed* (rational-intuitive) knowledge is possible; because reason and the senses are absorbed by the total reality, which is unique; and only in this way can one speak of unity.

2.2.5.7 The relationship between the philosophical assumptions from which the problem of the origin of knowledge can be solved and the philosophical assumptions from which the problem of the classification of knowledge can be solved.

It can be concluded that the *classification of knowledge* proposed in this paper is mainly based on the philosophical assumptions from which the problem of the *origin of knowledge* can be solved: rationalism, empiricism, intellectualism and apriorism.

If we assume that knowledge originates in reason (rationalism), then there can only be *rational* knowledge. If we assume that knowledge originates in the senses (empiricism), then we can conclude that there can only be *intuitive* knowledge. If it is assumed that knowledge arises both from the senses (empiricism) and from reason (rationalism), but that we first feel and then reason (intellectualism), then we can speak of a *mixed* type of knowledge (intuitive-rational). And, finally, if we conjecture that knowledge springs from both reason and the senses, but that we first reason and then think (apriorism), then it can be said that only *mixed* (intuitive-rational) knowledge exists. It is further granted that there are philosophically no other options. For, as has been recalled throughout this paper, the cognising subject has only his reason and his senses to relate to his object of knowledge.

It is also necessary to remember that the previous arguments are deduced from the fact that the cognising subjects only have their *reason* and their *senses* to know reality. As already mentioned, mathematically, only the four possibilities mentioned above are given, in each and every one of the problems of knowledge addressed and to be addressed in this study.

So much for the assumption that there can only be *mixed* (intuitive-rational) knowledge. The fifth and final problem of knowledge will now be discussed: the concepts and criteria of truth of knowledge.

2.2.5.8 *The philosophical assumptions from which the problem of the concept and the criterion of truth of knowledge can be solved.*

Scientific communities or research traditions, depending on the perspective, paradigm or epistemological orientation of the programme or mode of knowledge production to which they adhere, construct their objects of study using *transcendent* or *immanent concepts* and *criteria* of truth; depending on how they solve the philosophical problem of the concept and criterion of truth: with reason, with the senses or with both qualities of the cognising subject.

The fifth and final philosophical problem of knowledge concerns the *truth* of knowledge. Paraphrasing Hessen (2011: 73), if we assume that the *truth* of knowledge consists in the agreement of the "image" with the object, it is not enough that our judgements are *true*; we need the *certainty* that they are true. The educational researcher must ask the following questions: What is the *criterion* that tells us whether knowledge is *true* or not, what is the *concept* of *truth* to be applied in a given research?

In order to answer the above questions it is necessary to resort, once again, to the definition of knowledge understood as a process. It has already been said that knowledge is an endless process, in which two entities are related (the cognising subject and the object to be known). It has already been established that an entity (only the human being) becomes a cognising subject when it fixes its attention on another entity (material, as for example: a tree; or immaterial, as for example: God), with the purpose of knowing it; and that, in turn, the entity on which the cognising subject fixed its attention in order to know it, becomes an object to be known, by the mere fact that another entity (the cognising subject) fixed its attention on it, in order to know it.

The elements of knowledge, understood as a process, are: the cognising subject, which is in the psychological sphere; the object to be known, which is in the ontological sphere; and the relation, which is in the logical sphere. Why logical sphere? Because the only thing that the cognising subject can establish as a relation with the object to be known is a discourse about it. Reality, in itself, is unknowable. The subject will have to be satisfied with discussing what the object is like, what it is for, how it works, how it can be classified, what purpose it can serve, etc. The subject will never be able to know what the object is in itself, because it cannot penetrate it, to know it in essence. The subject will not be able to penetrate the sphere of the subject, to become one with it, to merge with it, to know it in essence; because both elements of knowledge are in different spheres, which cannot be united.

Once the relation of knowledge between the cognising subject and the object to be known has been established, it is observed that its realisation is not simple, that it is very complex; because the two poles between which the connection of discernment is intended to be established are on different planes, the mentioned link of cognition has to take place between entities belonging to different realities, the correspondence between the two parts of the process of knowledge will be difficult because these are in different situations: the subject is the human soul which, in seeking to establish the relation of knowledge with the object to be known, has moved from the ontological sphere (ontos=being) to the psychological sphere (psyche=soul); the object, on the other hand, remains in the otological sphere (ontos=being). When an entity (the human being) seeks to know another entity (any material or immaterial reality), it must leave its sphere (ontos=being), it must move from the ontological sphere (as the material or immaterial reality that is the human being) to the psychological sphere (as soul, psyche, reason, thought, spirit, etc.), i.e. it remains in a different reality from that of the object to be known (material or immaterial reality).

The cognising subject and the object to be known, due to the relation of knowledge that the former intends to establish with the latter, remain in different "worlds". The fundamental problem of knowledge consists in the fact that the cognising subject and the object to be known can never be mixed, brought together, united, etc., because they belong to different and contradictory "worlds", "spheres", "realities", etc.

The cognising subject (who is in the psychological sphere), separated from the object to be known (which remains in the ontological sphere), when attempting to establish a relation of knowledge with it, finds it impossible to penetrate the sphere of reality (material or immaterial) of the object he is trying to elucidate. The two are like water and oil, they cannot be mixed, united, brought together, etc.

How, then, *can the relation of knowledge be established between the cognising subject and the object to be known*? It has already been said that the link between the human soul and reality can only be established logically; that the connection between human reason and phenomena is reduced to mere discourse which the mind elaborates on the facts it studies.

If this is so, *how is the correspondence between the spirit and the events it investigates established*? Answer: the cognising subject, the individual human being, as an entity that can be both material and spiritual, has two qualities that allow him to establish the relation of knowledge with his object of study: his senses (sight, touch, smell, taste, hearing) and his reason (soul, spirit, mind, or whatever you want to call this "thing" with which we human beings reason).

In order to know reality, the educational researcher can use his senses and his reason. If he uses his senses, the cognising subject can explore, describe, explain, interpret, understand, the material reality. If he uses his reason, the researcher can explore, describe, explain, interpret, understand, the spiritual reality. If he uses both his senses and his reason, the researcher can explore, describe, explain, interpret, understand, both material and spiritual reality. And by using both his reason and his senses, the investigator can explore, describe, explain, interpret, understand, both spiritual and material reality.

A major problem of knowledge is that the reason and senses of human beings are not perfect. That is why the functions of the senses have had to be extended by artificial devices, as in the case of the telescope for sight. The functions of reason have also been extended by the use of computers.

But the most important problems of the relation of knowledge between a cognising subject and his object of study is the philosophical one: is it possible to know, where does knowledge come from, who determines whom in a relation of knowledge: the object to the subject, the subject to the object, or do both determine each other, how many types of knowledge can there be, what are the concepts and criteria of truth of knowledge, etc.?

It has already been mentioned that these problems do not have a single answer, that the proposed solution to them depends on what the researcher assumes. Why does the cognising subject have to assume what is the concept of truth that he must apply in the knowledge of his object of study? Answer: because the researcher is condemned to ignore the truth about the concept of truth that he must consider in the reality he studies, due to the fact that the phenomenon under study is in a sphere different from his own; and, therefore, he can only suppose, thus establishing the logical relation of knowledge. He could suppose from the senses, from reason, from both, first the senses and then reason; and from both, first reason and then the senses.

In the case at hand, the concepts and criteria of truth that the researcher assumes will depend on his personal and professional inclinations and his object of study. Concerning the concept of truth:

If the cognising subject has only his senses and his reason to relate to his object of study, in mathematical terms, he has only four possible solutions to the problem of the concept of truth:

FIRST: It can assume, but never be certain, by locating itself in the senses, that only a transcendent concept of truth can be elaborated: the concordance of thought with the object thought.

SECOND: It can assume, but never be certain, being located in reason, that only an immanent concept of truth can be elaborated: the concordance of thought with itself.

THIRD: It can assume, but never be certain, being located both in the senses and in reason, that only a mixed concept of truth can be elaborated: the concordance of thought with the object thought (first) and with itself (afterwards).

FOURTH: It can assume, but never be certain, being located both in reason and in the senses, that only a mixed concept of truth can be elaborated: the concordance of the thought with itself (first) and with the object thought (afterwards).

In the case at hand, the concepts and criteria of truth that the researcher assumes will depend on his personal and professional inclinations and his object of study. Concerning the criterion of truth:

If the cognising subject has only his senses and his reason to relate to his object of study, in mathematical terms, he has only four possible solutions to the problem of the criterion of truth:

FIRST: He can assume, but never be certain, by locating himself in the senses, that only a transcendent criterion of truth can be elaborated: that the cognising subject is confronted with real objects, which are supposed to exist independently of his thought and to be outside his mind.

SECOND: It can assume, but never be certain, by placing itself in reason, that only an immanent criterion of truth can be elaborated: that the cognising subject is confronted with ideal, mental entities, which have no existence in reality and which are to be found inside the mind.

THIRD: It can assume, but never be certain, being located both in the senses and in reason, that only a mixed criterion of truth can be elaborated: that the cognising subject is confronted with both real and ideal entities.

FOURTH: It can assume, but never be certain, being located both in reason and in the senses, that only a mixed criterion of truth can be elaborated: that the cognising subject is confronted with both ideal and real objects.

So much for the introduction to the subject. In what follows, the philosophical assumptions from which the problem about the concept of truth of knowledge can be solved are analysed. As already mentioned, the cognising subject can assume from the senses, from reason, from the senses (first) and reason (later) and from reason (first) and the senses (later) to solve the problem of truth (of the concept of truth). With the "small disappointment" that he is only presuming the solution, because, apparently, he was not born to know reality in essence and, therefore, it only remains for him to estimate that it is in a certain way.

2.2.5.8.1 The philosophical assumptions from which the problem of the concept of truth of knowledge can be solved.

One will never be certain of the essential knowledge of reality. To know reality in an essential way, the cognising subject would have to penetrate it and merge with it (literally), transforming both (subject and object) into a single reality, and this is impossible, because the cognising subject and the object to be known are in different "worlds": the subject is the soul, the spirit; the object, reality (concrete or abstract). Let us say, for example, that we would like to know what a tree is, in essence. In this case it is a concrete, tangible entity, which we can appreciate, but not know, with the senses. To know what a tree is, is impossible, because, in order to do so, we would have to enter (literally) into its sap, leaves, roots, trunk, branches, etc., and be one with it. Then we would know what a tree is, but, perhaps, we would cease to be ourselves and we would be transformed into another entity, who knows what kind of entity we would then be. In the case of abstract entities (God) the relation of knowledge becomes more complicated: where is God, how can we establish a relation of knowledge with God as an object?

In order to establish the logical relationship with the object of study, which in this case is the concept of truth (an abstract entity) and which therefore makes the relationship more difficult, the cognising subject can establish the following conjectures:

As cognising subjects we can solve the problem about the concept of truth of knowledge by assuming from the senses (transcendent concept of truth), from reason (immanent concept of truth), or from both (mixed concept of truth), in two different senses: starting with the senses and ending with reason or vice versa.

2.2.5.8.1.1 Transcendentally resolving the problem of the concept of the truth of knowledge.

Paraphrasing John Hessen (2011: 73-75), truth can be assumed to consist in the concordance of thought with the object thought. Objects of knowledge are deemed to be outside the mind of the cognising subject. Such objects are presumed to transcend the mind of the cognising subject. That is why Hessen calls this concept of truth: transcendent concept of truth. Transcendence is understood as meaning that something (the object) is outside something (the subject), i.e. the object of study (the concrete reality) transcends the cognising subject, because it is outside his mind, in the environment, in the material reality, which can be seen, smelled, touched, heard, tasted.

Objects of knowledge that lie outside the spirit, the cognising subject, are studied by the natural sciences. Thought relates to entities (from the mineral, plant and animal kingdoms) which are in front of thought; they are material entities which transcend thought.

In the transcendent philosophical assumption, the problem about the concept of truth of knowledge is solved from the senses.

In the four problems of knowledge discussed in sections 2.2.5.1 (the possibility of knowledge), 2.2.5.2 (the origin of knowledge), 2.2.5.3 (the essence of knowledge) and 2.2.5.4 (the classification of knowledge) one can observe philosophical assumptions akin to the assumption that there can be only one transcendent criterion of truth.

The philosophical assumptions of *scepticism, subjectivism, relativism* and *pragmatism*, from which the problem of the possibility of knowledge can be solved by affirming that no real contact between subject and object is possible, are perfectly related to the conjecture that there is only a transcendent concept of truth. In both cases the cognising subject is located in the senses, supposes from the sensations and, understanding that reality exists, independently of the mind, can conclude that one must only speak of a transcendent concept of truth.

The *empiricist* philosophical assumption, from which the problem of the origin of knowledge can be solved by affirming that the only source and basis of human knowledge is in the senses, in the experiences of the senses, is perfectly related to the assumption that only a transcendent concept of truth can exist. In both cases it can be asserted that if the source of human knowledge is in the senses (empiricism), then only a transcendent concept of truth is possible.

The *subjectivist* philosophical assumption, from which the pre-metaphysical problem about the essence of knowledge can be solved (claiming that, in a relation of knowledge, the cognising subject determines the object to be known), is perfectly related to the estimation that there can only be a transcendent concept of truth. In both cases it can be asserted that, if it is the passions, emotions, feelings, ambitions, prejudices, etc., of the subject that determine the knowledge of the object to be known, then educational researchers only have to use their senses to construct that knowledge; because knowledge can only be elaborated, according to John Locke, from the sensations of the senses.

The philosophical *realist* assumption, from which the metaphysical problem of the essence of knowledge can be solved (asserting that reality exists independently of whether a cognising subject fixes his reason and senses on it for the purpose of knowing it), is perfectly related to the estimation that only a transcendent concept of truth can exist. In both cases it can be asserted that, if reality (the object to be known) exists in and of itself (realism), independently of a cognising subject's relations to it (realism), then only a transcendent concept of truth is possible.

Finally, the *dualistic and theistic* philosophical assumption, from which the theological problem about the essence of knowledge can be solved (affirming that reality is dual), is perfectly related to the estimation that only a transcendent concept of truth can exist. In both cases it can be affirmed that, if reality is dual, then only a transcendent concept of truth is possible; because only from the senses can one speak of duality.

In summary, the transcendent concept of truth can be stated as "the concordance of the thought (cognising subject) with the object (to be known)".

Therefore, all judgements that rest on an immediate presence or reality of the object thought of are true. For example: "the sky is blue".

From realism, reality is assumed to exist independently of the cognising subject.

So far what has been said about the assumption that there can be only one transcendent concept of truth. The assumption that there can be only one immanent concept of truth will now be discussed.

2.2.5.8.1.2 . Immanently solving the problem of the concept of the truth of knowledge.

Paraphrasing Hessen (20011: 73-75) if we assume from reason, we can conclude that the essence of truth lies in the agreement of thought with itself, with something that resides within thought itself. A judgement is considered to be true when it is formed in accordance with the laws and norms of thought itself. According to this, truth is presumed to mean something purely formal; it coincides with the logical correctness of thought.

In the immanent philosophical assumption, the problem of the concept of the truth of knowledge is solved by reason.

As was done in the discussion of the assumption that there can be only one transcendent concept of truth, philosophical assumptions akin to the assumption that there can be only one immanent concept of truth can be observed in the four problems of knowledge discussed in sections 2.2.5.1 (the possibility of knowledge), 2.2.5.2 (the origin of knowledge), 2.2.5.4 (the essence of knowledge) and 2.2.5.6 (the classification of knowledge).

The *dogmatic* philosophical assumption, from which the problem of the possibility of knowledge can be solved by affirming that real contact between subject and object is possible, is perfectly related to the conjecture that there is only an immanent concept of truth. In both cases one has full confidence in human reason, one has faith that reason alone can provide us with true knowledge.

The *rationalist* philosophical assumption, from which the problem of the origin of knowledge can be solved by affirming that the only source and basis of human knowledge is reason, is perfectly related to the assumption that there can only be an immanent concept of truth. In both cases it can be asserted that if the source from which human knowledge springs is reason, then only an immanent concept of truth is possible.

The *objectivist* philosophical assumption, from which the pre-metaphysical problem about the essence of knowledge can be solved (claiming that, in a relation of knowledge, it is the object to be known that determines the cognising subject), is perfectly related to the estimation that there can only be an immanent concept of truth. In both cases it can be asserted that, if there is an objective world of ideas (objects to be known) that is determining the knowledge that cognising subjects can obtain, then educational researchers only have to use their reason to find that knowledge; for it can only be obtained, according to Plato, by rational means.

The *idealistic* philosophical assumption, from which the metaphysical problem of the essence of knowledge can be solved (by asserting that reality has spiritual forces, subjective or logical ideal entities as its background), is perfectly related to the estimation that only an immanent concept of truth can exist. In both cases it can be asserted that, if reality (the object to be known) does not exist in and of itself (realism), but is only a construct of the cognising subjects (idealism), then only an immanent concept of truth is possible.

Finally, the *monistic and pantheistic* philosophical assumption, from which the theological problem about the essence of knowledge can be solved (affirming that reality is one), is perfectly related to the estimation that only an immanent concept of truth can exist. In both cases it can be affirmed that, if reality is one, then only an immanent concept of truth is possible; for only from reason can one speak of such a concept as truth.

In short, the immanent concept of truth can be stated as "the agreement of thought with itself".

A judgement is true when it is formed according to the rules of thought.

Truth is something formal, it coincides with the correctness of thought. For example: education is the art by which the adult generations transmit culture to the younger generations for their preservation, recreation and enhancement.

Idealism assumes that reality is constructed by the subject.

So far what has been said about the assumption that there can only be one immanent concept of truth. The philosophical assumptions from which the problem of the truth criteria of knowledge can be solved will now be analysed.

2.2.5.8.1.3 The philosophical assumptions from which the problem of the truth criterion of knowledge can be solved.

The question of the concept of truth is very closely connected with the question of the criterion of truth.

As cognising subjects we can solve the problem about the criterion of truth of knowledge by assuming from the senses (transcendent criterion of truth), from reason (immanent criterion of truth), or from both (mixed criterion of truth), in two different senses: starting with the senses and ending with reason or vice versa.

1.1.1.1 .2.1 Resolving in a transcendent way the problem of the criterion of truth of knowledge.

Following Hessen (2011: 75-79), if by truth we mean the concordance of thought with the object thought (transcendent concept of truth), then we will say that all judgements that rest on an immediate presence or reality of the object thought are true.

It deals with real objects which are then transformed into objects of consciousness, data of consciousness. It is assumed that we possess immediate certainty about the red we see or the pain we feel, because they are real; they exist independently of the mind. The *criterion of truth* is considered to consist in the immediate presence or reality of an object (realism).

In short, the transcendent criterion of truth consists in the fact that the objects are outside the consciousness of the subjects. They are real objects. In the data of consciousness we possess an immediate certainty of their existence. Perception provides us with immediate evidence. For example: the leaves of the tree are green.

It is assumed, from realism, that reality exists, independently of the cognising subject.

1.1.1.2 .2.2 Immanently solving the problem of the truth criterion of knowledge.

Following Hessen (2011: 75-79), if by truth we mean the concordance of thought with itself, we will say that a judgement is true when it is formed in accordance with the laws and norms of thought. Truth is supposed to be something formal that coincides with the correctness of thought. This would be a conception that *logical idealism* makes its own. Truth is considered to mean the concordance of thought with itself. We can know this agreement in the absence of contradiction. Our thought agrees with itself when it is free of contradictions and only then. The immanent or idealistic concept necessarily entails considering the absence of contradiction as a criterion of truth.

In short, the immanent criterion of truth means that objects are within the consciousness of the subject. Thought encounters mental, ideal objects. Logic and mathematics are formal or ideal sciences. They are judgements proper to logic and mathematics. Example: "2 + 2 = 4", "the whole is greater than the part", "all bodies are large". It is assumed, from idealism, that reality is constructed by the mind.

Amanera of general summary on the subchapter just analysed, the problem about the concepts and criteria of truth of knowledge are irresolvable, in a definitive way; due to the reasons already considered. We can only assume from the senses, from reason or from both, that they can be solved in a transcendent, immanent or mixed way.

2.2.5.9 *The epistemological relationship between the philosophical assumptions from which the problem about the classification of knowledge can be solved and the philosophical assumptions from which the problem about the concept and the criterion of truth of knowledge can be solved.*

It can be concluded that the concepts and truth criteria proposed in this paper are based on the philosophical assumptions from which the problems of knowledge discussed in the previous subchapters (possibility, origin, essence and classification of knowledge) can be solved. In the following, the philosophical assumptions from which the problems about the *concept* and truth *criterion* of knowledge can be solved will be compared with the assumptions from which the problems about the origin and classification of knowledge can be solved.

If we assume that knowledge originates in reason (rationalism), then there can only be *rational* knowledge; and if only rational knowledge is possible, then the concept and the criterion of truth of this type of (rational) knowledge will be *immanent*. If it is assumed that knowledge springs from the senses (empiricism), then it can be concluded that only *intuitive* knowledge exists; and if only intuitive knowledge exists, then the criterion of truth of this type of (intuitive) knowledge will be *transcendent*. If it is presumed that knowledge is born both in the senses (empiricism) and in reason (rationalism), but that we first feel and then reason (intellectualism), then one can speak of a *mixed* type of knowledge (intuitive-rational); and if only knowledge of this type (mixed: rational-intuitive) is possible, then the concept and the criterion of truth of this type of knowledge (mixed: intuitive-rational) will also be mixed (transcendent-immanent) And, finally, if we conjecture that knowledge springs from both reason and the senses, but that we first reason and then think (apriorism), then it can be said that only *mixed* (rational-intuitive) knowledge exists; and if only mixed (rational-intuitive) knowledge is possible, then the concept and criterion of truth of this kind of knowledge (mixed: rational-intuitive) will also be mixed (immanent-transcendent). It is further granted that there are, philosophically, no other options.

It is also necessary to remember that the above arguments are deduced from the fact that the cognising subjects only have their *reason* and their *senses* to know reality. As already mentioned, mathematically, only the four possibilities mentioned above are given, in each and every one of the problems of knowledge addressed and to be addressed in this study.

2.2.5.10 *Summary of the sub-chapter.*

Philosophical assumptions, whether the cognising subject knows it or not, are estimates that the cognising subject makes using his reason, his senses, or both, to solve each and every one of the five main philosophical problems of knowledge, in the exploration, description, explanation, interpretation, etc., of his object of study.

The main characteristics, functions and purpose of philosophical assumptions are as follows:

- The main characteristic of a philosophical assumption is, precisely, that it is a conjecture that the cognising subject elaborates from his reason, his senses or from both qualities in order to solve some philosophical problem of knowledge.

- The function of any philosophical assumption, in accordance with the above, is to locate the cognising subject in one of its qualities (reason, senses or both) in order to solve some philosophical problem of knowledge, related to its object of study.

- The aim of each and every one of the philosophical assumptions studied is to solve each and every one of the five main problems of knowledge.

The problems of knowledge can be classified from reason, from the senses or from both qualities of the cognising subject.

It can be concluded that the major philosophical problems of knowledge (possibility, origin, essence, classification and criteria of truth) are essentially unsolvable. That the educational researcher will need to choose the philosophical assumptions to solve each and every one of the five problems of knowledge mentioned. And that this will depend on the quality he uses to relate to his object of study: reason, the senses, or both.

By way of summary, the following table shows the five main philosophical problems of knowledge and the main *philosophical assumptions* from which each and every one of them can be solved:

PROBLEM	POSSIBILITY	SUPPOSITIONS	
			DOGMATISM: The subject really apprehends the object.
			ESCEPTICISM: The subject cannot really apprehend the object.
			RELATIVISM: There are only truths in relation to a given humanity.
			SUBJECTIVISM: Truth is limited to the subject who knows and judges.
			PRAGMATISM: True means useful, valuable, life-founding.

			CRITICISM: It is possible to know, one must examine all claims of reason and accept nothing carelessly.	
S PHLOSOPHICAL KNOWLEDGE	**ORIGIN**	**SUPPOSITIONS**		**RATIONALISM**: The main source of human knowledge is in reason, in thought.
				EMPIRISM: The only source of human knowledge is experience.
				INTELLECTUALISM: The source and basis of knowledge is both experience (first) and reason (second).
				APRIORISM: Experience (after) and thought (first) are the sources of knowledge.
	ESSENCE	SOLUTIONS PRE-METAPHYSICS	ASSUMPTIONS	OBJECTIVISM: The object determines the subject.
				SUBJECTIVISM: The subject determines the object.
		SOLUTIONS METAPHYSICS	SUPPOSITIONS	REALISM: In addition to ideal objects there are real objects, independent of thought.
				IDEALISM: All objects possess an ideal, mental being.
				PHENOMENALISM: We know things not as they are, but as they appear to us.
		THEOLOGICAL SOLUTIONS	SUPPOSITIONS	DUALISM AND THEISM: Divinity is the common source of thought and being. The transcendent absolute
				MONISM AND PANTHEISM: The immanent absolute. Absorbing subject and object into a unity.
		TYPES OF KNOWLEDGE	ASSUMPTIONS	**RATIONAL** KNOWLEDGE: Mediate, discursive
				INTUITIVE KNOWLEDGE: Immediate. Knowing by seeing
		CRITERIA	ASSUMPTIONS	**TRASCENDENT**: Concordance of thought with the object.
				IMMANENT: Concordance of thought with itself.

2.3 THEORETICAL FOUNDATIONS, TO PROBLEMATISE THE OBJECTS OF STUDY FROM THE EDUCATIONAL SCIENCES.

Conceptual mapping" will be used for the analysis in this sub-chapter. Conceptual mapping" is a *concept* developed by Tobón (2010) which, in general terms, can be understood as a strategy to form and evaluate key academic concepts, through eight axes or essential questions. The essential questions refer to:

1. Notion (what is it?). A notion or definition of the concept or theory is given.

2. Categorisation (to which general class does it belong?). The major class in which the concept or theory falls is described.

3. Characteristics (what is it like?). The key aspects that give identity and particularity to the concept or theory are described and explained, considering the class within which it falls.

4. Differences (what other nearby concepts does it differ from). Concepts in the same class with which the concept or theory can be confused are indicated and explained.

5. Subdivision (into which classes is it divided?). The types or classes of the concept or theory are described and explained. Each type or class must meet the above characteristics. This is the opposite of categorisation.

6. Linkage (to which social, economic and historical categories and processes does it relate?) Approaches, theories, approaches and methodologies from other areas or contexts that help to better understand and apply the concept or theory are described and explained.

7. Methodology (what are the key elements of the methodology?). The minimum aspects to be taken into account in the application of the concept or theory are described and explained. The elements of the methodology can be in different orders.

8. Exemplification (what could be an example?). An example of the concept or theory is presented.

Why is it necessary to construct the concept of "theory" in this paper?

Because *epistemological orientations* are composed, as already noted, of philosophical assumptions, in order to observe reality;

Theoretical foundations, to problematise the objects of study; methodological procedures, to generate new knowledge; technical strategies, to learn about the phenomena; and instruments, to gather the information to be technically analysed.

It has already been mentioned that the difference between *science* and *philosophy* is the same as the difference between *philosophical assumptions* and *theoretical foundations* of epistemological orientations; science arises from philosophy, just as theoretical foundations arise from philosophical assumptions.

The *theory* or *theories* that the educational researcher uses to problematise his or her object of study will depend on the philosophical *assumption*(s) from which he or she solved the five main problems of knowledge (possibility, origin, essence, classification and concepts and criteria of truth).

This subchapter tries to relate the *philosophical assumptions* of *epistemological perspectives, paradigms* or *orientations* to their *theoretical foundations,* i.e. to determine how the *philosophical* level influences the *theoretical level* when constructing an object of study.

Thinking reality from *dogmatic* or *sceptical, pragmatic, subjectivist, relativist, critical,* etc., philosophical assumptions (as far as the *possibility of knowing* is concerned); observing it, surveying it, experiencing it or documenting it - technically - as a compact whole or as divided into parts; as if it were still or moving; as if it were stable or unstable; as if it were single or multiple; as if it were fixed or mobile; as if it were regular or irregular; etc., brings important consequences in the production of knowledge. If we assume that reality is fixed, for example, we are thinking of it in a *dogmatic* way; as if it were given and that we need only apprehend the object absolutely as it is given to us. On the other hand, if we reflect on phenomena *in a sceptical, subjective, relative, pragmatic,* etc. way, we begin to doubt their apprehension, universality, validity, limits, usefulness, reasons, etc.

The same is true of - and, indeed, relates to - the problems of knowledge concerning its origin, essence, types and criteria of truth. To understand phenomena in *objective terms*, for example, is to examine them as if they were still, as if they did not change in time, space and conditions, as if they were given forever, the same, and so on. To view facts *subjectively*, on the other hand, is to see them as moving, constantly changing, differentiated, conflicting, related, etc. Analysing things in an *idealistic* way leads us to observe them, survey them, document them, experience them, etc., in a *dogmatic* way; that is to say, thinking about what ought to be and neglecting what is. On the other hand, studying behaviours or behaviours *in a realist* way means knowing them in a *sceptical, subjectivist, relativist, pragmatic, critical*, etc. way; that is, considering beings in such a way that we observe, survey, experiment, document, etc., as if they were moving, changing, modifying, etc. Finally, thinking of reality in monistic terms implies thinking of it in itself, as a fixed, immobile, eternal, immutable, etc., whole. On the contrary, if we think of it in a dualistic way, we can analyse it in relation to other realities in conflict, conciliation, etc.

2.3.1 *The definition of "theory"*.

The concept of "*theory*" can be defined, in etymological terms, as "to observe" or "to contemplate" (from the Greek *Theorein*, to observe or contemplate). From its epistemological origin it can be assumed that the one who "observes" or "contemplates" is the cognising subject and the "observed" or "contemplated" must be the object to be known. What elements does the cognising subject have to "observe" or "contemplate" the object of study? Answer: his reason and his senses. The educational researcher can only use his reason and his senses to establish the relationship of knowledge with the phenomenon to be investigated.

Paraphrasing Cortés Morato, Jordi and Martínez Riu, Antoni (1996), Plato and Aristotle gave the etymological meaning to the term "*theory*", understood as contemplation of ideas or as contemplative knowledge and higher intellectual activity of man, respectively.

Plato assumes, from *objectivism*, that reason can remember *ideas*, because he considers that they exist independently of the cognising subject; Aristotle, on the other hand, assumes that *theory* is the product of man's intellectual activity; that is, the human being "observes" or "contemplates" nature, with his senses, and gives a meaning to "*that*" which he observes, using his reason (intellectualism).

For Popper (1980: 57) "*Theories are nets we cast in order to grasp that which we call "world": to rationalise it, explain it and dominate it...*". The educational researcher tries to apprehend reality, according to this, in order to rationalise, explain and master it.

From a critical rationalist assumption, Popper tries to explain reality and bring order to it by rationalising it, in order to dominate and exploit it.

According to Sautú, Ruth (2003: 155) "*we understand theory as conceptualisations, affirmations or propositions that postulate explanations*". From a pragmatic assumption, it is stated that a *theory* is a *concept* or *proposition* that explains some phenomenon. A *judgement*, expressed as a *proposition*, can be said to be a *theory*.

The aforementioned authors agree that the idea of *theory* refers to *concepts, affirmations* or *propositions* within a *domain*. For Gutiérrez (2005: 128) "... *the difference between idea and judgement is that the former neither affirms nor denies anything; and, on the other hand, the essence of judgement is in the affirmation or denial of something*". Paraphrasing Gutiérrez (2005: 128), *judgement* is psychological because it is an act of judging that a cognising subject (the human soul) performs on an object to be known (reality). A judgement (as a process) is a mental operation by means of which a cognising subject affirms or denies an idea with respect to another idea.

Judgement, as a process, is in the logical sphere, it is thought, discourse. Judgement, as a product, is the (already realised) affirmation of the relation between two ideas. The proposition is the external expression of the judgement. Judgements are expressed by means of propositions.

The cognising subject, who is in the psychological sphere (it is the human soul, his mind, his reason), in view of the fact that he cannot apprehend the essence of the object to be known, because he is in the ontological sphere (it is the concrete or abstract reality), and the two spheres represent different worlds, using his reason and/or his senses, elaborates a discourse (explorations, descriptions, explanations, interpretations, understandings, etc.) about his object of study. It is not reality, it is only a discourse about reality. That is why the term "pen" is nothing like "that thing" with which we write.

It should be made clear that this discourse, this theory, which the cognising subject elaborates about his object to be known, is constructed on the basis of the way in which the cognising subject, whether he knows it or not, solves the five main philosophical problems of knowledge (possibility, origin, essence, classification and concept and criterion of truth of knowledge). The philosophical problems of knowledge are solved depending on whether the subject is located in his reason (rationalism), his senses (empiricism), both: senses and reason (intellectualism) or both: reason and senses (apriorism).

Depending on what the cognising subject assumes, whether he solves the problems of knowledge with his reason or with his senses, he will elaborate his discourse on the object to be known. From one assumption, a theory is elaborated; from its opposite, a different theory will be elaborated. This is why there is so much contradictory knowledge about the same object of knowledge. Because this knowledge is elaborated by different subjects, from different philosophical assumptions.

Theories are developed in a domain. By domain we should understand the field of knowledge. The sciences can be classified, according to Bunge (1999), into two main branches: Factual Sciences (Natural Sciences and Social Sciences) and Formal Sciences (Logic and Mathematics). The factual sciences and the formal or ideal sciences would be the first two great fields of science, in general. From these two great fields of science there are innumerable divisions and subdivisions, up to education, which is within the field of social sciences.

It can be assumed that theory is a series of judgements, by means of which we affirm or deny an idea (or concept) with respect to another idea (or concept), within a field of knowledge. It is proposed that theory (as a product) be understood as a series of propositions that a cognising subject elaborates about an object to be known, within a field of knowledge, on the basis of certain philosophical assumptions.

The affirmations or negations, which a cognising subject elaborates about an object to be known, will depend on what the subject assumes about the reality he or she is analysing. Theory depends on philosophy.

2.3.2 *The characteristics of the theory*.

An important characteristic of theory is that it must frame or locate an aspect of reality, which can be natural or social. *"Every theory is based on a formal structure of a domain" Padilla,* G. Jesús (2000: 23) This means that theories gain meaning and strength when they form a constituent part of a conceptual structure within a general field of science identified as a domain, such as the social sciences or the natural sciences, where there is a basic conceptual system agreed upon by the scientific community.

Theories are explorations, descriptions, explanations, interpretations, understandings of natural or social reality.

According to Sautú, Ruth (2003: 34), theories are delimited by their scope, disciplines and areas of knowledge. *"Theories provide the framework through which we define reality and study it"*.

Theories are developed on the basis of certain philosophical assumptions. That is why the explorations, descriptions, explanations, interpretations, understandings, etc. that different subjects construct about the same object of study are different in content.

2.3.3 *The elements of the theory*.

Theories are composed of certain elements, which can be epistemological and logical.

2.3.3.1 *The epistemological elements of theories*.

The epistemological elements of theories are the philosophical assumptions, from which the philosophical problems of knowledge are solved; the intellectual operations or methodological procedures, with which theories are constructed; the technical strategies, which the cognising subject uses to learn about reality; and the instruments, with which information is recovered to analyse phenomena. Theory as a process is analysed here.

The epistemological elements of the theories are discussed more fully in chapter two of this paper.

2.3.3.2 *The logical elements of theories*.

The *logical elements* of theories are ideas or concepts, logical judgement and logical reasoning.

The *logical elements* of the theories are discussed more fully in subchapter 2.5 of this paper.

2.3.3.2.1 Ideas or concepts.

In a *theory*, *concepts* are the simplest elements. *"The word concept comes from the Latin conceptus, from concipere, to conceive; in the Latin philosophical tradition, that which is conceived by the mind. In a broad sense, it is equivalent to general idea or abstract idea. As understood by traditional philosophy, it is the result of the process of abstraction*" (Cortés, Jordi et al., 1996: 76).

Paraphrasing Gutiérrez (2005: 61-69), an *idea* is the mental representation of an object, without affirming or denying anything about it. This mental representation is obtained by means of an intellectual operation called simple apprehension or abstraction. As a product of this intellectual operation, an *idea* or *concept* (thought) is obtained. The *idea* or *concept* (thought) is expressed by means of a *term* or *word*. Example: tree.

It is necessary to clarify that the *term* "tree" is nothing like the "thing" it is referring to. It is only a logical discourse, a "convention" that the cognising subject elaborates about his object of knowledge; with the purpose of making himself understood by other people. "*A concept is a figurative content designated by a concrete term*" (Mayntz, Renate, 1975: 13).

Concepts can be broken down into their constituent parts: definition, characteristics, function or causes, purpose or consequences, classification, etc.

Within a theory, *concepts* are like the building blocks of a construction. They are elements known to the scientific community or research tradition that serve to construct more complete explanations: *propositions*, which are the expressions of *judgements*.

2.3.3.2.2 The trials.

A *judgement* is the affirmation or negation of an idea with respect to another idea. This affirmation or negation is obtained by means of an intellectual operation called psychological *judgement*. As a product of this intellectual operation, a logical *judgement* (thought) is obtained. The logical *judgement* (thought) is expressed by means of a *proposition* or *enunciation*. Example: the tree is dry.

It is necessary to clarify that the logical *judgement* "the tree is dry" is nothing like "that thing" that the subject is judging. It is only a logical discourse, a "convention" that the cognising subject elaborates on his object of knowledge; with the aim of making himself understood by other people.

2.3.3.2.3 Rationale.

A *ratiocination* is the obtaining of new knowledge from already established knowledge. This new knowledge is obtained by means of an intellectual operation called psychological *reasoning*. As a product of this intellectual operation, a logical *reasoning* (thinking) is obtained. Logical *reasoning* (thinking) is expressed by means of *argumentation*. Example: "The tree is dry because it has no water". An argument is made up of two or more propositions. In this case "the tree is dry" and "the tree has no water". There are two propositions. In the first proposition the idea "dry" of the idea "tree" is affirmed; in the second proposition the idea "water" of the idea "tree" is denied. Together they constitute an argument, derived from a reasoning.

It is necessary to clarify that the logical *reasoning* "the tree is dry because it lacked water" is nothing like "that thing" about which the subject is *arguing*. It is only a logical discourse, a "convention" that the cognising subject elaborates about his object of knowledge; with the aim of making himself understood by other people.

2.3.4 *The purpose of the theory*.

The *purpose* of the theory depends on the epistemological orientation of the researcher. For Cohen (1968: 238) *"all theories involve a process of abstraction from concrete questions"*. It can be argued that all knowledge developed by human beings is theoretical, because it involves an abstract explanation of reality.

The main *purposes* of theory could be to explore, describe, explain, interpret and understand reality.

For Cortés J. et al. (1996), *propositions "come from the Latin propositio, an assertive sentence, which affirms or denies something about something and is susceptible of being true or false"*. Cortés *assumes* that the main *characteristic* of *propositions* is the possibility of being qualified as false or true and, in estimating the falsity or veracity of a proposition, he reveals the *assumptions* from which he resolves each and every one of the five philosophical *problems* of knowledge: *dogmatism*, regarding the possibility of knowing; *rationalism*, regarding the origin of knowledge; *objectivism*, regarding the pre-metaphysical solution to the problem of the essence of knowledge; *idealism*, regarding the metaphysical solution to the problem of the essence of knowledge; *dualism* and theism, regarding the theological solution to the problem of the essence of knowledge; *rational* knowledge, regarding the classification of knowledge; and *immanent* concept and criteria of truth.

That about which something is affirmed is called the subject; and that which is affirmed about the subject is called the predicate. *Propositions* are complete sentences, with subject and predicate. *Propositions* are more explanatory than concepts, although they usually include them.

For Padilla, G. (2000: 19) *"...the result of the scientist's activity takes the form of propositions.... "*. *Propositions* are linguistic constructions that explain in a concrete way a given fact or phenomenon. For example: "learning is a change of behaviour". When a series of *propositions*, such as the above, can be analysed to determine whether they are true or false, they become *principles* or *postulates* that can form a logical system and constitute *science*. *"...for there to be science it is necessary that our propositions form a logical system, that is, that there is a relationship between them..."* (Cohen, Morris and Nagel, Ernest; 1968: 154).

For R. A. E. (2003) a *principle* or *postulate* refers to *".each of the first propositions or fundamental truths by which one begins to study the sciences or the arts* - also explained as the - *basis, origin, fundamental reason on which one proceeds in discourse in any subject"*. From the certainty (only from the assumptions mentioned above) that "learning is a change of behaviour", Skinner explained, at the time, how human beings learn. This *principle* or *postulate* allowed Skinner to elaborate a series of explanations about what learning is, how it is learnt, etc.

The *principles* or *postulates* constitute the elements from which the theories state their bases, questions and hypotheses.

The theories will be analysed below, based on the assumptions from which they solve each and every one of the five main philosophical problems of knowledge, depending on whether the cognising subject uses his reason, his senses or both qualities.

2.3.5 *The classification of theories*.

Any *classification* is arbitrary and follows the interests of the research. In this case, the second element of an epistemological orientation is *theory*. For the purposes of this study,

Theories are *classified* - on the basis of the *assumptions* from which they solve each and every philosophical *problem* of knowledge - into three main *branches*: general theories of knowledge, particular theories of the social sciences and specific theories of the educational sciences. Why they were given this name will be explained in due course.

The *theoretical foundations* of epistemological perspectives, paradigms or orientations, according to criteria of extension and understanding, as already indicated, can be classified as general, particular and specific to the field of educational sciences.

The proposed classification is also based on criteria of extension and comprehension, in a descending order, starting with the largest, the ones that include the most phenomena, and ending with the smallest, the most specific ones.

2.3.5.1 *General theories of knowledge*.

For the analysis of *general theories of knowledge* and *particular theories of social sciences*, we will mainly consider the work of Gabriel Gutiérrez Pantoja (1999), entitled: *Methodology of social sciences I*, specifically, chapter III, whose title is: "alternative links between thought and reality". The title of the aforementioned chapter suggests that there are many possibilities or forms of relationship between the cognising subject and the object to be known, in any process of knowledge. What are these alternatives of linkage (relationship) between thought (cognising subject) and reality (object to be known)? Gutiérrez (2009: 147 - 232) calls them *methodological worldviews* and develops three: mathematicism, mechanicism and organicism.

For Gutiérrez (1999: 153-154), *methodology* is the study of methods, and by *method* he understands the way to reach a goal. This is an explanation with which we agree. But, without further explanation, the author then goes on to discuss what he calls *methodological worldviews* (mathematicism, mechanicism and organicism). This is a subject with which we do not agree. For the purposes of this analysis, these "methodological worldviews" will be called "*general theories of objective knowledge*". In the course of the analysis of the aforementioned theories, it will become clear why they are so called. What needs to be clarified for the time being is that what for the author mentioned above is a method will be considered as a theory in this work.

Mathematicism, mechanicism, organicism, chaos, conflict, complexity, and any other *general theories of knowledge* that may exist, are so called because they explore, describe, explain, interpret, understand, etc. facts, phenomena, events, etc., both factual (within the natural and social sciences) and formal (logic and mathematics).

General theories of knowledge, depending on the philosophical *assumptions* from which they solve each and every problem of knowledge, can be classified as dogmatic, sceptical - including pragmatic, subjective, relative - or critical (if the problem of the possibility of knowledge is taken as a criterion for classification); rational, empirical, or intellectual and aprioristic (if the problem of the origin of knowledge is taken as a criterion for classification); objective, subjective or dialectical (if the problem of the origin of knowledge is taken as a criterion for classification); rational, empirical, or intellectual and aprioristic (if the problem of the origin of knowledge is taken as a criterion for classification); objective, subjective or dialectical (if the pre-metaphysical solution of the problem of the essence of knowledge is taken as a criterion for classification); idealist, realist or phenomenalist (if the metaphysical solution of the problem of the essence of knowledge is taken as a criterion of classification); dualist and theistic, monistic and pantheistic or mixed (if the theological solution of the problem of the essence of knowledge is taken as a criterion of classification); rational, intuitive or mixed (if the problem of the classification of knowledge is taken as a criterion of classification); and transcendent, immanent or mixed (if the problem of the truth criteria of knowledge is taken as a criterion of classification).

General theories of knowledge can be classified according to the above criterion as dogmatic, rational, objective, ideal, dualistic and theistic, rationalistic and transcendental (first) if they start from the above philosophical *assumptions*; sceptical, subjectivist, relativist, pragmatic, empiricist, subjectivist, realist, monist and pantheist, intuitive and immanent (secondly) if their philosophical *assumptions* are those stated; or critical, intellectualist and apriorist, dialectical, phenomenalist and mixed (thirdly) if their philosophical *assumptions* are those stated.

For the purposes of this section, *general theories of knowledge* will be *classified* according to the philosophical *assumptions* of the *pre-metaphysical* solution to the problem of the *essence* of knowledge, into general theories of objective knowledge, general theories of subjective knowledge and general theories of dialectical knowledge.

2.3.5.1.1 General theories of objective knowledge.

Following Gabriel Gutiérrez Pantoja (1984: 147-232), methods are alternatives for linking thought and reality. In this study, what Pantoja calls method will be called theory. Mathematicism, mechanicism and organicism will not be treated as methods but as theories, as *general theories of objective knowledge*, as will be explained throughout the analysis of this section. Some forms of *relationship* between the *philosophical* and *theoretical* levels (the exploration, description, explanation and/or understanding or interpretation of reality, from some epistemological orientation), in an *objective way* are: *mathematicism* (methodology derived from mathematics), *mechanicism* (methodology as mechanical function) and *organicism* (methodology as organic development), among others.

The analysis, in a first moment, will be carried out considering the definition, characteristics, function, purpose, classification, authors and works of each *general theory of objective knowledge*; and, in a second moment, the philosophical *assumptions* from which each and every one of the five main *problems* of knowledge are solved will be taken into account: possibility, origin, essence, classification and concepts and criteria of truth of knowledge.

2.3.5.1.1.1 Mathematicism

Mathematicism is a *general theory of objective knowledge* that compares reality with a mathematical logical ideal. This reality can be factual (the phenomena or facts studied by both the natural and social sciences) or formal (the symbols of logic and mathematics).

For the purposes of this research, *mathematics* is understood as a *theory* because it explores, describes, explains, interprets, understands, etc., reality, in general; it is explored as a *general* theory of knowledge, because logic and mathematics allow us to describe, explain, interpret, understand, etc., all kinds of realities: both factual (natural sciences and social sciences) and formal (logic and mathematics, in themselves); finally, it is described as a *general theory* of objective knowledge, because in this theory all kinds of realities are described, all kinds of realities: both factual (natural sciences and social sciences) and formal (logic and mathematics, in themselves); finally, it is described as a general theory of *objective* knowledge, because in this theory the problem of the essence of knowledge is solved on the basis of a pre-metaphysical solution assuming, from reason, that the object of knowledge determines the cognising subject.

That reality, in general, is *compared* to an ideal, to an idea that has no existence of its own in reality, to an entity suggested by reason because reason wants to put order in the chaos of reality (for example: "2"); it means that the only possibility for human beings to generate new knowledge is to use some of the *intellectual operations* or *methodological procedures* (capacities with which they come equipped to survive in this world), such as addition, subtraction, multiplication, division, analysis, synthesis, induction, deduction, *comparison*, classification, definition, etc.

It is known, by common sense, that human beings began to count with their fingers and toes, in a pictographic way; but when these were no longer enough, they had to resort to the *symbol*; an invention of *reason*, to put order in reality, a "convention", which allowed them to "regulate" their commercial transactions.

Granted that in *logic* and *mathematics*, as in the factual sciences (natural and social), each and every one of the *intellectual operations* or *methodological procedures*, ("chips" with which human beings are equipped to survive on this planet) are used to generate new knowledge; depending on the subfield of knowledge: arithmetic (numbers), geometry (figures), etc. But, in the case of the name of the mathematical theory, the *comparison* applies very well, because in logic and mathematics, in order to generate new knowledge, reality, in general, must be compared with an *objective ideal*. It is a "must be", not a "to be". Two and two must be four; neither more nor less; because it is convenient. That is why it is a "convention".

The fact that in logic and mathematics reality is generally compared to a logical or mathematical *ideal* means that the object of study of these sciences is an abstract entity, a being created by reason to bring order to reality, which has nothing to do with reality itself. The entities of logic and mathematics

102

have no existence in reality, they only exist in the mind of their creator (the human being who invented the symbol), in a first moment; and, in a second moment, in the subjects who apprehend them for practical purposes. For example: in reality there is no equilateral triangle, such a symbol, if we call it properly, only exists in the mind of its creator (Euclid), in a first moment; and, in a second moment, in the subjects who internalise it for practical purposes.

In *logic* and *mathematics*, by comparing reality with ideas, with symbols that have no real existence in reality, the problem of the *possibility* of knowledge is solved on the basis of a *dogmatic* assumption.

In *logic* and *mathematics* there is a need to invent symbols, to agree in our daily interpersonal relations, which allow the construction of judgements so that reality does not move. Reality must always remain the same, fixed, without any change. A judgement such as "the whole is greater than the part" must be eternal, forever; it is a judgement made from *reason*, not from the senses. A judgement such as "2 + 2 = 4" must also be eternal, immutable.

In *logic* and *mathematics*, we need reality not to move, so that the "conventions" we work out, to agree on in our daily transactions, do not change. Such judgements must be universally valid and logically necessary. It is logically necessary and universally valid, for example, that three plus three is six, it must not be something else; because reality would change and there would be problems of understanding between human beings. It is logically necessary and universally valid, for example, that "every body is extensive", such a judgement, elaborated from reason, must be eternal and immutable, always the same everywhere and at all times; as if it had an existence of its own, independent of the subjects we use it for.

In *logic* and *mathematics* it is *assumed*, from *reason*, that there are true judgements and false judgements: "5 + 5 = 10", five plus five must not be eight, because it would be a false judgement.

The judgements of *logic* and *mathematics* are logically necessary and universally valid judgements because it is *reason* that is putting order into reality, for practical purposes. The problem about the *origin* of knowledge is solved from a *rational assumption*.

In *logic* and *mathematics*, the object to be known determines the cognising subject. Children learn to add, subtract, multiply and divide in order to have elements that will enable them to carry out their future transactions with other people. If you ask someone how much is two plus two, without thinking too much, he or she will answer: four. This means that the cognising subject (that someone) has been determined by the object to be known (the sum). It works like a "brainwashing". The problem about the *essence* of knowledge is solved, in a *pre-metaphysical* way, from an *objectivist assumption*.

In *logic* and *mathematics* it is *assumed*, or it is *assumed*, for practical needs, that the symbols invented by certain *rationalities* have their own existence, independent of both the subjects who constructed them and the cognising subjects.

In *logic* and *mathematics*, the problem of the *essence* of knowledge is solved *metaphysically*, on the basis of an *idealistic assumption*. It is *assumed* that reality exists independently of the subjects that could account for it.

In logic and mathematics, reality can be assumed to be single, dual or multiple.

From the *mathematical* theory, there are three different ways of thinking reality: the first according to *diversity* (it is considered by itself, it is the subjects, each of which refers only to itself; e.g. law, education, etc.; it is thought separately, and not in relation to other things; such is the determination of identity with itself or independence), the second according to *contraposition* (the one is determined as simply opposed to the other; such is the determination of identity with itself or independence).It is thought of separately, and not in relation to other things; this is the determination of identity with itself or independence), the second according to *contraposition* (the one is determined as simply opposed to the other, e.g. good, bad, just and unjust, pious and impious, stillness and movement, etc.), and the third according to *opposition* (the one is determined as simply opposed to the other, e.g. good, bad, just and unjust, pious and impious, stillness and movement, etc.).) and the third according to the *relation* (determination of the object by the position it occupies in relation to another, such as right or left, up or down, double or half, etc.; the one is only understood on the basis of the other, since one cannot represent the left without imagining the right) (Gutiérrez, 1999:163 - 164).

The difference between *relation* and *contraposition* lies in the fact that in *contraposition* the emergence of one thing presupposes the disappearance of the other, and vice versa. Thus, when movement disappears, stillness appears and, conversely, when movement arises, stillness ends. On the other hand, when it is a question of *relation,* both things arise and end at the same time: if something is suppressed on the right, it is also suppressed on the left; the double disappears when the half is destroyed.

In *logic* and *mathematics*, the problem of the essence of knowledge is solved theologically by assuming that reality can be single, dual or multiple.

The *logical* and *mathematical* type of knowledge is *rational*, because it is constructed from *reason*.

The *concepts* and *criteria* of *truth* in *logic* and *mathematics* are *immanent*. A *logical* or *mathematical* judgement is true when it conforms to the rules, to the laws of human understanding, even if it has nothing to do with concrete reality. The concept of truth, in logic and mathematics, reads as follows: "the agreement of thought with itself".

In *logic* and *mathematics* the cognising subject is confronted with *ideal*, mental, *idealistic* objects to be known. They are "conventions", "agreements", "inventions", ideas created by other rationalities, which have nothing to do with reality.

The following table shows the philosophical *assumptions* from which each and every one of the five main philosophical *problems* of knowledge are solved in the construction of the *general theory of* mathematical *objective knowledge:*

<table>
<tr><td rowspan="3">GENERAL THEORY OF</td><td colspan="8">PHILOSOPHICAL PROBLEMS OF KNOWLEDGE</td></tr>
<tr><td rowspan="2">OBJECTIVE KNOWLEDGE</td></tr>
<tr></tr>
<tr>
<td></td>
<td rowspan="2">POSSIBILITY OF THE CONOCTION</td>
<td rowspan="2">ORIGIN OF KNOWLEDGE</td>
<td colspan="3">ESSENCE OF KNOWLEDGE</td>
<td rowspan="2">TYPE OF KNOWLEDGE</td>
<td rowspan="2">CONCEPT AND CRITERION OF TRUTH OF KNOWLEDGE</td>
</tr>
<tr>
<td></td>
<td colspan="3">SOLUTIONS</td>
</tr>
<tr>
<td></td>
<td></td>
<td></td>
<td>PRE-METAPHYSICAL SOLUTION</td>
<td>METAPHYSICAL SOLUTION</td>
<td>THEOLOGICAL SOLUTION</td>
<td></td>
<td></td>
</tr>
<tr>
<td></td>
<td colspan="7">ASSUMPTIONS ON THE BASIS OF WHICH IT IS POSSIBLE TO SOLVE THE PROBLEMS OF THE KNOWLEDGE</td>
</tr>
<tr>
<td>MATE-MATI-GOSIC</td>
<td>DOGMATISM</td>
<td>RATIONALISM</td>
<td>OBJECTIVISM</td>
<td>IDEALISM</td>
<td>DUALISM</td>
<td>RATIONAL</td>
<td>IMMANENT</td>
</tr>
</table>

2.3.5.5.1.1.1.2 Mechanism.

Mechanism can be *defined*, from reason, as a general theory of objective knowledge in which reality, in general, is compared to a machine.

Mechanism is a *theory* because it explores, describes, explains, interprets, understands, etc., vital (natural science) and social phenomena, assuming that there are laws in nature and society that can be discovered through reflection.

Mechanism is a *general* theory because it explores, describes, explains, interprets, understands, etc., both natural and social reality.

Mechanism is a general theory of *objective* knowledge because it explores, describes, explains, interprets, understands, etc., reality (phatic and formal) from the *reason* of the subject who constructs the theory, assuming that the *object* determines the *subject.*

The fact that in *mechanicism* reality (both factual and formal) is *compared* to a machine means that, of all the capacities that the subject has to generate new knowledge (addition, subtraction, multiplication, division, analysis, synthesis, induction, deduction, *comparison*, classification, definition, etc.), *comparison* is being used, preferably, to bring order to reality.

That in the *mechanistic* general theory of objective knowledge, both natural and social, the reality to be explored, described, explained, interpreted, understood, etc., is compared to a machine, means that reason, which is the quality of the subject being used to explain reality, assumes, or wants to assume in order to order phenomena, that it must not move, that it must remain forever and ever fixed, eternally immobile (dogmatism).

A characteristic of the *mechanistic* view (theory) of reality is that it seeks to explore, describe, explain, interpret, understand, etc., phenomena, both vital and social or formal, by means of the laws of *mechanics*; that is, it is based on the *assumption* of the existence of movement and balance of forces, of general laws of movement and rest in space (*classical physics*). All motion can only be understood in relation to rest in space; that is to say, to understand that a body is in motion can only be done in relation to another body that is at rest, in relation to the space that contains them. To think in this way presupposes an *ontological determinism* of space, movement and rest of bodies.

This ontological *determinism* makes it possible to assume, on the basis of *reason*, that in reality, whether factual (natural and/or social) or formal, there is an established *order* (rationalism) (by God, reason or the history of peoples), which human *reason* discovers through reflection. It is assumed, or one wants to assume, because it suits certain interests, that in reality, in general, there is an *order*, pre-established rules of the game, laws of movement and rest in space; that they are eternal and immutable, given forever and ever (dogmatism).

Thus Nicolaus Copernicus, *comparing* the solar planetary system to a clock (machine), estimated that its component *parts* (the sun, the planets, the moons, etc.) are in eternal motion (dogmatism), perhaps driven by the hand of God; and that they will remain so, forever and ever, performing the same motion (the moons revolving around their planets).) are in *eternal* motion (dogmatism), perhaps driven by the hand of God; and that they will remain so, forever and ever, performing the same motion (the moons revolving around their planets, the planets revolving around the sun, the sun revolving around another larger body), in the same time; without ever changing their times, because a catastrophe would happen (rationalism). Mechanics means machine.

The science Copernicus was creating was nothing less than *mechanical physics*. In mechanical physics, the parts that make up the whole must be performing the same function, forever and ever, in the same way and at the same time, totally synchronised (dogmatism). It is now known that things do not happen that way, that the universe is the product of an explosion and that we do not know where we are going to end up (which is assumed in chaos theory).

In *classical physics*, the general laws of motion and rest in space are investigated. In this way, *philosophy* is initially understood as a unitary system, based on the accuracy of *mathematics*, from which the other sciences will derive their certainty and foundation. The whole is equal to the sum of its parts and the parts exist only for the whole. In this way it is possible to analyse and synthesise observable and predictable regularities (rationalism) and predictable regularities (dogmatism), because the whole and the parts do not modify each other, they only interact and complement each other.

John Kepler applies the mathematical theory to the mechanical process of planetary motion, assuming that the planetary motion around the sun maintains its rotation in a specific (immutable and eternal) time that is proportional to its size (dogmatism).

Galileo Galilei assumed that in order to *master* nature it is necessary to know the *laws* (dogmatism) from which all the *principles* of classical *mechanics* are derived. He believed that there was a general, eternal and immutable *order* in nature (dogmatism). Classical *mechanics* was thought to allow the *analysis* and *synthesis* (analytical-synthetic *method* to generate new knowledge) of *regularities* (physical laws) and even *predictable regularities*, since any *mechanism*, real (nature) or instituted (society), can be disintegrated and integrated again.

For mechanism the whole is indispensable (dogmatism), but that whole exists by the sum of its parts, and only the total integration of these parts can form it (dogmatism). The whole is equal to the sum of its parts, and the parts exist only for the whole (laws of nature). But whole and parts do not modify each other, they interact, they complement each other (dogmatism). For *mechanicism* to work, each part needs to be in the right place and to complement the others in order to continue to fulfil the same function. The impulse, or lack of it, will determine the movement or passivity of the mechanism, but that movement or passivity will be determined in relation to another object in the opposite condition.

The aim of *mechanicism* or *mechanism* is the discovery of laws that are simple and unalterable, which must explain a set of elements that are simple and unalterable.

For Issac Newton, all the *principles* of *classical mechanics* follow from three *laws*:

1. Every body continues in its state of rest or uniform rectilinear motion unless it is forced to change its state of motion by forces acting upon it.

2. The change in motion is proportional to the driving force acting and operates in the direction of the straight line in which it acts.

3. Every action is always opposed by an equal reaction (Gutiérrez, 1984: 169-170). The relationship between two phenomena that act, one (independent variable) on the other (dependent variable) is demonstrated by means of a hypothesis. The hypothesis, in logical terms, is the way of proving a deductive argument.

It can be argued that the *method* used by a *mechanist* to generate new knowledge is *deductive* and, consequently, a *mechanist* (theory) is also a *rationalist* (philosophy) because the main intellectual operation to generate new knowledge, from a *rationalist assumption*, is the *deductive method*. The deductive method is explained below, in section 2.6 (the methodological procedures or intellectual operations to generate new knowledge).

The mechanistic (deduction) methodology was extended to the social sciences, with physics and social mechanics emerging, in order to interpret the behaviour of the individual and society, respectively.

The 18th century saw the birth of *social physics* and *social mechanics*, whose aim was to interpret the behaviour of the individual in society (Gutiérrez, 1984:170). Auguste Comte, following in Galileo's footsteps, compared social reality to a machine and founded social physics or sociology.

Social physics (or sociology) is based on the assumption that the human being is a *physical* object, a kind of complex *machine* whose actions and psychic processes can be analysed on the basis of the laws (dogmas) of *mechanics*. His behaviour responds to the activity of his brain, which acts on the basis of stimuli generated by society. Thus, the individual is composed of integrated elements and his individuality is an element of society, of *social mechanics*.

In *social mechanics*, the functioning of society is conceived as an astronomical system consisting of the totality of individuals. They are closely interrelated and form part of a *social machinery*. Society is made up of the human atom, which is united with some atoms by mutual attraction and separated from others by repulsion, so that societies or states are systems of opposition in equilibrium (Gutiérrez: 171).

Thomas Hobbes assumed that the behaviour of individuals can be *deduced* (by means of hypotheses) by reason and verified by observation (and experimentation), for the human being can be conceived of as a *machine*, since he works like a machine.

Starting from the supposed *laws* of nature discovered by his predecessors, Hobbes (2003: 578) estimates a social *law*: "...*To the laws of nature presented in Chapter XV I am to add the following: That every man is bound by nature, so far as it depends on him, to protect in war the authority which protects him in time of peace...*".

In the *mechanistic general theory of objective knowledge* - applied to the exploration, description, explanation, interpretation, understanding, etc., of human behaviour in society - the *object* (the idea, the instituted, the institutions, etc., constructed by certain subjects, assuming, from reason, that reality does not move) determines the *subject*. It is *assumed*, or one wants to assume, from *reason*. Whose reason? Answer: a reason, of a person or of several persons at the same time. What is assumed or supposed? Answer: that the *object* determines the *subject*. What does it mean that the *object* determines the subject? Answer: in a relation of knowledge (epistemological level), something like the following: that the world of ideas exists independently of the material world. For example: to consider that beyond this material world, where education is imperfect, on a metaphysical plane, lies true education, good teaching, perfect instruction, etc., and that human beings can discover it through reflection.

On the *ontological* level, the interpretation of social reality, from the *general theory of mechanistic objective knowledge*, means, more or less, the following: It is *assumed*, or one wants to *assume* (from certain rationalities), because it suits certain interests, that the *subject* is due to the *object*; that what is important is the whole, not the part; that the parts are due to the whole; that the reason for the existence of the parts is the conservation, preservation and enhancement of the whole; that what must be preserved are the *institutions* (ideas) not the *subjects*.

Example: when the royalists apprehended the father of Vicente Guerrero, during the struggle for Mexican independence, the aforementioned approached the hero of Mexican independence, more or less along the following lines: "if you don't lay down your arms, we will shoot your father, for being a traitor". Guerrero answered them, in the same way, more or less along the following lines: "The homeland comes first". An *idea* (the fatherland) was more important than his father's life.

Something similar happened with the Japanese suicide pilots, during the Second World War, when they launched themselves with everything and their plane, in order not to miss the enemy target; they said, more or less, the following: "for my emperor"; they were not considered as subjects, only within the *institution* (object) did their lives make sense. The word *target* is ontologically and epistemologically derived from the word object of knowledge.

Another important phenomenon that could be analysed, *assuming*, from *reason*, that the *object* determines the *subject*, are the Islamic fundamentalists. They offer their lives to "God".

In the *mechanistic general theory of objective knowledge*, explorations, descriptions, explanations, interpretations, understandings, etc. about human behaviour in society are constructed by solving the *metaphysical* problem from reason, using *idealistic* philosophical *assumptions*. It is *assumed* that the studied reality (the *object* to be known) exists independently of whether there is a *cognising subject* who is interested in knowing it or not.

For example, if a person does not know the true *definition* of the word "education", it is *assumed*, from *reason*, that the cause of this is because he has not *discovered* it in the *objective* world of *ideas* (through the *reflection* of his *reason*); because the "true", "eternal" and "immutable" definition of "education" exists (in the world of ideas) independently of whether or not there is a cognising subject who fixes his reason on it in order to know its essence.

In the *mechanistic general theory of objective knowledge*, explorations, descriptions, explanations, interpretations, understandings, etc. about human behaviour in society are constructed by solving the *theological* problem *of the essence of knowledge from reason*, using *dualistic* philosophical *assumptions*. The reality under study (the *object* to be known) is *assumed to be* divided into two opposing and irreconcilable poles: the good and the bad, the right and the wrong, the valid and the invalid, the beautiful and the ugly, the decent and the indecent, the normal and the abnormal, the wise and the ignorant, God and the Devil, the civilised and the uncivilised, and so on.

The *epistemological* has a lot to do with the *ontological*. For example, in past centuries, Europeans expressed themselves about the other peoples of Africa, Asia and America more or less along the following lines: the Americans are uncivilised, let's go and civilise them! In the course of time, this assertion proved to be false. Europeans used it to justify to the international community their plundering of the wealth of these peoples.

Assuming that reality is divided into two opposing and irreconcilable poles is very convenient for justifying exclusions and atrocities that can be committed against others.

The type of knowledge that is constructed in the *general theory of mechanistic objective knowledge* is *rational*. It is assumed, on the basis of *reason*, that the only *true* knowledge is that which is born of the reflection of the human *soul*.

In the *mechanistic general theory of objective knowledge*, the problem of the classification of knowledge is solved by reason, using rational philosophical assumptions.

The concepts and criteria of truth of knowledge that are constructed in the general theory of mechanistic objective knowledge are immanent. It is assumed, from reason, that truth is the concordance of thought with itself, not with reality. The cognising subjects are confronted with ideal, mental objects of knowledge, entities created by certain rationalities, which have no existence, properly speaking, in material reality.

The following table shows the philosophical *assumptions* from which each and every one of the five main philosophical *problems* of knowledge are solved in the construction of the *mechanistic general theory of objective knowledge*:

GENERAL THEORY OF OBJECTIVE KNOWLEDGE	PHILOSOPHICAL PROBLEMS OF KNOWLEDGE						
	POSSIBILITY OF KNOWLEDGE	ORIGIN OF KNOWLEDGE	ESSENCE OF KNOWLEDGE — SOLUTIONS			TYPE OF KNOWLEDGE	CONCEPT AND CRITERION OF TRUTH OF KNOWLEDGE
			PRE-METAPHYSICAL SOLUTION	METAPHYSICAL SOLUTION	THEOLOGICAL SOLUTION		
	ASSUMPTIONS FROM WHICH TO SOLVE KNOWLEDGE PROBLEMS						
MECHANISM	DOGMATISM	RATIONALISM	OBJECTIVISM	IDEALISM	DUALISM	RATIONAL	IMMANENT

In the mechanistic general theory of objective knowledge each and every one of the five main philosophical problems of knowledge is solved by reason.

2.3.5.5.1.1.1.3 Organicism

Organicism can be rightly *defined* as a general theory of objective knowledge in which social reality is compared to a living organism. The social conglomerate is understood and interpreted as if it were a living organism. This analogy makes it possible to analyse a social body as if it had a constantly evolving process, in which one can speak of both natural selection and survival of the fittest.

In order to generate new knowledge in the *social sciences*, the methods of the *natural sciences* are applied. An example of the application of intellectual operations or methodological procedures to generate new knowledge in the spiritual sciences is Popper's methodological monism, which will be discussed in the corresponding subchapter.

Organicism is a *theory* because it explores, describes, explains, interprets, understands, etc., social reality.

Organicism is a *general* theory of society because it explores, describes, explains, interprets, understands, etc., any social reality.

The *organicist worldview*, or *organic model*, is based on the idea that every living thing has an evolution in its organism, and that all living things must be explained within this framework. It is also known as *evolutionism* or *Darwinism*, after Charles Robert Darwin, its creator.

While *mathematics* and *mechanism* develop in mathematics and physics, *evolutionism* develops in biology.

It should be borne in mind that the first science invented by man is mathematics, that mathematics made the birth of physics possible and, in turn, physics helps in the construction of biology.

In the social sciences, the conglomerate is understood as a living organism, as a social body with a constantly *evolving* process, in which both natural selection and survival of the fittest take place. There is a similarity between the general principles of *evolutionism* and social groups, such as the mutual dependence between the whole and its constituent parts; the difference with *mechanicism* is that the integrated parts are made up of multiple particularities which, interrelated, achieve the evolution of the whole.

In this way, the subject-object relationship, in the problem of the essence of knowledge, is posed in terms of an epistemological monism and pantheism; which differs from the statism provoked by the dualism of the *mathematical* and *mechanistic* worldviews.

Society is an organism, and as organic wholes grow, so society grows. All were born by evolution at some point, both living bodies and societies show in their development an increase in mass. Societies, like organisms, grow throughout their lives, until they divide or collapse. Every living organism, while increasing in size, increases in structure, as its parts multiply and differentiate; the same happens with societies as their populations increase, divisions and subdivisions increase their structure (Gutiérrez, 1984:170-174). Some proposals for understanding the individual and society from an *organicist* viewpoint, for example, are those of Charles Robert Darwin and Herbert Spencer.

Carlos Roberto Darwin (2002) understands and interprets the social conglomerate as a living organism, as a social body that has at its disposal a constantly evolving process, involving both natural selection and survival of the fittest.

Herbert Spencer exposed the similarity between the more general principles of Darwinian evolutionism and social groups: mutual dependence between the whole and its constituent parts. The whole is the organic unity of the given object which is composed of multiple particularities, which, interacting with each other, bring about its evolution. Every society is an *organism*, and as *organic* wholes grow, so does society grow. Everyone was born by evolution at some point, both living bodies and societies present in their development a minuscule but constant increase of their mass, which is another of the most general principles of *organicism*. In the case of *organisms*, many grow throughout their lives, and others only at certain moments of momentum; in the case of societies, they grow steadily until they split up or collapse.

Every living *organism* as it increases in size, increases in structure, as its parts multiply and differentiate, the same happens with societies as populations increase, divisions and subdivisions increase the structure.

As societies multiply, structures acquire greater complexity, which are necessary for their *organisation* (Gutiérrez, 1984: 173-174).

In living *organisms*, in addition to changes in their structure, there are also changes in their functions, because each structure has a direct correlation with the functions that it performs (Gutiérrez, 1984: 175).

Organicism is a general theory of *objective* knowledge because it explores, describes, explains, interprets, understands, etc., social reality from the *reason* of the subject who constructs the theory, assuming that the *object* determines the *subject.*

The fact that *organicism compares* social reality with a living organism means that, of all the capacities that the subject has to generate new knowledge (addition, subtraction, multiplication, division, analysis, synthesis, induction, deduction, *comparison*, classification, definition, etc.), *comparison* is being used, preferably, to bring order to reality.

The fact that in the general theory of objective, *organicist* knowledge, the social reality to be explored, described, explained, interpreted, understood, etc., is compared to a living organism, means that reason, which is the quality of the subject being used to explain reality, assumes, or wants to assume in order to order phenomena, that it must not move, that it must remain forever and ever fixed, eternally immobile (dogmatism).

A *characteristic* of the *organicist* view of society is that it seeks to explain social phenomena by means of the laws of *nature*. Social facts are understood and interpreted by analogy with a living organism, as if they were natural phenomena. It is assumed that a social body, like a living organism, has an evolutionary process in which both natural selection and survival of the fittest take place.

This ontological *determinism* makes it possible to assume, on the basis of *reason*, that there is an established *order* (rationalism) in social reality (by God, reason or the history of peoples), which human *reason* discovers through reflection. It is assumed, or one wants to assume, because it suits certain interests, that in social reality, in general, there is an *order*, pre-established rules of the game; that they are eternal and immutable, given forever and ever (dogmatism).

Organicism only *works* when each part is integrated in the right place and complements the others in order to continue to fulfil the same function (rationalism).

The *aim* of *organicism* is the discovery of laws that are simple and unalterable, which must explain a set of elements that are simple and unalterable (dogmatism).

In the *organicist general theory of objective knowledge* - applied to the exploration, description, explanation, interpretation, understanding, etc., of human behaviour in society - the *object* (the idea, the instituted, the institutions, etc., constructed by certain subjects, assuming, from reason, that reality does not move) determines the *subject*. It is *assumed*, or one wants to assume, from *reason*. Whose reason? Answer: a reason, of a person or of several persons at the same time. What is assumed or supposed? Answer: that the *object* determines the *subject*. What does it mean that the *object* determines the subject? Answer: in a relation of knowledge (epistemological level), something like the following: that the world of ideas exists independently of the material world. For example: to consider that beyond this material world, where education is imperfect, on a metaphysical plane, lies true education, good teaching, perfect instruction, etc., and that human beings can discover it through reflection (rationalism).

On the *ontological* level, the interpretation of social reality from the *general theory of objective organicist knowledge* means, more or less, the following: It is *assumed*, or one wants to *assume* (from certain rationalities), because it suits certain interests, that the *subject* is due to the *object*; that what is important is the whole, not the part; that the parts are due to the whole; that the reason for the existence of the parts is the conservation, preservation and enhancement of the whole; that what must be preserved are the *institutions* (ideas) not the *subjects.*

Example: Analyse the state education subsystem (of the State of Mexico) by comparing it, by analogy, to a living organism. In a school (institution) (let's say a primary school), pupils are "like living cells", which make up a tissue: that of the students. The teachers are "like living cells" that constitute another tissue: that of the teachers. The school secretary, vice-principal and principal, if any, are likewise "like living cells" that make up another tissue: that of the management. The people in charge of cleaning are "like living cells" that make up another fabric: that of the custodial staff. The watchmen are "like living cells" that are part of another fabric: the watch staff. The shorthand secretaries are "like living cells" that are part of another fabric: the administrative staff. The union of all these "tissues" constitute the school "organ" called: Escuela Primaria Estatal "Miguel Hidalgo y Costilla", Morning Shift, belonging to School Zone No. 2, of the Department of Primary Education, of the Subdirección de Educación Básica, of the Dirección General de Educación Básica y Normal, of the Subsecretaría de Educación de Educación Normal y Desarrollo Docente, of the Secretaría de Educación del Gobierno del Estado de México. The union of all primary education institutions are like "living organs" that make up the state educational "apparatus". The state educational apparatus is united with the federal educational "apparatus" and, together with the individual, they constitute the national educational "system".

"All for one and one for all". The same thing happens to cells that do not fulfil their function as they should: they are excluded, separated from the whole, exterminated. Cancer cells, for example, are eliminated. Pupils who do not "do what they are supposed to do" are failed.

As *subjects*, in themselves, they are not considered, only within the *institution* (object) did their lives make sense. The word *objective* is detached, in ontological and epistemological terms, from the word object of knowledge.

Another important phenomenon that could be analysed, *assuming* from *reason* that the *object* determines the *subject*, is the situation of workers in companies. In the *organicist general theory of objective knowledge*, explorations, descriptions, explanations, interpretations, understandings, etc. about human behaviour in society are constructed by solving the metaphysical problem of the essence of knowledge, using *idealistic* philosophical *assumptions*. It is *assumed* that the reality under study (the *object* to be known) exists independently of whether there is a *cognising subject* interested in knowing it or not.

For example, if a person does not know the "true" definition of the word "learning", it is *assumed*, from *reason*, that the cause of this is because he has not *discovered* it in the *objective* world of *ideas* (through the *reflection* of his *reason*); because the "true", "eternal" and "immutable" definition of "learning" exists (in the world of ideas) whether or not there is a cognising subject who fixes his reason on it in order to know its essence.

In the *organicist general theory of objective knowledge*, explorations, descriptions, explanations, interpretations, understandings, etc. about human behaviour in society are constructed by solving the theological problem of the essence of knowledge using *dualistic* philosophical ass*umptions*. The reality under study (the *object* to be known) is *assumed to be* divided into two opposing and irreconcilable poles: pass and fail pupils, good and bad teachers, punctual and unpunctual, etc.

The *epistemological* has a lot to do with the *ontological*. For example, if a teacher assumes that a pupil does not know, he will fail him. Failing a person indicates that this subject is a nullity, that he or she is good for nothing. The main consequence is the expulsion of the pupil in question from the education system.

Assuming that reality is divided into two opposing and irreconcilable poles is very convenient for justifying exclusions and atrocities that can be committed against others.

The *type* of knowledge that is constructed in the *general theory of objective organicist knowledge* is rational. It is assumed, on the basis of reason, that the only *true* knowledge is that which is born of the reflection of the human soul. The *concepts* and *criteria* of truth of knowledge that are constructed in the *general theory of objective organicist knowledge* are immanent. It is assumed, from reason, that truth is the concordance of thought with itself, not with reality. The cognising subjects are confronted with ideal, mental objects of knowledge, entities created by certain rationalities, which have no existence, properly speaking, in material reality.

The general objective organicist theory of knowledge can serve purposes such as the following: to make the members of a social group feel that it must function and evolve as if it were a living organism, regardless of the differences (economic, political, social, etc.) between its constituent parts.

The following table shows the philosophical *assumptions* from which each and every one of the five main philosophical *problems* of knowledge are solved in the construction of the *general theory of objective organicist knowledge*:

GENERAL THEORY OF OBJECTIVE KNOWLEDGE	PHILOSOPHICAL PROBLEMS OF KNOWLEDGE						
	POSSIBILITY OF KNOWLEDGE TO	ORIGIN OF KNOWLEDGE	ESSENCE OF KNOWLEDGE — SOLUTIONS			TYPE OF KNOWLEDGE	CONCEPT AND CRITERION OF TRUTH OF KNOWLEDGE
			PRE-METAPHYSICAL SOLUTION	METAPHYSICAL SOLUTION	THEOLOGICAL SOLUTION		
	ASSUMPTIONS FROM WHICH TO SOLVE KNOWLEDGE PROBLEMS						
ORGANISM	DOGMATISM	RATIONALISM	OBJECTIVISM	IDEALISM	DUALISM	RATIONAL	IMMANENT

2.3.5.1.1.2 General theories of subjective knowledge.

General theories of subjective knowledge are derived from *philosophical assumptions* that are sceptical, subjectivist, relativist and pragmatist (thus solving the problem of the possibility of knowledge); empiricist (thus solving the problem of the origin of knowledge); empiricist (thus solving the problem of the origin of knowledge); subjectivists, realists and dualists (thus solving the problem of the essence of knowledge as regards the pre-metaphysical, metaphysical and theological solutions, respectively); intuitionists (thus solving the problem of the classification of knowledge); and transcendentalists (thus solving the problem of the concepts and criteria of truth of knowledge). In general theories of subjective knowledge, each and every one of the five main philosophical problems of knowledge is resolved from the senses of the cognising subject.

Some *general theories of subjective knowledge* that solve each of the five major philosophical problems of knowledge from the above-mentioned assumptions are *chaos* and *conflict* theories.

Just as the *general theories of objective knowledge* (mathematicism, mechanicism and organicism) were worked on, the analysis of the *general theories of subjective knowledge* (chaos and conflict), in a first moment, will be carried out considering the definition, characteristics, function, purpose, classification, authors and works of each *general theory of subjective knowledge*; and, in a second moment, the philosophical *assumptions* from which each and every one of the five main philosophical *problems* of knowledge are solved will be taken into account: Possibility, Origin, Essence, Classification, and Concepts and Criteria of Truth of Knowledge.

It is necessary to recall, for the purposes of this analysis, that the *classification* and *names* assigned to each and every one of the *general theories of knowledge* discussed in this section;

They are due to the way in which one of the five main philosophical *problems* of knowledge is solved: the problem of the *essence* of knowledge. This philosophical problem of knowledge (the essence) was chosen and no other, because this difficulty of knowledge refers to the *relation* of knowledge that is established between the cognising *subject* and the *object* to be known.

It has already been made clear that, of the different philosophical *assumptions* from which the problem of the *essence* of knowledge can be solved and which can be found in three different *solutions* (pre-metaphysical, metaphysical and theological), we have chosen the *pre-metaphysical* solution, because this solution addresses the problem of the following question: *who determines whom in a relation of knowledge: the object to the subject, the subject to the object, or do the two determine each other?*

If *philosophy* determines *theory*, then *theory* depends on *philosophy*. If *we assume*, from reason, that, in a relation of knowledge, the object determines the subject, then we can speak of *objective* theories. On the contrary, if we assume, from the senses, that, in a relation of knowledge, the subject determines the object, then we can speak of *subjective* theories. Finally, if we assume, from both qualities of the cognising subject that, in a relation of knowledge, both elements of knowledge determine each other, then we can speak of *dialectical* theories.

So far we have analysed the general theories of objective knowledge (mathematicism, mechanicism and organicism). In this section we will analyse the second group of general theories of knowledge: the *general theories of subjective knowledge* (*chaos* and *conflict* theories). Subsequently, one of the general theories of dialectical knowledge will be analysed: the theory of complex thinking.

It has already been said that *objective* theories are constructed from reason (objectivist), *subjective* theories from the senses (subjectivist) and *dialectical* theories from both qualities of the cognising subject: from reason and from the senses; being able to start first from reason and then from the senses; or vice versa (dialectical).

2.3.5.5.1.2.2.1 Chaos.

Chaos is a *general theory of subjective knowledge* that explores, describes, explains, interprets, understands, etc., reality, phenomena, facts, things, etc. in terms of permanent *chaos* (relativism), of disturbances (movement) that have repercussions on the whole. Everything is relative (reality moves). Disorder (irregularities), irregularities, unpredictability (uncertainty), chaos are accepted.

Chaos is a *theory* because it explains, interprets, understands, etc., reality, phenomena, facts, things, etc.

Chaos is a *general theory of knowledge* because it explains, interprets, understands, etc., any reality, phenomenon, fact, thing, etc.; both natural and social.

Chaos is a *general theory of subjective knowledge* because it explains, interprets, understands, etc., any reality, phenomenon, event, thing, etc., both natural and social, in a *subjective* way. The explorations, descriptions, explanations, interpretations, comprehensions, etc., which, about reality, phenomena, events, things, etc., are carried out in *chaos* theory, are done by solving the great *problems* of knowledge (possibility, origin, essence, classification and concepts and criteria of truth) from the senses, based on sceptical, subjectivist, relativist, pragmatic, empirical, *subjectivist*, realist, monist, intuitive, transcendent philosophical *assumptions*, respectively.

Chaos theory, from the *senses*, allows us to analyse turbulence, disorganisation, relativism and the unexpected, i.e. randomness (relativism).

With *chaos theory*, from the senses, from *subjectivist* philosophical assumptions, it is possible to observe reality in constant movement. Nature is not linear (rational), as theories based on objectivist philosophical assumptions would have us believe; nothing is simple; randomness, unpredictability; movement and its fluctuations predominate over structures, organisations and permanence (mathematics, mechanicism and organicism). Dynamics is not linear, it gives access to less apparently ordered phenomena. Reality is said to oscillate between states of regularity and chaos, so the research questions are more or less along these lines: how can some kind of organisation emerge from *chaos*, how does it again emerge from order and escape the constraints (dogmas) it defines?

In rational science (based on objectivist philosophical assumptions of mathematical, mechanistic and organicist theories), the answers are subjected to the test of verification and continuous revision; the great myths of the societies of tradition give a total explanation, they affirm and say what is and what must be (objectivism). In empirical science - from *subjectivist* philosophical assumptions such as those used in *chaos* theory - no attempt is made to arrive at a totally definitive explanation of the world, the vision produced is partial and provisional; this science is confronted with an uncertain reality, with imprecise or moving boundaries; it studies the play of possibilities; it explores the complex, the unpredictable, the unprecedented; it is no longer obsessed with harmony; it gives a place to entropy and disorder, discovering its own (subjective) limitations.

There are systems in which tiny perturbations can be drastically amplified over time (Poncairé, 1980).

The myths of *origin* (engendered by the general theories of mathematical, mechanistic and organicist objective knowledge) express a primordial *order* out of *chaos*; the rites work for order and, in this way, tradition works cunningly with movement; that is, being must be transformed, modified, because of its imperfection (objectivism).

In the evolution of science, the history of the ways of dialoguing with nature, the passage from a world defined by harmony to a world in movement, free to an incessant turbulence (proclaimed by theories based on subjectivist philosophical assumptions) leads us to privilege *disorder* over *order*; that is, being must not be transformed, nor modified, towards an egoistic ideal that pretends to be universal, but interpreted and understood.

What can be affirmed about reality will always be relative, because the world is chaotic and we can hardly order it in and with our thinking (Balandier, 2003: 9-13).

In *chaos* theory, each and every one of the five main problems of knowledge is solved from the senses.

The philosophical assumptions from which each and every one of the five main philosophical problems of knowledge (possibility, origin, essence, classification and concept and criterion of truth of knowledge) are solved in *chaos* theory are the following:

In the *general theory of subjective knowledge of chaos*, it is *assumed*, from the senses, that *reality* is very complex and very difficult to understand, due to the permanent *chaos* (change) in which it is found. The problem of the *possibility* of knowledge is solved on the basis of sceptical, subjectivist, relativist and pragmatic philosophical *assumptions*.

What prevails in *reality* is disorder, irregularities, unpredictability. In the case of behavioural psychology, it was claimed that human behaviour depended on certain regularities and was explained by means of explanatory models. It is now known that human behaviour is *chaotic*, so that no explanatory model can be established, but that each case will depend on the understanding that can be had of the most fundamental aspects that are perceived; ruling out the possibility of predicting human behaviour.

The supposed "regularities" that some people have tried to "discover" in phenomena from reason (using dogmatic philosophical assumptions), in order to try to explain them, have led them to form an idea of the world that does not correspond to *reality*, but, on the contrary, to the conformation of an ideal world, and from this they think that this is the *real* world.

In the *general theory of subjective knowledge of chaos*, it is *assumed*, from the senses, that the origin of knowledge is to be found in sensations. It is believed that human beings (each one in particular) perceive reality differently from others. Each human being experiences the same sensations in a different way. A distinction is made between perception (which is universal) and representation (which is particular). The *problem* of the origin of knowledge is solved on the basis of *empirical* philosophical *assumptions*.

In the *general subjectivist chaos theory of knowledge*, it is *assumed*, from the *senses*, that (in a knowledge relation) the cognising *subject* determines the *object* to be known. It is presumed that if two cognising *subjects relate* to the same *object* of knowledge, both will apprehend their object to be known in a totally different way; because their life history, feelings, emotions, passions, complexes, ambitions, etc. "contaminate" the object of study. "contaminate" the object of study. Science is not neutral, it obeys philosophical assumptions and ontological interests. The pre-metaphysical problem about the essence of knowledge is solved from subjectivist philosophical assumptions.

For example: in the Chamber of Deputies of the Congress of the Union, the discourse of the supporters of the Institutional Revolutionary Party (PRI) - on the economic, political and social situation of Mexico - can be totally different from that of the supporters of the Party of the Democratic Revolution (PRD); because both factions solve each and every one of the five main philosophical problems of knowledge (possibility, origin, essence, classification and concepts and criteria of truth) from different *assumptions*. The former are *objectivists*; the latter are *subjectivists*. The former, from *reason*; the latter, from the *senses*. The former want reality to move (scepticism, subjectivism, relativism, pragmatism); the latter want it to remain static (dogmatism). The former are located in what ought to be; the latter in what is.

In the *general subjectivist chaos theory of knowledge*, it is *assumed*, based on the *senses*, that *reality* exists independently of whether or not it is apprehended by the cognising subjects. It is believed that the impressions of the objects that surround us impact our senses and produce sensations that different subjects perceive, but represent them differently. The metaphysical problem about the *essence* of knowledge is solved on the basis of *realist* philosophical *assumptions*.

In the *general subjectivist chaos theory of knowledge*, it is *assumed*, from the *senses*, that reality is divided into two opposing and contradictory poles: order - disorder, regularities - irregularities, certainty - uncertainty, and so on. The theological problem of the *essence* of knowledge is solved on the basis of *dualistic* philosophical *assumptions*.

In the *general subjectivist chaos theory of knowledge*, it is *assumed*, from the *senses*, that the only *kind* of knowledge that a cognising subject can obtain of an object to be known is *intuitive*. Everything we know about reality is considered to have been obtained by means of the senses. The problem of the *classification* of knowledge is solved on the basis of *intuitive* philosophical assumptions.

In the *general theory of subjective knowledge of chaos*, it is *assumed*, from the *senses*, that the *concepts* and *criteria* of truth of knowledge are *transcendent*. Truth is considered to be the concordance of thought with the object thought. Because it is assumed that the cognising subject is confronted with objects that have their own existence in *reality*. The problem of *concepts* and *criteria* of truth is solved on the basis of *transcendent* philosophical *assumptions*.

The following table shows the philosophical *assumptions* from which each and every one of the five main philosophical *problems* of knowledge are solved in the construction of the *general theory of subjective knowledge of chaos*:

GENERAL THEORY OF SUBJECTIVE KNOWLEDGE	PHILOSOPHICAL PROBLEMS OF KNOWLEDGE						
	POSSIBILITY OF KNOWLEDGE	ORIGIN OF KNOWLEDGE	ESSENCE OF KNOWLEDGE **SOLUTIONS**			TYPE OF KNOWLEDGE	CONCEPT AND CRITERION OF TRUTH OF KNOWLEDGE
			SOLUCION PRE GOAL PHYSICS	SOLUTION GOAL PHYSICS	SOLUTION TEO LOGICA		
	ASSUMPTIONS FROM WHICH THE PROBLEMS OF KNOWLEDGE CAN BE SOLVED.						
CHAOS	SCEPTICISM, SUBJECTIVISM AND PRAGMATISM	EMPIRISM	SUBJECTIVISM	REALISM	DUALISM	INTUITIVE	TRASCENDENT

3.2.5.1.2.2.2 Conflict.

Conflict is a *general theory of subjective knowledge* that explores, describes, explains, interprets, understands, etc., reality, phenomena, facts, things, etc. in terms of combat, struggle, conflict.

Conflict is a *theory* because it explains, interprets, understands, etc. reality, phenomena, facts, things, etc.

Conflict is a *general theory of knowledge* because it explains, interprets, understands, etc., any reality, phenomenon, fact, thing, etc.; both natural and social.

Conflict is a *general theory of subjective knowledge* because it explains, interprets, understands, etc., any reality, phenomenon, event, thing, etc., both natural and social, in a *subjective* way. The explorations, descriptions, explanations, interpretations, comprehensions, etc., which, about reality, phenomena, events, things, etc., are carried out in the theory of *conflict*, are done by solving the great *problems* of knowledge (possibility, origin, essence, classification and concepts and criteria of truth) through the senses, from sceptical, subjectivist, relativist, pragmatic, empirical, *subjectivist*, realist, monist, intuitive, transcendent philosophical *assumptions*, respectively.

In the *general theory of subjective knowledge of conflict,* it is assumed, from the *senses,* that reality moves. Phenomena are problematised in terms of combat, struggle, antagonism, pugnacity, opposition, anguish, predicament, etc. In other words, privileging the *subjective, reality* and the *dualism* of subject and object (seeing reality in terms of opposing opposites). It is possible to analyse three approaches in the evolution of the theory:

In the traditional (objective) approach, from the point of view of *reason*, all *conflict* is thought to be bad, as synonymous with violence, destruction, and irrationality and that, for this reason, it must be avoided, because it negatively affects individuals, groups and organisations. In order to solve or prevent it, it is only necessary to attack its causes, which, according to this approach, are poor communication, lack of frankness and trust, etc. The pre-metaphysical problem about the *essence* of knowledge is solved on the basis of *objectivist* philosophical *assumptions*.

In the (subjective) human relations approach, it is *assumed*, from the *senses*, that the presence of *conflicts* in human relations is a natural process and that it is therefore inevitable and should be accepted as such. It is also said that it is not always bad or negative and that it can be beneficial for the performance of individuals and groups.

The interactive (dialogic) approach accepts conflict as something natural, to be encouraged, because a harmonious, peaceful, calm and cooperative group tends to be static, apathetic and unresponsive to the needs of change and innovation. It is said that conflict should be encouraged to a manageable degree that encourages creativity, reflection, more efficient decision making, teamwork, a willingness to change and the setting of ambitious and achievable goals; contributing to a sense of achievement.

The principles of conflict theory are: that it is neither positive nor negative, it can simply be generated; that it is part of life; that it affects us all; and finally, that understanding and analysing it helps to resolve it effectively and productively.

A key element in understanding why things happen is to know why people make decisions the way they do. To do this we need to know the protagonists of the conflict, their culture, the prevailing paradigms, the causes that led to the conflict, the underlying communication problems, emotions, perceptions of the parties, values and principles, ways of reacting, the influence of external factors and, above all, the positions, interests and needs of the protagonists.

The philosophical *assumptions* from which each and every one of the five main philosophical *problems* of knowledge (possibility, origin, essence, classification and concept and criterion of truth of knowledge) are solved in the general subjectivist *conflict* theory of knowledge are the following:

In the *general theory of subjective knowledge of conflict*, it is *assumed*, from the senses, that *reality* is very complex and very difficult to understand, due to the permanent *conflict* (struggle, debate, fight) in which the elements that make it up are found. The problem of the *possibility* of knowledge is solved on the basis of sceptical, subjectivist, relativist and pragmatic philosophical *assumptions*.

In the *general theory of subjective conflict knowledge*, it is *assumed*, from the senses, that the origin of knowledge is to be found in sensations. It is believed that human beings (each one in particular) perceive reality differently from others. Each human being experiences the same sensations in a different way. A distinction is made between perception (which is universal) and representation (which is particular). The *problem* of the origin of knowledge is solved on the basis of *empirical* philosophical *assumptions*.

In the *general subjectivist chaos theory of knowledge*, it is *assumed*, from the *senses*, that (in a relation of knowledge) the cognising *subject* determines the *object* to be known. It is presumed that if two cognising *subjects relate* to the same *object* of knowledge, both will apprehend their object to be known in a totally different way; because their life history, feelings, emotions, passions, complexes, ambitions, etc. "contaminate" the object of study. "contaminate" the object of study. Science is not neutral, it obeys philosophical assumptions and ontological interests. The pre-metaphysical problem about the essence of knowledge is solved from subjectivist philosophical assumptions.

In the four possibilities of realisation of the human spirit (philosophy, science, art and religion) there is a constant struggle between the various *scientific communities* or *traditions of research* (empirical-analytical; phenomenological, hermeneutic and linguistic; and dialectical or critical-hermeneutic) for the prevalence, over the others, of their respective explorations, descriptions, explanations, interpretations, understandings of reality, of things, of phenomena, etc.These are elaborated on the basis of different philosophical assumptions and are therefore contradictory and irreconcilable with each other.

In the *general subjectivist conflict theory of knowledge*, it is *assumed*, based on the *senses*, that *reality* exists independently of whether or not it is apprehended by the cognising subjects. It is believed that the impressions of the objects that surround us impact our senses and produce sensations that different subjects perceive, but represent them differently. The metaphysical problem about the *essence* of knowledge is solved on the basis of *realist* philosophical *assumptions*.

In the *general subjectivist conflict theory of knowledge*, it is *assumed*, from the *senses*, that reality is divided into two opposing and mutually contradictory poles: order - disorder, regularities - irregularities, certainty - uncertainty, etc. The theological problem of the *essence* of knowledge is resolved on the basis of *dualistic* philosophical *assumptions*.

In the *general subjectivist conflict theory of knowledge*, it is *assumed*, from the *senses*, that the only *kind* of knowledge that a cognising subject can obtain of an object to be known is *intuitive*. Everything we know about reality is considered to have been obtained by means of the senses. The problem of the *classification* of knowledge is solved on the basis of *intuitive* philosophical assumptions.

In the *general theory of subjective conflict knowledge*, it is *assumed*, from the *senses*, that the *concepts* and *criteria* of truth of knowledge are *transcendent*. Truth is considered to be the concordance of thought with the object thought. Because it is assumed that the cognising subject is confronted with objects that have their own existence in *reality*. The problem of *concepts* and *criteria* of truth is solved on the basis of *transcendent* philosophical *assumptions*.

The following table shows the philosophical *assumptions* from which each and every one of the five main philosophical *problems* of knowledge are solved on the basis of the senses in the construction of the *general theory of subjective knowledge of conflict*:

GENERAL THEORY OF SUBJECTIVE KNOWLEDGE	PHILOSOPHICAL PROBLEMS OF KNOWLEDGE						
	POSSIBILITY OF KNOWLEDGE	ORIGIN OF KNOWLEDGE	ESSENCE OF KNOWLEDGE			TYPE OF KNOWLEDGE	CONCEPT AND CRITERION OF TRUTH OF KNOWLEDGE
			SOLUTIONS				
			PRE-METAPHYSICAL SOLUTION	METAPHYSICAL SOLUTION	THEOLOGICAL SOLUTION		
	ASSUMPTIONS FROM WHICH TO SOLVE KNOWLEDGE PROBLEMS						
CONFLICT	SCEPTICISM, SUBJECTIVISM AND PRAGMATISM	EMPIRISM	SUBJECTIVISM	REALISM	DUALISM	INTUITIVE	TRASCENDENT

2.3.5.1.3 The general theories of dialectical knowledge.

General theories of dialectical knowledge are derived from *critical philosophical assumptions* (thus solving the problem about the possibility of knowledge); *intellectualist* and *apriorist* (thus solving the problem about the origin of knowledge); *dialectical, phenomenological* and *monistic* (thus solving the problem about the essence of knowledge, with respect to the pre-metaphysical, metaphysical and theological solutions, respectively); *mixed* - knowledge is both rational and intuitive - (thus solving the problem about the classification of knowledge); and *mixed* - concepts and criteria of truth must be both transcendent and immanent - (thus solving the problem about concepts and criteria of truth of knowledge).

In the general theories of dialectical knowledge, each and every one of the five main philosophical problems of knowledge is solved from both qualities of the cognising subject: reason and the senses.

Two of the *general theories of dialectical knowledge* that solve each and every one of the five great philosophical problems of knowledge from the aforementioned assumptions are the analogical and complexity theories.

Just as the *general theories of subjective knowledge* (chaos and conflict) were worked on, the analysis of the *general theories of dialectical knowledge* (analogy and complexity), in a first moment, will be carried out considering the definition, characteristics, function, purpose, classification, authors and works of each *general theory of dialectical knowledge*; and, in a second moment, the philosophical *assumptions* from which each and every one of the five main philosophical *problems* of knowledge are solved will be taken into account: Possibility, Origin, Essence, Classification and Concepts and Criteria of Truth of Knowledge.

It is necessary to remember, for the purposes of this analysis, that the *classification* and the *names* assigned to each and every one of the *general theories of knowledge* analysed in this section, obey the way in which one of the five main philosophical *problems* of knowledge is solved: the problem of the *essence* of knowledge. This philosophical problem of knowledge (the essence) was chosen and no other, because this difficulty of knowledge refers to the *relation* of knowledge that is established between the cognising *subject* and the *object* to be known.

It has already been made clear that, of the different philosophical *assumptions* from which the problem of the *essence* of knowledge can be solved and which can be found in three different *solutions* (pre-metaphysical, metaphysical and theological), we have chosen the *pre-metaphysical* solution, because this solution addresses the problem of the following question: *who determines whom in a relation of knowledge: the object to the subject, the subject to the object, or do the two determine each other?*

If *philosophy* determines *theory*, then *theory* depends on *philosophy*. If *we assume* that, in a relation of knowledge, the object determines the subject, then we can speak of *objective* theories. On the contrary, if we assume that, in a relation of knowledge, the subject determines the object, then we can speak of *subjective* theories. Finally, in the following cases, if we assume that, in a relation of knowledge, both elements of knowledge determine each other, then we can speak of *dialectical* theories.

So far we have analysed the general theories of objective knowledge (mathematics, mechanicism and organicism) and subjective knowledge (chaos and conflict). In this section we will analyse the third group of general theories of knowledge: the *general theories of dialectical knowledge* (analogy and complexity).

It has already been said that *objective* theories are constructed from reason (objectivist), *subjective* theories from the senses (subjectivist) and *dialectical* theories from both qualities of the cognising subject: from reason and from the senses; being able to start first from reason and then from the senses (apriorism); or vice versa (intellectualism).

One of the *general theories of knowledge,* which starts from *critical* philosophical assumptions (possibility of knowing); *intellectualist* and/or *apriorist* (origin of knowledge); *dialectical*, and *monistic* and pantheistic (pre-metaphysical, metaphysical and theological solutions, respectively, to the problem of the essence of knowledge); *intuitive-rational* (type of knowledge); and *transcendent-immanent* (criteria of truth), is Mauricio Beachot's *analogical theory* (Robles, 2000: 11-18).

2.3.5.1.3.1 Analogy.

Analogy is a *general theory of dialectical knowledge* that explores, describes, explains, interprets, understands, etc., reality, phenomena, facts, things, etc. in analogical terms.

Analogy is a *theory* because it explains, interprets, understands, etc., the reality, phenomena, facts, thing, etc.

Analogy is a *general theory of knowledge* because it explains, interprets, understands, etc., any reality, phenomenon, fact, thing, etc.; both natural and social.

Analogy is a *general theory of dialectical knowledge* because it explains, interprets, understands, etc., any reality, phenomenon, fact, thing, etc., both natural and social, in a dialectical way.

The explorations, descriptions, explanations, interpretations, comprehensions, etc., which, about reality, phenomena, events, things, etc., are made in the *analogical* theory, are made solving the great *problems* of knowledge (possibility, origin, essence, classification and concepts and criteria of truth) from both qualities of the cognising subject: reason and the senses (but first the senses work and then reason), from critical philosophical *assumptions*; intellectualist and/or apriorist; dialectic, phenomenalist, and monist; mixed <intuitive - rational>; and mixed <transcendent - immanent>; respectively.

In the *general analogical dialectical theory of knowledge*, it is *assumed*, from the senses and reason (Aristotelian intellectualism), that knowledge is possible (dogmatism), but not in essence (scepticism), because each cognising subject feels and thinks differently from others (subjectivism), because truth changes in time, space and circumstances (relativism), and because any discourse that is developed about a certain object of knowledge must be useful to humanity (pragmatism). The problem of the *possibility* of knowledge is solved on the basis of critical philosophical *assumptions*.

Paraphrasing Beauchot (Gutiérrez, 2000: 11-13), analogical hermeneutics, the interpretation of reality by resemblance, understanding by resemblance, similarity, affinity, tries to reconcile, mediate, balance between univocism (dogmatism) and equivocism (scepticism, subjectivism, relativism, preagmatism), in a proportional way, but predominating the second (univocism) over the first (equivocism). By univocism we mean the scientism and positivism of postmodernity. Scientism and positivism solve the problem of the possibility of knowledge on the basis of dogmatic assumptions. By equivocism we mean postmodern thinking (subjective predominates over objective). Postmodernists (equivocists) solve the problem of the possibility of knowledge on the basis of sceptical, subjectivist, relativist and pragmatic philosophical assumptions. Beauchot proposes a mediation between dogmatism and scepticism: solving the problem of the possibility of knowledge critically. It is something like the application of the Aristotelian middle ground.

In the *general analogue dialectical theory of knowledge*, it is *assumed*, from the senses and reason (first the senses and then reason), that the origin of knowledge is to be found both in the senses and in the reason of the cognising subject. The *problem* of the origin of knowledge is solved on the basis of intellectualist philosophical *assumptions* (first we think and then we feel).

According to Beauchot (Gutiérrez, 2000: 13), "...*one can only understand if we believe in something, and only if we understand something, we can believe more...*". Belief is related to dogmatism and understanding to scepticism (including subjectivism, relativism and pragmatism); together they give us intellectualist criticism: the origin of knowledge is located in both reason and experience, only that we think first and then we feel (intellectualism).

In the *general theory of dialectical knowledge of analogical hermeneutics*, it is *assumed*, from the *senses and from reason*, that in a relation of knowledge, the cognising *subject* determines the *object* to be known and, in turn, the object to be known determines the cognising subject. This dialectical relation between the cognising subject and the object to be known determines that the pre-metaphysical problem of the essence of knowledge is resolved on the basis of dialectical philosophical assumptions.

To paraphrase Beauchot (Gutiérrez, 2000: 13), reality is perceived (subjectivism) and understood (objectivism). First we perceive reality and then we understand it.

In the *general analogue dialectical theory of knowledge*, it is *assumed*, from the *senses and from reason*, that *reality* exists (realism), but that the subjects apprehend it in a different way (subjective idealism), as it is presented to the limitations of our senses and our reason; that is, the object to be known is presented to the different cognising subjects, as a phenomenon, as an appearance. It is believed that the impressions of the objects that surround us impact our senses and produce sensations that different subjects perceive, but that they represent them differently and, moreover, as phantoms, as phenomena, in time and space. The *metaphysical problem* about the *essence* of knowledge is solved on the basis of *phenomenalist* philosophical *assumptions*.

Paraphrasing Beauchot (Gutiérrez, 2000: 16), in the understanding of phenomena, the cognising subject must avoid extreme realism (equivocalism) and extreme idealism (univocism); phenomenalism must be fought for.

In the *general analogical dialogical theory of knowledge*, it is *assumed*, from the *senses* and from *reason*, that reality is unique. The problem of the *essence* of knowledge is solved on the basis of *monistic* philosophical *assumptions* by means of a *theological* solution.

If reality is unique, there is no such separation between the cognising subject and the object to be known; neither are explanation (objectivist) and understanding (subjectivist) separated"... *analogue hermeneutics tries to merge explanation with understanding, but by considering things and activities as texts it finds the need to explain contextually and not only causally*" (Alcalá, 2000: 20).

In the *general analogical dialectical theory of knowledge*, it is *assumed*, from the *senses* and from *reason*, that the *type* of knowledge that a cognising subject can obtain of an object to be known is *mixed* (intuitive-rational). It is considered that everything we know about reality was obtained by means of the senses (first) and reason (later). The problem of the *classification* of knowledge is solved on the basis of *mixed* (intuitive-rational) philosophical assumptions.

Paraphrasing Beauchot (2000: 01), *analogy* tries to find what is attainable of similarity (rational) in things without forgetting that the different predominates (intuitive), diversity (intuitive), respecting the difference (intuitive) without renouncing the similarity (rational) that allows to achieve some universalisation (rational).

In the *general analogue dialectical theory of knowledge*, it is *assumed*, from the *senses* and from *reason*, that the *concepts* and *criteria* of truth of knowledge are *mixed* (transcendent and immanent). The truth of knowledge is considered to be the concordance of thought with the object thought and of thought with itself. For it is assumed that the cognising subject is confronted both with objects that have their own existence in *reality* and with ideal objects, which exist only in the mind of the cognising subject. The problem of *concepts* and *criteria* of truth is solved on the basis of mixed philosophical *assumptions* (transcendent and immanent).

The following table shows the philosophical *assumptions* from which each and every one of the five main philosophical *problems* of knowledge are solved, from the senses and reason, in the construction of the *general theory of dialectical knowledge of analogy*:

GENERAL THEORY OF DIALECTICAL KNOWLEDGE	PHILOSOPHICAL PROBLEMS OF KNOWLEDGE						
	POSSIBILITY OF KNOWLEDGE	ORIGIN OF KNOWLEDGE	ESSENCE OF KNOWLEDGE			TYPE OF KNOWLEDGE	CONCEPT AND CRITERION OF TRUTH OF KNOWLEDGE
			SOLUTIONS				
			PRE-METAPHYSICAL SOLUTION	METAPHYSICAL SOLUTION	THEOLOGICAL SOLUTION		
	ASSUMPTIONS FROM WHICH THE PROBLEMS OF KNOWLEDGE CAN BE SOLVED.						
ANALOGY	CRITICISM	INTELLECTUALISM	DIALECTICS	PHENOMENALISM	MONISM	MIXED: (INTUITIVE-RATIONAL)	MIXED: (TRANSCENDENT-IMMANENT)

2.3.5.1.3.2 Complexity.

Another of the *general theories of knowledge,* which starts from *critical* philosophical assumptions (possibility of knowing); *intellectualist* and/or *apriorist* (origin of knowledge); *dialectical, phenomenalist* and *monistic* and pantheistic (pre-metaphysical, metaphysical and theological solutions, respectively, to the problem of the essence of knowledge); *intuitive-rational* (type of knowledge); and *transcendent-immanent* (criteria of truth), is Edgar Morin's (2001) *theory of complexity.*

Complex thinking is a *general theory of dialectical knowledge* that explores, describes, explains, interprets, understands, etc., reality, phenomena, facts, things, etc. in dialectical terms.

Complex thinking is a *theory* because it explains, interprets, understands, etc., reality, phenomena, facts, thing, etc.

Complex thinking is a *general theory of knowledge* because it explains, interprets, understands, etc., any reality, phenomenon, fact, thing, etc.; both natural and social.

Complex thinking is a *general theory of dialectical knowledge* because it explains, interprets, understands, etc., any reality, phenomenon, fact, thing, etc., both natural and social, in a dialectical way.

The explorations, descriptions, explanations, interpretations, comprehensions, etc., about reality, phenomena, events, things, etc., are made in the theory of *complexity,* are made solving the great *problems* of knowledge (possibility, origin, essence, classification and concepts and criteria of truth) from critical philosophical *assumptions*; intellectualist and/or apriorist; dialectic, phenomenalist, and monist; mixed <intuitive - rational>; and mixed <transcendent - immanent>; respectively.

In complexity each and every one of the five main philosophical problems of knowledge are solved from both qualities of the cognising subject: reason and the senses (only that, unlike analogy, reason works first and then the senses). In the *general theory of complex dialectical knowledge*, it is *assumed*, from reason and the senses (Kantian apriorism), that knowledge is possible (dogmatism), but not in essence (scepticism), because each cognising subject feels and thinks differently from others (subjectivism), because truth changes in time, space and circumstances (relativism), and because any discourse that is developed about a certain object of knowledge must be useful to humanity (pragmatism). The problem of the *possibility* of knowledge is solved on the basis of critical philosophical *assumptions*.

According to the *theory of complex thought*, the cognising subject, faced with the movements, changes and instability of reality, must try to bring order (dogmatism) and clarity to reality (rationalism) in order to discover the laws that govern it. Complexity means disturbance, confusion and inability of the human soul to apprehend the object of knowledge simply and clearly.

In the *complex dialectical general theory of knowledge*, it is *assumed*, from reason and the senses (first reason and then the senses), that the origin of knowledge is to be found both in reason and in the senses of the cognising subject. The *problem* of the origin of knowledge is solved on the basis of apriorist philosophical *assumptions* (first we think and then we feel).

While the theories that solve the problem of the origin of knowledge from rationalist philosophical assumptions (mathematics, mechanicism and organicism) and empiricism (chaos and conflict) claim that the *mission of science is* to eliminate the complexity of phenomena and discover the order to which they obey (explanation) or their interpretation (understanding), respectively; the *theory of complexity*, based on dialectical philosophical assumptions, seeks to explain and understand them at the same time.

In the *complex dialectical general theory of knowledge*, it is *assumed*, from reason and the senses, that in a relation of knowledge, the cognising *subject* determines the *object* to be known and, in turn, the object to be known determines the cognising subject. This dialectical relationship between the cognising subject and the object to be known determines that the pre-metaphysical problem about the essence of knowledge is solved from reason and the senses, on the basis of dialectical philosophical assumptions.

The question to be asked is, according to the above, how to approach complexity in a non-simplifying way, how to apprehend phenomena in a way that is neither objective nor subjective, but dialectical?

The term *complexity*, as Morín (2001) puts it, implies confusion, uncertainty, disorder, etc. The definition of complexity cannot be reduced to a single word, referred to a single law or reduced to a simple idea. Complexity cannot be summarised in the term complexity, reduced to a law of complexity, reduced to the idea of complexity. Complexity cannot be defined in a simple way to take the place of simplicity; because it is a problem word and not a solution word. The complexity of the term "complexity" is the reason why a true knowledge of what it means will never be achieved, because through the dialectic of subject and object only approximations to the concept can be achieved in time and space. There will never be a definitive concept of the term "complexity". Nevertheless, there remains the hope that if we do not have a "true" knowledge, at least, each approximation to the concept, in time and space, will provide us with the best explanation of the moment.

In the *general theory of complex dialectical knowledge*, it is *assumed*, from reason and the senses, that *reality* exists (realism), but that subjects apprehend it in a different way (subjective idealism), as it is presented to the limitations of our senses and our reason; that is, the object to be known is presented to the different cognising subjects, as a phenomenon, as an appearance. It is believed that the impressions of the objects that surround us impact our senses and produce sensations that different subjects perceive, but that they represent them differently and, moreover, as phantasms, as phenomena, in time and space. The *metaphysical problem* about the *essence* of knowledge is solved on the basis of *phenomenalist* philosophical *assumptions*.

Instead of trying to explain reality, to control and dominate it (in accordance with the simple thinking of theories based on idealistic philosophical assumptions) in order to solve the metaphysical problem of the essence of knowledge, or to understand the particular phenomena (as it is thought from the theories that start from realist philosophical assumptions), the cognising subject must reconcile, negotiate with the reality to be known (as it is proposed by the *theory of complexity*, when solving the metaphysical problem about the essence of knowledge, from phenomenological philosophical assumptions).

In the *complex dialectical general theory of knowledge*, it is *assumed*, on the basis of reason and the senses, that reality is unique. The theological problem of the *essence* of knowledge is solved on the basis of *monistic* philosophical *assumptions*.

The *simplifying* thinking of theories based on dualistic philosophical assumptions (mathematics, mechanicism, organicism, chaos and conflict) distances the cognising subject from *complex* thinking, because reality is divided into two opposing and irreconcilable poles: the cognising subject and the object to be known. In contrast, complex thinking allows for the reconciliation of subject-object seen as a unity, as a complex whole.

In the *general theory of complex dialectical knowledge*, it is *assumed*, from reason and the senses, that the *type* of knowledge that a cognising subject can obtain of an object to be known is *mixed* (rational-intuitive). It is considered that everything we know about reality, we obtained by means of reason (first) and the senses (later). The problem of the *classification* of knowledge is solved on the basis of *mixed* philosophical assumptions (rational-intuitive).

Complexity arises where the *simplifying* thinking of theories based on objectivist (mathematics, mechanicism and organicism) and subjectivist (chaos and conflict) philosophical assumptions fail to explore, describe, explain, understand, analyse, etc., reality. Complexity theory integrates everything that brings order, clarity, distinction, precision, etc. to the knowledge of phenomena.

In the *general theory of complex dialectical knowledge*, it is *assumed*, from reason and the senses, that the *concepts* and *criteria* of truth of knowledge are *mixed* (immanent/transcendent). The truth of knowledge is considered to be the concordance of thought with the object thought and of thought with itself. For it is assumed that the cognising subject is confronted both with objects that have their own existence in *reality* and with ideal objects, which exist only in the mind of the cognising subject. The problem of *concepts* and *criteria* of truth is solved on the basis of mixed philosophical *assumptions* (immanent-transcendent).

General theories of knowledge that assume that knowledge is rational (mathematics, mechanicism, organicism) or intuitive (chaos and conflict), because they solve the problem about the classification of science from reason (general theories of objective knowledge) or from the senses (general theories of subjective knowledge), only; they construct a simplifying knowledge; because they solve the mentioned problem from rational or intuitive philosophical assumptions, only; disintegrating the complexity of the real, which can be apprehended by assuming, from reason and senses (at the same time), from *mixed* philosophical assumptions (rational-intuitive).

Complex thinking tries to account for the articulations between the various disciplinary fields of science that simplifying thinking has broken down. Simplistic thinking isolates, separates, etc., the subject from the object, and thus hides everything that connects, interacts or interferes. Complex thinking constructs

n multidimensional and multi-referential knowledge, understanding, at the same time, that total knowledge of the complex is impossible for the cognising subject.

Complex thinking starts from the principle of incompleteness and uncertainty in knowledge. Totalisations are not true, they do not exist, they are impossible. But the links between the objects of knowledge that the human soul must distinguish, but not isolate, from each other are recognised.

For the complex dialectical general theory of knowledge, unlike the objective (mathematicism, mechanicism and organicism) and subjective (chaos and conflict) general theories of knowledge, which construct knowledge from reason or from the senses alone, on the basis of objective and subjective philosophical assumptions, respectively, all phenomena are governed by the law of cause and effect: all things are caused and causing, aided and aiding, mediate and immediate; and yet all things subsist united by a natural and insensible bond which binds the most remote and the most different. In the general dialectical theory of complexity, on the other hand, we can observe a permanent tension between a totalising knowledge and the incompleteness and incompleteness of all knowledge; because it starts from monistic philosophical assumptions, solving in a theological way the problem of the essence of knowledge. In order to construct knowledge, using the theory of complexity, the cognising subject must use both his reason (first) and his senses (second) (Morín, 2001:21-24).

The following table shows the philosophical *assumptions* from which each and every one of the five main philosophical *problems* of knowledge are solved in the construction of the *general theory of dialectical knowledge of complexity*:

GENERAL THEORY OF DIALECTICAL KNOWLEDGE	PHILOSOPHICAL PROBLEMS OF KNOWLEDGE						
	POSSIBILITY OF KNOWLEDGE	ORIGIN OF KNOWLEDGE	ESSENCE OF KNOWLEDGE			TYPE OF KNOWLEDGE	CONCEPT AND CRITERION OF TRUTH OF KNOWLEDGE
			SOLUTIONS				
			PRE-METAPHYSICAL SOLUTION	METAPHYSICAL SOLUTION	THEOLOGICAL SOLUTION		
	ASSUMPTIONS FROM WHICH TO SOLVE KNOWLEDGE PROBLEMS						
COMPLEXITY	CRITICISM	APRIORISM	DIALECTICS	PHENOMENOLOGY	MONISM	MIXED: (RATIONAL INTUITIVE)	MIXED: IMMANEN TETRASCENDENTE)

So far, so much for the general theory of complex dialectical knowledge.

The following synoptic table shows the main *general theories of* objective, subjective and dialectical *knowledge*, respectively, and the respective philosophical assumptions from which they were created:

GENERAL THEORY OF KNOWLEDGE	PHILOSOPHICAL PROBLEMS OF KNOWLEDGE						
	POSSIBILITY OF KNOWLEDGE	ORIGIN OF KNOWLEDGE	ESSENCE OF KNOWLEDGE			TYPE OF KNOWLEDGE	CONCEPT AND CRITERION OF TRUTH OF KNOWLEDGE
			SOLUTIONS				
			PRE-METAPHYSICAL SOLUTION	METAPHYSICAL SOLUTION	THEOLOGICAL SOLUTION		
	ASSUMPTIONS FROM WHICH TO SOLVE KNOWLEDGE PROBLEMS						
MATHEMATICISM	DOGMATISM	RATIONALISM	OBJECTIVISM	IDEALISM	DUALISM	RATIONAL	IMMANENT
MECANICISM	DOGMATISM	RATIONALISM	OBJECTIVISM	IDEALISM	DUALISM	RATIONAL	IMMANENT
ORGA-NICISM	DOGMATISM	RATIONALISM	OBJECTIVISM	IDEALISM	DUALISM	RATIONAL	IMMANENT
CHAOS	**SCEPTICISM, SUBJECTIVISM AND PRAGMATISM**	EMPIRISM	**SUBJECTIVISM**	**REALISM**	**DUALIS-MO**	**INTUITIVE**	**TRASCENDENT**
CONFLICTO	**SCEPTICISM, SUBJECTIVISM AND PRAGMATISM**	EMPIRISM	**SUBJECTIVISM**	**REALISM**	**DUALISMO**	**INTUITIVE**	**TRASCENDENT**
ANALOGY	CRITICISM	INTELLECTUALISM	DIA READING	FENO MENOLOGY	MONISM	MIXED	MIXED
COMPLEXITY	CRITICISM	APIORISM	DIALECTICS	PHENOMENOLOGY	MONISM	MIXED	MIXED

The general theories of knowledge that have just been analysed constitute the general theoretical foundation for problematising the objects of study of the particular theories of the social sciences that seek to explore, describe, explain, interpret, etc., social reality.

2.3.5.1.3.3 *The particular theories of the social sciences.*

The *particular theories of the social sciences* explore, describe, explain, interpret, etc., uniquely social phenomena, facts, events, etc.,. Educational sciences are social sciences, because their object of study is the social human being.

The classification of science proposed in this paper goes from the general to the particular: general theories of knowledge (already discussed), *particular theories of social sciences* (described in this section) and specific theories of education (to be discussed later).

The criterion for classifying the *particular theories of the social sciences* will be the same as that adopted for classifying the general theories of knowledge: first, the theories that explore, describe, explain, interpret, etc., will be analysed. social reality, from *reason*, and that solve, by the same token, each and every one of the five philosophical problems of knowledge, from *dogmatic* (possibility of knowledge), *rational* (origin of knowledge), *objectivist*, *idealist* and *dualist* assumptions (pre-metaphysical, metaphysical and theological solutions, respectively, to the problem of the essence of knowledge), *rational* (types of knowledge) and *immanent* (concepts and criteria of truth of knowledge). We will call these theories *particular theories of the objective social sciences*; in attention to the agreed criterion of classification, the way they solve the following question: who determines whom in a knowledge relation: the object to the subject, the subject to the object, or both determine each other?

This will be followed by an analysis of the *particular theories of the social sciences* that explore, describe, explain, interpret, etc., from *the senses*, social reality, from the *senses*, and which, by the same token, solve each and every one of the five main philosophical problems of knowledge, from *sceptical*, *subjectivist*, *relativist* and *pragmatic* (possibility of knowledge), *empiricist* (origin of knowledge), *subjectivist*, *realist* and *dualist* (pre-metaphysical, metaphysical and theological solutions, respectively, to the problems of the essence of knowledge), *intuitive* (types of knowledge) and *transcendent* (concepts and criteria of truth of knowledge) assumptions. We will call these theories *particular theories of the subjective social sciences*, in accordance with the classification criterion already indicated.

Finally, we will analyse the *particular theories of the social sciences* that explore, describe, explain, interpret, etc., from the point of view of reason and the senses, social reality, from *reason* and the *senses*, and which, by the same token, solve each and every one of the five philosophical problems of knowledge from *critical* (possibility of knowledge), *intellectualist* and/or *apriorist* (origin of knowledge), *dialectical*, *phenomenological* and *monistic* (pre-metaphysical, metaphysical and theological solutions, respectively, to the problem of the essence of knowledge), *mixed* (types of knowledge) and *mixed* (concepts and criteria of truth of knowledge) assumptions. We will call these theories *particular theories of dialectical social sciences*; for the same reason of classification already mentioned.

2.3.5.2.1 The particular theories of objective social sciences.

The *particular theories of the objective social sciences* explore, describe, explain, interpret, etc., social reality from the standpoint of *reason*. Therefore, the philosophical assumptions from which they solve each and every one of the five main problems of knowledge are *dogmatism* (possibility of knowledge), *rationalism* (origin of knowledge), *objectivism, idealism* and *dualism* (pre-metaphysical, metaphysical and theological solutions, respectively, to the problem of the essence of knowledge), *rational* (type of knowledge) and *immanent* (concepts and criteria of truth of knowledge).

The *particular theories of the objective social sciences* explore, describe, explain, interpret, etc., the social reality, comparing it with a logical-mathematical ideal, with a machine, with a living organism, with a structure, with a cybernetic system, etc. Social objects of study are constructed using *reason* and, therefore, on the basis of the philosophical assumptions mentioned above.

The *particular theories of objective social science* resemble the general theories of objective knowledge. The philosophical *assumptions* from which both theories solve each of the five main *problems* of knowledge are the same. The only difference that can be observed between the two classifications of theory is one of degree. General theories of objective knowledge explore, describe, explain, interpret, etc., any phenomenon, whether factual (natural or social) or formal (logical-mathematical); the particular theories of objective social science deal only with social phenomena.

The analysis, as was done with the general theories of objective knowledge, will be carried out, in a first moment, considering the definition, characteristics, function, purpose, classification, authors and works of each *particular theory of objective social sciences*; and, in a second moment, the philosophical *assumptions* from which each and every one of the five main *problems* of knowledge are solved will be taken into account: possibility, origin, essence, classification and concepts and criteria of truth of knowledge. Some of the *particular theories of objective social science* discussed in this section are: positivism, functionalism, structuralism and systems theory.

2.3.5.2.1.1 Positivism.

Positivism can be rightly *defined as a particular theory of objective social science* in which social reality is *compared* to an *ideal*. Social groups are explored, described, explained, interpreted, etc. on the basis of the *ought to be* (idea). For example: students in teacher training have to study hard in order to graduate with a degree in education. The idea "Graduates in Education" is an ideal (should be) to be achieved by the students (to be).

Positivism is a *theory* because it explores, describes, explains, interprets, understands, etc., social reality.

Positivism is a *particular theory of social science* because it explores, describes, explains, interprets, understands, etc., only social reality.

Positivism is a *particular theory of objective social sciences* because it explores, describes, explains, interprets, understands, etc., social reality from the *reason* of the subject who constructs the theory; *assuming* that, in a knowledge relationship, the object to be known determines the cognising subject (objectivism).

The fact that *positivism* compares social reality with an ideal means that, of all the capacities that the subject has to generate new knowledge (addition, subtraction, multiplication, division, analysis, synthesis, induction, deduction, *comparison*, classification, definition, etc.), *comparison* is preferentially used to bring order to reality.

That in the *particular theory of the positivist objective social sciences,* the social reality to be explored, described, explained, interpreted, understood, etc., is *compared* to an ideal, means that *reason*, which is the quality of the subject being used to explain reality, *assumes*, or wants to assume in order to order the phenomena, that it must not move, that it must remain forever and ever fixed, eternally immobile (dogmatism).

A *characteristic feature* of the *positivist* view of *social* reality is that it seeks to explain social phenomena by means of the laws of *nature*. Social facts are understood and interpreted by analogy with an ideal, as if they were natural phenomena. It is assumed, on the basis of reason, that the only authentic knowledge is scientific knowledge (dogmatism), and that such knowledge can only arise from the positive affirmation of theories through the scientific method.

This ontological *determinism* makes it possible to assume, on the basis of *reason*, that there is an established *order* (rationalism) in social reality (by God, reason or the history of peoples), which human *reason* discovers through reflection. It is assumed, or one wants to assume, because it suits certain interests, that in social reality, in general, there is an *order*, pre-established rules of the game; that they are eternal and immutable, given forever and ever (dogmatism).

Comte (1997) assumes, from reason, to have discovered the fundamental law of progress and development of the human spirit (dogmatism). According to Comte (1997), this law (dogma) consists of three stages through which humanity has passed:

1 The first of these (the theological state) corresponds to the infancy of humanity, when it questions the what of all things. At this stage there are three moments: fetishism, where things are personified and magical or divine power is attributed to them; polytheism, where material things are replaced by divine beings and natural processes are made dependent on the will of the gods; and monotheism, where the plurality of gods is replaced by a single, unique and omnipotent divinity which, with its laws (dogmas), governs the whole universe.

2 The second of the three stages through which, according to Auguste Comte (1997), humanity has passed, is the metaphysical stage. It is a modification of the theological stage and is indispensable for the development of mankind and just as transitory and imperfect. Instead of discovering causes, the aim is to know essences; substituting natural entities with abstractions, such as the ideas of principle, substance, essence, cause, etc.

3 The third and perfect stage is the *positive* stage. The development of the human spirit. This stage is reached when one no longer aspires to absolute

knowledge which explains the origin and meaning of the universe, when one ceases to seek the why of all things and man limits himself to observing the facts of experience, to describe them and to discover the laws (dogmatism) which govern their behaviour; that is to say, the constant relations (rationalism) which exist between the phenomena observed.

Positivism, like the general theories of objective knowledge (mathematicism, mechanicism and organicism) only *works* when each part is integrated in the right place and complements the others in order to continue to fulfil the same function (rationalism).

The *function* of *positivism*, like that of the general theories of objective knowledge (mathematicism, mechanism and organicism) is the discovery of laws that are simple and unalterable, which must explain a set of elements that are simple and unalterable (dogmatism).

According to positivist theory, we can only know what science allows us to know; and the only method of knowledge is that of the natural sciences.

In the *particular theory of positivist objective social science* - applied to the exploration, description, explanation, interpretation, understanding, etc., of human behaviour in society - the *object* (the idea, the instituted, the institutions, etc., constructed by certain subjects, assuming, from reason, that reality does not move) determines the *subject*. It is *assumed*, or one wants to assume, from *reason* that, in a relation of knowledge, the object determines the subject. That human beings, as *subjects* in themselves, are less important than institutions, that only within the *institution* (object) do their lives make sense. The word *objective* is derived, in ontological and epistemological terms, from the word object of knowledge.

The interpretation of social reality, from the *particular theory of positivist objective social science*, as in the general theories of objective knowledge (mathematics, mechanicism and organicism), *assumes*, or wants to *assume* (from certain rationalities and because it suits certain interests), that the *subject* is due to the *object*; that what is important is the whole, not the part; that the parts owe the whole; that the reason for the existence of the parts is the conservation, preservation and enhancement of the whole; that what must be preserved are the *institutions* (ideas) to which the *subjects* are indebted.

The method of natural science (discovery of causal laws and their control over facts) applies not only to the study of nature, but also to the study of society (epistemological monism).

In the *particular theory of positivist objective social science*, explorations, descriptions, explanations, interpretations, understandings, etc. about human behaviour in society are constructed by solving the pre-metaphysical problem of the essence of knowledge, using *idealistic* philosophical *assumptions*. It is *assumed* that the studied reality (the *object* to be known) exists independently of whether there is a *cognising subject* interested in knowing it or not.

That is why sociology, understood as the science of social facts, constituted by human relations, is the characteristic result of the positivist programme.

In the *particular theory of positivist social science*, explorations, descriptions, explanations, interpretations, understandings, etc. about human behaviour in society are constructed by solving the theological problem of the essence of knowledge, using *dualistic* philosophical ass*umptions*. It is *assumed* that the reality under study (the *object* to be known) is divided into two opposing and irreconcilable poles: pass and fail students, good and bad teachers, punctual and unpunctual students, etc.

Methodological monism, based on the *positivist* scientific method, would be the solution to all of humanity's social problems: to know in order to control.

The *type* of knowledge that is constructed, in the *particular theory of positivist social science*, is *rational*. It is assumed, on the basis of *reason*, that the only *true* knowledge is that which is born of the reflection of the human *soul*.

Positivism gives optimism to humanity based on the certainty (rationalism) of an unstoppable process (sometimes conceived as the result of human ingenuity and work, sometimes as something necessary and automatic) that advances towards conditions of generalised well-being, in a peaceful society permeated by solidarity among men (idealism).

The *concepts* and *criteria* of truth of knowledge that are constructed in the *particular theory of positivist social science* are *immanent*. It is assumed, from reason, that truth is the concordance of thought with itself, not with reality. The cognising subjects are confronted with ideal, mental objects of knowledge, entities created by certain rationalities, which have no existence, properly speaking, in material reality.

It is about knowing in order to control and controlling in order to dominate, both nature and society.

The *particular theory of the positivist target society* can serve purposes such as the following: to realise the "ideals" of certain rationalities of particular subjects or groups, regardless of the differences (economic, political, social, etc.) between the constituent parts.

According to the *particular theory of objective social sciences*, called *positivism*, the sciences can be classified into: astronomy, physics, chemistry, physiology, and social physics or sociology.

To study social reality, we must start from *philosophical assumptions* that imply order, harmony, stillness, etc. (dogmatic, rationalist, objectivist, idealist, etc.).

Mathematical, mechanistic and organicist theoretical foundations are very useful to reinforce the problematisation of the objects of study using the particular theory of positive objective social science.

The following table shows the philosophical *assumptions* from which each and every one of the five main philosophical *problems* of knowledge are solved in the construction of the *particular theory of positivist objective social science*:

<table>
<tr>
<td rowspan="3">PARTICULAR THEORY OF OBJECTIVE SOCIAL SCIENCES</td>
<td colspan="6">PHILOSOPHICAL PROBLEMS OF KNOWLEDGE</td>
</tr>
<tr>
<td rowspan="2">POSSIBILITY OF KNOWLEDGE</td>
<td rowspan="2">ORIGIN OF KNOWLEDGE</td>
<td colspan="3">ESSENCE OF KNOWLEDGE
SOLUTIONS</td>
<td rowspan="2">TYPE OF KNOWLEDGE</td>
<td rowspan="2">CONCEPT AND CRITERIA TRUTHFULLY OF KNOWLEDGE</td>
</tr>
<tr>
<td>SOLUTION PREMETAFISICA</td>
<td>METAPHYSICAL SOLUTION</td>
<td>SOLUTION THEOLOGY</td>
</tr>
<tr>
<td></td>
<td colspan="6">ASSUMPTIONS FROM WHICH TO SOLVE KNOWLEDGE PROBLEMS</td>
</tr>
</table>

POSITIVISM	DOGMATISM	RATIONALISM	OBJECTIVISM	IDEALISM	DUALISM	RATIONAL	IMMANENT

2.3.5.2.2.1.2 Functionalism

Functionalism can be *defined*, from reason, as a *particular theory of objective social sciences* in which social reality is *compared* to a *vital organic function*, to be explored, described, explained, interpreted, understood, etc., as a system of vital movements and the corresponding needs of the organism: digestive, respiratory, etc. function.

Durkheim (1999) understands *function* as the satisfaction of a need of a living organism. For example: the respiratory *function*, the digestive *function*, etc., in a living organism. This idea of *function*, which is constructed in the natural sciences - particularly in biology - is applied in the social sciences, by *analogy*. It is *assumed* that just as living organisms have needs for validity, integration, etc., which are met by the digestive, respiratory, etc., *functions,* so societies have needs for harmony, order, integration, validity, etc., which are met by the digestive, respiratory, etc., functions, so societies have needs for harmony, order, integration, validity, etc., which are met by the digestive, respiratory, etc., functions.

The problem is solved through associations and combinations, aggregations, penetrations and mergers of individuals.

Functionalism is a theory because it explores, describes, explains, interprets, understands, etc., social reality.

Functionalism is a particular theory of social science because it explores, describes, explains, interprets, understands, etc., only social reality.

Functionalism is a particular theory of the objective social sciences because it explores, describes, explains, interprets, understands, etc., social reality from the reason of the subject who constructs the theory; assuming that, in a knowledge relationship, the object to be known determines the cognising subject (objectivism).

The fact that *functionalism* compares social reality with the vital organic functions of a living being means that, of all the capacities that the subject has to generate new knowledge (addition, subtraction, multiplication, division, analysis, synthesis, induction, deduction, *comparison*, classification, definition, etc.), *comparison* is being used, preferably, to bring order to reality. That in the particular theory of the objective *functionalist* social sciences, the social reality that is to be explored, described, explained, interpreted, understood, etc., is compared to the vital organic functions, means that reason, which is the quality of the subject that is used to explain reality, assumes, or wants to assume, in order to order phenomena, that it must not move, that it must remain forever and ever fixed, eternally immobile (dogmatism).

Some characteristics of the *functionalist* view of *social* reality are the following:

1 The aim is to explain social phenomena by means of analogies with natural phenomena. Where the social whole under study can only be understood as a unit.

2 This unit is considered to be made up of component parts that acquire significance and meaning in their relationship to the whole.

3 The social body is presumed to maintain a state of relative equilibrium when each part is in its proper place and performing its proper function within the whole.

4 In the face of any disturbance to disorganise the system, the system defends itself to restore the threatened equilibrium.

5 The proper way to maintain equilibrium is through the normalisation of human behaviour to accept the values and patterns of the status and social role it is expected to play in the function of the system.

6 . Functionalism aims at explaining and substantiating social equilibrium, which means the preservation of established social structures.

This ontological *determinism* makes it possible to assume, on the basis of *reason*, as in the general theories of objective knowledge (mathematics, mechanicism and organicism) and the particular theory of objective social sciences (positivism) that we have just analysed, that in social reality there is an established *order* (rationalism) (by God, reason or the history of peoples), which human *reason* discovers through reflection. It is assumed, or one wants to assume, because it suits certain interests, that in social reality, in general, there is an *order*, pre-established rules of the game; that they are eternal and immutable, given forever and ever (dogmatism).

Those who believe in order explain society dogmatically, rationally, rationally, objectively, ideally, dualistically, etc., in terms of integrating (*relating*) the separate, the *opposed*, involving associations, combinations, aggregations, penetrations, mergers, etc. of individuals.

Order is understood as a social fact that regulates individual actions, with a view to the integration of the parts into the whole.

The social fact is every way of making social consciousness and a social action implies a set of individual behaviours regulated by coercion.

An example, from *functionalism*, any society is comparable to a vital function, in which it is necessary to exercise certain coercion (set of individual behaviours) in the face of a social *dysfunction*; to satisfy - that is to say - to establish general harmony, social order, the need for validity and integration of society; through the aggregation, penetration, fusion, etc. of individuals; ordering them, that is to say, to do in such a way that individual actions are regulated, with a view to a general end.

In *functionalism*, like the general theories of objective knowledge (mathematicism, mechanicism and organicism) and the particular theory of positive objectivist social science, it only *works* when each part is integrated in the right place and complements the others in order to continue to fulfil the same function (rationalism).

The *function* of *functionalism*, like that of the general theories of objective knowledge (mathematicism, mechanicism and organicism) and the particular theory of positivist social science, is the discovery of laws that are simple and unalterable, which must explain a set of elements that are simple and unalterable (dogmatism).

The aim is to explain and underpin the social equilibrium, in order to preserve the established structures.

The "cells" that make up the social "fabric" must perform their function so that this "fabric", together with other social "fabrics", forms certain vital "organs" which, in turn, in connection with other fundamental "organs", form vital apparatuses and systems which, together, satisfy the needs of the "whole". The objectives of the "whole" must be achieved.

Society is understood as an organism in which there is mutual dependence between the whole and the parts and between the parts themselves.

According to *functionalist* theory, we can only know what science allows us to know; and the only method of knowledge is that of the natural sciences.

In the particular theory of objective *functionalist* social science (as in the general theories of objective mathematical, mechanistic and organicist knowledge; and the particular theory of positive social science) - applied to the exploration, description, explanation, interpretation, understanding, etc., of human behaviour in society - the *object* (the idea, the instituted, the institutions, etc., constructed by certain subjects, assuming, from reason, that reality does not move) determines the *subject.* It is *assumed,* or one wants to assume, from *reason* that, in a relation of knowledge, the object determines the subject. That human beings, as *subjects* in themselves, are less important than institutions, that only within the *institution* (object) do their lives make sense. The word *objective* is derived, in ontological and epistemological terms, from the word object of knowledge.

Functionalism is idealistic because it explores, describes, explains, interprets, understands, etc. social reality by comparing it to what it is not in reality: an organic function.

The interpretation of social reality, from the *particular theory of objective functionalist social science,* as in the general theories of objective knowledge (mathematics, mechanicism and organicism) and the particular theory of positive objective social science, *assumes,* or wants to *assume* (from certain rationalities and because it suits certain interests), that the *subject* is due to the *object;* that what is important is the whole, not the part; that the parts owe the whole; that the reason for the existence of the parts is the conservation, preservation and enhancement of the whole; that what must be preserved are the *institutions* (ideas) to which the *subjects* are indebted.

The method of natural science (discovery of causal laws and their control over facts) is not only applied to the study of nature, but also to the study of society (epistemological monism).

Methodological monism, based on the *positivist* and *functionalist* scientific method, is supposed to be the solution to all of humanity's social problems: to know in order to control.

In the particular theory of objective *functionalist* social science, as in the general theories of objective knowledge (mathematicism, mechanicism and organicism) and the particular theory of positive objective social science, explorations, descriptions, explanations, interpretations, understandings, etc. about human behaviour in society are constructed by solving the metaphysical problem of the essence of knowledge using *idealistic* philosophical *assumptions*. It is *assumed* that the studied reality (the *object* to be known) exists independently of whether there is a *cognising subject* who is interested in knowing it or not.

That is why sociology, understood as the science of social facts, constituted by human relations, is the characteristic result of the positivist and *functionalist* programmes.

In the particular theory of social *functionalist* science, as in positivism, explorations, descriptions, explanations, interpretations, understandings, etc. about human behaviour in society are constructed by solving the theological problem of the essence of knowledge, using *dualistic* philosophical *assumptions*. It is *assumed* that the reality under study (the *object* to be known) is divided into two opposing and irreconcilable poles: pass and fail students, good and bad teachers, punctual and unpunctual students, etc.

The type of knowledge that is constructed, in the particular theory of *functionalist* social science, as in positivist social science, is rational. It is assumed, on the basis of reason, that the only true knowledge is that which is born of the reflection of the human soul.

Functionalism, like positivism, gives optimism to humanity on the basis of the certainty (rationalism) of an unstoppable process (sometimes conceived as the result of human ingenuity and work, and in other cases as something necessary and automatic) that advances towards conditions of generalised well-being, in a peaceful society permeated by solidarity among men (idealism).

The concepts and criteria of truth of knowledge that are constructed in the particular theory of objective *functionalist* social science, as in positivism, are *immanent*. It is assumed, from reason, that truth is the concordance of thought with itself, not with reality. Cognitive subjects are confronted with ideal, mental objects of knowledge, entities created by certain rationalities, which have no existence, properly speaking, in material reality.

Functionalism is a particular theory of objective social science because social groups are not living organisms, that idea is only in the mind of the originator of the theory. Durkheim constructed the concept of social function in analogical terms with the biological organism. He understands that both social systems and living organisms have certain needs to be satisfied. He says that just as in the living organism physiological satisfaction is what maintains the validity of a corporeality, so the existence of the organism, in the case of a society, its validity, its integration, depends on the establishment of a general harmony, of an order.

The particular theory of the objective *functionalist* society, like the positivist one, can serve purposes such as the following: to realise the "ideals" of certain rationalities of particular subjects or groups, regardless of the differences (economic, political, social, etc.) between the constituent parts.

In *functionalism*, as in positivism, the aim is to explain and substantiate social equilibrium in order to preserve established social structures.

To study social reality from *functionalism*, as in positivist theory, we must start from philosophical assumptions that imply order, harmony, stillness, etc. (dogmatic, rationalist, objectivist, idealist, etc.).

As in positivism, it is a matter of knowing in order to control and controlling in order to dominate, both nature and society.

The general theoretical foundations of knowledge (mathematical, mechanistic, mechanistic, organicist) and particular objective-positivist social sciences are very useful to reinforce the problematisation of the objects of study using the particular theory of objective-functionalist social science.

The categories that, in order to explain society, have been elaborated from this particular theory of objective social sciences, have evolved and increased over time, starting with authors such as the English anthropologist Radcliffe Brown, Bronislaw Malinowsky, Max Weber, Talcot Parsons, Robert Merton, etc. (Gutiérrez, 1984).

The following table shows the philosophical *assumptions* from which each and every one of the five main philosophical *problems* of knowledge are solved in the construction of the *particular theory of objective functionalist social science*:

PARTICULAR THEORY OF OBJECTIVE SOCIAL SCIENCE	PHILOSOPHICAL PROBLEMS OF KNOWLEDGE						
	POSSIBILITY OF KNOWLEDGE	ORIGIN OF KNOWLEDGE	ESSENCE OF KNOWLEDGE			TYPE OF KNOWLEDGE	CONCEPT AND CRITERION OF TRUTH OF KNOWLEDGE
			SOLUTIONS				
			SOLUTION PREMETAFISCA	METAPHYSICAL SOLUTION	THEOLOGICAL SOLUTION		
	ASSUMPTIONS ON THE BASIS OF WHICH KNOWLEDGE PROBLEMS CAN BE SOLVED						
FUNCTIONALISM	DOGMATISM	RATIONALISM	OBJECTIVISM	IDEALISM	DUALISM	RATIONAL	IMMANENT

2.3.5.2.2.1.3 Structuralism.

Structuralism can be *defined*, from reason, as a *particular theory of objective social science* in which social reality is *compared* to a structure (construct), in order to be explored, described, explained, interpreted, understood, etc., as a structured whole, united, in conjunction, in structure.

Structuralism is a theory because it explores, describes, explains, interprets, understands, etc., social reality.

Structuralism is a particular theory of social science because it explores, describes, explains, interprets, understands, etc., only social reality.

Structuralism is a particular theory of the objective social sciences because it explores, describes, explains, interprets, understands, etc., social reality from the reason of the subject who constructs the social reality.

theory; assuming that, in a knowledge relation, the object to be known determines the cognising subject (objectivism).

The fact that *structuralism* compares social reality with a construction means that, of all the capacities that the subject has to generate new knowledge (addition, subtraction, multiplication, division, analysis, synthesis, induction, deduction, *comparison*, classification, definition, etc.), *comparison* is preferentially used to bring order to reality.

That in the particular theory of objective *structuralist* social science, the social reality to be explored, described, explained, interpreted, understood, etc., is compared to a structure, means that reason, which is the quality of the subject being used to explain reality, assumes, or wants to assume, in order to order the phenomena, that it must not move, that it must remain forever and ever fixed, eternally immobile (dogmatism).

The philosophical assumption from which the particular theory of objective *structuralist* social science solves the problem of the possibility of knowledge, preferably using reason, is dogmatism.

Some general characteristics of the particular theory of structuralist social science are as follows:

1. Reality is a structured whole.
2. Reality is transformed.
3. Reality is self-regulating.

This ontological *determinism* makes it possible to assume, on the basis of *reason*, that there is an established *order* (rationalism) in social reality (by God, reason or the history of peoples), which human *reason* discovers through reflection. It is assumed, or one wants to assume, because it suits certain interests, that in social reality, in general, there is an *order*, pre-established rules of the game; that they are eternal and immutable, given forever and ever (dogmatism).

In the particular theory of structuralist social science, the philosophical problem of the origin of knowledge is solved on the basis of rationalist assumptions.

Those who believe in order explain society dogmatically, rationally, rationally, objectively, ideally, dualistically, etc., in terms of integrating (*relating*) the separate, the *opposed*, involving associations, combinations, aggregations, penetrations, mergers, etc. of individuals.

Structuralism, like the general theories of objective knowledge (mathematicism, mechanicism and organicism) and the particular theories of positive objectivist and functional objectivist social sciences, only *works* when each part is integrated in the right place and complements the others to continue to fulfil the same function (rationalism).

The *function of* structuralism, like that of the general theories of objective knowledge (mathematicism, mechanicism and organicism) and the particular theories of positivist and functionalist social sciences, is the discovery of laws that are simple and unalterable, which must explain a set of elements that are simple and unalterable (dogmatism).

The aim is to explain and underpin the social equilibrium, in order to preserve the established structures.

In the particular theory of objective *structuralist* social science (as in the general theories of objective mathematical, mechanistic and organicist knowledge; and the particular theories of positive and functional social science) - applied to the exploration, description, explanation, interpretation, understanding, etc., of human behaviour in society - the *object* (the idea, the instituted, the institutions, etc., constructed by certain subjects, assuming, from reason, that reality does not move) determines the *subject*. It is *assumed*, or one wants to assume, from *reason* that, in a relation of knowledge, the object determines the subject. That human beings, as *subjects* in themselves, are less important than institutions, that only within the *institution* (object) do their lives make sense. The word *objective* is derived, in ontological and epistemological terms, from the word object of knowledge.

In *structuralism*, starting from reason, the problem of the essence of knowledge is solved from a pre-metaphysical solution, using objectivist philosophical assumptions.

The function of *structuralism*, the need it satisfies, is to discover the laws that govern structure.

The interpretation of social reality, from the *particular theory of structuralist objective social science*, as in the general theories of objective knowledge (mathematicism, mechanicism and organicism) and the particular theories of positive and functional objective social sciences, *assumes*, or wants to *assume* (from certain rationalities and because it suits certain interests), that the *subject* is due to the *object*; that what is important is the whole, not the part; that the parts owe the whole; that the reason for the existence of the parts is the conservation, preservation and enhancement of the whole; that what must be preserved are the *institutions* (ideas) to which the *subjects* are indebted.

In the particular theory of *structuralist* objective social science, as in the general theories of objective knowledge (mathematicism, mechanicism and organicism) and the particular theories of objective positive and functional social science, the explorations, descriptions, explanations, interpretations, understandings, etc. of human behaviour in society are constructed by solving the metaphysical problem of the essence of knowledge on the basis of *idealistic* philosophical assumptions. It is assumed that the studied reality (the *object* to be known) exists independently of whether or not there is a *cognising subject* interested in knowing it or not.

In the particular theory of *structuralist* social science, as in positivism and functionalism, explorations, descriptions, explanations, interpretations, understandings, etc. of human behaviour in society are constructed from reason, solving the theological problem of the essence of knowledge by using *dualistic* philosophical ass*umptions*. It is *assumed* that the reality under study (the *object* to be known) is divided into two opposing and irreconcilable poles: students who pass and those who fail, good and bad teachers, those who are punctual and those who are unpunctual, etc.

The aim of *structuralism* is to maintain the state of affairs, that the social structure remains stable, regardless of structural inequalities.

The type of knowledge that is constructed, in the particular theory of *structuralist* social science, as in positivist and functionalist social science, is rational. It is assumed, on the basis of reason, that the only true knowledge is that which is born of the reflection of the human soul.

Structuralism solves the problem of the classification of knowledge, from the point of view of reason, on the basis of rationalist philosophical assumptions.

Structuralism, like positivism and functionalism, gives optimism to humanity on the basis of the certainty (rationalism) of an unstoppable process (sometimes conceived as the result of human ingenuity and labour, sometimes as something necessary and automatic) that advances towards conditions of generalised well-being, in a peaceful society permeated by solidarity among men (idealism).

The concepts and criteria of truth of knowledge that are constructed in the particular theory of objective *structuralist* social science, as in positivism and functionalism, are *immanent*. It is assumed, from reason, that truth is the concordance of thought with itself, not with reality. Cognitive subjects are confronted with ideal, mental objects of knowledge, entities created by certain rationalities, which have no existence, properly speaking, in material reality.

In *structuralism*, the philosophical problem of the concept and criterion of the truth of knowledge is solved by reason, using immanent assumptions.

Structuralism is a particular theory of objective social science because social groups are not structures, buildings. That idea is only in the mind of the originator of the theory. Claude Levi Straus assumed that human thought can discover and explain the structure of objects of knowledge.

The particular theory of the objective *structuralist* society, like the positivist and functionalist ones, can serve purposes such as the following: to realise the "ideals" of certain rationalities of particular subjects or groups, regardless of the differences (economic, political, social, etc.) between the constituent parts.

In *structuralism*, as in positivism and functionalism, it tries to explain and substantiate social equilibrium, in order to preserve established social structures.

To study social reality in *structuralism*, as in positivist and functionalist theories, we must start from philosophical assumptions that imply order, harmony, stillness, etc. (dogmatic, rationalist, objectivist, idealist, etc.).

It is, as in positivism and functionalism, about knowing in order to control and controlling in order to dominate, both nature and society.

The general theoretical foundations of knowledge (mathematical, mechanistic, mechanistic, organicist) and particular objective social sciences (positivist and functionalist) are very useful to reinforce the problematisation of the objects of study using the particular theory of *structuralist* objective social science.

The categories to explain society that have been elaborated from this particular theory of objective social sciences have evolved and increased over time, starting with authors such as Claude Levi Straus, Piaget, Jacques Lacan, Althusser, Schaff, etc.

Structuralism, whose concept (arising from chemistry, passing from there to language and other sciences) means "to construct", according to Schaff, and in agreement with Matallman, Ferdinand de Saussure, Levi Strauss, Piaget, Althusser, etc., differs from *functionalism*, mainly in that the object, as something exposed, given in itself, only has significance at the moment when thought can discover and explain its structure (phenomenalism), differs from functionalism mainly in that the object, as something exposed, given in itself, only has significance at the moment when thought can discover and explain its structure (phenomenalism), which is immanent to the object, but not manifest, we only grasp the phenomenon as it appears to us, not in itself (phenomenalism), as functionalism naively pretends.

According to this theory the object is constructed, thus beginning the explanation. Reality is empirically observable, but the objects that are presented are given in a primitive, crude and simple way to our senses; so our thought must, in a second instance, elaborate a model (dogmatism) of reality to try to find the structure (rationalism) that is found in those objects; a structure that, being immanent to them, is proper to those objects. Thought does not have to intervene (objectivism), since otherwise it would destroy the order that exists in perceptible phenomena.

Seeks unity, conjunction, structure, order. Reality is seen (in a dogmatic, rationalist, objective, idealist, dualist way) as related to the whole. The diverse, the heterogeneous, does not fit into this current (Gutiérrez, 1984:195-207).

Structuralism, together with Marxism, bridges the gap between the objective and the subjective in the construction of its objects of study.

The following table shows the philosophical *assumptions* from which each and every one of the five main philosophical *problems* of knowledge are solved in the construction of the *particular theory of structuralist objective social science*:

PARTICULAR THEORY OF OBJECTIVE SOCIAL SCIENCE	PHILOSOPHICAL PROBLEMS OF KNOWLEDGE						
	POSSIBILITY OF KNOWLEDGE	ORIGIN OF KNOWLEDGE	ESSENCE OF KNOWLEDGE			TYPE OF KNOWLEDGE	CONCEPT AND CRITERION OF TRUTH OF KNOWLEDGE
			SOLUTIONS				
			PRE-METAPHYSICAL SOLUTION	METAPHYSICAL SOLUTION	THEOLOGICAL SOLUTION		
	ASSUMPTIONS FROM WHICH TO SOLVE KNOWLEDGE PROBLEMS						
STRUCTURALISM	DOGMATISM	RATIONALISM	OBJECTIVISM	IDEALISMO	DUALISM	RATIONAL	IMMANENT

2.3.5.2.2.1.4 Systems.

Systems can be defined, from reason, as a particular theory of objective social sciences in which social reality is compared to a whole, to a totality that can be a machine, a living organism, a structure (concrete or abstract), etc., in order to explore, describe, explain, interpret, understand, etc., as a systemic, ideal, mechanical, organic, positive, functional, structured, etc., whole.

The *system* is a theory because it explores, describes, explains, interprets, understands, etc., social reality.

The *system* is a particular theory of social science because it explores, describes, explains, interprets, understands, etc., only social reality.

The *system* is a particular theory of the objective social sciences because it explores, describes, explains, interprets, understands, etc., the social reality from the reason of the subject who constructs the theory; assuming that, in a relation of knowledge, the object to be known determines the cognising subject (objectivism).

The fact that in a *system* social reality is compared to a whole, to a totality that can be a machine, a living organism, a structure (concrete or abstract), etc., means that, of all the capacities that the subject has to generate new knowledge (addition, subtraction, multiplication, division, analysis, synthesis, induction, deduction, *comparison*, classification, definition, etc.), *comparison* is being used, preferably, to bring order to reality.

A *system* should be considered as an integrated entity or phenomenon that encompasses all the aspects and levels that compose it, characterised by their mutual interrelation (Gutiérrez, 1984: 220). An example of this can be from a cell to a living being, from a simple mechanical machine to a self-regulating computer, from a social group to the international social context; that is, any entity or phenomenon of any type or class that is identified as a totality (Gutierrez, 1984: 221). (Gutierrez, 1984: 221).

That in the particular theory of objective *systemic* social science, the social reality to be explored, described, explained, interpreted, understood, etc., is compared to a whole, to a totality, which can be a machine, a living organism, a structure (concrete or abstract, etc.), with a whole, with a totality which can be a machine, a living organism, a structure (concrete or abstract), etc.; it means that reason, which is the quality of the subject that is being used to explain reality, assumes, or wants to assume, in order to order the phenomena; that it must not move, that it must remain forever and ever fixed, eternally immobile (dogmatism).

The philosophical assumption from which the particular theory of *systemic* objective social science solves the problem of the possibility of knowledge, preferably using reason, is dogmatism.

General systems theory, starting with authors such as the Viennese biologist Bertalanffy, the economist Kennet E. Boulding, the biomathematician Anatol Rapoport, the physiologist Ralph Gerard, etc., applies mathematics to the knowledge of society, using biological and conceptual theoretical, mechanistic and organicist models. He claims total explanations (dogmatism) of any mathematical, biological, mechanistic or social system (Gutiérrez, 1984: 219-232).

The most important characteristic of the particular theory of *systemic* social science is that it understands the possibility of embracing systems as wholes and totalities.

This ontological *determinism* makes it possible to assume, on the basis of *reason*, that there is an established *order* (rationalism) in social reality (by God, reason or the history of peoples), which human *reason* discovers through reflection. It is assumed, or one wants to assume, because it suits certain interests, that in social reality, in general, there is an *order*, pre-established rules of the game; that they are eternal and immutable, given forever and ever (dogmatism).

In the particular theory of systemic objective social science, the philosophical problem of the origin of knowledge is solved on the basis of rationalist assumptions.

Those who believe in order explain society dogmatically, rationally, rationally, objectively, ideally, dualistically, etc., in terms of integrating (*relating*) the separate, the *opposed*, involving associations, combinations, aggregations, penetrations, mergers, etc. of individuals.

Systems, like the general theories of objective knowledge (mathematicism, mechanism and organicism) and the particular theories of positive objectivist, functional and structuralist social sciences, only *work* when each part is integrated in the right place and complements the others in order to continue to fulfil the same function (rationalism).

The function of *systems*, like that of the general theories of objective knowledge (mathematicism, mechanicism and organicism) and the particular theories of positivist, functionalist and structuralist social sciences, is the discovery of laws that are simple and unalterable, which must explain a set of elements that are simple and unalterable (dogmatism). It tries to give a scientific explanation of all and of totalities.

The function of systemic order, the need it satisfies, is to discover the laws that govern the system.

The aim is to explain and underpin the social equilibrium, in order to preserve the established structures.

In the particular theory of *systemic* objective social science (as in the general theories of objective knowledge (mathematical, mechanistic and organicist) and the particular theories of social science (positive, functional and structural) - applied to the exploration, description, explanation, interpretation, understanding, etc., of human behaviour in society - the object (the idea, the instituted, the institutions, etc., constructed by certain subjects, assuming, from reason, that reality does not move) determines the subject. It is assumed, or one wants to assume, from reason that, in a relation of knowledge, the object determines the subject. That human beings, as subjects in themselves, are less important than institutions, that only within the institution (object) do their lives make sense. The word objective is derived, in ontological and epistemological terms, from the word object of knowledge.

In the *systemic* order, the pre-metaphysical problem about the essence of knowledge is solved, on the basis of reason, using objectivist philosophical assumptions.

The interpretation of social reality, from the particular theory of *systemic* objective social science, as in the general theories of objective knowledge (mathematicism, mechanicism and organicism) and the particular theories of objective social sciences (positive, functional and structuralist), assumes, or wants to assume (from certain rationalities and because it suits certain interests), that the subject is due to the object; that what is important is the whole, not the part; that the parts owe the whole; that the reason for the existence of the parts is the conservation, preservation and enhancement of the whole; that what must be preserved are the institutions (ideas) to which the subjects are indebted.

In the particular theory of systemic objective social science, as in the general theories of objective knowledge (mathematicism, mechanicism and organicism) and the particular theories of objective social science (positive, functional and structural), explorations, descriptions, explanations, interpretations, understandings, etc. about human behaviour in society are constructed by solving the metaphysical problem of the essence of knowledge from reason, using idealistic philosophical assumptions. It is assumed that the studied reality (the object to be known) exists independently of whether there is a cognising subject who is interested in knowing it or not.

In the particular theory of *systemic* social science, as in positivism, functionalism and structuralism, explorations, descriptions, explanations, interpretations, understandings, etc. about human behaviour in society are constructed by solving the theological problem of the essence of knowledge from reason, using dualistic philosophical assumptions. It is *assumed* that the reality under study (the *object* to be known) is divided into two opposing and irreconcilable poles: students who pass and those who fail, good and bad teachers, those who are punctual and those who are unpunctual, etc.

The purpose of the *system* is to maintain the state of affairs, that the social structure remains stable, regardless of systemic inequalities.

The type of knowledge that is constructed, in the particular theory of systemic social science, as in positivist, functionalist and structuralist theory, is rational. It is assumed, on the basis of reason, that the only true knowledge is that which is born of the reflection of the human soul.

The *system* solves the problem of the classification of knowledge, from reason, on the basis of rationalist philosophical assumptions.

The *system*, like positivism, functionalism and structuralism, gives optimism to humanity based on the certainty (rationalism) of an unstoppable process (sometimes conceived as the result of human ingenuity and labour and sometimes as necessary and automatic) that advances towards conditions of generalised well-being, in a peaceful society permeated by solidarity among men (idealism).

The concepts and criteria of truth of knowledge that are constructed in the particular theory of *systemic* objective social science, as in positivism, functionalism and structuralism, are *immanent*. It is assumed, from reason, that truth is the concordance of thought with itself, not with reality. Cognitive subjects are confronted with ideal, mental objects of knowledge, entities created by certain rationalities, which have no existence, properly speaking, in material reality.

In the *system*, the philosophical problem of the concept and criterion of truth of knowledge is solved by reason, using immanent assumptions.

The *system* is a particular theory of objective social science because social groups are not *systems*, they are not a systemic, ideal, mechanical, organic, positive, functional, structured, etc. whole. That idea is only in the mind of the originator of the theory. To explain the process of theory formation, Bertalanffy () considered it necessary to identify, for his research in biology, the conceptual-theoretical, mechanistic and organicist models.

The particular theory of the *systemic* target society, like positivist, functionalist and structuralist theories, can serve purposes such as the following: to realise the "ideals" of certain rationalities of particular subjects or groups, regardless of the differences (economic, political, social, etc.) between the constituent parts.

The *system*, like positivism, functionalism and structuralism, tries to explain and substantiate social equilibrium, in order to preserve established social structures.

To study social reality from the *system*, as in positivist, functionalist and structuralist theories, we must start from philosophical assumptions that imply order, harmony, stillness, etc. (dogmatic, rationalist, objectivist, idealist, etc.). As in positivism, functionalism and structuralism, it is a matter of knowing in order to control and controlling in order to dominate society.

The general theoretical foundations of knowledge (mathematical, mechanistic, mechanistic, organicist) and particular objective social sciences (positivist, functionalist and structuralist) are very useful to reinforce the problematisation of the objects of study using the particular theory of objective-systemic social science.

The categories to explain society that have been elaborated from this particular theory of objective social sciences have evolved and increased over time, starting with authors such as Berthalanffy, John Von Neuman, Oran R. Young, Merton D. Davism, D. J. White, etc.

In *general systems theory*, unity, conjunction, structure, order are sought. Reality is seen (in a dogmatic, rationalist, objective, idealist, dualist way) as related to the whole. The diverse, the heterogeneous, does not fit into this current (Gutiérrez, 1984:195-207).

The following table shows the philosophical assumptions from which each and every one of the five main philosophical *problems* of knowledge are solved in the construction of the particular theory of *systemic* objective social science:

PARTICULAR THEORY OF OBJECTIVE SOCIAL SCIENCES	PHILOSOPHICAL PROBLEMS OF KNOWLEDGE						
	POSSIBILITY OF KNOWLEDGE	ORIGIN OF KNOWLEDGE	ESSENCE OF KNOWLEDGE			TYPE OF KNOWLEDGE	CONCEPT AND CRITERION OF TRUTH OF KNOWLEDGE
			SOLUTIONS				
			PRE-METAPHYSICAL SOLUTION	METAPHYSICAL SOLUTION	THEOLOGICAL SOLUTION		
	ASSUMPTIONS FROM WHICH TO SOLVE KNOWLEDGE PROBLEMS						
GENERAL SYSTEMS THEORY	DOGMATISM	RATIONALISM	OBJECTIVISM	IDEALISM	DUALISM	RATIONAL	IMMANENT

2.3.5.2.2 The particular theories of subjective social sciences.

Particular theories of subjective knowledge are derived, like general theories of subjective knowledge, from philosophical assumptions that are sceptical, subjectivistic, relativistic and pragmatic (thus solving the problem of the possibility of knowledge); empiricist (thus solving the problem of the origin of knowledge); empiricist (thus solving the problem of the origin of knowledge); subjectivists, realists and dualists (thus solving the problem of the essence of knowledge as regards the pre-metaphysical, metaphysical and theological solutions, respectively); intuitionists (thus solving the problem of the classification of knowledge); and transcendentalists (thus solving the problem of the concepts and criteria of truth of knowledge).

Some *particular theories of the subjective social sciences* that resolve each of the five major philosophical problems of knowledge from the above-mentioned assumptions are historicism and dialectical historical materialism. Just as the *particular theories of the objective social sciences* (mathematicism, mechanicism and organicism) were worked on, the analysis of the *particular theories of the subjective social sciences* (historicism and historical-dialectical materialism), in a first moment, will be carried out considering the definition, characteristics, function, purpose, classification, authors and works of each *particular theory of the subjective social sciences*; and, in a second moment, the philosophical assumptions from which each and every one of the five main philosophical problems of knowledge are solved will be taken into account: Possibility, Origin, Essence, Classification, and Concepts and Criteria of Truth.

It is necessary to remember, for the purposes of this analysis, that the *classification* and the *names* assigned to each and every one of the *particular theories of the subjective social sciences* analysed in this section, obey the way in which one of the five main philosophical problems of knowledge is solved: the problem of the essence of knowledge. This philosophical problem of knowledge (the essence) was chosen and no other, because this difficulty of knowledge refers to the *relation* of knowledge that is established between the cognising subject and the object to be known.

It has already been made clear that, of the different philosophical assumptions from which the problem of the *essence* of knowledge can be solved and which can be found in three different solutions (pre-metaphysical, metaphysical and theological), we have chosen the pre-metaphysical solution, because this solution addresses the problem of the following question: *who determines whom in a relation of knowledge: the object to the subject, the subject to the object, or do the two determine each other?*

If philosophy determines theory, then theory depends on philosophy. If we assume that, in a relation of knowledge, the object determines the subject, then we can speak of objective theories. On the contrary, if we suppose that, in a relation of knowledge, the subject determines the object, then we can speak of *subjective* theories. Finally, if we assume that, in a relation of knowledge, both elements of knowledge determine each other, then we can speak of dialectical theories.

So far we have analysed the particular theories of objective social science (positivism, functionalism, structuralism and general systems theory). In this section we will analyse the second group of particular theories of social science: the *particular theories of subjective social science* (historicism and historical-dialectical materialism). Subsequently, two of the particular dialectical social science theories will be analysed: phenomenology and critical dialectics.

It has already been said that objective theories are constructed from reason (objectivist), *subjective* theories from the senses (subjectivist) and dialectical theories from both qualities of the cognising subject: from reason and from the senses; being able to start first from reason and then from the senses; or vice versa.

2.3.5.2.2.1 Historicism.

Historicism is a particular theory of subjective social science that explores, describes, explains, interprets, understands, etc., reality, phenomena, facts, things, etc. in historical terms (relativism).

Historicism emerged in Germany at the end of the 19th century from the work of W. Dilthey (), who distinguished between the sciences of nature (explanation) and the sciences of the spirit (understanding); based on the ontological distinction between the natural world and the historical world, which he considered to be the result of the unique and unrepeatable action of human beings (ontological subjectivism). According to Dilthey, the facts, to which such action gives rise, are linked to the context in which they occur and to the relationship between the past and the present (relativism), the only elements that can allow their understanding.

Other German thinkers who promoted *historicism* in the world were W. Windelband, H. Rickert, G. Simmel, and O. Spengler. The same was done in Italy by B. Croce and A. Gramcsi.

Historicism influenced the development of other theories particular to the social sciences, such as existentialism, phenomenology and hermeneutics.

Structuralism and neo-positivism reject *historicism*. The epistemological reasons for this are understood: these particular theories of objective social science solve each of the five main philosophical problems of knowledge on different and contradictory assumptions from those used by *historicism*.

Historicism is a *theory* because it explains, interprets, understands, etc., reality, phenomena, facts, thing, etc.

Historicism is a *particular theory of social science* because it explains, interprets, understands, etc., social reality.

Historicism is a particular theory of the subjective social sciences because it explains, interprets, understands, etc., reality subjectively. The explorations, descriptions, explanations, interpretations, understandings, etc., of reality, phenomena, events, things, etc., which are carried out in *historicist* theory, are done by solving the great problems of knowledge (possibility, origin, essence, classification and concepts and criteria of truth) from reason, using sceptical, subjectivist, relativist, pragmatic, empirical, subjectivist, realist, monistic, intuitive, transcendent philosophical assumptions, respectively.

With the theory of *historicism*, from subjectivist philosophical assumptions, it is possible to observe reality in constant movement.

The philosophical assumptions from which each and every one of the five main philosophical problems of knowledge (possibility, origin, essence, classification and concept and criterion of truth of knowledge) are solved in *historicism* are the following:

In the particular theory of *historicist* social sciences, as in the general theory of subjective knowledge of chaos and conflict, it is assumed, from the senses, that reality is very complex and very difficult to understand, due to the permanent change in which it finds itself. The problem of the possibility of knowledge is solved on the basis of sceptical, subjectivist, relativist and pragmatic philosophical assumptions.

According to Dilthey (1978), *historicism* considers reality as the product of historical becoming (relativism); being is essentially an event, a temporal process, which cannot be grasped by reason; it is about experiences, concrete facts, conclusions, the fruit of experiences; it works on a transcendental level; it is lived experience, personal and non-transferable (empiricism).

In the particular theory of the subjective *historicist* social sciences, it is assumed, as in the general theories of knowledge of chaos and conflict, that the origin of knowledge is to be found in sensations. It is believed that human beings (each one in particular) perceive reality differently from others. Each human being experiences the same sensations differently. A distinction is made between perception (which is universal) and representation (which is particular). The problem of the origin of knowledge is solved on the basis of empirical philosophical assumptions.

Historicism considers man and reality as history (relativism) and, by extension, all knowledge as historical (Heideger, 1993).

In the particular theory of subjective *historicist* social sciences, it is assumed, from the senses, as in general theories of subjective knowledge (chaos and conflict), that (in a knowledge relation) the cognising subject determines the object to be known. It is presumed that if two cognizing subjects relate to the same object of knowledge, both will apprehend their object to be known in a totally different way; because their life history, feelings, emotions, passions, complexes, ambitions, etc. "contaminate" the object of study. "contaminate" the object of study. Science is not neutral, it obeys philosophical assumptions and ontological interests. The pre-metaphysical problem about the essence of knowledge is solved from subjectivist philosophical assumptions.

Historical knowledge is not objective, it is not exact, it depends on the historian subject (subjectivism); the subjective vision of history does not allow the establishment of historical laws; historical knowledge is relative, because the historical event is one and non-transferable.

In the particular theory of subjective *historicist* social sciences, it is *assumed*, from the senses, as in general subjectivist theories of knowledge (chaos and conflict), that reality exists independently of whether or not it is apprehended by the cognising subjects. It is believed that the impressions of the objects around us impact our senses and produce sensations that different subjects perceive, but represent them differently. The metaphysical problem of the *essence* of knowledge is solved on the basis of realist philosophical assumptions.

Dilthey (1978) opposes the idealists' conceptions of history. For him, truths and values are relative to each epoch. He does not believe in manifestations of the absolute or in any other universal essence. He denies any ultimate and transcendent finality of history.

In the particular theory of subjective *historicist* social sciences, it is *assumed*, from the senses, as in general theories of subjective knowledge (chaos and conflict), that reality is divided into two opposing and contradictory poles: order - disorder, regularities - irregularities, certainty - uncertainty, etc. The theological problem about the essence of knowledge is solved on the basis of dualistic philosophical assumptions.

The theory of *historicism*, from the senses, allows us to analyse phenomena in time and space (relativism).

In the particular theory of the subjective *historicist* social sciences, it is assumed, from the senses, as in the general theories of subjective knowledge of chaos and conflict, that the only kind of knowledge that a cognising subject can obtain of an object to be known is intuitive. Everything we know about reality is considered to have been obtained by means of the senses. The problem of the classification of knowledge is solved on the basis of intuitive philosophical assumptions.

Historicism encompasses a set of diverse currents that coincide in underlining the historical character of man; in this sense, everything that man is, he experiences through history.

In the particular theory of the subjective historicist social sciences, it is assumed, from the senses, as in the general theories of subjective knowledge of chaos and conflict, that the concepts and criteria of truth of knowledge are transcendent. Truth is considered to be the concordance of thought with the object thought. Because it is assumed that the cognising subject is confronted with objects that have their own existence in reality. The problem of concepts and criteria of truth is solved on the basis of transcendent philosophical assumptions.

The following table shows the philosophical assumptions from which each and every one of the five main philosophical problems of knowledge are solved in the construction of the particular theory of *historicist* subjective social science:

GENERAL THEORY OF SUBJECTIVE KNOWLEDGE	PHILOSOPHICAL PROBLEMS OF KNOWLEDGE						
	POSSIBILITY OF KNOWLEDGE	ORIGIN OF KNOWLEDGE	ESSENCE OF KNOWLEDGE			TYPE OF KNOWLEDGE	CONCEP TO AND CRITERIA OF TRUTH OF KNOWLEDGE
			SOLUTIONS				
			PRE-METAPHYSICAL SOLUTION	METAPHYSICAL SOLUTION	SOLUTION THEOLOGY		
	ASSUMPTIONS FROM WHICH KNOWLEDGE PROBLEMS CAN BE RESOLVED						
HISTORICISM	SCEPTICISM, SUBJECTIVISM AND PRAGMATISM	EMPIRISM	SUBJECTIVISM	REALISM	DUALISM	INTUITIVE	TRASCENDENTE

2.3.5.2.2.2 Dialectical historical materialism.

Dialectical historical materialism is a particular theory of the subjective social sciences which, like the general theories of subjective knowledge (chaos and conflict), explores, describes, explains, interprets, understands, etc., reality, phenomena, facts, things, etc., from the senses, in terms of combat, struggle, conflict. Social reality is analysed in terms of the struggle of opposites: social classes.

Historical materialism is a term constructed by Georgi Plekhanov and refers to the philosophical assumptions from which Karl Marx and Fiedrich Engels solved each of the five main problems of knowledge in their explorations, descriptions, explanations, interpretations and understandings of human history.

Dialectical historical materialism is a theory because it explains, interprets, understands, etc., reality, phenomena, facts, things, etc.

Dialectical historical materialism is a *particular theory of social science* because it explains, interprets, understands, etc. any social reality, phenomenon, fact, thing, etc.

Dialectical historical materialism is a *particular theory of the subjective social sciences* because it explains, interprets, understands, etc., any social reality, phenomenon, event, thing, etc., in a subjective way. The explorations, descriptions, explanations, interpretations, understandings, etc., which, about reality, phenomena, events, thing, etc., are carried out in *dialectical historical materialism,* are done by solving the great *problems* of knowledge (possibility, origin, essence, classification and concepts and criteria of truth) from the senses, using sceptical, subjectivist, relativist, pragmatic, empirical, subjectivist, realist, monist, intuitive, transcendent philosophical assumptions, respectively.

In the *particular theory of the dialectical historical materialist social sciences,* it is assumed, from the senses, that reality moves. Phenomena are problematised in terms of combat, struggle, antagonism, pugnacity, opposition, anguish, predicament, etc. That is to say, privileging the *subjective*, reality and the dualism of subject and object (seeing reality in terms of opposing opposites).

The assumptions from which each and every one of the five main philosophical problems of knowledge (possibility, origin, essence, classification and concept and criterion of truth of knowledge) are solved in the particular theory of dialectical historical materialist social sciences are the following:

In the *particular theory of the dialectical historical materialist social sciences*, it is assumed, as in the general theories of knowledge of chaos and conflict, from the senses, that *reality* is very complex and very difficult to understand, due to the permanent conflict (struggle, debate, fight) in which the elements that make it up are found. The problem of the possibility of knowledge is solved on the basis of sceptical, subjectivist, relativist and pragmatic philosophical assumptions.

For example, in Marx (n/d: 182) one can read that *"...in the social production of their lives, men establish certain necessary relations independent of their will, relations of production, which correspond to a certain stage of development of their material productive forces. The totality of these relations of production forms the economic structure of society, the basis on which the legal and political superstructure is built and to which certain forms of social consciousness correspond. The mode of production of material life conditions the process of political and spiritual social life in general. It is not man's consciousness that determines his being, but, on the contrary, it is his social being that determines his consciousness".*

This discourse was constructed on the assumption that each subject can explore, describe, explain, interpret, understand, etc., his or her own reality (depending on his or her relations with other cognising subjects).

In the *particular theory of the dialectical historical materialist subjective social sciences*, it is assumed, as in the general theories of subjective knowledge (chaos and conflict), from the senses, that the origin of knowledge is to be found in sensations. It is believed that human beings (each one in particular) perceive reality differently from others. Each human being experiences the same sensations in a different way. A distinction is made between perception (which is universal) and representation (which is particular). The *problem* of the origin of knowledge is solved on the basis of *empirical* philosophical *assumptions*.

Marx (n/d: 182) also observes that *"...both juridical relations and forms of state cannot be understood in themselves or by the so-called general evolution of the human spirit, but lie, on the contrary, in the material conditions of life, the whole of which Hegel, following the precedent of the English and French of the 18th century, summarises under the name of <civil society>, and that the anatomy of civil society is to be sought in Political Economy.... "*.

This discourse was constructed on the assumption that the origin of knowledge is to be found in the experiences of the cognising subjects (the material conditions of life in civil society).

In the *particular theory of the dialectical historical materialist subjectivist social sciences*, it is assumed, as in general theories of subjective knowledge (chaos and conflict), from the senses, that (in a knowledge relation) the cognising subject determines the object to be known. It is presumed that if two cognizing subjects relate to the same object of knowledge, both will apprehend their object to be known in a totally different way; because their life history, feelings, emotions, passions, complexes, ambitions, etc. "contaminate" the object of study. "contaminate" the object of study. Science is not neutral, it obeys philosophical assumptions and ontological interests. The pre-metaphysical problem about the essence of knowledge is solved from subjectivist philosophical assumptions.

Dialectical historical materialism investigates human society, trying to do so without ideological assumptions, starting from empirical individuals and the relations they establish between them *"... the premises from which we start are not arbitrary, they are not dogmas, but real premises, from which it is only possible to abstract in the imagination. They are the real individuals, their action and their material conditions of life, both those they have already encountered and those engendered by their own action. These premises can therefore be verified purely empirically..."* (Karl Marx and Friedrich Engels (1886). *The German Ideology*).

This discourse was constructed on the assumption that, in a knowledge relationship, the cognising subject (the real individual) determines the object to be known (human society). Each individual feels and thinks differently, depending on his or her experiences. The social class (cognising subject) determines the type of acceptable discourse about society (object to be known).

In the *particular theory of the dialectical historical materialist subjective social sciences*, it is assumed, as in the general theories of knowledge of chaos and conflict, from the senses, that reality exists independently of whether or not it is apprehended by the cognising subjects. It is believed that the impressions of the objects that surround us impact our senses and produce sensations that different subjects perceive, but represent them differently. The metaphysical problem about the *essence* of knowledge is solved on the basis of realist philosophical assumptions.

It is assumed that the subject can reproduce the real concrete, the existing reality, by means of his perception, through his senses; and this reproduction is the constitution of, the formation of categories.

The definition of history, understood as "class struggle" and divided into modes of production (primitive communism, slavery, feudalism, capitalism, socialism and scientific communism) (Brom, 1975: 54-100), is constructed from reality, from the senses.

In the *particular theory of the dialectical historical materialist subjectivist social sciences*, it is assumed, as in the general theories of subjective knowledge (chaos and conflict), from the senses, that reality is divided into two opposing and mutually contradictory poles: master and slave, lord and deer, employer and worker, and so on. The theological problem of the *essence* of knowledge is resolved on the basis of *dualistic* philosophical *assumptions*.

In the particular theory of the dialectical historical materialist subjective social sciences, social facts are studied as if they were real (realism), with particular characteristics (subjectivism) but not absolute. The historical fact is momentary, transient and contradictory (relativism). Facts are in constant movement, in continuous transformation. Social reality is dialectical. Reasoning must be adapted to reality (subjectivism), not reality to reasoning (objectivism).

In the *particular theory of the dialectical historical materialist subjectivist social sciences*, it is assumed, as in the general theories of knowledge of chaos and conflict, from the senses, that the only kind of knowledge that a cognising subject can obtain of an object to be known is intuitive. It is considered that everything we know about reality was obtained by means of the senses. The problem of the *classification* of knowledge is solved on the basis of intuitive philosophical assumptions.

Knowledge is constructed on the basis of the object. The totality and concreteness is the structuring and reproduction that we can do intellectually aimed at the conceptualisation and categorisation of reality. But this is not achieved by simple perception, it is part of a process of continuous interaction between the subject and the object.

In the *particular theory of the dialectical historical materialist subjectivist social sciences*, it is assumed, as in the general theories of subjective knowledge (chaos and conflict), from the senses, that the *concepts* and *criteria* of truth of knowledge are transcendent. Truth is considered to be the concordance of thought with the object thought. Because it is assumed that the cognising subject is confronted with objects that have their own existence in reality. The problem of the concepts and criteria of truth of knowledge is solved on the basis of transcendent philosophical assumptions.

In the particular theory of the *dialectical historical materialist* subjectivist social sciences the materialist conception of reality, the particularity of the historical moment and the dynamicity of the dialectical movement are united. The following table shows the assumptions from which each and every one of the five main philosophical problems of knowledge are solved in the construction of the particular theory of the *dialectical historical materialist subjective social sciences*:

GENERAL THEORY OF SUBJECTIVE KNOWLEDGE	PHILOSOPHICAL PROBLEMS OF KNOWLEDGE						
	POSSIBILITY OF KNOWLEDGE	ORIGIN OF KNOWLEDGE	ESSENCE OF KNOWLEDGE			TYPE OF KNOWLEDGE	CONCEPT AND CRITERION OF TRUTH OF KNOWLEDGE
			SOLUTIONS				
			PRE-METAPHYSICAL SOLUTION	METAPHYSICAL SOLUTION	THEOLOGICAL SOLUTION		
	ASSUMPTIONS FROM WHICH KNOWLEDGE PROBLEMS CAN BE SOLVED						
HISTORICAL-DIALECTICAL MATERIALISM	ESCEP-TICIS-MO, SUBJECTIVISM, RELATIVISM AND PRAGMATISM	EMPIRISM	SUBJECTIVISM	REALISM	DUALISMO	INTUITIVE	TRASCENDENT

The *general theoretical foundations* for problematising their objects of study are mainly the *general theories of* objective *knowledge*, chaos and conflict.

2.3.5.2.3 The particular theories of dialectical social sciences.

The *particular theories of dialectical social sciences* are derived, like the general theories of analogical and complex dialectical knowledge, from *critical philosophical assumptions* (thus solving the problem of the possibility of knowledge); *intellectualist* and *apriorist* (thus solving the problem of the origin of knowledge); dialectical, phenomenological and monistic (thus solving the problem of the essence of knowledge with respect to the pre-metaphysical, metaphysical and theological solutions, respectively); mixed - with respect to the pre-metaphysical, metaphysical and theological solutions; *dialectical, phenomenological* and *monistic* (thus solving the problem about the essence of knowledge, as regards the pre-metaphysical, metaphysical and theological solutions, respectively); *mixed* - knowledge is both rational and intuitive - (thus solving the problem about the classification of knowledge); and *mixed* - concepts and criteria of truth must be both transcendent and immanent - (thus solving the problem about the concepts and criteria of truth of knowledge).

Two of the *particular dialectical social science theories* that solve each of the five major philosophical problems of knowledge on the basis of the above-mentioned assumptions are *phenomenological* and critical *hermeneutic* theories.

Just as the *general theories of dialectical knowledge* (analogy and complexity) were worked on, the analysis of the *particular theories of dialectical social sciences* (phenomenology and critical hermeneutics), in a first moment, will be carried out considering the definition, characteristics, function, purpose, classification, authors and works of each *particular theory of dialectical social sciences*; and, in a second moment, the philosophical *assumptions* from which each and every one of the five main philosophical *problems* of knowledge are solved will be taken into account: possibility, origin, essence, classification, and concepts and criteria of truth of knowledge.

It is necessary to recall again, for the purposes of this analysis, that the *classification* and the *names* assigned to each and every one of the *particular theories of the social sciences* analysed in this section obey the way in which one of the five main philosophical *problems* of knowledge is solved: the problem of the *essence* of knowledge. This philosophical problem of knowledge (the essence) was chosen and no other, because this difficulty of knowledge refers to the *relation* of knowledge that is established between the cognising *subject* and the *object* to be known.

It has already been made clear that, of the different philosophical *assumptions* from which the problem of the *essence* of knowledge can be solved and which can be found in three different *solutions* (pre-metaphysical, metaphysical and theological), we have chosen the *pre-metaphysical* solution, because this solution addresses the problem of the following question: *who determines whom in a relation of knowledge: the object to the subject, the subject to the object, or do the two determine each other?*

If *philosophy* determines *theory*, then *theory* depends on *philosophy*. If *we assume* that, in a relation of knowledge, the object determines the subject, then we can speak of *objective* theories. On the contrary, if we assume that, in a relation of knowledge, the subject determines the object, then we can speak of *subjective* theories. Finally, in the following cases, if we assume that, in a relation of knowledge, both elements of knowledge determine each other, then we can speak of *dialectical* theories.

So far we have analysed the particular theories of subjective social science (historicism and dialectical historical materialism). In this section we will analyse the third group of particular social science theories: the *particular dialectical social science theories* (phenomenology and critical hermeneutics).

It has already been said that *objective* theories are constructed from reason (objectivist), *subjective* theories from the senses (subjectivist) and *dialectical* theories from both qualities of the cognising subject: from reason and from the senses; being able to start first from reason and then from the senses (apriorism); or vice versa (intellectualism).

One of the *particular theories of the social sciences*, which starts from *critical* philosophical assumptions (possibility of knowing); *intellectualist* and/or *apriorist* (origin of knowledge); *dialectical*, and *monistic* and pantheistic (pre-metaphysical, metaphysical and theological solutions, respectively, to the problem of the essence of knowledge); *intuitive-rational* (type of knowledge);

and *transcendent-immanent* (criteria of truth), is the *phenomenological theory*.

2.3.5.2.3.1 Phenomenology.

Phenomenology is a particular theory of the dialectical social sciences that explores, describes, explains, interprets, understands, etc., reality, phenomena, facts, things, etc.; solving each and every one of the five main philosophical problems of knowledge from critical (possibility of knowledge), intellectualist and/or apriorist (origin of knowledge), dialectical, phenomenological and monistic (pre-metaphysical, meta-physical and theological solutions, respectively, to the problems of the essence of knowledge), mixed (rational intuitive) (classification of knowledge) and mixed (transcendent-immanent) (concept and criterion of truth of knowledge) assumptions.

Phenomenology is a theory because it explains, interprets, understands, etc., reality, phenomena, facts, things, etc.

Phenomenology is a particular theory of the social sciences because it explores, describes, explains, interprets, understands, etc., any social reality, phenomenon, fact, thing, etc., in the social sciences.

Phenomenology is a general theory of dialectical knowledge because it explains, interprets, understands, etc., any social reality, phenomenon, fact, thing, etc., from dialectical assumptions.

The term "phenomenology" assigned as a name to the theory is due to the philosophical assumption that gives it its origin: Kantian phenomenalism. Another great developer of the theory is Edmund Gustav Albrecht Husserl.

The explorations, descriptions, explanations, interpretations, comprehensions, etc., which, about reality, phenomena, events, things, etc., are made in *phenomenological* theory, are made, as already mentioned, solving the great philosophical problems of knowledge (possibility, origin, essence, classification and concepts and criteria of truth) from critical *assumptions*; intellectualist and/or apriorist; dialectic, phenomenalist, and monist; mixed <intuitive - rational>; and mixed <transcendent - immanent>; respectively.

In the *particular theory of the phenomenological dialectical social sciences*, it is assumed, from reason and the senses (Kantian apriorism), that knowledge is possible (dogmatism), but not in essence (scepticism), because each cognising subject feels and thinks differently from others (subjectivism), because truth changes in time, space and circumstances (relativism), and because every discourse that is elaborated on a certain object of knowledge must be useful to humanity (pragmatism). The problem of the *possibility* of knowledge is solved on the basis of critical philosophical *assumptions*.

Phenomenology describes the different types of experiences, their genres and species, and the essential relations between them. Consciousness is not limited to knowledge: perception, memory, imagination, thought, love, hatred, desire, willing, etc. are different forms of the living of consciousness (criticality).

In the *particular theory of the dialectical phenomenological social sciences*, it is assumed, from both qualities of the cognising subject: reason and senses (first reason and then senses), that the origin of knowledge is to be found both in the senses and in the reason of the cognising subject. The *problem* of the origin of knowledge is solved on the basis of apriorist philosophical assumptions (first we think and then we feel).

In contrast to empiricist currents, phenomenology is not limited to the perceptual world, but also to reason. Mental structures precede experience. Mental structures filter experience. If two people have different structures, then their experiences will be different.

In the *particular theory of the dialectical phenomenological social sciences*, it is assumed, from reason and the senses, that in a relation of knowledge, the cognising *subject* determines the *object* to be known and, in turn, the object to be known determines the cognising subject. This dialectical relation between the cognising subject and the object to be known determines that the pre-metaphysical problem of the essence of knowledge is resolved on the basis of dialectical philosophical assumptions.

Phenomenological (appearance) *theory* aims to study the phenomena thrown into consciousness, i.e. the essences of things. It studies the relationship between the facts (phenomena) and the sphere in which they become present (psyche, consciousness). It is the study of the different ways in which things appear or manifest themselves in consciousness.

In the *particular theory of the dialectical phenomenological social sciences*, it is assumed, from reason and the senses, that reality exists (realism), but that the subjects apprehend it in a different way (subjective idealism), as it is presented to the limitations of our reason and our senses; that is, the object to be known is presented to the different cognising subjects, as a phenomenon, as an appearance. It is believed that the impressions of the objects that surround us impact our senses and produce sensations that different subjects perceive, but that they represent them differently and, moreover, as phantoms, as phenomena, in time and space. The metaphysical *problem* about the *essence* of knowledge is solved on the basis of *phenomenalist* philosophical *assumptions*.

The object of knowledge does not exist outside the consciousness of the subject; the object is discovered and recreated as a result of the intentionality of the intuition directed towards it. There is no object without a subject; that is, consciousness is intentional (Husserl, 1995).

In the *particular theory of the dialectical phenomenological social sciences*, it is assumed, on the basis of reason and the senses, that reality is unique. The theological problem of the essence of knowledge is solved on the basis of monistic philosophical assumptions.

Reality is unique but complex, its essence cannot be known; the only thing that the cognising subject can do is to explore it, describe it, explain it, interpret it, understand it, etc., by means of his reason and his senses.

In the *particular theory of the dialectical phenomenological social sciences*, it is assumed, from reason and from the senses, that the type of knowledge that a cognising subject can obtain of an object to be known is *mixed* (rational-intuitive). It is considered that everything we know about reality was obtained by means of reason (first) and the senses (later). The problem of the *classification* of knowledge is solved on the basis of *mixed* philosophical assumptions (rational-intuitive).

Consciousness is the realm where reality, the phenomenon, is made present or shown (the extent to which reality is made present or shown in consciousness). The extent to which reality is made present in our consciousness is deliberate, intentional.

In the *particular theory of the dialectical phenomenological social sciences*, it is assumed, on the basis of reason and the senses, that the *concepts* and *criteria* of truth of knowledge are *mixed* (immanent-transcendent). The truth of knowledge is considered to be the concordance of thought with the object thought and of thought with itself. For it is assumed that the cognising subject is confronted both with objects that have their own existence in reality and with ideal objects, which exist only in the mind of the cognising subject. The problem of concepts and criteria of truth is solved on the basis of mixed philosophical assumptions (immanent-transcendent).

The following table shows the philosophical *assumptions* from which each and every one of the five main philosophical problems of knowledge are solved in the construction of the *particular theory of the phenomenological dialectical social sciences*:

GENERAL THEORY OF DIALECTICAL KNOWLEDGE	PHILOSOPHICAL PROBLEMS OF KNOWLEDGE						
	POSSIBILITY OF KNOWLEDGE	ORIGIN OF KNOWLEDGE	ESSENCE OF KNOWLEDGE			TYPE OF KNOWLEDGE	CONCEPT AND CRITERION OF TRUTH OF KNOWLEDGE
			SOLUTIONS				
			PRE-METAPHYSICAL SOLUTION	METAPHYSICAL SOLUTION	THEOLOGICAL SOLUTION		
	ASSUMPTIONS FROM WHICH TO SOLVE KNOWLEDGE PROBLEMS						
PHENOMENOLOGY	CRITICISM	APRIORISM	DIALECTICS	PHENOMENALISM	MONISM	MIXED	MIXED

The general theories of dialectical knowledge (analogy and complexity) can serve as theoretical foundations in the construction of the objects of study of the *particular theory of the phenomenological dialectical social sciences*, because they start from the same philosophical assumptions to solve each and every one of the five main problems of knowledge.

2.3.5.2.3.1 Critical hermeneutics.

Another particular theory of dialectical social science, which, like phenomenology, starts from critical philosophical assumptions (possibility of knowing); intellectualist (origin of knowledge); dialectical, phenomenalist and monistic and pantheistic (pre-metaphysical, metaphysical and theological solutions, respectively, to the problem of the essence of knowledge); intuitive-rational (type of knowledge); and transcendent-immanent (concepts and criteria of truth of knowledge), is *critical hermeneutics*.

The philosophical difference between phenomenology and *critical hermeneutics* is one of order: while in phenomenology we first think and then we feel (Kantian apriorism), in *critical hermeneutics* we first feel and then we think (Aristotelian intellectualism).

The main proponents of critical hermeneutics are the Germans Jurgen Habermas and Karl Otto Apel.

Critical hermeneutics is a theory because it explains, interprets, understands, etc. reality, phenomena, facts, things, etc.

Critical hermeneutics is a particular theory of the social sciences because it explains, interprets, understands, etc., any social reality, phenomenon, fact, thing, etc., of a social kind.

Critical hermeneutics is a particular theory of dialectical social sciences because it explains, interprets, understands, etc., any social reality, phenomenon, fact, thing, etc., from dialectical philosophical assumptions.

The explorations, descriptions, explanations, interpretations, comprehensions, etc., which, about reality, phenomena, events, things, etc., are carried out in *critical hermeneutics*, are done by solving the great problems of knowledge (possibility, origin, essence, classification and concepts and criteria of truth) from both qualities of the cognising subject: reason and the senses (first the senses work and then reason), using critical philosophical assumptions; intellectualist; dialectical, phenomenological, and monistic; mixed <intuitive - rational>; and mixed <transcendent - immanent>; respectively.

In *critical hermeneutics*, it is assumed, from the senses and reason (Aristotelian intellectualism), as in phenomenalism, that knowledge is possible (dogmatism), but not in essence (scepticism), because each cognising subject feels and thinks differently from others (subjectivism), because truth changes in time, space and circumstances (relativism), and because any discourse that is developed about a certain object of knowledge must be useful to humanity (pragmatism). The problem of the possibility of knowledge is solved on the basis of critical philosophical assumptions.

In *critical hermeneutics*, it is assumed, from the senses and reason (first the senses and then reason), that the origin of knowledge is to be found both in the senses and in the reason of the cognising subject. The problem of the origin of knowledge is solved on the basis of intellectualist philosophical assumptions (first we sense and then we weigh).

In *critical hermeneutics*, it is assumed, from the senses and reason, that in a relation of knowledge, the cognising subject determines the object to be known and, in turn, the object to be known determines the cognising subject. This dialectical relationship between the cognising subject and the object to be known determines that the pre-metaphysical problem of the essence of knowledge is resolved on the basis of dialectical philosophical assumptions.

In *critical hermeneutics*, it is assumed, from the senses and reason, that reality exists (realism), but that subjects apprehend it in a different way (subjective idealism), as it is presented to us within the limitations of our senses and our reason; that is, the object to be known is presented to the different cognising subjects as a phenomenon, as an appearance. It is believed that the impressions of the objects that surround us impact our senses and produce sensations that different subjects perceive, but that they represent them differently and, moreover, as phantoms, as phenomena, in time and space. The metaphysical problem about the *essence* of knowledge is solved on the basis of phenomenalist philosophical assumptions.

In *critical hermeneutics*, it is assumed, on the basis of the senses and reason, that reality is unique. The theological problem of the *essence* of knowledge is solved on the basis of monistic philosophical assumptions.

In *critical hermeneutics*, it is assumed, from the senses and reason, that the type of knowledge that a cognising subject can obtain of an object to be known is mixed (intuitive-rational). It is considered that everything we know about reality, we obtained by means of the senses (first) and reason (later). The problem about the classification of knowledge is solved on the basis of mixed philosophical assumptions (intuitive-rational).

In *critical hermeneutics*, it is assumed, on the basis of the senses and reason, that the concepts and criteria of truth of knowledge are *mixed* (transcendent-immanent). The truth of knowledge is considered to be the concordance of thought with the object thought and of thought with itself. For it is assumed that the cognising subject is confronted both with objects that have their own existence in reality and with ideal objects, which exist only in the mind of the cognising subject. The problem of the concepts and criteria of truth of knowledge is solved on the basis of mixed (transcendent-immanent) philosophical assumptions.

The following table shows the assumptions from which each and every one of the five main philosophical problems of knowledge are solved in the construction of *critical hermeneutics*:

GENERAL THEORY OF DIALECTICAL KNOWLEDGE	PHILOSOPHICAL PROBLEMS OF KNOWLEDGE						
	POSIBILIDAD OF KNOWLEDGE	ORIGIN OF KNOWLEDGE	ESSENCE OF KNOWLEDGE **SOLUTIONS**			TYPE OF KNOWLEDGE	CONCEP TO Y CRITE RIO DE TRUTH OF KNOWLEDGE TO
			SOLU-CION PRE META-FISCA	SOLUCION TARGET PHYSICS	SOLUCION TEO LOGICA		
	ASSUMPTIONS FROM WHICH KNOWLEDGE PROBLEMS CAN BE SOLVED						
CRITICAL HERMENEUTICS	CRITICISM	INTELEC-TUALISM	DIALECTICS	FENO MENA LISMO	MONISM	MIXED	MIXED

So much for *critical hermeneutics*.

The following synoptic table shows some of the main *particular theories of the objective, subjective* and *dialectical social sciences*, respectively, that were analysed philosophically and the respective assumptions from which they solve each of the five main problems of knowledge:

PARTICULAR THEORY OF	PHILOSOPHICAL PROBLEMS OF KNOWLEDGE			
	POSSIBILITY OF	ORIGIN OF KNOWLEDGE	ESSENCE OF KNOWLEDGE **SOLUTIONS**	CONCEPT AND

SOCIAL SCIENCES	KNOWLEDGE		PRE-METAPHYSICAL SUN	METAPHYSICAL SOLUTION	THEOLOGICAL SOLUTION	TYPE OF KNOWLEDGE	CRITERION OF TRUTH OF KNOWLEDGE
	ASSUMPTIONS ON THE BASIS OF WHICH KNOWLEDGE PROBLEMS CAN BE SOLVED						
POSITIVISM	**DOGMATISM**	**RATIONALISM**	**OBJECTIVISM**	**IDEALISM**	**DUALISM**	**RATIONAL**	**IMMANENT**
FUNCTIONALISM	**DOGMATISM**	**RATIONALISM**	**OBJECTIVISM**	**IDEALISM**	**DUALISM**	**RATIONAL**	**IMMANENT**
STRUCTU-RALISM	**DOGMATISM**	**RATIONALISM**	**OBJECTIVISM**	**IDEALISM**	**DUALISM**	**RATIONAL**	**IMMANENT**
SYSTEMS	**DOGMATISM**	**RATIONALISM**	**OBJECTIVISM**	**IDEALISM**	**DUALISM**	**RATIONAL**	**IMMANENT**
HISTORICISM	SCEPTICISM, SUBJECTIVISM AND PRAGMATISM	EMPIRISM	SUBJECTIVISM	REALISM	DUALISM	INTUITIVE	TRACENDY
MATERIALIS MO HISTORICODIAL ECTICAL	SCEPTICISM, SUBJECTIVISM AND PRAGMATISM	EMPIRISM	SUBJECTIVISM	REALISM	DUALISM	INTUITIVE	TRACENDY
PHENOMENOLOGY	**CRITICISM**	**APIORISM**	**DIALECTICS**	**PHENOMENOLOGY**	**MONISM**	**MIXED**	**MIXED**
CRITICAL HERMENEUTICS	**CRITICISM**	**INTELLECTUALISM**	**DIALECTICS**	**PHENOMENOLOGY**	**MONISM**	**MIXED**	**MIXED**

The *particular theories of the objective, subjective and dialectical social sciences* that have just been analysed constitute the particular theoretical foundation for problematising the objects of study of the specific theories of the educational sciences that seek to explore, describe, explain, interpret, understand, etc., the educational reality.

2.3.5.3 *The philosophical relationship between general theories of knowledge and particular theories of the social sciences.*

Certain similarities and differences can be established between general theories of knowledge and particular theories of social science.

2.3.5.3.1 philosophical differences between general theories of knowledge and particular theories of the social sciences:

- General theories of knowledge try to explore, describe, explain, interpret, understand, etc., any fact, phenomenon, event, thing, occurrence, etc., be it natural, social or ideal. On the other hand, the particular theories of the social sciences, as their name indicates, deal only with social problems.

- General theories of knowledge can serve as a theoretical foundation for the construction of the objects of study of the particular theories of the social sciences.

- Particular theories of social science derive from general theories of knowledge because they solve each of the five main problems of knowledge from the same philosophical assumptions.

2.3.5.3.3.2 Philosophical similarities between general theories of knowledge and particular theories of the social sciences.

-Both types of theories need to solve each of the five main problems of knowledge on the basis of certain philosophical assumptions.

-The philosophical assumptions from which the two types of theories solve each of the five main problems of knowledge allow them to be classified as objective, subjective and mixed.

-The general theories of objective, subjective and dialectical knowledge and the particular theories of objective, subjective and dialectical social sciences, respectively, start from the same philosophical assumptions to construct their objects of study.

The following table shows schematically the relationship between the general theories of knowledge and the particular theories of the social sciences:

GENERAL THEORIES OF KNOWLEDGE			PARTICULAR THEORIES OF SOCIAL SCIENCES		
OBJECTIVES	MATHEMATICIS M	THE OBJECT DETERMINES TO THE SUBJECT	OBJECTIVES	POSITIVISM	THE OBJECT DETERMINES THE SUBJECT
	MECHANISM			FUNCTIONALISM	
				ESTRUCTURALIS	
	ORGANISM			MO SYSTEMS	
SUBJECTIVE S	CHAOS	THE SUBJECT DETERMINES THE OBJECT	SUBJECTIVE S	HISTORICISM	THE SUBJECT DETERMINES THE OBJECT
	CONFLICT			HISTORICAL- DIALECTICAL MATERIALISM	
DIALECTICS	ANALOGY	BOTH ELEMENTS OF THE KNOWLEDGE RELATIONSHI P MUTUALLY DETERMINE EACH OTHER	DIALEC TICAS	PHENOMENOLOG Y	BOTH ELEMENTS OF THE KNOWLEDGE RELATIONSHI P MUTUALLY DETERMINE EACH OTHER
	COMPLEXITY			CRITICAL HERMENEUTICS	

2.3.5.4 *The specific theories of educational sciences.*

The *particular theories of the social sciences*, which have just been described, constitute the foundation for problematising the objects of study of the *specific theories of the educational sciences* that seek to explore, describe, explain, understand, interpret, etc., the educational reality.

The *specific theories of the educational sciences*, depending on the general and particular theoretical foundations of the social sciences, from which they start to problematise their objects of study, study educational phenomena on the basis of objective, subjective or dialectical philosophical assumptions.

The *particular theories of the social sciences* explore, describe, explain, interpret, etc., social phenomena, facts, events, etc., of a social nature. The educational sciences are social sciences because their object of study is the social human being.

As already mentioned, the classification of science proposed in this paper goes from the general to the particular: general theories of knowledge, particular theories of social sciences (already discussed), and *specific theories of educational sciences* (to be discussed in this section).

The criterion for classifying *theories specific to the educational sciences* will be the same as that adopted for classifying general theories of knowledge and the particular theories of the social sciences: theories that explore, describe, explain, interpret, etc. social reality from the standpoint of reason, and which therefore resolve each and every one of the five main philosophical problems of knowledge from dogmatic assumptions, will be analysed first.

(possibility of knowledge), rational (origin of knowledge), objectivist, idealist and dualist (pre-metaphysical, metaphysical and theological solutions, respectively, to the problem of the essence of knowledge), rational (types of knowledge) and immanent (concepts and criteria of truth of knowledge). We will call these theories *specific theories of the objective sciences of education*; in attention to the agreed classification criterion, the way they solve the following question: who determines whom in a knowledge relation: the object to the subject, the subject to the object, or both determine each other?

Then the *specific theories of the objective sciences of education* that explore, describe, explain, interpret, etc. will be analysed, social reality, from the senses, and which, by the same token, solve each and every one of the five main philosophical problems of knowledge, from *sceptical, subjectivist, relativist* and *pragmatic* (possibility of knowledge), *empiricist* (origin of knowledge), *subjectivist, realist* and *dualist* (pre-metaphysical, metaphysical and theological solutions, respectively, to the problems of the essence of knowledge), *intuitive* (types of knowledge) and *transcendental* (concepts and criteria of truth of knowledge) assumptions. We will call these theories *specific theories of the subjective sciences of education*, according to the classification criterion already indicated.

Finally, the *specific theories of the educational sciences* that explore, describe, explain, interpret, etc., will be analysed, social reality, from *reason* and the *senses*, and which, by the same token, solve each and every one of the five main philosophical problems of knowledge from *critical* (possibility of knowledge), *intellectualist* and/or *apriorist* (origin of knowledge), *dialectical, phenomenological* and *monistic* (pre-metaphysical, metaphysical and theological solutions, respectively, to the problem of the essence of knowledge), *mixed* (types of knowledge) and *mixed* (concepts and criteria of truth of knowledge) assumptions. We will call these theories *specific theories of the dialectical sciences of education*; for the same reason of classification already mentioned.

The analysis, as it was done with the general theories of objective knowledge and with the particular theories of objective social sciences, will be carried out, in a first moment, considering the definition, characteristics, function, purpose, classification, authors and works of each *particular theory of objective social sciences*; in a second moment, the philosophical *assumptions* from which each and every one of the five main *problems* of knowledge are solved will be taken into account: possibility, origin, essence, classification, and concepts and criteria of truth of knowledge; and, finally, the following problems will be analysed: goals of education, concept of learning, role of the teacher, concept of the learner, motivation, methodology of teaching and evaluation.

2.3.5.4.1 The specific theories of the objective sciences of education.

The *specific theories of the objective sciences of education* explore, describe, explain, interpret, understand, etc., the educational reality from *reason*. Therefore, the philosophical assumptions from which they solve each and every one of the five main problems of knowledge are *dogmatism* (possibility of knowledge), *rationalism* (origin of knowledge), *objectivism, idealism* and *dualism* (pre-metaphysical, metaphysical and theological solutions, respectively, to the problem of the essence of knowledge), *rational* (type of knowledge) and *immanent* (concepts and criteria of truth of knowledge).

The *specific theories of the objective sciences of education* explore, describe, explain, interpret, understand, etc., the educational reality, comparing it with a logical-mathematical ideal, with a machine, with a living organism, with a structure, with a cybernetic system, etc. The objects of educational study are constructed using *reason* and, therefore, from the philosophical assumptions mentioned above.

The *specific theories of the objective sciences of education* resemble the general theories of objective knowledge (mathematicism, mechanicism and organicism) and the particular theories of the objective social sciences (positivism, functionalism, structuralism and systems). The philosophical *assumptions* from which both theories solve each of the five main *problems* of knowledge are the same.

The only difference that can be observed between the three classifications of theory is one of degree. The general theories of objective knowledge explore, describe, explain, interpret, etc., any phenomenon, whether factual (natural or social) or formal (logical-mathematical); the particular theories of the objective social sciences deal only with social phenomena; and the specific theories of the objective sciences of education, with educational social phenomena.

A *specific theory of the objective sciences of education* that is analysed in this section is: *behaviourism.*

2.3.5.4.1.1 Behaviourism.

Behaviourism can be *defined*, from reason, as a *specific theory of the objective sciences of education* in which educational reality is compared to a mathematical logical ideal, to a machine, to a living organism, to a structure, to a cybernetic system, etc. Educational phenomena are explored, described, explained, interpreted, understood, etc., from the point of view of a *must be* (idea).

As stated in previous pages, the mathematical theory (from the formal sciences: logic and mathematics), together with mechanicism (from the factual sciences: physics and chemistry) and organicism (from the factual sciences: biology), according to Mario Bunge's classification (1977), are transplanted to the social sciences.

In other words, for its study, social reality will have to be compared with a mathematical ideal, with a machine or with a living organism; in other words, the objects of social study will have to be constructed from dogmatic philosophical assumptions (possibility of knowing); rationalist (origin of knowledge); objectivist, idealist and dualist and theistic (pre-metaphysical, metaphysical and theological solutions, respectively, to the problem of the essence of knowledge); rational (types of knowledge); and immanent (criteria of truth of knowledge).

In turn, the particular theories of the social sciences (positivist, functionalist, structuralist, systemic, among others), served as a basis for the development of specific theories in the field of psychology, which have been applied to explore, describe, explain, interpret, understand, etc., the educational phenomenon. One of them is *behaviourism*.

Behaviourism assumes that human *behaviour* can be studied objectively, away from subjective speculations and ambiguities (Guzmán, Jesús Carlos and Gerardo Hernández Rojas; 1993: 13).

Behaviourism is a *theory* because it explores, describes, explains, interprets, understands, etc., *behaviour*.

Behaviour must be observable so that it can be measured, quantified and eventually reproduced under controlled conditions.

Behaviourism is a *theory specific to the educational sciences* because, although it originates in psychology, it can be used to explore, describe, explain, interpret, understand, etc., educational *behaviour*. Psychology is one of the sciences that has had the greatest influence on education.

Behaviourism assumes that interactions between the *behaviour* of individuals and environmental events can be identified in a functional way: as one element changes, the other changes as well. The cause of everything is the environment.

Behaviourism is a *specific theory of the objective sciences of education* because it can be used to explore, describe, explain, interpret, understand, etc., the educational reality from the reason of the subject who constructs the theory; assuming that, in a knowledge relationship, the object to be known determines the cognising subject (objectivism).

In *behaviourist* theory it is assumed that human behaviour is subject to laws (dogmatism). It is assumed that these dogmas can be discovered by means of reason (rationalism). It is believed that by using the same method as the natural sciences: the scientific method (inductive-deductive), the laws or dogmas that regulate human *behaviour* can be discovered. It is presumed that if the laws of *behaviour* can be known, then behaviour can be predicted and controlled.

The fact that in *behaviourism* the educational reality is compared with an ideal means that, of all the capacities that the subject has to generate new knowledge (addition, subtraction, multiplication, division, analysis, synthesis, induction, deduction, comparison, classification, definition, etc.), comparison is being used, preferably, to put order in reality.

That in *behaviourism* the educational reality to be explored, described, explained, interpreted, understood, etc., is compared to an ideal, means that reason, which is the quality of the subject being used to explain reality, assumes, or wants to assume in order to order phenomena, that it must not move, that it must remain forever and ever fixed, eternally immobile (dogmatism).

In *behaviourism*, as in the general theories of objective knowledge (mathematicism, mechanicism and organicism) and the particular theories of objective social sciences (positivism, functionalism, structuralism, systems theory, etc.) the philosophical problem of the possibility of knowledge is solved by reason, by means of dogmatic assumptions. It is believed that if there are general and universal laws that regulate behaviour and if these dogmas can be discovered by reason, then it is possible to know human behaviour in order to predict and control it.

A characteristic of the *behaviourist* view of educational reality is that it seeks to explain social phenomena by means of the laws of nature. Social facts (and with them educational facts) are understood and interpreted by analogy with an ideal, as if they were natural phenomena. It is assumed, from reason, that the only authentic knowledge is scientific knowledge (dogmatism), and that such knowledge can only arise from the positive affirmation of theories, through the scientific method.

This ontological determinism makes it possible to assume, on the basis of reason, that in social reality (and therefore also in education) there is an established order (rationalism) (by God, reason or the history of peoples), which human reason discovers through reflection. It is assumed, or one wants to assume, because it suits certain interests, that in social (educational) reality, in general, there is an order, pre-established rules of the game; that they are eternal and immutable, given forever and ever (dogmatism).

Behaviourism, like the general theories of objective knowledge (mathematicism, mechanicism and organicism) and the particular theories of objective social sciences (positivism, functionalism, structuralism, systems theory, etc.) only *works* when each part is integrated in the right place and complements the others in order to continue to fulfil the same function (rationalism).

The function of *behaviourism*, like that of the general theories of objective knowledge (mathematicism, mechanicism and organicism) and the particular theories of objective social sciences (positivism, functionalism, structuralism, systems theory, etc.) is the discovery of laws that are simple and unalterable, which must explain a set of elements that are simple and unalterable (dogmatism).

According to *behaviourist* theory, the goals of education are: to control human behaviour, to transmit cultural patterns and innovation of these patterns, and to develop the potential of the human organism to the maximum extent possible (rationalism).

According to *behaviourist* theory, we can only know what science allows us to know; and the only method of knowledge is that of the natural sciences (inductive-deductive).

Learning is explained as the relatively permanent modification of the observable behaviour of organisms as a result of experience. The ought to be (reason) putting order in the being (passion). In *behaviourism* the problem of the origin of knowledge is solved on the basis of rationalist philosophical assumptions.

In *behaviourist* theory - applied to the exploration, description, explanation, interpretation, understanding, etc., of human behaviour in society and, therefore, of education - the object (the idea, the instituted, the institutions, etc., constructed by certain subjects, assuming, from reason, that reality does not move) determines the subject. It is assumed, or one wants to assume, from reason that, in a relation of knowledge, the object determines the subject. That human beings, as subjects in themselves, are less important than institutions, that only within the institution (object) do their lives make sense. The word objective is derived, in ontological and epistemological terms, from the word object of knowledge.

The pupil is the "object" of the educational act. It is like an "empty pitcher" to be "filled" with the "waters of wisdom" of the teacher. It is the object (the educational contents) determined to the subject (the pupil). In *behaviourism* the pre-metaphysical problem about the essence of knowledge is solved from objectivist philosophical assumptions.

In the interpretation of social (and therefore also educational) reality, from the *behaviourist theory*, as well as in the general theories of objective knowledge (mathematics, mechanicism and organicism) and the particular theories of objective social sciences (positivism, functionalism, structuralism, systems theory, etc.), it is assumed, or it is wanted to be assumed (from certain rationalities and because it may be convenient for certain interests), that the subject is due to the object; that what is important is the whole, not the part; that the parts are due to the object.), it is assumed, or it is assumed (from certain rationalities and because it may suit certain interests), that the subject owes the object; that what is important is the whole, not the part; that the parts owe the whole; that the reason for the existence of the parts is the conservation, preservation and enhancement of the whole; that what must be preserved are the *institutions* (ideas) to which the *subjects* are indebted.

The method of natural science (discovery of causal laws and their control over facts) is not only applied to the study of nature, but also to the study of society (epistemological monism).

In *behaviourist* theory, explorations, descriptions, explanations, interpretations, understandings, etc. about human behaviour in society are constructed by solving the metaphysical problem of the essence of knowledge, using *idealistic* philosophical ass*umptions*. It is *assumed* that the studied reality (the *object* to be known) exists independently of whether there is a *cognising subject* who is interested in knowing it or not.

That is why the teaching methodology proposed by behaviourism mainly contains the following tasks:
- The teacher develops instructional objectives.
- Tasks are analysed.
- Pre-currents are identified.
- Instructional materials and techniques are designed and/or selected.
- New responses are taught through verbal instruction, shaping, demonstration or discovery (learning by doing).

In *behaviourism*, the metaphysical problem of the essence of knowledge is solved on the basis of idealistic philosophical assumptions. The metaphysical part means that we place ourselves above reality and assume that reality exists independently of the cognising subject.

In *behaviourist* theory, explorations, descriptions, explanations, interpretations, understandings, etc. about human *behaviour* in society are constructed by solving the theological problem about the essence of knowledge, using dualistic philosophical assumptions. The reality under study (the *object* to be known) is considered to be divided into two opposing and irreconcilable poles: students who pass and those who fail, good and bad teachers, those who are punctual and those who are unpunctual, etc.

The role of the teacher is to be a "technologist of education", a director and controller of the learning process, a behavioural engineer. The teacher is the one who "knows" and the pupil is the one who "does not know".

The type of knowledge that is constructed, in *behaviourist* theory, is rational. It is assumed, from reason, that the only true knowledge is that which is born of the reflection of the human soul.

When the "to be" wants to influence the "to be", incentives and rewards (material or social) are given. This is why behavioural motivation is extrinsic: the aim is for pupils to assimilate the "good news" of the system. It is reason bringing order to passion.

In *behaviourism*, the problem of the classification of knowledge is solved, from reason, using rationalist philosophical assumptions.

The concepts and criteria of truth of knowledge that are constructed in *behaviourist* theory are immanent. It is assumed, from reason, that truth is the concordance of thought with itself, not with reality. Cognitive subjects are confronted with ideal, mental objects of knowledge, entities created by certain rationalities, which have no existence, properly speaking, in material reality.

It is about knowing in order to control and controlling in order to dominate, both nature and society.

That is why the evaluation proposed in behaviourism is based on the application of objective instruments. The aim is for the subjects to assimilate the given objects of knowledge.

In behaviourism, the problem of the concept and the criterion of truth of knowledge is solved, from reason, on the basis of immanent philosophical assumptions.

Behaviourist theory can serve purposes such as the following: to realise the "ideals" of certain rationalities of particular subjects or groups, regardless of the differences (economic, political, social, etc.) between the constituent parts.

In order to study educational reality, we must start from *philosophical assumptions* that imply order, harmony, stillness, etc. (dogmatic, rationalist, objectivist, idealist, etc.).

The general theoretical foundations of knowledge (mathematical, mechanistic and organicist) and those particular to the social sciences (positivism, functionalism, structuralism, systems theory, etc.) are very useful to reinforce the problematisation of the objects of study carried out using *behaviourist* theory.

The following table shows the philosophical assumptions from which each and every one of the five main problems of knowledge are solved in the construction of *behaviourist* theory:

SPECIFIC THEORY OF EDUCATIONAL SCIENCES	PHILOSOPHICAL PROBLEMS OF KNOWLEDGE						
	POSSIBILITY OF KNOWLEDGE	ORIGIN OF KNOWLEDGE	ESSENCE OF KNOWLEDGE SOLUTIONS			TYPE OF KNOWLEDGE	CONCEPT AND CRITERION OF TRUTH OF KNOWLEDGE
			PRE-METAPHYSICAL SOLUTION	METAPHYSICAL SOLUTION	THEOLOGICAL SOLUTION		
	ASSUMPTIONS FROM WHICH TO SOLVE THE PROBLEMS OF THE KNOWLEDGE						
CONDUCTISM	DOGMATISM	RATIONALISM	OBJECTIVISM	IDEALISM	DUALISM	RATIONAL	IMMANENT

2.3.5.4.4.2 Theories specific to the subjective sciences of education.

The *specific theories of the subjective sciences of education* are derived, like the general theories of subjective knowledge (chaos, conflict, etc.) and the particular theories of the subjective social sciences (historicism, historical-dialectical materialism, etc.), of sceptical, subjectivist, relativist and pragmatic philosophical assumptions (thus solving the problem of the possibility of knowledge); empiricists (thus solving the problem of the origin of knowledge); subjectivists, realists and dualists (thus solving the problem of the essence of knowledge as regards the pre-metaphysical, metaphysical and theological solutions, respectively); intuitionists (thus solving the problem of the classification of knowledge); and transcendentalists (thus solving the problem of the concepts and criteria of truth of knowledge).

Some *specific theories of the subjective sciences of education* that solve each of the five major philosophical problems of sense-knowledge on the basis of the above-mentioned assumptions are psychoanalysis, humanism and cognoscitivism. As the *behaviourist theory* was worked on, the analysis of the *specific theories of the subjective sciences of education* (psychoanalysis, humanism and cognoscitivism), will be carried out, in a first moment, considering the definition, characteristics, function, purpose, classification, authors and works of each *specific theory of the subjective sciences of education*; in a second moment, the philosophical assumptions from which each and every one of the five main philosophical problems of knowledge are solved will be taken into account: possibility, origin, essence, classification, and concepts and criteria of truth of knowledge; and, finally, the following problems will be analysed: goals of education, concept of learning, role of the teacher, concept of the learner, motivation, methodology of teaching and evaluation.

It is necessary to remember, for the purposes of this analysis, that the *classification* and the *names* assigned to each and every one of the *specific theories of the subjective sciences of education* that are analysed in this section, obey the way in which one of the five main philosophical problems of knowledge is solved: the problem of the essence of knowledge. This philosophical problem of knowledge (the essence) was chosen and no other, because this difficulty of knowledge refers to the *relation* of knowledge that is established between the cognising subject and the object to be known.

It has already been made clear that, of the different philosophical assumptions from which the problem of the *essence* of knowledge can be solved and which can be found in three different solutions (pre-metaphysical, metaphysical and theological), we have chosen the pre-metaphysical solution, because this solution addresses the problem of the following question: *who determines whom in a relation of knowledge: the object to the subject, the subject to the object, or do the two determine each other?*

If philosophy determines theory, then theory depends on philosophy. If we assume that, in a relation of knowledge, the object determines the subject, then we can speak of objective theories. On the contrary, if we suppose that, in a relation of knowledge, the subject determines the object, then we can speak of *subjective* theories. Finally, if we assume that, in a relation of knowledge, both elements of knowledge determine each other, then we can speak of dialectical theories.

So far we have analysed one of the theories specific to the objective sciences of education (behaviourism). In this section we will analyse the second group of theories specific to the educational sciences: *theories specific to the subjective sciences of education* (psychoanalysis, humanism and cognitivism). Subsequently, two of the specific theories of the dialectical sciences of education will be analysed: genetic theory (Piaget) and socio-cultural theory.

It has already been said that objective theories are constructed from reason (objectivist), *subjective* theories from the senses (subjectivist) and dialectical theories from both qualities of the cognising subject: from reason and from the senses; being able to start first from reason and then from the senses; or vice versa.

2.3.5.4.4.2.1 Psychoanalysis.

Psychoanalysis is a specific theory of the subjective sciences of education that explores, describes, explains, interprets, understands, etc., from the senses, the teaching reality, educational phenomena, school facts, the formative thing, etc. from the senses, through subjective (possibility of knowledge), empirical (origin of knowledge), subjectivist (pre-metaphysical solution to the problem of the essence of knowledge), realist (metaphysical solution to the problem of the essence of knowledge), dualist (theological solution to the problem of the essence of knowledge), intuitive (type of knowledge) and transcendent (concept and criterion of truth of knowledge) philosophical assumptions.

Psychoanalysis is "... *both a technique of psychotherapy and a theory of personality created by Sigmund Freud in an attempt to solve the problems presented by psychopathological behaviour...*" (Guzmán, Jesús Carlos and Gerardo Hernández Rojas; 1993: 59).

In the field of education, Freud influenced A. S. Neill (creator of the Sumerhill school in England), the precursor of the "active school", which aims to train for freedom, love, respect and non-coercion towards pupils. The autonomy and independence of the pupil is encouraged. Students are autonomous and independent to enter or not to enter classes, to learn or not to learn, to attend or not to attend school, etc. All this while trying to avoid falling into debauchery. Everyone must respect the rules and regulations and abide by the decisions taken democratically by the student community in assemblies.

Psychoanalysis is a theory; because it explores, describes, explains, interprets, understands, etc., reality, phenomena, facts, things, etc.

Psychoanalysis is a theory specific to the educational sciences; because, although it arises in the field of education, it is not a theory that is specific to the educational sciences.

psychology, can be used to explore, describe, explain, interpret, understand, etc., the educational reality.

Psychoanalysis is a specific theory of the subjective sciences of education because it can be used to explore, describe, explain, interpret, understand, etc., the educational reality in a subjective way. The explorations, descriptions, explanations, interpretations, comprehensions, etc., about the educational reality, the teaching phenomena, school events, the formative thing, etc., that are carried out using as a theoretical foundation, which are carried out using psychoanalysis as a theoretical basis, are done by solving the great problems of knowledge (possibility, origin, essence, classification and concepts and criteria of truth) from the senses, through sceptical, subjectivist, relativist, pragmatic, empirical, subjectivist, realist, monist, intuitive, transcendent philosophical assumptions, respectively.

With the theory of *psychoanalysis* as a theoretical foundation, from subjectivist philosophical assumptions, it is possible to explore, describe, explain, interpret, understand, etc. the educational reality, privileging the cognising subject over the object to be known.

The philosophical assumptions from which each and every one of the five main philosophical problems of knowledge (possibility, origin, essence, classification and concept and criterion of truth of knowledge) are solved, using the senses, in *psychoanalysis*, are the following:

- In *psychoanalytic* theory, as in the general theories of subjective knowledge (chaos, conflict, etc.) and the particular theories of the subjective social sciences (historicism, historical-dialectical materialism, etc.) it is assumed, from the senses, that reality is very complex and very difficult to understand, due to the permanent change in which it finds itself. The problem of the possibility of knowledge is solved on the basis of sceptical, subjectivist, relativist and pragmatic philosophical assumptions.

When *psychoanalysis* is used as a theoretical basis for exploring, describing, explaining, interpreting, understanding, etc., it is assumed, from the senses, that learner motivation is governed by external (social) and internal (self-satisfaction) factors, so that the satisfaction of affective, security and achievement needs in learners must be sought.

- In *psychoanalytic* theory, as in general theories of subjective knowledge (chaos, conflict, etc.) and the particular theories of the subjective social sciences (historicism, historical-dialectical materialism), it is believed that the origin of knowledge is to be found in sensations. It is believed that human beings (each one in particular) perceive reality differently from others. Each human being experiences the same sensations in a different way. A distinction is made between perception (which is universal) and representation (which is particular). The problem of the origin of knowledge is solved on the basis of empirical philosophical assumptions.

When *psychoanalysis* is used as a theoretical basis for exploring, describing, explaining, interpreting, understanding, etc., the role of the teacher in the student's learning, it is considered, from the senses, that the teacher is reduced to a mere mediator of the student's knowledge acquisition processes.

- In psychoanalytic theory, it is presumed, from the senses, as in general theories of subjective knowledge (chaos, conflict, etc.) and particular theories of subjective social sciences (historicism, historical-dialectical materialism), that (in a relation of knowledge) the cognising subject determines the object to be known. It is presumed that if two cognizing subjects relate to the same object of knowledge, both will apprehend their object to be known in a totally different way; because their life history, feelings, emotions, passions, complexes, ambitions, etc. "contaminate" the object of study. "contaminate" the object of study. Science is not neutral, it obeys philosophical assumptions and ontological interests. The pre-metaphysical problem about the essence of knowledge is solved on the basis of subjectivist philosophical assumptions.

When *psychoanalysis* is used as a theoretical basis for exploring, describing, explaining, interpreting, understanding, etc. the concept of the learner, it is presumed, from the senses, that the learner is the planner, executor and evaluator of his or her knowledge.

- In *psychoanalytic* theory, it is conjectured, from the senses, as in general theories of subjective knowledge (chaos, conflict, etc.) and particular theories of subjective social sciences (historicism, historical-dialectical materialism), that reality exists independently of whether the cognising subjects apprehend it or not. It is believed that the impressions of the objects that surround us impact our senses and produce sensations that different subjects perceive, but represent them differently. The metaphysical problem about the *essence* of knowledge is solved on the basis of realist philosophical assumptions.

When *psychoanalysis* is used as a theoretical basis for exploring, describing, explaining, interpreting, understanding, etc., the concept of learning, it is conjectured, from the senses, that it refers to an unconscious process that generates comprehensive changes in the behavioural patterns of learners.

- In *psychoanalytic* theory, as in the general theories of subjective knowledge (chaos, conflict, etc.) and the particular theories of the subjective social sciences (historicism, historical-dialectical materialism), it is conceded, from the senses, that reality is divided into two opposing and contradictory poles: order - disorder, regularities - irregularities, certainty - uncertainty, etc. The theological problem of the essence of knowledge is solved on the basis of dualistic philosophical assumptions.

When *psychoanalysis* is used as a theoretical basis for exploring, describing, explaining, interpreting, understanding, etc., the aims of education, it is granted, from the senses, that these should consist of forming psychologically healthy personalities and favouring healthy psycho-emotional development.

- In *psychoanalytic* theory, as in the general theories of subjective knowledge (chaos, conflict, etc.) and the particular theories of subjective social sciences (historicism, historical-dialectical materialism), the only type of knowledge that a cognising subject can obtain of an object to be known is intuitive. Everything we know about reality is considered to have been obtained by means of the senses. The problem of the classification of knowledge is solved on the basis of intuitive philosophical assumptions.

When *psychoanalysis* is used as a theoretical basis for exploring, describing, explaining, interpreting, understanding, etc., teaching methodology, it is attributed, from the senses, that it should be based on operational groups.

- In *psychoanalytic* theory, as in the general theories of subjective knowledge (chaos, conflict, etc.) and the particular theories of the subjective social sciences (historicism, historical-dialectical materialism), it is presupposed, from the senses, that the concepts and criteria of truth of knowledge are transcendent. Truth is considered to be the concordance of thought with the object thought. Because it is assumed that the cognising subject is confronted with objects that have their own existence in reality. The problem of concepts and criteria of truth is solved on the basis of transcendent philosophical assumptions.

The following table shows the philosophical assumptions from which each of the five main philosophical problems of knowledge are resolved in the construction of *psychoanalytic* theory:

SPECIFIC THEORY OF EDUCATIONAL SCIENCES	PHILOSOPHICAL PROBLEMS OF KNOWLEDGE						
SPECIFIC THEORY OF EDUCATIONAL SCIENCES	POSSIBILITY OF KNOWLEDGE	ORIGIN OF KNOWLEDGE	ESSENCE OF KNOWLEDGE			TYPE OF KNOWLEDGE	CONCEPT AND CRITERION OF TRUTH OF KNOWLEDGE
			SOLUTIONS				
			PREMETA-FISCA SOLUTION	SOLUTION METAPHYSICS	SOLUTION TEO LOGICA		
	ASSUMPTIONS FROM WHICH KNOWLEDGE PROBLEMS CAN BE RESOLVED						
PSYCHOANALYTICS SIS	SCEPTICISM, SUBJECTIVISM, RELATIVISM AND PRAGMATISM	EMPIRISM	SUBJECTIVISM	REALISM	DUALISM	INTUITIVE	TRASCENDENT

2.3.5.4.4.2.2 Humanism.

Humanism, like psychoanalysis, is a specific theory of the subjective sciences of education that explores, describes, explains, interprets, understands, etc., the reality of teaching, educational phenomena, school events, the formative thing, etc., from the senses, using subjective (possibility of knowledge), empirical (origin of knowledge), subjectivist (pre-metaphysical solution to the problem of the essence of knowledge) philosophical assumptions.using subjective (possibility of knowledge), empirical (origin of knowledge), subjectivist (pre-metaphysical solution to the problem of the essence of knowledge), realist (metaphysical solution to the problem of the essence of knowledge), dualist (theological solution to the problem of the essence of knowledge), intuitive (type of knowledge) and transcendent (concept and criterion of truth of knowledge) philosophical assumptions.

Humanism or existentialism "... was founded by Abraham Maslow, who conceives it as a psychology of <being> and not of <having>. This current proposes a science of man that takes into account conscience, ethics, individuality and spiritual values". (Guzmán, Jesús Carlos and Gerardo Hernández Rojas; 1993: 41). Humanism, like existentialism, shares a vision of man as a creative, free and conscious being (subjectivism).

The most important representatives of this theory, with applications in sociology, psychology, psychiatry and education, are Maslow, Aliport, Rogers, R. May and V. Frankl. Frankl.

Humanism is a theory; because it explores, describes, explains, interprets, understands, etc., reality, phenomena, facts, things, etc.

Humanism is a theory specific to the educational sciences; because, although it arose in the field of sociology, and then moved on to psychology and psychiatry, it can be used to explore, describe, explain, interpret, understand, etc., the reality of education.

Humanism is a specific theory of the subjective sciences of education because it can be used to explore, describe, explain, interpret, understand, etc., the educational reality; from the senses; in a subjective way. The explorations, descriptions, explanations, interpretations, comprehensions, etc., about the educational reality, the teaching phenomena, school events, the formative thing, etc., that are carried out using a theoretical foundation, that are carried out using *humanism* as a theoretical basis, are done by solving the great problems of knowledge (possibility, origin, essence, classification and concepts and criteria of truth) from philosophical assumptions that are sceptical, subjectivist, relativist, pragmatic, empirical, subjectivist, realist, monist, intuitive, transcendent, respectively.

With the theory of *humanism* as a theoretical foundation, from the senses and using subjectivist philosophical assumptions, the educational reality can be explored, described, explained, interpreted, understood, etc., privileging the cognising subject over the object to be known. The cognising subject determines the object to be known.

The philosophical assumptions from which each and every one of the five main philosophical problems of knowledge (possibility, origin, essence, classification and concept and criterion of truth of knowledge) are resolved in *humanism* are the following:

- In *humanism*, as in psychoanalysis, it is assumed, from the senses, that reality is very complex and very difficult to understand, due to the permanent change in which it finds itself. The problem of the possibility of knowledge is solved on the basis of sceptical, subjectivist, relativist and pragmatic philosophical assumptions. When *humanism* is used as a theoretical basis for exploring, describing, explaining, interpreting, understanding, etc., the aims of education, it is assumed, from the senses, that these should consist of promoting the self-realisation of human beings, stimulating their potentialities, so that they may reach the maximum height that the human species can attain.

- In humanism, it is considered, from the senses, as in psychoanalysis, that the origin of knowledge is to be found in sensations. It is believed that human beings (each one in particular) perceive reality differently from others. Each human being experiences the same sensations in a different way. A distinction is made between perception (which is universal) and representation (which is particular). The problem of the origin of knowledge is solved on the basis of empirical philosophical assumptions.

When *humanism* is used as a theoretical basis for exploring, describing, explaining, interpreting, understanding, etc.; the

teaching methodology; it is considered, from the senses, that one should work with problems perceived as real, provide resources, make agreements, divide the class into teams, investigate and promote encounter groups. Because learning is acquired more by experimenting than by reasoning.

- In humanism, it is presumed, from the senses, as in psychoanalysis, that (in a relation of knowledge) the cognising subject determines the object to be known. It is presumed that if two cognizing subjects relate to the same object of knowledge, both will apprehend their object to be known in a totally different way; because their life history, feelings, emotions, passions, complexes, ambitions, etc. "contaminate" the object of study. "contaminate" the object of study. Science is not neutral, it obeys philosophical assumptions and ontological interests. The pre-metaphysical problem about the essence of knowledge is solved from subjectivist philosophical assumptions.

When *humanism* is used as a theoretical basis for exploring, describing, explaining, interpreting, understanding, etc., the concept of the learner, it is assumed, from the senses, that the learner is a completely unique and different individual entity; a being with initiative, with self-determination needs and with the potential to develop activities and solve problems; a total person who possesses affections and has particular experiences.

- In *humanism*, it is conjectured, from the senses, as in psychoanalysis, that reality exists independently of whether the cognising subjects apprehend it or not. It is believed that the impressions of the objects that surround us have an impact on our senses and produce sensations that different subjects perceive, but that they represent them differently. The metaphysical problem about the *essence* of knowledge is solved on the basis of realist philosophical assumptions.

When *psychoanalysis* is used as a theoretical foundation to explore, describe, explain, interpret, understand, etc., the concept of learning; it is conjectured, from the senses, that this consists of a process that modifies the perception of reality, derived from the reorganisation of the self. The learning that is promoted must be meaningful or experiential: cognitive and affective (self-motivated).

- In humanism, it is conceded, from the senses, as in psychoanalysis, that reality is divided into two opposing and contradictory poles: order - disorder, regularities - irregularities, certainty - uncertainty, etc. The theological problem of the essence of knowledge is solved on the basis of dualistic philosophical assumptions.

When *psychoanalysis* is used as a theoretical basis for exploring, describing, explaining, interpreting, understanding, etc., evaluation, it is conceded, from the senses, that the only type of evaluation that should be privileged is self-evaluation.

- In *humanism*, it is attributed, from the senses, as in psychoanalysis, that the only type of knowledge that a cognising subject can obtain of an object to be known is intuitive. It is considered that everything we know about reality was obtained through the senses. The problem about the classification of knowledge is solved on the basis of intuitive philosophical assumptions.

When *psychoanalysis* is used as a theoretical basis for exploring, describing, explaining, interpreting, understanding, etc., motivation, it is attributed, from the senses, that it must consist of experiences, occupations and communication.

- In humanism, it is presupposed, from the senses, as in psychoanalysis, that the concepts and criteria of truth of knowledge are transcendent. Truth is considered to be the concordance of thought with the object thought. Because it is assumed that the cognising subject is confronted with objects that have their own existence in reality. The problem of concepts and criteria of truth is solved on the basis of transcendent philosophical assumptions.

When *humanism* is used as a theoretical basis for exploring, describing, explaining, interpreting, understanding, etc., the role of the teacher in the learning process is attributed, from the senses, that this should consist of facilitating the student's learning by providing the conditions for it to take place autonomously, and starting from individual potentialities and needs by fostering a social climate. The following table shows the philosophical assumptions from which each and every one of the five main philosophical problems of knowledge, from the senses, are resolved in the construction of *psychoanalytic* theory:

SPECIFIC THEORY OF THE SCIENCES OF EDUCATION CION	PHILOSOPHICAL PROBLEMS OF KNOWLEDGE						
	POSSIBILITY OF KNOWLEDGE	ORIGIN OF KNOWLEDGE TO	ESSENCE OF KNOWLEDGE			TYPE OF KNOWLEDGE	CONCEPT AND CRITERION OF TRUTH OF KNOWLEDGE
			SOLUTIONS				
			PRE-METAPHYSICAL SOLUTION	METAPHYSICAL SOLUTION	THEOLOGICAL SOLUTION		
	ASSUMPTIONS FROM WHICH THE PROBLEMS OF KNOWLEDGE CAN BE SOLVED.						
HUMANISM	SCEPTICISM, SUBJECTIVISM AND PRAGMATISM	EMPIRISM	SUBJECTIVISM	REALISM	DUALISM	INTUITIVE	TRASCENDENT

2.3.5.4.4.2 Cognitivism.

Cognoscitivism, like psychoanalysis and humanism, is a specific theory of the subjective sciences of education that explores, describes, explains, interprets, understands, etc.; the reality of teaching, educational phenomena, school events, the formative thing, etc.using subjective (possibility of knowledge), empirical (origin of knowledge), subjectivist (pre-metaphysical solution to the problem of the essence of knowledge), realist (metaphysical solution to the problem of the essence of knowledge), dualist (theological solution to the problem of the essence of knowledge), intuitive (type of knowledge) and transcendent (concept and criterion of truth of knowledge) philosophical assumptions.

Cognoscitivism is the result of "*... different psychological approaches and related disciplines, such as linguistics, artificial intelligence, epistemology, among others. Despite their different origins, they all share the purpose of studying, analysing and understanding mental processes*" (Guzmán, Jesús Carlos and Gerardo Hernández Rojas; 1993: 25).

Cognitivism has its origins in Gestalt psychology, a school of psychology developed at the end of the 20th century in Germany.

Gestalt is characterised by the consideration of perceptual processes in problem solving. The form, pattern or configuration (Gestalt) consists of asking questions such as: how did the learner learn to perceive the situation? Learning means exchanging one *gestalt* for another; one form, one situation, one pattern for another. The change can be brought about by new experience, reflection or the mere passage of time.

The most representative currents of *cognitivism* are the theories of information processing, meaningful learning (David Ausubel), instructional learning (Jerome Bruner) and the work of Piaget.

- *Information processing* theory studies the way in which the cognitive subject incorporates, transforms, stores, retrieves and uses the information it receives. It is very influential in the development of artificial intelligence.

- David Ausubel's theory of *meaningful learning* investigates the functioning of people's cognitive structures and tries to determine the mechanisms for achieving meaningful learning in teaching.

- Instructional theory attempts to explain discovery learning.

- For the purposes of this part of the study, since it is a matter of exploring, describing, explaining, interpreting, understanding, etc.the relationship between theory and philosophy, mainly; Piaget's work will be analysed in the following section, corresponding to the specific theories of the dialectical sciences of education; for considering *constructivism* as a theory that deals or can deal with the educational phenomenon from critical philosophical assumptions (possibility of knowledge), apriorist (origin of knowledge), dialectical, phenomenological and monistic (pre-metaphysical, metaphysical and theological solutions, respectively, to the problem of the essence of knowledge), mixed <rational-intuitive> (classification of knowledge) and mixed <immanent-transcendent> (concepts and criteria of truth of knowledge).

The most important proposal of *cognitivism* is "learning to learn", an aspect that is totally related to the aspirations of the present work.

Cognoscitivism is a theory; because it explores, describes, explains, interprets, understands, etc., reality, phenomena, facts, thing, etc.

Cognoscitivism is a specific theory of educational sciences; because, although it comprises several aspects (linguistics, artificial intelligence, epistemology, etc.), it can be used to explore, describe, explain, interpret, understand, etc., mental processes in education.

Cognoscitivism is a specific theory of the subjective sciences of education because it can be used to explore, describe, explain, interpret, understand, etc., the mental processes of learning; from the senses; in a subjective way. The explorations, descriptions, explanations, interpretations, comprehensions, etc., about the educational reality, teaching phenomena, school events, the formative thing, etc., which are carried out using a theoretical basis, that are carried out using *humanism* as a theoretical basis, are done by solving the great problems of knowledge (possibility, origin, essence, classification and concepts and criteria of truth) from philosophical assumptions that are sceptical, subjectivist, relativist, pragmatic, empirical, subjectivist, realist, monist, intuitive, transcendent, respectively.

With the theory of *cognoscitivism* as a theoretical foundation, from the senses and using subjectivist philosophical assumptions, the educational reality can be explored, described, explained, interpreted, understood, etc., privileging the cognising subject over the object to be known. The cognising subject determines the object to be known.

The philosophical assumptions from which each and every one of the five main philosophical problems of knowledge (possibility, origin, essence, classification and concept and criterion of truth of knowledge) are solved, from the senses, in *cognoscitivism* are the following:

- In *cognoscitivism*, as in psychoanalysis and humanism, it is assumed, from the senses, that reality is very complex and very difficult to understand, due to the permanent change in which it finds itself. The problem of the possibility of knowledge is solved on the basis of sceptical, subjectivist, relativist and pragmatic philosophical assumptions.

When *cognitivism* is used as a theoretical basis for exploring, describing, explaining, interpreting, understanding, etc., the aims of education, it is assumed, from the senses, that these should consist of the long-term retention of significant bodies of knowledge, developing cognitive processes (learning to learn), and the development of curiosity, doubt, creativity, reasoning and imagination.

- In *cognoscitivism*, it is believed, as in psychoanalysis and humanism, that the origin of knowledge is to be found in sensation. It is believed that human beings (each one in particular) perceive reality differently from others. Each human being experiences the same sensations differently. A distinction is made between perception (which is universal) and representation (which is particular). The problem of the origin of knowledge is solved on the basis of empirical philosophical assumptions.

When *cognoscitivism* is used as a theoretical basis for exploring, describing, explaining, interpreting, understanding, etc., teaching methodology is used.The teaching methodology; it is considered, from the senses, that the mastery of cognitive, meta-cognitive (knowing that one knows), self-regulatory strategies and the induction of more elaborated and inclusive representations of knowledge (schemas) should be promoted; for this, instructional strategies should be used (design of teaching situations: advance organiser, summaries, illustrations, questions, semantic networks, concept maps, etc.), induced or learning strategies (skills, habits, techniques and skills: self-interrogation, imagination, imagination, etc.).) induced or learning (skills, habits, techniques and skills: self-interrogation, imagination, identification and elaboration.

- In cognoscitivism, it is presumed, from the senses, as in psychoanalysis and humanism, that (in a relation of knowledge) the cognising subject determines the object to be known. It is presumed that if two cognising subjects relate to the same object of knowledge, both will apprehend their object to be known in a totally different way; because their life history, feelings, emotions, passions, complexes, ambitions, etc., are different.

"contaminate" the object of study. Science is not neutral, it obeys philosophical assumptions and ontological interests. The pre-metaphysical problem about the essence of knowledge is solved on the basis of subjectivist philosophical assumptions.

When *cognitive scientism* is used as a theoretical basis for exploring, describing, explaining, interpreting, understanding, etc., the concept of the learner, it is assumed, from the senses, that the learner is an active processor of information and responds to his or her own learning.

- In *cognoscitivism*, it is conjectured, from the senses, as in psychoanalysis and humanism, that reality exists independently of whether or not cognitive subjects apprehend it. It is believed that the impressions of the objects that surround us have an impact on our senses and produce sensations that different subjects perceive, but represent them differently. The metaphysical problem about the *essence* of knowledge is solved on the basis of realist philosophical assumptions.

When *cognitive scientism* is used as a theoretical basis for exploring, describing, explaining, interpreting, understanding, etc., the concept of learning; it is conjectured, from the senses, that this consists of the qualitative restructuring of people's schemas, ideas, perceptions or concepts: this is meaningful learning.

- In *cognoscitivism*, as in psychoanalysis and humanism, it is conceded that reality is divided into two opposing and contradictory poles: order - disorder, regularities - irregularities, certainty - uncertainty, etc. The theological problem of the essence of knowledge is solved on the basis of dualistic philosophical assumptions.

When *cognitive scientism* is used as a theoretical basis for exploring, describing, explaining, interpreting, understanding, etc., motivation, it is attributed, from the senses, that motivation should consist in

to provoke imbalances in the learner so that the search for balance becomes the driving force for learning.

- In cognoscitivism, as in psychoanalysis and humanism, the only type of knowledge that a cognitive subject can obtain from an object to be known is intuitive. Everything we know about reality is considered to have been obtained through the senses. The problem of the classification of knowledge is solved on the basis of intuitive philosophical assumptions.

When *cognitive scientism* is used as a theoretical basis for exploring, describing, explaining, interpreting, understanding, etc., assessment, it is conceded, from the senses, that students' thinking and reasoning skills should be assessed.

- In *cognoscitivism*, it is assumed, as in psychoanalysis and humanism, that the concepts and criteria for the truth of knowledge are transcendent. Truth is considered to be the concordance of thought with the object thought. Because it is assumed that the cognising subject is confronted with objects that have their own existence in reality. The problem of concepts and criteria of truth is solved on the basis of transcendent philosophical assumptions.

When *cognoscitivism* is used as a theoretical basis for exploring, describing, explaining, interpreting, understanding, etc., the role of the teacher in the learning process is attributed, from the senses, that this should consist of encouraging the development and practice of the student's cognitive processes: identifying prior knowledge and relating it to new knowledge in order to achieve meaningful learning.

The following table shows the philosophical assumptions from which each and every one of the five main philosophical problems of knowledge are solved in the construction of the *cognoscitivist* theory:

SPECIFIC THEORY OF EDUCATIONAL SCIENCES	PHILOSOPHICAL PROBLEMS OF KNOWLEDGE						
	POSSIBILITY OF KNOWLEDGE	ORIGIN OF KNOWLEDGE	ESSENCE OF KNOWLEDGE			TYPE OF KNOWLEDGE	CONCEPT AND CRITERION OF TRUTH OF KNOWLEDGE
			SOLUTIONS				
			PRE-METAPHYSICAL SOLUTION	METAPHYSICAL SOLUTION	THEOLOGICAL SOLUTION		
	ASSUMPTIONS FROM WHICH KNOWLEDGE PROBLEMS CAN BE RESOLVED						

COGNOSCITIVISM	SCEPTICISM, SUBJECTIVISM, RELATIVISM AND PRAGMATISM	EMPIRISM	SUBJECTIVISM	REALISM	DUALISM	INTUITIVE	TRASCENDENT

The theoretical foundations that allow the objects of study to be problematised with greater cognitive depth from *cognoscitivism* are the general subjective theories of knowledge (chaos, conflict, etc.), the particular theories of the subjective social sciences (historicism, historical-dialectical materialism, etc.) and the specific theories of the subjective sciences of education that were analysed prior to *cognoscitivism* (psychoanalysis and humanism).

2.3.5.4.4.3 Theories specific to the dialectical sciences of education

The *specific theories of the dialectical sciences of education* derive, like the general theories of dialectical knowledge (analogy, complexity, etc.) and the particular theories of the dialectical social sciences (phenomenology, critical hermeneutics, etc.), of *critical philosophical assumptions* (thus solving the problem about the possibility of knowledge); *intellectualist* and *apriorist* (thus solving the problem about the origin of knowledge); *dialectical, phenomenological* and *monistic* (thus solving the problem about the essence of knowledge, in terms of pre-metaphysical, metaphysical and theological solutions, respectively); *mixed* - knowledge is both rational and intuitive - (thus solving the problem about the classification of knowledge); and *mixed* - concepts and criteria of truth must be both transcendent and immanent - (thus solving the problem about concepts and criteria of truth of knowledge).

Two of the *specific theories of the dialectical sciences of education* that solve each and every one of the five great philosophical problems of knowledge from both qualities of the cognising subject: reason and the senses, using the aforementioned assumptions, are the genetic theory (Piaget) and the socio-cultural theory (Vygostky).

Just as the *general theories of dialectical knowledge* (analogy and complexity) and the particular theories of the dialectical social sciences (phenomenology, hermeneutics, etc.), the analysis of the *specific theories of the dialectical sciences of education* (genetic and sociocultural), in a first moment, will be carried out considering the definition, characteristics, function, purpose, classification, authors and works of each *specific theory of the dialectical sciences of education*; in a second moment, the philosophical *assumptions* from which each and every one of the five main philosophical *problems* of knowledge are solved will be taken into account: possibility, origin, essence, classification, and concepts and criteria of truth of knowledge; and, finally, the following aspects will be analysed: aims of education, concept of learning, role of the teacher, concept of the learner, motivation, teaching methodology and evaluation.

It is necessary to remember, for the purposes of this analysis, that the *classification* and the *names* assigned to each and every one of the *specific theories of the educational sciences* analysed in this section are based on the way in which one of the five main philosophical *problems* of knowledge is solved: the problem of the *essence* of knowledge. This philosophical problem of knowledge (the essence) was chosen and no other, because this difficulty of knowledge refers to the *relation* of knowledge that is established between the cognising *subject* and the *object* to be known.

It has already been made clear that, of the different philosophical *assumptions* from which the problem of the *essence* of knowledge can be solved and which can be found in three different *solutions* (pre-metaphysical, metaphysical and theological), we have chosen the *pre-metaphysical* solution, because this solution addresses the problem of the following question: *who determines whom in a relation of knowledge: the object to the subject, the subject to the object, or do the two determine each other?*

If *philosophy* determines *theory*, then *theory* depends on *philosophy*. If *we assume* that, in a relation of knowledge, the object determines the subject, then we can speak of *objective* theories. On the contrary, if we suppose that, in a relation of knowledge, the subject determines the object, then we can speak of *subjective* theories. Finally, in the following cases, if we assume that, in a relation of knowledge, both elements of knowledge determine each other, then we can speak of *dialectical* theories.

So far we have analysed the specific theories of the subjective sciences of education (psychoanalysis, humanism and cognitivism). In this section we will analyse the third group of theories specific to the educational sciences: *theories specific to the dialectical sciences of education* (genetic and socio-cultural).

It has already been said that *objective* theories are constructed from reason (objectivist), *subjective* theories from the senses (subjectivist) and *dialectical* theories from both qualities of the cognising subject: from reason and from the senses; being able to start first from reason and then from the senses (apriorism); or vice versa (intellectualism).

One of the *specific theories of the dialectical sciences of education*, which starts from *critical* philosophical assumptions (possibility of knowing); *apriorist* (origin of knowledge); *dialectical*, and *monistic* (pre-metaphysical, metaphysical and theological solutions, respectively, to the problem of the essence of knowledge); rational-intuitive (type of knowledge); and immanent-transcendent (criteria of truth), is *the genetic theory* constructed by Piaget.

2.3.5.4.4.3.1 Genetic theory (Piaget).

Genetic theory is a specific theory of the dialectical sciences of education that explores, describes, explains, interprets, understands, etc., the reality, phenomena, facts, things, etc., of education, educational; solving each and every one of the five main philosophical problems of knowledge from both qualities of the cognising subject: reason and the senses (first reason and then the senses), using critical (possibility of knowledge), apriorist (origin of knowledge), dialectical, phenomenological and monistic (pre-metaphysical, meta-physical and theological solutions, respectively, to the problems of the essence of knowledge), mixed (rational-intuitive) (classification of knowledge) and mixed (immanent-transcendent) assumptions (concept and criterion of truth of knowledge).

Genetic theory emerged in the third decade of the 20th century, based on Piaget's studies of logic and verbal thinking in children.

Paraphrasing Guzmán, Jesús Carlos and Gerardo Hernández Rojas (1993: 71-73), Piaget's epistemological studies on how to move from a certain level of knowledge to others of greater validity, searching for the purely instrumental and methodological part of learning, led him to try to describe and explain the nature of knowledge and how it is constructed: how do subjects know and learn, what are the mechanisms involved in this process?

Among the most important of his followers are Cesar Coll, De Vries, Kohlberg, Kamil and Marro.

The two main conclusions reached by the theory are as follows: *"... 1) There is no univocity in the interpretations or readings of the theory for subsequent use in the field of education, given that different <uses> can be made according to the different aspects that are taken from it (e.g. functional, structural aspects) or the different conceptions of how psychological theories should be used in the field of education (e.g. crude extrapolations or critical readings that propose the need for an adequate re-contextualisation). 2) Despite the enormous efforts made to date on the implications of the theory, there is still much research work to be done (especially in the field of psychogenetics of learning school content), which has not yet resulted in the expected great impact of the theory in the field of education"*. (Guzmán, Jesús Carlos and Gerardo Hernández Rojas; 1993: 73).

Genetic theory is also known as *constructivist*, in the understanding that Piaget assumes that knowledge is not acquired only by internalisation of the social environment <empiricism> (as proposed by Freud and Vygostky), but that the construction carried out from within by the subject predominates (rationalism). It is a matter of finding the path of the constructive process of knowledge.

If in the *genetic* or *constructivist* theory it is assumed that the origin of knowledge is to be found in reason and the senses, with reason predominating over the senses, then in this theory knowledge of educational reality is constructed on the basis of aprioristic conjectures. The theory is based more on Kant (apriorism) than on Aristotle (intellectualism). This is only with regard to the philosophical problem of the source and basis of our knowledge.

Genetics, or *constructivism*, is a theory because it explains, interprets, understands, etc., reality, phenomena, facts, things, etc., about how knowledge is constructed.

Genetics, or *constructivism*, is a particular theory of the social sciences because it explores, describes, explains, interprets, understands, etc., any reality, phenomenon, fact, thing, etc., related to knowledge, understood as a process, not as a product. Knowledge, understood as a product, is of more interest to behaviourist theory.

Genetics or *constructivism* is a specific theory of the dialectical sciences of education because, as it deals with the study of epistemological questions, it can be used to explore, describe, explain, interpret, understand, etc., any reality, phenomenon, fact, thing, etc., that is related to the way in which knowledge is constructed, from reason and the senses, using apriorist dialectical assumptions.

The explorations, descriptions, explanations, interpretations, comprehensions, etc., which, about reality, phenomena, events, things, etc., are made in the *genetic* or *constructivist* theory, are made, as already mentioned, solving the great philosophical problems of knowledge (possibility, origin, essence, classification and concepts and criteria of truth) from both qualities of the cognising subject: reason and the senses (first reason and then the senses), using critical *assumptions*; aprioristic; dialectical, phenomenalist, and monistic; mixed <intuitive - rational >; and mixed < transcendent - immanent >; respectively; from reason and the senses.

- in the *genetic or constructivist* theory, it is assumed, from reason and the senses <first reason and then the senses> (Kantian apriorism), that knowledge is possible (dogmatism), but not in essence (scepticism), because each cognising subject feels and thinks differently from others (subjectivism), because truth changes in time, space and circumstances (relativism), and because any discourse that is developed about a certain object of knowledge must be useful to humanity (pragmatism). The problem of the *possibility* of knowledge is solved on the basis of critical philosophical *assumptions*.

When *genetic* theory or *constructivism* is used as a theoretical foundation to explore, describe, explain, interpret, understand, etc., the aims of education are assumed, from reason and the senses (first reason and then the senses), to be the following:

1. Education is the appropriate element to enhance the learner's development and promote his or her moral and intellectual autonomy.
2. Education must develop creative, inventive and discovering learners.
3. Education must develop critical learners.
4. Education should contribute to the development of rational thinking and moral and intellectual autonomy.

- In the *genetic* or *constructivist* theory, it is assumed, from reason and the senses (first reason and then the senses), that the origin of knowledge is to be found both in the senses and in the reason of the cognising subject. The *problem* of the origin of knowledge is solved on the basis of apriorist philosophical assumptions (first we think and then we feel).

When *genetic* theory or *constructivism* is used as a theoretical basis for exploring, describing, explaining, interpreting, understanding, etc., the concept of learning, it is assumed, from reason and the senses (first reason and then the senses), that learning is a process of acquiring knowledge. Learning is a process of assimilation of content that requires accommodation by the cognising subject.

- In the *genetic* or *constructivist* theory, it is assumed, from reason and the senses (first reason and then the senses), that in a relation of knowledge, the cognising *subject* determines the *object* to be known and, in turn, the object to be known determines the cognising subject. This dialectical relation between the cognising subject and the object to be known determines that the pre-metaphysical problem about the essence of knowledge is solved on the basis of dialectical philosophical assumptions.

When *genetic* theory or *constructivism* is used as a theoretical basis for exploring, describing, explaining, interpreting, understanding, etc., the concept of the learner, it is assumed, from reason and the senses (first reason and then the senses), that the learner is the active constructor of his or her own knowledge.

- In the *genetic* or *constructivist* theory, it is estimated, from reason and the senses (first reason and then the senses), that reality exists (realism), but that the subjects apprehend it in a different way (subjective idealism), as it is presented to the limitations of our reason and our senses; that is, the object to be known is presented to the different cognising subjects, as a phenomenon, as an appearance. It is believed that the impressions of the objects that surround us impact our senses and produce sensations that different subjects perceive, but that they represent them differently and, moreover, as phantasms, as phenomena, in time and space. The metaphysical *problem* about the *essence* of knowledge is solved on the basis of *phenomenalist* philosophical *assumptions*.

When *genetic* theory or *constructivism* is used as a theoretical basis for exploring, describing, explaining, interpreting, understanding, etc., school motivation, it is assumed, from reason and the senses (first reason and then the senses), that it must be intrinsic: the product of imbalances (cognitive conflicts) caused by contradiction (conscious thematisation) and thus move to a higher level of understanding. That motivation must promote cognitive conflicts in order to induce states of imbalance that motivate to learn.

- In the *genetic* or *constructivist* theory, it is presumed, from reason and the senses (first reason and then the senses), that reality is unique. The theological problem about the essence of knowledge is solved on the basis of monistic philosophical assumptions.

When *genetic* theory or *constructivism* is used as a theoretical basis for exploring, describing, explaining, interpreting, understanding, etc., the teaching methodology assumes, from reason and the senses (first reason and then the senses), that it must be direct: activity, initiative and curiosity. That the right conditions must be created (logical-mathematical), situations must be designed to acquire it through the experience of discovery (rationalism) or direct contact (physical) <empiricism> and teaching (socially or conventionally) or animation for its appropriation or reconstruction (non-conventional social).

- In the *genetic or constructivist theory*, it is conjectured, from reason and from the senses, that the type of knowledge that a cognising subject can obtain of an object to be known is *mixed* (rational-intuitive). It is considered that everything we know about reality was obtained by means of reason (first) and the senses (later). The problem of the *classification* of knowledge is solved on the basis of *mixed* philosophical assumptions (rational-intuitive).

When *genetic* theory or *constructivism* is used as a theoretical basis for exploring, describing, explaining, interpreting, understanding, etc., the evaluation of teaching, it is assumed, from reason and the senses (first reason and then the senses), that cognitive and scholastic processes must be ascertained.

- In the *genetic* or *constructivist* theory, it is attributed, from reason and the senses (first reason and then the senses), that the *concepts* and *criteria* of truth of knowledge are *mixed* (immanent-transcendent). The truth of knowledge is considered to be the concordance of thought with the object thought and of thought with itself. For it is assumed that the cognising subject is confronted both with objects that have their own existence in reality and with ideal objects, which exist only in the mind of the cognising subject. The problem of concepts and criteria of truth is solved on the basis of mixed philosophical assumptions (immanent-transcendent).

The following table shows the philosophical assumptions from which each and every one of the five main philosophical problems of knowledge are solved, from both qualities of the cognising subject: reason and the senses (first reason and then the senses), in the construction of the *genetic* or *constructivist* theory:

SPECIFIC THEORY OF THE DIALECTICAL SCIENCES OF EDUCATION	**PHILOSOPHICAL PROBLEMS OF KNOWLEDGE**						
	POSSIBILITY OF KNOWLEDGE	ORIGIN OF KNOWLEDGE	ESSENCE OF KNOWLEDGE			TYPE OF KNOWLEDGE	CONCEPT AND CRITERION OF TRUTH OF KNOWLEDGE
			SOLUTIONS				
			PRE-METAPHYSICAL SOLUTION	METAPHYSICAL SOLUTION	THEOLOGICAL SOLUTION		
	ASSUMPTIONS ON THE BASIS OF WHICH KNOWLEDGE PROBLEMS CAN BE SOLVED						
GENETICS OR COSNSTRUCTIVIST	CRITICISM	APRIORISM	DIALECTICS	PHENOMENALISM	MONISM	MIXED	MIXED

The general theories of dialectical knowledge (analogy and complexity) and the particular theories of dialectical social sciences (phenomenology, critical hermeneutics, etc.), can serve as theoretical foundations in the construction of the objects of study of *genetic* or *constructivist* theory, because they start from the same philosophical assumptions to solve each and every one of the five main problems of knowledge.

2.3.5.4.4.3.2 Socio-cultural theory.

Another of the specific theories of the dialectical sciences of education, which solves each and every one of the five main philosophical problems of knowledge from both qualities of the cognising subject: the senses and reason (but which, unlike the genetic or constructivist theory, first the senses and then reason intervene) starting from critical philosophical assumptions (possibility of knowing); intellectualist (origin of knowledge); dialectical, phenomenalist and monistic and pantheistic (pre-metaphysical, metaphysical and theological solutions, respectively, to the problem of the essence of knowledge); intuitive-rational (type of knowledge); and transcendent-immanent (concepts and criteria of truth of knowledge), is the *socio-cultural* theory.

The philosophical difference between the genetic or constructivist theory and the *socio-cultural* theory, *as already mentioned in the previous paragraph*, is one of order: while in the genetic or constructivist theory we first think and then we feel (Kantian apriorism), in the socio-cultural theory we first feel and then we think (Aristotelian intellectualism).

In *socio-cultural* theory, man is studied as a product of social and cultural processes.

L. S. Vigotsky founded the sociocultural theory in psychology, between 1925 and 1934, trying to articulate psychological and sociocultural processes; from the fields of literature, linguistics, philosophy and other humanistic disciplines (Guzmán, Jesús Carlos and Gerardo Hernández Rojas; 1993: 73).

Vigotsky's work is mainly based on the particular theory of the subjective social sciences which in this study was analysed in previous sections under the name of dialectical historical materialism of Karl Marx and Friedrich Engels.

Socio-cultural theory is a theory, pardon the pleonasm, because it explores, describes, explains, interprets, understands, etc., reality, phenomena, facts, things, etc.

Socio-cultural theory is a theory specific to the educational sciences because it explains, interprets, understands, etc., any educational reality, phenomenon, fact, thing, etc., etc.

Sociocultural theory is a specific theory of the dialectical sciences of education because it explains, interprets, understands, etc., any educational reality, phenomenon, fact, thing, etc., from dialectical philosophical assumptions.

The explorations, descriptions, explanations, interpretations, comprehensions, etc., about reality, phenomena, events, things, etc., that are carried out in sociocultural theory are done by solving the great problems of knowledge (possibility, origin, essence, classification and concepts and criteria of truth) from critical philosophical assumptions; intellectualist, dialectic, phenomenalist and philosophical criteria, are carried out in *socio-cultural* theory by solving the great problems of knowledge (possibility, origin, essence, classification and concepts and criteria of truth) from critical philosophical assumptions; intellectualist; dialectical, phenomenological, and monistic; mixed <intuitive - rational>; and mixed <transcendent - immanent>; respectively.

- In *socio-cultural* theory, it is assumed, from the senses and reason (Aristotelian intellectualism), as in genetic theory, that knowledge is possible (dogmatism), but not in essence.

(scepticism), because each cognising subject feels and thinks differently from others (subjectivism), because truth changes in time, space and circumstances (relativism), and because any discourse that is developed about a certain object of knowledge must be useful to humanity (pragmatism). The problem of the possibility of knowledge is solved on the basis of critical philosophical assumptions.

When *sociocultural* theory is used as a theoretical basis for exploring, describing, explaining, interpreting, understanding, etc., the aims of education, it is assumed, from reason and the senses (first the senses and then reason), that these are to promote the socio-cultural and holistic development of learners.

- In *sociocultural* theory, it is assumed, from the senses and reason (first the senses and then reason), that the origin of knowledge is to be found both in the senses and in the reason of the cognising subject. The problem of the origin of knowledge is solved on the basis of intellectualist philosophical assumptions (first we feel and then we weigh).

When *sociocultural* theory is used as a theoretical basis for exploring, describing, explaining, interpreting, understanding, etc., the concept of learning, it is assumed, from reason and the senses (first the senses and then reason), that it consists of negotiating zones of proximal development, integrating the current level of development with the potential and in a dialogue between the child and his or her future.

- In *socio-cultural* theory, it is assumed, from the senses and reason (first the senses and then reason), that in a knowledge relation, the cognising subject determines the object to be known and, in turn, the object to be known determines the cognising subject. This dialectical relationship between the cognising subject and the object to be known determines that the pre-metaphysical problem about the essence of knowledge is solved on the basis of dialectical philosophical assumptions.

When *sociocultural* theory is used as a theoretical foundation to explore, describe, explain, interpret, understand, etc., the role of the teacher in education, it is assumed, from reason and the senses (first the senses and then reason), that the role of the teacher is to create and negotiate zones of proximal development in the learner, as an expert who guides and mediates the sociocultural knowledge that learners must learn and internalise.

- In *sociocultural* theory, it is assumed, based on the senses and reason (first the senses and then reason), that reality exists (realism), but that subjects apprehend it differently (subjective idealism), as it is presented to us within the limitations of our senses and our reason; that is, the object to be known is presented to the different cognising subjects as a phenomenon, as an appearance. It is believed that the impressions of the objects that surround us impact our senses and produce sensations that different subjects perceive, but that they represent them differently and, moreover, as phantasms, as phenomena, in time and space. The metaphysical problem about the *essence* of knowledge is solved on the basis of phenomenalist philosophical assumptions.

When *sociocultural* theory is used as a theoretical basis to explore, describe, explain, interpret, understand, etc., the concept of the learner, it is assumed, from reason and the senses (first the senses and then reason), that the learner is a social entity, protagonist (subjectivism) and product (objectivism) of multiple social interactions (dialectics).

- In *socio-cultural* theory, it is assumed, on the basis of the senses and reason, that reality is unique. The theological problem of the *essence* of knowledge is solved on the basis of monistic philosophical assumptions.

When *sociocultural* theory is used as a theoretical basis for exploring, describing, explaining, interpreting, understanding, etc., teaching methodology, it is assumed, from reason and the senses (first the senses and then reason), that this consists of creating zones of proximal development and moving the learner from the lower to the higher levels of the zone; seeking a certain necessary degree of cognitive competence and guiding with a very fine sensitivity; starting from the performances gradually achieved by the learners.

- In *sociocultural* theory, it is assumed, from the senses and reason, that the type of knowledge that a cognising subject can obtain of an object to be known is mixed (intuitive-rational). It is considered that everything we know about reality, we obtained by means of the senses (first) and reason (later). The problem about the classification of knowledge is solved on the basis of mixed philosophical assumptions (intuitive-rational).

When *socio-cultural* theory is used as a theoretical basis for exploring, describing, explaining, interpreting, understanding, etc., assessment, it is assumed, from reason and the senses (first the senses and then reason), that assessment is about determining the level of learners' potential development (the emergent competences that are brought to light by interactions with others who provide context for them).

- In *sociocultural* theory, it is assumed, from the senses and reason, that the concepts and criteria of truth of knowledge are *mixed* (transcendent-immanent). The truth of knowledge is considered to be the concordance of thought with the object thought and of thought with itself. For it is assumed that the cognising subject is confronted both with objects that have their own existence in reality and with ideal objects, which exist only in the mind of the cognising subject. The problem of the concepts and criteria of truth of knowledge is solved on the basis of mixed (transcendent-immanent) philosophical assumptions.

The following table shows the assumptions from which each of the five main philosophical problems of knowledge are solved in the construction of *socio-cultural* theory:

GENERAL THEORY OF DIALECTICAL KNOWLEDGE	PHILOSOPHICAL PROBLEMS OF KNOWLEDGE						
	POSSIBILITY OF KNOWLEDGE	ORIGIN OF KNOWLEDGE	ESSENCE OF KNOWLEDGE			TYPE OF KNOWLEDGE	CONCEPT AND CRITERION OF TRUTH OF KNOWLEDGE
			SOLUTIONS				
			PRE-METAPHYSICAL SOLUTION	METAPHYSICAL SOLUTION	THEOLOGICAL SOLUTION		
	ASSUMPTIONS FROM WHICH TO SOLVE THE PROBLEMS OF THE KNOWLEDGE						
SOCIOCULTURAL THEORY	CRITICISM	INTELLECTUALISM	DIALECTICS	PHENOMENMENOLOGY	MONISM	MIXED	MIXED

The general theories of dialectical knowledge (analogy and complexity) and the particular theories of dialectical social sciences (phenomenology, critical hermeneutics, etc.) can serve as theoretical foundations in the construction of the objects of study of socio-cultural theory, because they start from the same philosophical assumptions to solve each and every one of the five main problems of knowledge.

So far, so much for socio-cultural theory.

The following synoptic table shows some of the main *theories specific to the objective, subjective and dialectical sciences of education*, respectively, which were analysed epistemologically; and the respective philosophical assumptions from which they solve each of the five main problems of knowledge.

SPECIFIC THEORY OF EDUCATIONAL SCIENCES	PROBLEMS OF KNOWLEDGE						
	POSSIBILITY OF KNOWLEDGE	ORIGIN OF KNOWLEDGE	ESSENCE OF KNOWLEDGE			TYPE OF KNOWLEDGE	CONCEPT AND CRITERION OF TRUTH OF KNOWLEDGE
			SOLUTIONS				
			PRE-METAPHYSICAL SOLUTION	METAPHYSICAL SOLUTION	THEOLOGICAL SOLUTION		
	ASSUMPTIONS ON THE BASIS OF WHICH THE PROBLEMS OF CO-KNOWLEDGE CAN BE SOLVED						

CONDUCT ISM	DOGMA TISM	RATIONALI SM	OBJECTI VISM	IDEALISM	DUALIS M	RATIONAL	IMMANENT
PSYCHOA NALYSIS	SCEPTIC ISM, SUBJEC TIVISM AND PRAGM ATISM	EMPIRISM	SUBJECTI VISM	REALISM	DUALIS M	INTUITIVE	TRASCENDENT
HUMANIS M	SCEPTIC ISM, SUBJEC TIVISM AND PRAGM ATISM	EMPIRISM	SUBJECTI VISM	REALISM	DUALIS M	INTUITIVE	TRASCENDENT
COGNOSCI TIVISM	SCEPTIC ISM, SUBJEC TIVISM AND PRAGM ATISM	EMPIRISM	SUBJECTI VISM	REALISM	DUALIS M	INTUITIVE	TRASCENDENT
GENE- ETHICAL THEORY (PIAGET)	CRITICI SM	APRIORISM	DIALECT ICS	PHENOME NALISM	MONIS M	MIXED: (RATIONALI NTUITIVE)	MIXED: (IMMANENT- TRANSCENDEN T)
THEORY SOCIOCU LTURAL	CRITICI SM	INTELLECT UALISM	DIALECT ICS	NALISM PHENOME NA	MONIS M	MIXED: (INTUITI VORACIO NAL)	MIXED: (TRACENDENTE INMANENT)

2.3.5.5 The philosophical relationship between the particular theories of the social sciences and the specific theories of the educational sciences.

Certain similarities and differences can be established between particular theories in the social sciences and specific theories in the educational sciences:

2.3.5.5.1 Philosophical differences between particular social science theories and specific educational science theories:

- The particular theories of the social sciences try to explore, describe, explain, interpret, understand, etc., any fact, phenomenon, event, thing, occurrence, etc., of a social nature. On the other hand, the specific theories of the educational sciences, as their name indicates, deal only with educational problems.

- Particular theories of the social sciences can serve as a theoretical foundation for the construction of the objects of study of specific theories of the educational sciences.

- The specific theories of the educational sciences are derived from the particular theories of the social sciences, because they solve each of the five main problems of knowledge from the same philosophical assumptions.

2.3.5.5.2 Philosophical similarities between particular theories in the social sciences and specific theories in the educational sciences:

- Both types of theories need to solve each of the five main problems of knowledge on the basis of certain philosophical assumptions.

- The philosophical assumptions from which the two types of theories solve each of the five main problems of knowledge allow them to be classified as objective, subjective and mixed.

- The particular theories of objective, subjective and dialectical social sciences and the particular theories of objective, subjective and dialectical social sciences, respectively, start from the same philosophical assumptions to construct their objects of study.

The following table shows schematically the relationship between the particular theories of the social sciences and the specific theories of the educational sciences:

PARTICULAR THEORIES OF SOCIAL SCIENCES			SPECIFIC THEORIES OF EDUCATIONAL SCIENCES		
OBJECTIVES	POSITIVISM	THE OBJECT DETERMINES TO THE SUBJECT	OBJECTIVES	CONDUCTISM	THE OBJECT DETERMINES TO THE SUBJECT
	FUNCTIONALISM				
	STRUCTURALISM				
	SYSTEMS				
SUBJECTIVES	**HISTORICISM**	**THE SUBJECT DETERMINES THE OBJECT**	**SUBJECTIVES**	**PSYCHOANALYSIS**	**THE SUBJECT DETERMINES THE OBJECT**
	HISTORICAL-DIALECTICAL MATERIALISM			**HUMANISM**	
				COGNOSCITIVISM	
DIALECTICS	PHENOMENOLOGY	BOTH ELEMENTS OF THE KNOWLEDGE RELATIONSHIP MUTUALLY DETERMINE EACH OTHER	DIALECTICS	GENETIC THEORY (PIAGET)	BOTH ELEMENTS OF THE KNOWLEDGE RELATIONSHIP MUTUALLY DETERMINE EACH OTHER
	HEERMENEUTICA CRITICA			SOCIOCULTURAL THEORY (VIGOTSKY)	

The *particular theories of the objective social sciences* (positivism, functionalism, structuralism, systems theory, etc.) can be used as a theoretical foundation in the construction of the objects of study of the *specific theories of the objective sciences of education* (behaviourism), because in both types of theory knowledge is constructed from reason.

The *particular theories of the subjective social sciences* (historicism, historical-dialectical materialism, etc.) can be used as theoretical foundations in the construction of the objects of study of the *specific theories of the subjective sciences of education* (psychoanalysis, humanism, cognoscitivism, etc.), because in both types of theory knowledge is constructed from the senses.

The *particular theories of the dialectical social sciences* (phenomenology, critical hermeneutics, etc.) can be used as a theoretical foundation in the construction of the objects of study of the *specific theories of the dialectical sciences of education* (genetic <Piaget>, sociocultural <Vigotsky>), because in both types of theory knowledge is constructed from reason and the senses (Piaget) and from the senses and reason (Vigotsky).

2.4 THE PHIOSOPHY - THEORY RELATIONSHIP

As has been demonstrated in the previous sections, the *relationship* between *philosophy* and *theory* can be established, more or less, in the following sense: all discourse (theory) depends on what the speaker assumes (philosophy). Whoever explores, describes, explains, interprets, understands, etc., any reality, whether he knows it or not, will construct it from the philosophical assumptions with which he solves each and every one of the five main problems of knowledge (possibility, origin, essence, classification and criteria of truth).

Such philosophical problems of knowledge can be solved from the senses, from reason or from both qualities of the cognising subject.

1) If the philosophical problems of knowledge are solved by reason, one can speak of dogmatic (possibility of knowledge), rationalist (origin of knowledge), objectivist, idealist and dualist (pre-metaphysical, metaphysical and theological solutions, respectively, to the problem of the essence of knowledge), rational (classification of knowledge) and immanent (concept and criterion of truth of knowledge) philosophical assumptions.

From these philosophical assumptions, the discourses of the general theories of objective knowledge (mathematics, mechanicism, organicism, etc.); the particular theories of the objective social sciences (positivism, functionalism, structuralism, systems theory, etc.); and the specific theories of the objective sciences of education (behaviourism, etc.) were constructed.

2) If the philosophical problems of knowledge are solved from the senses, one can speak of sceptical, subjectivist, relativist and pragmatic (possibility of knowledge), empiricist (origin of knowledge), subjectivist, realist and dualist (pre-metaphysical, metaphysical and theological solutions, respectively, to the problem of the essence of knowledge), intuitive (classification of knowledge) and transcendental (concept and criterion of truth of knowledge) philosophical assumptions.

From these philosophical assumptions, the discourses of the general theories of subjective knowledge (chaos, conflict, etc.); the particular theories of the subjective social sciences (historicism, dialectical historical materialism, etc.); and the specific theories of the subjective sciences of education (psychoanalysis, humanism and cognoscitivism) were constructed.

3) If the philosophical problems of knowledge are solved from both qualities of the cognising subject (reason and senses), two things can happen:

3.1). If the philosophical problems of knowledge are solved from reason and the senses (first reason and then the senses), one can speak of critical (possibility of knowledge), aprioristic (origin of knowledge), dialectical, phenomenological and monistic philosophical assumptions (pre-metaphysical, metaphysical and theological solutions, respectively, to the problem of the essence of knowledge), mixed <rational-intuitive> (classification of knowledge) and mixed <immanent-transcendent> (concepts and criteria of truth of knowledge).

From these philosophical assumptions, the discourses of the general theories of dialectical knowledge (complexity, etc.); the particular theories of the dialectical social sciences (phenomenology, etc.); and the specific theories of the subjective sciences of education (genetics <Piaget>, etc.) were constructed.

2) If the philosophical problems of knowledge are solved from the senses and reason (first the senses and then reason), one can speak of critical (possibility of knowledge), intellectualist (origin of knowledge), dialectical, phenomenological and monistic philosophical assumptions (pre-metaphysical, metaphysical and theological solutions, respectively, to the problem of the essence of knowledge), mixed <intuitive-rational > (classification of knowledge) and mixed <transcendental-immanent > (concepts and criteria of truth of knowledge).

From these philosophical assumptions, the discourses of the general theories of dialectical knowledge (analogy, etc.); the particular theories of dialectical social sciences (critical hermeneutics, etc.); and the specific theories of dialectical educational sciences (socio-cultural <Vigotsky>, etc.) were constructed.

The goals of education, the concept of learning, the role of the teacher, the concept of the learner, motivation, teaching methodology, evaluation, etc. from the specific theories of the objective sciences (behaviourism), subjective sciences (psychoanalysis),

humanism, cognoscitivism, etc.) and dialectics (genetic, sociocultural, etc.) of education, differ; because the discourses are constructed from different attributes of the cognising subject (reason, senses, or both); and, for the same reason, the philosophical assumptions from which each and every one of the five problems of knowledge are solved, are also different.

One can conclude with the following popular saying: "nothing is true and nothing is a lie, everything is the colour of the glass you look through".

The discourses we elaborate are neither true nor false, they just are; and they derive from the philosophical assumptions from which each and every one of the five main problems of knowledge are solved. In turn, these assumptions depend on whether reason, the senses or both qualities of the cognising subject are used to relate to its object of knowledge.

2.5 SUMMARY OF THE SUB-CHAPTER.

As a summary of the sub-chapter, in the following table it is possible to appreciate the definitions of some of the *general theories of knowledge, particular theories of social sciences* and *specific theories of educational sciences,* described above:

THEORETICAL UNDERPINNINGS	GENERAL THEORIES OF KNOWLEDGE	**OBJECTIVES**	MATEMATICISM: Comparing reality to an ideal
			MECHANICISM: Comparing reality to a machine
			ORGANICISM: To compare reality to a biological organ, apparatus or system.
		SUBJECTIVES	CHAOS: Reality is unpredictable, but not anarchic
			CONFLICT: Antagonism, opposition, combat, etc., involving innovation and change.
		DIALECTICS	ANALOGY: Similarity
			COMPLEXITY: There is no such thing as simple, only simplified.
	PARTICULAR THEORIES OF SOCIAL SCIENCE	**OBJECTIVES**	POSITIVISM: The only authentic knowledge is scientific knowledge.
			FUNCTIONALISM: Satisfaction of a need
			STRUCTURALISM: Comparing reality with a structure
			SYSTEMS THEORY: Comparing reality with a system
		SUBJECTIVES	HISTORICISM: Looking at reality in terms of movement, of change
			HISTORICAL-DIALECTIVE MATERIALISM: Looking at reality in terms of conflict (class struggle).
		DIALECTICS	PHENOMENOLOGY: We do not know things as they are, but as they appear to us.
			CRITICAL HERMENEUTICS: Art of explaining, translating or interpreting.

SPECIFIC THEORIES OF EDUCATIONAL SCIENCES	**OBJECTIVES**	CONDUCTISM: Controlling behaviour
	SUBJECTIVES	PSYCHOANALYSIS: Developing cognitive processes
		HUMANISM: To promote healthy psycho-emotional development.
		COGNOSCITIVISM: To promote the development of sociocultural and integral
	DIALECTICS	PSYCHOGENETICS (PIAGET): Enhancing development and promoting moral and intellectual autonomy.
		SOCIO-CULTURAL: Promoting self-fulfilment

2.6 METHODOLOGICAL PROCEDURES OR INTELLECTUAL OPERATIONS, TO GENERATE NEW KNOWLEDGE IN THE EDUCATIONAL FIELD.

In this section, research methods will be discussed. Conceptual mapping will also be used to construct *methodological procedures* or *intellectual operations* that can be used to generate new knowledge.

Just as *theory* (second level of an epistemological orientation) depends on *philosophy* (first level of an epistemological orientation), *methodology* (third level of an epistemological orientation) depends on *theory*.

If the educational researcher solves each and every one of the five main philosophical problems of knowledge from reason, he can construct his objects of study from dogmatic (possibility of knowledge), rational (origin of knowledge), objective, idealistic and dualistic (pre-metaphysical, metaphysical and theological solutions, respectively, to the problem of the essence of knowledge), rational (classification of knowledge) and rational philosophical assumptions (classification of knowledge).

and immanent (concept and criterion of truth of knowledge); problematising the reality it investigates by means of the general theories of objective knowledge (mathematics, mechanicism, organicism, etc.); the particular theories of objective social sciences (positivism, functionalism, structuralism, systems, etc.); and the specific theories of objective educational sciences (behaviourism).

If the educational researcher solves each and every one of the five main philosophical problems of knowledge from the senses, he can construct his objects of study from sceptical, subjectivist, relativist and pragmatic (possibility of knowledge), empirical (origin of knowledge), subjective, realist and dualist (pre-metaphysical, metaphysical and theological solutions, respectively, to the problem of the essence of knowledge), intuitive (classification of knowledge) and transcendental (concept and criterion of truth of knowledge) philosophical assumptions; problematising the reality it investigates by means of the general theories of subjective knowledge (chaos, conflict, etc.); the particular theories of the subjective social sciences (historicism, historical-dialectical materialism, etc.); and the specific theories of the subjective sciences of education (psychoanalysis, humanism, cognoscitivism, etc.).

If the educational researcher solves each and every one of the five main philosophical problems of knowledge from reason and senses (first thinking and then feeling), or from senses and reason (first feeling and then thinking) he can construct his objects of study from critical philosophical assumptions (possibility of knowledge) apriorist or intellectualist, respectively (origin of knowledge), dialectical, phenomenalist and monistic (pre-metaphysical, metaphysical and theological solutions, respectively, to the problem of the essence of knowledge), mixed <rational-intuitive> or <intuiotive-rational> (classification of knowledge) and mixed <immanent-transcendent> or <transcendent-immanent>, respectively (concept and criterion of truth of knowledge); problematising the reality it investigates by means of the general theories of dialectical knowledge (<complexity-analogy> or <analogy-complexity, etc.); the particular theories of the dialectical social sciences (historicism, historical-dialectical materialism, etc.); and the specific theories of the dialectical sciences of education (<genetics-humanism> or humanism-genetics>, etc.).

Let us remember that an *epistemological orientation* is made up of five elements or levels of knowledge: the *philosophical* assumptions, from which each and every one of the five main problems of knowledge are resolved; the *theoretical* foundations, with which the objects of study can be problematised; the *methodological* procedures or intellectual operations, with which the cognising subject generates new knowledge; the *technical* strategies with which reality is known; and the *instruments* with which information is gathered.

If *theory* (second level of knowledge of an epistemological orientation) depends on philosophy (first level of knowledge of an epistemological orientation) and if method (third level of knowledge of an epistemological orientation) is derived from theory, then: What is to be understood by method of knowledge?

2.6.1 *The definition of knowledge methods*.

Paraphrasing Gutiérrez Pantoja (1999: 153-154), *method* is a way, a path, a route, to reach or obtain an end, an objective. *Methodology*, on the other hand, is the study of methods.

For reasons of space and time, the following definition of educational research *method* is suggested: the *method* or *methods* in educational research consist of those intellectual operations or *methodological* procedures that the cognising subject carries out to generate new knowledge in the educational field, from reason, from the senses or from both qualities of the cognising subject.

2.6.2 *The characteristics of knowledge methods*.

The most important characteristic of intellectual operations or methodological procedures for generating new knowledge is precisely that, that their purpose is to produce new knowledge.

Another important characteristic of the intellectual operations or methodological procedures, which the cognising subject performs in order to generate new knowledge, is that this activity depends on the research question.

The research question is the one that determines the method to be used to produce the new knowledge. For example: if the research question were the following: *what are the similarities and differences between capitalist and socialist education with respect to the sponsorship of education*, the main *intellectual operation* or *methodological procedure* with which the answer could be given is *comparison*. *Comparison* is an intellectual operation or methodological procedure that the cognising subject carries out in order to give an answer to the aforementioned question, looking for *similarities* and *differences* between one type of education and the other. In this way, the answer to this question would constitute new knowledge that would not have been available before if research had not been carried out beforehand.

2.6.3 . *The role of knowledge methods*.

The main need satisfied by an intellectual operation or methodological procedure is to answer the research question.

2.6.4 *The purpose of knowledge methods*.

The main *purpose* of an intellectual operation or methodological procedure is to generate new knowledge.

2.6.5 . *The classification of knowledge methods*.

The main *methodological procedures* or *intellectual operations* (third level of knowledge of an epistemological orientation) that we carry out in order to generate new knowledge are: addition, subtraction, multiplication, division, analysis, synthesis, induction, deduction, definition, classification, comparison, etc. These methods can be classified, according to the philosophical assumptions from which the pre-metaphysical problem of the essence of knowledge is solved, into objective, subjective and dialectical. The same classification criterion was followed for the theoretical foundations (second level of knowledge of an epistemological orientation).

2.6.5.1 *Methodological procedures or intellectual operations to generate new knowledge from reason (objectively)*.

The main methodological procedures or intellectual operations for generating new knowledge from reason, and which are therefore philosophically assumed to be objective, are addition, multiplication, deduction, synthesis, comparison and definition.

2.6.5.1.1 The sum.

The intellectual operation or methodological procedure called *addition* consists of combining or adding two numbers to obtain a final quantity or total. It is a process in which two or more collections of objects are put together in order to obtain a single object.

Paraphrasing Juvencio Reyes Parra (1982: 1) a set is a group, a list, a collection of objects or a gathering of people, called elements or members of the set. Sets can be finite (because they can have a certain number of elements, for example: the planets of the Solar Planetary System) or infinite (because it is unknown how many elements the set can contain, for example: the stars that make up the universe).

Elements can belong to a given set or not, e.g. the horse belongs to the set of horses, the goose does not belong to the set of horses.

Sets are comparable when all the elements of one set are in another set, e.g.: high and low; big and small; bigger than, smaller than; much, little, none; same, different; same, unequal; etc.

The intellectual operation called *addition* is the union of two or more sets of objects in order to obtain a single object.

Empirically speaking, one can only group equal elements, both material (gold with gold, mahogany with mahogany, cows with cows, people with people, etc.) and spiritual (righteous with righteous, good with good, equals with equals, etc.). The problem arises in rational terms, when one wants the union of unequals.

The definition, characteristics, function, purpose, classification, etc., of *addition*, as in multiplication, is constructed from reason. The philosophical assumptions of the concept of *addition* are dogmatic (possibility of knowing), rationalist (origin of knowledge), objectivist, idealist and dualist (pre-metaphysical, metaphysical and theological solutions, respectively, to the problem of the essence of knowledge), rational (classification of knowledge) and immanent (concept and criterion of truth of knowledge).

In *addition,* it is assumed that some elements can be joined, added, added, added to others, increasing their size. With unity it is claimed that reality does not move, that it always remains the same, immobile. This is the truly philosophical aspect of addition: that reality is unique and that phenomena do not change, that they do not move. If reality were to move, two plus two would no longer be four and the international convention would collapse, causing serious financial problems in the world.

In the *sum*, the problem of the *possibility* of knowing is solved preferably from reason, using dogmatic philosophical assumptions. Only from reason can the cognising subject assume that two collections of objects can be brought together to obtain a single one. The object of study can be explored, described, explained, interpreted, understood as a series of parts which, when joined together, can form a whole.

In *addition*, the problem of the origin of knowledge is preferably solved by reason, using rationalist philosophical assumptions. If the cognising subject assumes that reason can discover the essence of his object of knowledge, by means of reflection, he will try to combine or add two or more numbers to obtain a final quantity or total. Addition is a rational operation because the cognising subject uses his reason, not his senses, to suppose or want to suppose that two or more real or ideal objects must be grouped together to form a single one, with a single objective.

It is a matter of putting order into reality. Only this "order" that is proposed is not the eternal, immutable, universal, uncreated, etc. order that the reason of the cognising subject who proposes it or imposes it on others would have us believe. It is an order engendered by the reason of the cognising subject whose intelligence makes him see that, in order to satisfy his needs to possess goods, for example, he needs to establish a series of conventions with other subjects to justify his possessions.

In *addition*, the problem about the essence of knowledge is solved, preferably, from reason; using objectivist philosophical assumptions. If the cognising subject assumes that a *sum* is a set, a group, a list, a collection, etc., of objects or a gathering of persons, called elements or members of the set; then he can estimate that in the relation of knowledge, the object determines the subject; that is to say, that one can know what reality is in itself, in its essence. This would be a pre-metaphysical solution to the problem of the essence of knowledge. In the relation between the cognising subject and the object to be known, it is considered, on the basis of reason, that the object determines the subject.

In the *sum*, the problem about the essence of knowledge is solved, preferably, from reason; using idealistic philosophical assumptions. It is assumed, from reason, that reality contains elements that can be integrated. That the elements of reality can be integrated is an idea that has nothing to do with reality. This would be a metaphysical solution to the problem of the essence of knowledge.

In the *sum*, the problem about the *essence* of knowledge is solved, preferably, from reason; using dualistic philosophical assumptions. Only from reason can the cognising subject assume that reality can be explored, described, explained, interpreted, understood, etc., by dividing it into parts, and then comparing these elements with each other, in terms of equality or inequality, greater than ($<$) and less than ($>$). This would be a theological solution to the problem of the essence of knowledge in which reality is considered to be divided into two opposing and irreconcilable poles.

In the *sum*, the problem about the classification of knowledge is solved, preferably, from reason; using rational philosophical assumptions. Only from reason can the cognising subject assume that the only true knowledge is rational knowledge. It is considered that the cognising subject can and must group, combine, add, etc., two or more collections of objects to form a single one.

If the research question is how much does two plus two give us, the intellectual operation or methodological procedure our mind performs to answer it is an *addition*:

RESEARCH QUESTION	INTELLECTUAL OPERATION OR METHODOLOGICAL PROCEDURE	RESPONSE
How much is two plus two? 2 + 2 =	Addition (grouping, addition)	4

In *sum*, the problem of the concepts and criteria of truth of knowledge is solved, preferably, from reason; using immanent philosophical assumptions. Only from reason can the cognising subject assume that truth is the concordance of thought with its own rules of creation. It is estimated, from reason, that it is possible to combine or add two numbers to obtain a final or total quantity. The concept of truth of the definition being used is immanent, because the ideas "two", "four", "more", "equal", etc., do not exist in reality, it is an invention of reason to bring order to reality. It is presumed, from reason, that the criteria of truth of the *sum* are immanent because the cognising subject relates to ideal, mental objects to be known, which do not have their own existence in reality, which only exist in thought.

2.6.5.1.1.2 Multiplication.

The intellectual operation or methodological procedure called *multiplication* consists of an abbreviated addition. It is an arithmetic operation of composition that consists of repeatedly adding the first quantity as many times as the second quantity indicates.

The definition, characteristics, function, purpose, classification, etc., of *multiplication*, as in addition, is constructed from reason. The philosophical assumptions of the concept of *addition* are dogmatic (possibility of knowing), rationalist (origin of knowledge), objectivist, idealist and dualist (pre-metaphysical solutions), metaphysical and theological, respectively, to the problem of the essence of knowledge), rational (classification of knowledge) and immanent (concept and criterion of truth of knowledge).

2.6.5.1.3 Deduction.

Deduction is an intellectual operation or methodological procedure to generate new knowledge, which the cognising subject carries out from reason, aiming to obtain particular conclusions from general laws.

Deduction (from the Latin *deductio*, to lead). "*... One of the fundamental forms of reasoning (conclusion) and methods for research.... Deduction is analysed as the movement of knowledge from the general to the particular...*" (I Blauberg et al., 1993: 43).

In the intellectual operation or methodological procedure to generate new knowledge called *deduction*, the reasoning process starts from laws (dogmas), which are assumed to be universally valid and logically necessary, to explain particular cases.

The logical model of the *deductive* method is the syllogism. "*From the Greek syllogismós (gathering, counting, calculating).is a deductive argument that has two premises and a conclusion*". (I Blauberg et al., 1993: 522). For example:

MAJOR PRIZE	EVERY MAN MAKES MISTAKES
MINOR PRIZE	EVERY WISE MAN IS A MAN
CONCLUSION	THEN, EVERY WISE MAN IS WRONG

For Aristotle (1983 B), the syllogism (*deductive* method) is "*... an argument (logos) in which, having established certain things, something different necessarily results from them, because they are what they are...*".

The *deductive* (syllogistic) method consists of a demonstration. A demonstration is the "*...substantiation of the truth (or falsity) of an isolated judgement (of an opinion)...by demonstration in a narrow sense we mean a logical reasoning that makes it possible to substantiate the truth of this or that assertion. The demonstration consists of: the conclusion to be demonstrated (thesis) and the premises (arguments or reasons) from which the thesis is deduced. The premises of the demonstration are considered true, and if the demonstrated thesis is deduced from these premises by observing certain logical rules, it is recognised as true (for example, the truth of the thesis: <some metals do not sink in water>, is deduced from the true premises" <potassium is a metal> and <potassium does not sink in water>...*" (I.Blauberg et al., 1983: 44-45).

The *syllogism* (*deductive* method) can also be expressed as a *hypothesis* (from the Greek *hypothesis*, foundation, conjecture), as a "*... theoretical construction not yet demonstrated... supposition...*" (I: Blauberg et al., 1983: 83). The *hypothesis* (intellectual operation or methodological procedure to generate new knowledge from reason) is an assumption, estimation, presumption, conjecture, etc.

In the *hypothesis* (*deductive* method) the aim is to demonstrate an interaction between two phenomena. Interaction is a "*.universal form of connections between objects and phenomena, which is expressed in the influence of one on the other and their modifications. It links their elements, determines their whole, their structural organisation and the changes occurring in them*". (I. Blauberg et al.,

1983: 101). It is assumed that in reality there are entities (objects and phenomena, both concrete and abstract) that interact with each other causing modifications between them, one (independent variable) on the other (dependent variable); governed by laws that can be discovered by reason.

The *hypothesis* relates a cause (independent variable) to an effect (dependent variable). Cause and effect are "*.philosophical categories reflecting the necessary general link between objects and phenomena*". (I. Blauberg et al., 1983: 25). It is assumed that, necessarily, a relationship is established between objects and/or phenomena (concrete and/or abstract). Causal phenomena (independent variable) give rise to effectual phenomena (dependent variable).

"*...the material content of the causal link between objects and phenomena consists ultimately in the influence of some objects and phenomena on others, in the interaction between them, and this interaction constitutes the process of transmission of substance, energy and information from one object to another*" (I. Blauberg *et al.*, 1983: 25-26). (I. Blauberg et al., 1983: 25-26). It is assumed that to every cause there is an effect. It is a cause-effect relationship. Some objects and/or phenomena determine others.

"*Cause always precedes effect. In the frameworks of a certain connection between two phenomena, one of them will be only a cause and the other an effect. At the same time, the effect can influence the cause, i.e. appear in its turn as a cause influencing the phenomenon that was previously the cause of it*". (I. Blauberg et al., 1983: 26). This will depend on whether the cognising subject elaborates his judgements using reason or his senses. If reason is used, it is because it assumes that reality is determined, that everything that happens in this world is due to some cause or causes, brought about by certain phenomena.

The judgements that the cognising subject elaborates from reason are supposed to be logically necessary and universally valid. Necessity and chance are "*.philosophical categories which reflect the various aspects of the objects and phenomena of the external world, their different nexuses. Necessity is the indispensable internal nexus, which arises from the fundamental peculiarities of phenomena and objects. It is what must inevitably happen and, moreover, precisely in this way and not in any other way. Chance, on the other hand, is external to the phenomenon in question. It is conditioned by extraneous factors, not connected with the essence of this phenomenon. It is* which under certain conditions can happen or not happen, be realised in one way or another...*" (I. Blauberg et al., 1983: 133).

Paraphrasing Gutiérrez Sáenz (2005: 169-171), *deduction* - or syllogism - is the reasoning (we would say intellectual operation or methodological procedure) in which the premises link two terms with a third, and the conclusion expresses the relationship of these two terms with each other. Example:

MAJOR PRIZE	EVERY **MAN** IS A RATIONAL ANIMAL
MINOR PRIZE	SOCRATES IS A **MAN**
CONCLUSION	SOCRATES IS A RATIONAL ANIMAL

The *syllogism* consists of proximate and remote matter. The proximate matter of the syllogism is constituted by the premises (major, minor) and the conclusion.

The premises and the conclusion are expressed by three propositions. The remote matter is in the three terms: major, minor and middle. The middle term (MAN) is the one repeated in the two premises. In the conclusion the lesser (SOCRATES) is linked to the greater (RATIONAL ANIMAL).

The major premise (EVERY **MAN** IS A RATIONAL ANIMAL) expresses that the middle term (SOCRATES) is contained in the major (RATIONAL ANIMAL). The minor premise (SOCRATES IS **MAN**) indicates that the minor term (SOCRATES) is contained in the middle (RATIONAL ANIMAL). From this it follows, thanks to the middle term (**MAN**), that the lesser term (SOCRATES) must be contained in the greater (RATIONAL ANIMAL).

The middle term (**MAN**) is the reason or cause of the link of the middle term (**MAN**) with the greater term (RATIONAL ANIMAL). The syllogism is knowledge by causes. That is why it is called scientific knowledge. The syllogism is an ordinary *deduction* that makes it possible to establish the causes or reasons of phenomena.

The definition, characteristics, function, purpose, classification, etc. of *deduction* is constructed from the senses. The philosophical assumptions of the concept of *induction* are dogmatic (possibility of knowing), rationalist (origin of knowledge), objectivist, idealist and dualist (pre-metaphysical, metaphysical and theological solutions, respectively, to the problem of the essence of knowledge), rational (classification of knowledge) and immanent (concept and criterion of truth of knowledge).

In *deduction*, the problem of the possibility of knowing is solved preferably from reason, using dogmatic philosophical assumptions. Only from reason can the cognising subject assume that there is a normative order from which the truth and validity of particular judgements can be deduced. The object of study can be explored, described, explained, interpreted, understood as a universal whole from which all particular phenomena can be derived, because it is considered that reality does not move. It is reason putting order in reality, according to the needs of the cognising subject. The syllogism is a demonstrative instrument.

In *deduction*, the problem of the origin of knowledge is resolved, preferably, from reason, using rationalist philosophical assumptions. If the cognising subject assumes that reason allows him to know his object of study, he will try to explain the causes of phenomena from the discovery of universally valid and logically necessary laws, derived from reason, by means of reflection.

In *deduction*, the problem of the essence of knowledge is preferably solved by reason, using objectivist philosophical assumptions. If the cognising subject assumes that a *deduction* consists in explaining particular phenomena on the basis of universally valid and logically necessary laws that exist on the metaphysical plane, then he may consider that in the relation of knowledge, the object determines the subject, i.e., that knowledge is obtained by means of syllogisms (deductions). This would be a pre-metaphysical solution to the problem of the essence of knowledge. In the relation between the cognising subject and the object to be known, it is considered, from reason, that the object to be known determines the cognising subject.

In *deduction*, the problem of the essence of knowledge is solved, preferably from reason, using idealistic philosophical assumptions. It is assumed, from reason, that reality exists independently of the cognising subject. This would be a metaphysical solution to the problem of the essence of knowledge.

In *deduction*, the problem about the essence of knowledge is solved, preferably, from reason; using dualistic philosophical assumptions. It is assumed, from reason, that the cognising subject can explore, describe, explain, interpret, understand, etc., reality in a Manichean way. It is considered that explanations of reality can be true or false. This would be a theological solution to the problem of the essence of knowledge in which reality is considered to be divided into two opposing and irreconcilable poles.

In *deduction*, the problem about the classification of knowledge is solved, preferably, from reason; using rational philosophical assumptions. Only from reason can the cognising subject assume that the only true knowledge is rational knowledge. It is considered that the cognising subject can and must seek new truths from those already known.

In *deduction*, the problem of the concepts and criteria of truth of knowledge is solved, preferably, from reason; using immanent philosophical assumptions. Only from reason can the cognising subject assume that truth is the concordance of thought with itself, that is, with its own rules of creation. It is considered, from reason, that the act of reasoning consists of obtaining new truths from those already known; that thought is made up of several judgements where the last one (consequent) is linked by a necessary nexus with the former (antecedent). The concept of truth of the definition being used is immanent, because it is conceded that the cognising subject is confronted with ideal objects of knowledge, which have nothing to do with reality. It is presumed, from the senses, that the truth criteria of *deduction* are immanent; because the cognising subject relates to ideal objects to be known, which have no existence of their own in reality, which are pure thought.

2.6.5.1.4 . The synthesis.

Synthesis is an intellectual operation or methodological procedure, which the cognising subject carries out with his object of study, in order to construct new knowledge from reason, reconstructing and reintegrating the parts into the whole. For I. Blauberg et al. (1983:12) analysis and *synthesis* (from the Greek analysis: decomposition, division, and *synthesis*: composition, union), are "*...processes of practical or mental division of the whole into parts, and the reunification of the whole on the basis of its parts (parts and whole)...*". Synthesis is a method of investigation that consists in reconstructing, in reintegrating the parts into the whole. Synthesis is an intellectual operation or methodological procedure that the cognising subject carries out with his object of study in order to generate new knowledge about it. Decomposition (analysis) is carried out from the senses and composition (synthesis) is carried out from reason. As processes of practical or mental division, they can be used to generate new knowledge both in the formal sciences (logic and mathematics) and in the factual sciences (natural and social).

It can be observed, as the authors mentioned above show when they state that both analysis and *synthesis* are "processes of practical or mental division of the whole into parts and the reunification of the whole on the basis of its parts", that one can analyse from the senses (processes of practical division) and synthesise from reason (processes of mental division). Analysis is an intellectual operation or methodological procedure (method) that the cognising subject can carry out with his object of study from the senses in order to generate new knowledge about it. On the other hand, synthesis is an intellectual operation or methodological procedure (method) that the cognising subject can carry out with his reason to generate new knowledge about his object of study.

Together these two methods (or methodological procedures or intellectual operations to generate new knowledge) constitute a new method: the analytic-synthetic method.

To paraphrase I. Blauberg et al. (1983:12), objects of study are complex, their apprehension cannot be limited to the sum of their parts (synthesis); for their reunification in thought (synthesis), with all the richness of their mutual relations, it is necessary to apply another methodological procedure or intellectual operation (method) to generate new knowledge: *synthesis*. By means of this intellectual operation or methodological procedure for generating new knowledge it is possible to reunify the whole in thought as a "*rich whole with numerous definitions and links*" (Marx, quoted by I. Blauberg et al. (1983:12), as a concrete whole.

The cited authors consider that knowledge of the objects of study is neither simple nor schematic, but complex. They state that *analysis* and *synthesis* are not isolated stages of knowledge, that they only complement and follow each other. They say that at each stage *analysis* and *synthesis* are inextricably linked; that *analysis* is not understood without *synthesis*, nor *synthesis* without *analysis*. They say that through *analysis* we separate in the object the properties that make it part of the whole, on the basis of a synthetic representation, even if it is the most general (prior) representation of the whole, while through *synthesis* we recognise the whole as composed of parts, related to each other in a certain way.

In the process of knowledge, *synthesis* is realised through *analysis* and analysis through *synthesis*. *<thought is composed both of the dismemberment of objects, by consciousness, into their elements, and of the reunification of the linked elements into a whole. Without analysis there is no synthesis >* (Engels, quoted by I. Blauberg et al. (1983:12).

For Ortiz (2003: 146) *synthesis* is a "...method of demonstration that proceeds from principles to consequences, from causes to effects. It is the gathering of the elements of a whole". Note that the author refers to the rational aspect. Synthesis is an intellectual operation or methodological procedure (method) to generate new knowledge from reason.

The *synthesis* of any entity is obtained by solving the five main philosophical problems of knowledge from reason: assuming that it is possible to know (dogmatism), believing that the source and basis of our knowledge is to be found in reason (rationalism), assuming that the object determines the subject in the relation of knowledge (objectivism), conjecturing that reality exists independently of the cognising subject (idealism), conceding that reality is divided into two opposing and irreconcilable poles (dualism), attributing that only rational knowledge can be valid (rationalism) and accepting that truth is the concordance of thought with its own laws of creation (concept and immanent criteria).

In the *synthesis*, the problem of the *possibility* of knowing is resolved, preferably, from *reason*; using *dogmatic* philosophical assumptions. Only from reason can the cognising subject assume that a proposition or set of things can have the general and differentiating properties of something material or immaterial.

In the *synthesis*, the problem of the *origin* of knowledge is preferably solved by *reason*, using *rationalist* philosophical assumptions. If the cognising subject assumes that reason can discover the essence of his object of knowledge, by means of reflection, he will try to demonstrate that it is possible to reconstruct and reintegrate the parts that make up a whole by proceeding from principles to consequences, from causes to effects. It is assumed, on the basis of reason, that synthesis is the reunion of the elements of a whole.

In the *synthesis*, the problem of the essence of knowledge is solved preferably from the standpoint of *reason*, using *objectivist* philosophical assumptions. If the cognising subject assumes that his object of knowledge is made up of parts that can be reconstructed and reintegrated into the whole, then he can consider that in the relation of knowledge, the object determines the subject; that is, that one can know what reality is in itself, in its essence. This would be a *pre-metaphysical* solution to the problem of the essence of knowledge: the relation between the cognising subject and the object to be known, in which it is estimated, from reason, that the object determines the subject.

In the *synthesis*, the problem of the essence of knowledge is preferably solved by *reason*, using *idealistic* philosophical assumptions. If the cognising subject assumes that the parts that make up the object to be known can be reconstructed and integrated into a whole, then he can estimate that he can arrive at the idea of what the object of knowledge really is. This would be a *metaphysical* solution to the problem of the essence of knowledge, in which it is conceded, from reason, that all reality is constructed by the cognising subject.

In the synthesis, the problem of the *essence* of knowledge is solved, preferably, from *reason*; using *dualistic* philosophical assumptions. Only from reason can the cognising subject suppose that one can speak of composition and decomposition, construction and deconstruction, etc. This would be a *theological* solution to the problem of the essence of knowledge in which reality is considered to be divided into two opposing and irreconcilable poles.

In the synthesis, the problem of the *classification* of knowledge is solved preferably from *reason*, using *rational* philosophical assumptions. Only from reason can the cognising subject assume that the object of study can be integrated into the parts that make it up. Between the question (What are the parts that make up the whole?) and the answer (x number) there is an intellectual operation or methodological procedure which, in this case, is a synthesis. The cognising subject considers, on the basis of reason, that the only true knowledge is rational knowledge.

In the synthesis, the problem about the *concepts* and *criteria* of truth of knowledge is solved, preferably, from *reason*; using *immanent* philosophical assumptions. Only from reason can the cognising subject assume that truth is the concordance of thought with its own rules of creation. It is considered, from reason, that *synthesising* consists in reconstructing, in reintegrating the parts into the whole. The concept of truth of *synthesis* that is being used is immanent, because the idea of "integrating the parts into the whole" does not exist in reality, it is an invention of reason to bring order to reality. It is presumed, from reason, that the criteria of truth of the *synthesis* are immanent because the cognising subject relates to ideal, mental objects to be known, which do not have their own existence in reality, which only exist in thought.

2.6.5.1.5 Classification.

Classification is an intellectual operation or methodological procedure that the cognising subject carries out from reason to generate new knowledge, which consists of grouping the elements of a set into subsets, classes or classificatory concepts that divide it in a disjunctive or exhaustive way.

According to Ortiz (3003: 28), *classification "...is the simplest way of simultaneously discriminating the elements of a set and of grouping them into subsets, that is, the simplest way of analysing and synthesise...* ". Discriminating, grouping, analysing and synthesising with reason and/or from the senses.

The *classification* of any entity is obtained by solving the five main philosophical problems of knowledge from reason: assuming that it is possible to know (dogmatism), estimating that the source and basis of our knowledge is to be found in reason (rationalism), assuming that the object determines the subject in the relation of knowledge (objectivism), conjecturing that reality exists independently of the cognising subject (idealism), conceding that reality is divided into two opposing and irreconcilable poles (dualism), attributing that only rational knowledge can be valid (rationalism) and accepting that truth is the concordance of thought with its own laws of creation (concept and immanent criteria).

As already mentioned, *classification* is an intellectual operation or methodological procedure to generate new knowledge from reason. In order to *classify*, it is necessary to "order", to simultaneously discriminate the elements of a set and group them into subsets, that is, the simplest way of analysing and synthesising. The analysed reality is discriminated, grouped, analysed and synthesised with reason. It is a matter of exploring, describing, explaining, interpreting, understanding, etc., the object of study, simultaneously discriminating the elements of a set and grouping them into subsets; analysing and synthesising them. In short: *classification* is an intellectual operation or methodological procedure that the reason of the cognising subject performs to generate new knowledge by answering questions such as the following: how many objects of knowledge can I find that resemble the reality being studied.

In *classification*, the problem of the *possibility* of knowing is preferably solved by *reason*, using *dogmatic* philosophical assumptions. Only from reason can the cognising subject assume that it is possible to discriminate simultaneously the elements of a set and group them into subsets, i.e. reality can be analysed and synthesised.

In *classification*, the problem of the *origin* of knowledge is resolved, preferably, from *reason*, using *rationalist* philosophical assumptions. If the cognising subject assumes that reason can discover the essence of his object of knowledge, by means of reflection, he will try to discriminate the elements that make up a set from the others, in order to group them into subsets of his object of study.

In *classification*, the problem of the essence of knowledge is preferably solved by *reason*, using *objectivist* philosophical assumptions. If the cognising subject assumes that the elements of a set can be grouped into subsets, then he can estimate that in the relation of knowledge, the object determines the subject; that is, that one can know what reality is in itself, in its essence. This would be a *pre-metaphysical* solution to the problem of the essence of knowledge: the relation between the cognising subject and the object to be known, in which it is estimated, from reason, that the object determines the subject.

In *classification*, the problem about the essence of knowledge is solved, preferably, from *reason*; using *idealistic* philosophical assumptions. If the cognising subject assumes that the elements of a set can be grouped into subsets, classes or classificatory concepts that divide it disjunctively and exhaustively, then he may consider that without a subject no object is possible (subjective idealism), i.e. that the idea of what the object of knowledge really is can be arrived at. This would be a *metaphysical* solution to the problem of the essence of knowledge, in which it is conceded, from reason, that all reality is constructed by the cognising subject.

In *classification*, the problem of the *essence* of knowledge is solved, preferably, from *reason*; using *dualistic* philosophical assumptions. Only from reason can the cognising subject suppose that the elements of a set can be grouped into subsets, classificatory concepts, which divide it in a disjunctive or exhaustive way. This would be a *theological* solution to the problem of the essence of knowledge in which reality is considered to be divided into two opposing and irreconcilable poles.

In *classification*, the problem of the types of knowledge is solved, preferably, from *reason*; using *rational* philosophical assumptions. Only from reason can the cognising subject assume that the elements of a set can be grouped into subsets, classes or classificatory concepts, which divide it disjunctively or exhaustively. The cognising subject considers, on the basis of reason, that the only true knowledge is rational knowledge.

In *classification*, the problem of the *concepts* and *criteria* of truth of knowledge is solved preferably from the standpoint of *reason*, using *immanent* philosophical assumptions. Only from reason can the cognising subject assume that truth is the concordance of thought with its own rules of creation. It is considered, from reason, that to *classify* is to group the elements of a set into subsets, classes or *classificatory* concepts, which divide it in a disjunctive or exhaustive way. The concept of truth of *classification* that is being used is immanent, because the idea of "grouping" does not exist in reality, it is an invention of reason to bring order to reality. It is presumed, from reason, that the criteria of truth of *classification* are immanent because the cognising subject relates to ideal, mental objects to be known, which do not have their own existence in reality, which only exist in thought.

2.6.5.1. 6The definition.

Definition is an intellectual operation or methodological procedure that the cognising subject performs with its object of knowledge.

study in order to generate new knowledge about it using reason and/or the senses. Paraphrasing I. Blauberg et al. (1983: 43-44), *definition* (from the Latin *definitio*, consists in the explanation of a *concept*. The cognizing subject will try to explore, describe, explain, interpret, understand, etc. what his object of study is and what it is not. *To define*, in this sense, means to set limits. It is a proposition or set of things that brings together the general and differentiating properties of something material or immaterial. In Aristotelian terms, it is a matter of finding the relation between the proximate genus and the specific difference. A *definition* must express the fundamental characteristics that constitute the content of the *concept*.

Definition is the first intellectual operation that the cognising subject must perform in order to explore, describe, explain, understand, interpret, etc., the characteristics, function, purpose, classification, elements, etc., of a *concept*. The content of a *concept* is broader than its *definition*. The *definition* is only one of the parts into which a *concept* can be divided for its construction.

To paraphrase Gutiérrez Sáenz (2005: 109-110) *to define* means "to set limits". It is something like the expression of what an object is without adding or subtracting anything from it. The term comes from the Latin *definire* = to set limits. To delimit what an entity is and is not.

Concepts refer to objects. To specify exactly what kind of objects these *concepts* refer to is to *define*: to set limits to what an entity is, without adding or subtracting anything from it. To construct a *concept*, from conceptual mapping, the first step is to *define it*, to set limits between what it is and what it is not.

The difference between a *concept* and a *definition* is one of degree; the *definition* is only a part of the *concept*: its notion. It answers the question of what the entity we want to talk about is: what is it? Other parts that make up the concept are its characteristics, the function it fulfils in a discourse, the purpose of this function, its classification, etc.

Definition refers to the understanding and extension of an entity. To develop an understanding of a *concept* accurately and faithfully, without missing or missing essential notes, is to *define it*. A well-done *definition* is a sign of correct thinking. In the *definition,* the law of logic applies: the longer a concept is, the less it is understood, and vice versa.

Some characteristics of the *definition* are:
1. Brief, but complete, i.e. accurate.
2. Applicable to everything and only what is defined.
3. Clara.
4. The defined word should not be used in the definition.
5. It should not be negative.
6. Must indicate essential attributes (if possible the proximate gender and the specific difference).

A definition is useful to the extent that it removes ambiguity of vocabulary, and makes uniformity of thought possible, leading us to the purpose of the definition: the understanding of the concept in question.

There are several types of definition:

7. *Nominal* definition: This refers to the name or word. This type of *definition* can guide the researcher about the meaning of the *defined* word. Synonyms can be used for the most common words that are close to the *defined word*. The *etymology* of the word should be used.

8. *Actual* definition: Refers to the thing or object signified. It is a matter of clarifying the constitutive notes of a *concept*, insofar as its extension encompasses precisely the notes it comprises. It brings us closer to the desired end: the understanding of the *concept*. The understanding of the *concept* can be reached in two ways: by describing it: the most typical properties of the object to be defined are listed (example: iron is a grey metal with atomic weight 55.84, atomic number 26 and density 7.86); or by decomposing it into its proximate genus and its specific difference (for example: man: animal <proximate genus> rational <specific difference>).

The *definition* of any entity is obtained by solving the five main philosophical problems of knowledge from reason: assuming that it is possible to know (dogmatism), estimating that the source and basis of our knowledge is to be found in reason (rationalism), assuming that the object determines the subject in the relation of knowledge (objectivism), conjecturing that reality exists independently of the cognising subject (idealism), conceding that reality is divided into two opposing and irreconcilable poles (dualism), attributing that only rational knowledge can be valid (rationalism) and accepting that truth is the concordance of thought with its own laws of creation (concept and immanent criteria).

As already mentioned, *definition* is an intellectual operation or methodological procedure to generate new knowledge from reason. In order to define, it is necessary to "order" the analysed reality, to set "limits" between what the object is and what it is not; it is a matter of exploring, describing, explaining, interpreting, understanding, etc., what is, in itself, an object of knowledge, without adding or subtracting anything from it.

The definition is a proposition or set of things that brings together the general and distinguishing properties of something material or immaterial.

In the *definition*, the problem of the *possibility* of knowing is solved preferably from *reason*, using *dogmatic* philosophical assumptions. Only from reason can the cognising subject assume that it can establish the limits between what is and what is not its object of knowledge. To pretend to know what reality is, as we have already seen, is an illusion.

In the *definition*, the problem of the *origin* of knowledge is preferably solved by *reason*, using *rationalist* philosophical assumptions. If the cognising subject assumes that reason can discover the essence of his object of knowledge, by means of reflection, he will try to find the proximate kind and the specific difference of his object of study by enumerating the most typical properties of the object.

In *definition*, the problem of the essence of knowledge is preferably solved by *reason*, using *objectivist* philosophical assumptions. If the cognising subject assumes that a definition must be brief, complete, exact, clear, applicable to everything and only what is defined and indicating essential attributes, then he can estimate that in the relation of knowledge, the object determines the subject; that is to say, that one can know what reality is in itself, in its essence. This would be a *pre-metaphysical* solution to the problem of the essence of knowledge: the relation between the cognising subject and the object to be known, in which it is estimated, from reason, that the object determines the subject.

In the *definition*, the problem about the essence of knowledge is solved preferably from *reason*; using *idealistic* philosophical assumptions. If the cognising subject assumes that the idea of the object to be known can be constructed, then he can estimate that without a subject no object is possible (subjective idealism), i.e. that the idea of what the object of knowledge really is can be arrived at. This would be a *metaphysical* solution to the problem of the essence of knowledge, in which it is conceded, on the basis of reason, that all reality is constructed by the cognising subject.

In *definition*, the problem of the *essence* of knowledge is solved, preferably, from *reason*; using *dualistic* philosophical assumptions. Only from reason can the cognising subject assume that one can speak of complete or incomplete, short or long, exact or inexact, clear or confused, negative or positive, etc. definitions of his object of study. This would be a *theological* solution to the problem of the essence of knowledge in which reality is considered to be divided into two opposing and irreconcilable poles.

In the *definition*, the problem about the *classification* of knowledge is solved, preferably, from *reason*; using *rational* philosophical assumptions. Only from reason can the cognising subject assume that boundaries can be drawn between what a thing is and what it is not. Between the question (what is the definition?) and the answer (expression of what an object is without adding or subtracting anything from it) there is an intellectual operation or methodological procedure which, in this case, is a definition. The cognising subject considers, on the basis of reason, that the only true knowledge is rational knowledge.

In the *definition*, the problem of the *concepts* and *criteria* of truth of knowledge is solved, preferably, from *reason*; using immanent philosophical assumptions. Only from reason can the cognising subject assume that truth is the concordance of thought with its own rules of creation. It is considered, from reason, that to define is to set limits to what a thing is and what it is not. The concept of truth of the definition being used is immanent, because the idea of "setting limits to what a thing is and what it is not" does not exist in reality, it is an invention of reason to bring order to reality. It is presumed, from reason, that the criteria of truth of the definition are immanent because the cognising subject relates to ideal, mental objects to be known, which do not have their own existence in reality, which only exist in thought.

2.6.5.2 *Methodological procedures or intellectual operations to generate new knowledge from the senses (subjectively).*

The main methodological procedures or intellectual operations for generating new knowledge from the senses, and which are therefore philosophically assumed to be subjective, are: subtraction, division, induction, analysis, and comparison.

2.6.5.2.1 Subtraction.

The intellectual operation or methodological procedure called *subtraction* is an operation of decomposition, which consists of, given a certain quantity, eliminating a part of it and the result is known as the difference. It is the inverse of addition.

Paraphrasing Juvencio Reyes Parra (1982: 24), subtraction is called difference; it is the set of elements that a set lacks in order to be equal to another set.

The definition, characteristics, function, purpose, classification, etc., of *subtraction*, as in division, is constructed from the senses. The philosophical assumptions of the concept of *subtraction* are sceptical, subjectivist, relativist and pragmatic (possibility of knowing), empiricist (origin of knowledge), subjectivist, realist and dualist (pre-metaphysical, metaphysical and theological solutions, respectively, to the problem of the essence of knowledge), intuitive (classification of knowledge) and transcendent (concept and criterion of truth of knowledge).

It is assumed, from the senses, that elements can be removed, separated or subtracted from one set because they belong to another set. The remaining elements are called a difference.

In *subtraction*, the problem of the *possibility* of knowing is resolved, preferably, from the senses; using sceptical, subjectivist, relativist and pragmatic philosophical assumptions. Only from the senses can the cognising subject assume that one set can be separated, subtracted or subtracted from another. The object of study can be explored, described, explained, interpreted, understood as a series of parts that, united, can form a whole.

In *subtraction*, the problem about the origin of knowledge is solved, preferably, from the senses; using empiricist philosophical assumptions. If the cognising subject supposes that, given a certain quantity, a part of it can be eliminated, he will concede, from the senses, that subtraction is an operation of decomposition, not of union, as in addition.

In *subtraction*, the problem about the essence of knowledge is resolved, preferably, from the senses; using subjectivist philosophical assumptions. If the cognising subject assumes that to subtract is to separate, to take away, one set from another; then he can estimate that in the relation of knowledge, the cognising subject determines the object to be known; that is to say, that in a subtraction, the difference is the set of elements that are missing from one set to make it equal to another set. This would be a pre-metaphysical solution to the problem of the essence of knowledge. In the relation between the cognising subject and the object to be known, it is estimated, from the senses, that the subject determines the object.

In *subtraction*, the problem of the essence of knowledge is solved preferably from the senses, using realist philosophical assumptions. It is assumed, from the senses, that reality contains elements that can be disintegrated from the wholes of which they are part. This would be a metaphysical solution to the problem of the essence of knowledge.

In *subtraction*, the problem about the *essence* of knowledge is solved, preferably, from the senses; using dualistic philosophical assumptions. Only from the senses can the cognising subject assume that reality can be explored, described, explained, interpreted, understood, etc., by dividing it into parts, and then comparing these elements with each other, in terms of equality or inequality, greater than (<) and less than (>). This would be a theological solution to the problem of the essence of knowledge in which reality is considered to be divided into two opposing and irreconcilable poles.

In *subtraction*, the problem about the classification of knowledge is solved preferably from the senses; using empiricist philosophical assumptions. Only from the senses can the cognising subject assume that the only true knowledge is intuitive knowledge. It is considered that the cognising subject can and must suppose that a difference or subtraction is the set of elements that a set lacks in order to be equal to another set.

If the research question is how much is four minus two, the intellectual operation or methodological procedure our mind performs to answer it is a *subtraction*:

RESEARCH QUESTION	INTELLECTUAL OPERATION OR METHODOLOGICAL PROCEDURE	RESPONSE
What is four minus two? 4 - 2 =	Subtract	2

In *subtraction*, the problem about the concepts and criteria of truth of knowledge is resolved, preferably, from the senses; using transcendent philosophical assumptions. Only from the senses can the cognising subject assume that truth is the concordance of thought with the object thought. It is estimated, from the senses, that it is possible to separate, subtract or subtract one set from another. The concept of truth of the definition being used is transcendent, because the ideas "minus", "subtract", etc., are empirical. It is presumed, from the senses, that the truth criteria of *subtraction* are transcendent because the cognising subject relates to real objects to be known, independent of the cognising subject.

2.6.5.2.2 The division.

Division is the operation that consists of dividing a whole into its parts. Paraphrasing Gutiérrez Sáenz (2005: 114-117), *division* is the distribution of a whole into its constituent parts. It refers to the extension of an idea or concept. *Division* helps to better understand the meaning of a concept.

Division moves in the realm of extension, *definition* in the realm of comprehension. The greater the extension (division) of a concept, the lesser the understanding (definition) of it; the smaller the extension of an idea (division), the greater the understanding (definition) of it.

The division is related to the analysis (division of the concept into its constituent parts or classes).

This intellectual operation or methodological procedure is very useful to achieve clarity and precision in the meaning of a concept.

The *division*, according to the aforementioned author, can be of different kinds:

- *Classification*: To mention the different species (or classes) contained in a genus (or whole). One starts from a universal whole and obtains parts called classes or species. It is a matter of ordering the different groups of individuals found in a *concept*. All the individuals included in a *concept* can be grouped into classes and subclasses, according to one or more characteristics that they have in common and that will serve as *classification criteria*. The *classification criterion* is the basis of the *division*. Every *concept* can be considered as a genus. *Dividing* or *classifying* consists of finding the different species contained in the genus. This form of *division* (the most illustrative example of which is the "tree of Porphyry") is called *dichotomous*. The whole under consideration is called the universal whole or genus and the parts into which it is or can be *divided* are the classes or species.

-Physical division: To mention the different material parts that make up a whole. We start from an integral whole and obtain physical parts. It is a matter of breaking down a whole into the physical parts that materially compose it.

-Logical or metal division: To mention the different elements that contain the understanding of a concept. The separation of these elements is only possible in the mind, but not in sensible reality. It is a question of penetrating into the elements contained in the understanding of a concept. These elements can only be separated in the mind, not in reality.

The main rules of a division are:

-It must be complete.

-One part should not include another. They are mutually exclusive.

-It should be orderly and gradual.

-It should be brief.

The definition, characteristics, function, purpose, classification, etc., of *division*, as in subtraction, is constructed from the senses. The philosophical assumptions of the concept of *division* are sceptical, subjectivist, relativist and pragmatist (possibility of knowing), rationalist (origin of knowledge), subjectivist, realist and dualist (pre-metaphysical, metaphysical and theological solutions, respectively, to the problem of the essence of knowledge), intuitive (classification of knowledge) and transcendent (concept and criterion of truth of knowledge).

In the *division*, the problem of the possibility of knowing is solved preferably from the senses, using sceptical, subjectivist, relativist and pragmatic philosophical assumptions. Only from the senses can the cognising subject assume that the object of knowledge can be distributed into its constituent parts. The object of study can be explored, described, explained, interpreted, understood as a universal whole that can be broken down into its constituent parts (classes or species), because it is believed that reality moves.

Division, like subtraction, are intellectual operations or methodological procedures to generate new knowledge, from the senses, of decomposition, not of union, as in addition and multiplication; that is why the philosophical assumptions of the mentioned methods are different.

In the *division*, the problem of the origin of knowledge is solved preferably from the senses, using empiricist philosophical assumptions. If the cognising subject assumes that reason can describe the object of knowledge by means of the senses, he will try to find the parts and characteristics that make it up.

In *division*, the problem of the essence of knowledge is solved preferably from the senses, using subjectivist philosophical assumptions. If the cognising subject assumes that a division must be complete, orderly, gradual and brief, then he may consider that in the relation of knowledge, the subject determines the object, i.e., that reality is constructed by each subject. This would be a *pre-metaphysical* solution to the problem of the essence of knowledge. In the relation between the cognising subject and the object to be known, it is estimated, from the senses, that the subject determines the object.

In *division*, the problem of the essence of knowledge is solved preferably from the senses, using realist philosophical assumptions. It is assumed, from the senses, that reality can be divided. This would be a metaphysical solution to the problem of the essence of knowledge.

In the *division*, the problem about the essence of knowledge is solved, preferably, from the senses; using *dualistic* philosophical assumptions. Only from the senses can the cognising subject suppose that reality can be explored, described, explained, interpreted, understood, etc., by means of complete, excluding, ordered, gradual, brief *divisions* with excluding parts, etc. This would be a *theological* solution to the problem of the essence of knowledge in which reality is considered to be divided into two opposing and irreconcilable poles.

In the *division*, the problem about the classification of knowledge is solved, preferably, from the senses; using intuitive philosophical assumptions. Only from the senses can the cognising subject assume that the only true knowledge is intuitive knowledge. It is considered that the cognising subject can and must distribute the whole into its constituent parts in order to be able to apprehend it.

In the *division*, the problem about the concepts and criteria of truth of knowledge is resolved, preferably, from the senses; using transcendent philosophical assumptions. Only from the senses can the cognising subject assume that truth is the concordance of thought with the object thought. It is estimated, from the senses, that to divide is to distribute a whole into its parts. The concept of truth of the *definition* being used is transcendent, because concrete or abstract entities that can have their own existence in reality are divided. It is presumed, from the senses, that the truth criteria of the division are transcendent because the cognising subject relates to real objects to be known, which have their own existence in reality, independently of the cognising subjects.

2.6.5.2.3 Induction.

Induction is an intellectual operation or methodological procedure, which the cognising subject carries out with his object of study, in order to generate new knowledge from the senses; and which consists of obtaining general conclusions from premises that contain particular data.

Induction (from the Latin *inductio*, to guide, to lead) "*... is one of the fundamental types of reasoning (conclusion) and method of investigation. The inductive conclusion is the movement of knowledge from isolated statements to general conclusions. A distinction is made between complete induction, when the conclusion about a class of objects in general is made on the basis of the analysis of all objects of that class, and the various types of incomplete induction, when the conclusion about the class of objects is made on the basis of the analysis of some objects of that class (in this case their essential properties, nexuses, etc. are analysed)...*" (I: Blauberg et al., 7983: 100). Induction is an intellectual operation or methodological procedure that can be performed by the cognising subject in order to generate new knowledge from the senses.

Paraphrasing Gutiérrez Sáenz (2005: 206-210), "*.induction is an inverse process to deduction*". *Induction* starts from the particular to end up in the universal, from the singular to the general, from the observation of some singular things to a universal law.

A constant relation between phenomena is observed and an essential relation (logically necessary and universally valid) is obtained. The author cites as an example the observation of some metals: if one observes that gold, iron, copper, etc., are good conductors of electricity, one can infer (inductively) a universally valid and logically necessary law: all metals are good conductors of electricity.

The process of *induction* depends on an essential relation. When we are able to grasp an essential relation in a series of singular experiences, it is valid to infer that all cases related to that essence possess the indicated property.

The laws of the experimental sciences (natural and physical sciences) have been obtained from this intellectual operation or methodological procedure, called the scientific method.

Induction can be total or partial:

- Total *induction*: observe all the cases contained in a lesson and grasp the property that relates them. For example: Mercury revolves around the sun, Venus revolves around the sun, the Earth revolves around the sun... Pluto...; therefore, all the planets of the solar planetary system revolve around the sun.

- Partial *induction*: observe a property in a sufficient (not total) number of singular cases, and from there infer the universal law. For example: Venus has no light of its own, mercury has no light of its own, etc., so all the planets of the solar planetary system have no light of their own.

The definition, characteristics, function, purpose, classification, etc. of *induction* is constructed from the senses. The philosophical assumptions of the concept of *induction* are sceptical, subjectivist, relativist, and pragmatic (possibility of knowing), empiricist (origin of knowledge), subjectivist, realist and dualist (pre-metaphysical, metaphysical and theological solutions, respectively, to the problem of the essence of knowledge), intuitive (classification of knowledge) and transcendent (concept and criterion of truth of knowledge).

In *induction*, the problem about the possibility of knowing is solved preferably from the senses; using sceptical, subjectivist, relativist and pragmatic philosophical assumptions. Only from the senses can the cognising subject assume that by observing a property in a sufficient (not total) number of singular cases, it can lead the cognising subject to infer a universal law.

In *induction*, the problem of the origin of knowledge is solved preferably from the senses, using empiricist philosophical assumptions. If the cognising subject assumes that the senses allow him to know his object of study, he will try to document several particular cases where an essence can be grasped, from there to a necessary nexus and then to a universal law.

In *induction*, the problem of the essence of knowledge is solved preferably from the senses, using subjectivist philosophical assumptions. If the cognising subject assumes that an *induction* consists in observing a property in a sufficient (not total) number of singular cases, and from there inferring the universal law, then he can estimate that in the relation of knowledge, the subject determines the object, i.e., that knowledge is obtained by means of experience (experiments). This would be a pre-metaphysical solution to the problem of the essence of knowledge. In the relation between the cognising subject and the object to be known, it is estimated, from the senses, that the cognising subject determines the object to be known.

In *induction*, the problem of the essence of knowledge is solved preferably from the senses, using realist philosophical assumptions. It is assumed, from the senses, that reality exists independently of the cognising subject. This would be a metaphysical solution to the problem of the essence of knowledge.

In *induction*, the problem about the essence of knowledge is solved, preferably, from the senses; using *dualistic* philosophical assumptions. It is assumed, from the senses, that the cognising subject can explore, describe, explain, interpret, understand, etc., reality in a Manichean way. This would be a theological solution to the problem of the essence of knowledge in which reality is considered to be divided into two opposing and irreconcilable poles.

In *induction*, the problem about the classification of knowledge is solved preferably from the senses; using intuitive philosophical assumptions. Only from the senses can the cognising subject assume that the only true knowledge is intuitive knowledge. It is considered that the cognising subject can and must look for a property common to a sufficient number of particular cases to be able to infer a universal law, derived from that empirical nexus.

In *induction*, the problem about the concepts and criteria of truth of knowledge is solved, preferably, from the senses; using transcendent philosophical assumptions. Only from the senses can the cognising subject assume that truth is the concordance of thought with the characteristics of the object thought. It is estimated, from the senses, that the mind reflects, in the manner of a "mirror", the real characteristics of the object thought. The concept of truth in the definition being used is transcendent, because it is conceded that reality exists independently of thought. It is presumed, from the senses, that the truth criteria of *induction* are transcendent; because the cognising subject relates to real objects to be known, which have their own existence in reality, independently of thought.

2.6.5.2.4 The analysis.

Analysis is an intellectual operation or methodological procedure, which the cognising subject carries out from the senses, in order to generate new knowledge, breaking down the whole (the object of study) into its constituent parts.

Analysis is understood in terms of "... *categorising, ordering, manipulating and summarising the data of an investigation in order to answer the questions posed in it; it is the intellectual operation that considers separately the parts of a whole...*" (Ortiz, 2003: 14). Note that the cited author considers, as we do, that we are talking about "intellectual operations". The method for generating new knowledge called *analysis* consists of an intellectual operation or methodological procedure that the cognising subject carries out to "answer the research question(s)", categorising, ordering, manipulating and summarising the parts that make up the whole, in order to be able to analyse them one by one.

For I. Blauberg et al. (1983:12) "*.analysis is a method of investigating objects which makes it possible to break down the whole into its parts and subject them to individual study. As they are separated from their links, from their interactions with the other parts and with the whole, abstract, incomplete, one-sided definitions are obtained. Analysis, however, is an indispensable stage in the knowledge of the whole. It makes it possible to study the isolated parts of the whole, to unravel the general relationships for all the parts, and thus to recognise the peculiarities of the emergence and development of the whole object (the whole)*". Analysis is a method that consists of breaking down a whole into its constituent parts.

To analyse is to break down a whole into its constituent parts. It is an intellectual operation or methodological procedure that the cognising subject carries out, from the senses, to put order in the various aspects of the object of study, with a view to exploring, describing, explaining, interpreting, understanding, in a better way the reality under analysis, as a whole that only the senses can divide into the parts that make it up.

The classifications of analysis can be infinite. The scope of the present study limits us to the philosophical aspect. For this reason, we will not go into the study of the classifications mentioned.

The definition, characteristics, function, purpose, classification, etc. of *analysis* are constructed from the senses. The philosophical assumptions of the concept of *analysis* are sceptical, subjectivist, relativist and pragmatic (possibility of knowing), empirical (origin of knowledge), subjectivist, realist and dualist (pre-metaphysical, metaphysical and theological solutions, respectively, to the problem of the essence of knowledge), intuitive (classification of knowledge) and transcendent (concept and criterion of truth of knowledge).

In *analysis*, the problem about the possibility of knowing is solved preferably from the senses; using sceptical, subjectivist, relativist and pragmatic philosophical assumptions. If the cognising subject assumes that it is not possible to know in essence his object of study, he will try to categorise, order, manipulate and summarise the data of an investigation in order to answer the questions posed in it. In *analysis*, it is considered that reality moves and that, therefore, it can be broken down into its constituent parts, in order to study them separately and, in a second stage, to explore, describe, explain, interpret, understand, etc., in a better way the whole.

In *analysis*, the problem of the *origin* of knowledge is solved preferably from the senses, using empirical philosophical assumptions. If the cognising subject assumes that the origin of knowledge is to be found in the senses, he will try to use it to decompose a whole into its constituent parts and thus analyse it part by part.

In the *analysis*, the problem of the essence of knowledge is solved preferably from the senses, using subjectivist philosophical assumptions. If the cognising subject assumes that in a relation of knowledge the cognising subject determines the object to be known, then he can estimate that reality, the whole, is constructed by each cognising subject, and, by the same token, the researcher has to construct his object of study. This would be a *pre-metaphysical* solution to the problem of the essence of knowledge. In the relationship between the cognising subject and the object to be known, it is estimated, from the senses, that the cognising subject determines his object of knowledge.

In *analysis*, the problem of the essence of knowledge is solved preferably from the senses, using realist philosophical assumptions. If the researcher assumes that reality exists independently of the cognising subject, then he will estimate that reality can be broken down into its constituent parts. This would be a metaphysical solution to the problem of the essence of knowledge.

In *analysis*, the problem of the essence of knowledge is preferably solved from the senses, using dualistic philosophical assumptions. If the researcher assumes that reality is divided into two opposing and irreconcilable poles, then he will consider that the object of study can be broken down into its different parts. It is granted, from the senses, that the cognising subject can explore, describe, explain, interpret, understand, etc., reality in a Manichean way. This would be a *theological* solution to the problem of the essence of knowledge in which reality is presumed to be divided into two opposing and irreconcilable poles.

In the *analysis*, the problem about the classification of knowledge is solved preferably from the senses; using intuitive philosophical assumptions. Only from the senses can the cognising subject assume that the only true knowledge is intuitive knowledge. It is considered that the cognising subject can and must break down his object of study into its constituent parts, with a view to a better understanding of it.

In the *analysis*, the problem of the *concepts* and *criteria* of truth of knowledge is resolved, preferably, from the senses; using transcendent philosophical assumptions. Only from the senses can the cognising subject assume that truth is the concordance of thought with the object thought. From the senses, it is considered that the senses describe the relations between phenomena. The concept of truth of the definition being used is transcendent, because it is conceded that reality exists independently of thought. It is presumed, from the senses, that the criteria of truth of the *analysis* are transcendent; because the cognising subject relates to real objects to be known, which have their own existence in reality, independently of thought.

2.6.5.2.5 The comparison.

Comparison is an intellectual operation or methodological procedure that the cognising subject carries out from the senses to generate new knowledge, which consists of fixing the attention on two or more objects to discover their relations or estimate their differences and/or similarities.

The definition, characteristics, function, purpose, classification, etc. of *comparison* is constructed from the senses. The philosophical assumptions of the concept of comparison are sceptical, subjectivist, relativist and pragmatic (possibility of knowing), empirical (origin of knowledge), subjectivist, realist and dualist (pre-metaphysical, metaphysical and theological solutions, respectively, to the problem of the essence of knowledge), intuitive (classification of knowledge) and transcendent (concept and criterion of truth of knowledge).

In *comparison*, the problem of knowability is preferably solved from the senses, using sceptical, subjectivist, relativist and pragmatic philosophical assumptions. If the cognising subject assumes that it is not possible to know in essence his object of study, he will try to discover the relations between two or more objects or estimate their differences or similarities in order to give an answer to the research question. In the comparison, it is estimated that reality moves and that, therefore, relationships between the objects of study can be discovered and, in a second moment, the whole can be explored, described, explained, interpreted, understood, etc., in a better way, estimating their differences and/or similarities.

In *comparison*, the problem of the *origin* of knowledge is solved preferably from the senses, using empirical philosophical assumptions. If the cognising subject assumes that the origin of knowledge is to be found in the senses, he will try to use comparison to break down a whole into its constituent parts and thus analyse it part by part.

In the *comparison*, the problem of the essence of knowledge is solved preferably from the senses, using subjectivist philosophical assumptions. If the cognising subject assumes that in a relation of knowledge the cognising subject determines the object to be known, then he can estimate that reality, the whole, is constructed by each cognising subject, and, by the same token, the researcher has to construct his object of study. This would be a *pre-metaphysical* solution to the problem of the essence of knowledge. In the relationship between the cognising subject and the object to be known, it is estimated, from the senses, that the cognising subject determines his object of knowledge.

In *comparison*, the problem of the essence of knowledge is preferably solved from the senses, using realist philosophical assumptions. If the researcher assumes that reality exists independently of the cognising subject, then he will consider that reality is composed of parts that may be similar or different from each other. This would be a metaphysical solution to the problem of the essence of knowledge.

In *comparison*, the problem of the essence of knowledge is preferably solved from the senses, using dualistic philosophical assumptions. If the researcher assumes that reality is divided into two opposing and irreconcilable poles, then he will consider that the object of study is composed of two or more parts that can be similar or different from each other. It is granted, from the senses, that the cognising subject can explore, describe, explain, interpret, understand, etc., reality in a Manichean way. This would be a theological solution to the problem of the essence of knowledge in which reality is presumed to be divided into two opposing and irreconcilable poles.

In the *comparison*, the problem about the classification of knowledge is solved preferably from the senses; using intuitive philosophical assumptions. Only from the senses can the cognising subject assume that the only true knowledge is intuitive knowledge. It is considered that reality can be divided into two or more objects of study for the purpose of comparing them with each other and discovering their similarities and differences.

In the *comparison*, the problem of the *concepts* and *criteria* of truth of knowledge is resolved, preferably, from the senses; using transcendent philosophical assumptions. Only from the senses can the cognising subject assume that truth is the concordance of thought with the object thought. It is estimated, from the senses, that relations of similarity and/or difference between phenomena can be discovered by comparing them with each other. The concept of truth in the definition being used is transcendent, because it is conceded that reality exists independently of thought. It is presumed, from the senses, that the criteria of truth of the *analysis* are transcendent; because the cognising subject relates to real objects to be known, which have their own existence in reality, independently of thought.

2.6.5.3 *Methodological procedures or intellectual operations to generate new knowledge from the senses and reason (dialectically).*

The main methodological procedures or intellectual operations to generate new knowledge from the senses and/or from reason, and which are therefore philosophically assumed to be dialectical, are: the inductive-deductive method or vice versa, the analytical-synthetic method or vice versa, and so on. These methods constitute a combination of the others (inductive, deductive; and analytical, synthetic; respectively).

2.6.5.3.1 The inductive-deductive method.

The inductive-deductive method is an intellectual operation or methodological procedure to generate new knowledge from both qualities of the cognising subject: reason and the senses, which consists of obtaining general conclusions from premises containing particular data (induction) and then obtaining particular conclusions from these general laws (deduction).

The *inductive-deductive* method sees science as rational, systematic, exact, verifiable and therefore fallible knowledge; *scientific knowledge* as a tentatively established system of ideas; and scientific research as an activity producing new ideas (Bunge, 1970: 9).

In the *inductive-deductive* method, science begins with observation (induction). It is a matter of recording what is seen, heard, etc. with the sense organs, reliably and without prejudice. Observational statements are derived into laws and theories (induction). Once a scientist has universal laws and theories at his disposal, he can draw from them various consequences that will serve as explanations and predictions (deduction).

Methodologically, the *inductive-deductive* method believes that, under certain conditions, it is permissible to generalise from a finite list of singular observational statements to a universal law; provided that the number of observational statements that form the basis of the generalisation is large, the observations are repeated under a wide variety of conditions and that no statement

The generalisations can be singular, referring to a particular event or state of affairs in a particular place at a particular time. Generalisations can be singular, referring to a particular event or state of affairs in a particular place at a particular time; general, expressing statements about the properties or behaviour of some aspect of the universe referring to all events of a particular kind in all places and at all times; and universal, all the laws and theories that constitute scientific knowledge.

The techniques used to collect data (facts) are observation, experimentation, survey and documentation.

The research model they follow is as follows: "if under a wide variety of conditions a large number of A's are observed and if all observed A's possess property B without exception, then all A's have property B".

And its graphic expression is as follows:

		LAWS AND THEORIES		
	INDUCTION		DEDUCTION	
FACTS ACQUIRED THROUGH EXPERIENCE				PREDICTIONS AND EXPLANATIONS

According to them science progresses by explaining and predicting. The source of truth is experience (empiricism). General principles are derived from experience by *induction*. Either *inductions* satisfy the prescribed conditions or they do not. The reliability of science follows from the *inductivist*'s claims about observation and *induction*. Observational statements are certain and reliable because their truth can be determined by using the senses.

The reliability of observational statements is transmitted to laws and theories. To the extent that scientific theories can be justified, they are justified because they rest inductively on the more or less secure basis provided by experience. Truth is established by careful observation and tested using the senses. Logically valid deduction is as follows: "if the premises of a logically valid deduction are true, then the conclusion must be true" (Chalmers, 1999: 11-23).

The definition, characteristics, function, purpose, classification, etc. of the *inductive-deductive* method is constructed from both qualities of the cognising subject: the senses and reason. The philosophical assumptions of the concept of the *inductive-deductive* method are critical (possibility of knowing), intellectualist or apriorist (origin of knowledge), dialectical, phenomenological and monistic (pre-metaphysical, metaphysical and theological solutions, respectively, to the problem of the essence of knowledge), mixed <intuitive-rational or rational-intuitive> (classification of knowledge) and mixed <transcendent-immanent or immanent-transcendent> (concept and criterion of truth of knowledge).

In the *inductive-deductive* method, the problem of the possibility of knowing is solved preferably from the senses and reason, using critical philosophical assumptions. If the cognising subject assumes that it is possible to know (dogmatism), but not in essence (scepticism), because each and every one of the cognising subjects thinks and feels differently (subjectivism), because truth changes in time, space and circumstances (relativism) and because, furthermore, all knowledge must have some utility for the subject who constructs it; he will try to use his senses and his reason to obtain general conclusions from premises containing particular data and to obtain particular conclusions from general laws.

In the *inductive-deductive* method, the problem about the origin of knowledge is solved, preferably, from both qualities of the cognising subject: the senses and reason; using intellectualist or apriorist philosophical assumptions (depending on whether he uses first his senses and then his reason or vice versa, respectively). If the cognising subject assumes that the origin of knowledge lies both in the senses and in reason, he will try to use the *inductive-deductive* method to generate new knowledge about his object of study by obtaining general conclusions from premises containing particular data and particular conclusions from general laws.

In the *inductive-deductive* method, the pre-metaphysical problem about the essence of knowledge is solved preferably from the senses and reason, using dialectical philosophical assumptions. If the cognising subject assumes that in a relation of knowledge the two elements of knowledge (subject-object) determine each other in a never-ending dialectical relation (because we never finish knowing objects), then he can estimate that the explorations, descriptions, explanations, interpretations, understandings of reality, the whole, must be *induced* and *deduced* as many times as necessary due to the constant change in which he finds himself. In the relationship between the cognising subject and the object to be known, it is considered, from the senses and reason, that the cognising subject and the object to be known determine each other mutually and endlessly.

In the *inductive-deductive* method, the metaphysical problem about the essence of knowledge is solved preferably from the senses and reason; using phenomenological philosophical assumptions. If the educational researcher assumes that reality exists, independently of the cognising subject, but that each subject knows it differently and only in appearance, never in an essential way, but only as a phenomenon located in time and space, then he/she will consider that it can be *induced* and *deduced*, in order to know it better.

In the *inductive-deductive* method, the theological problem about the essence of knowledge is solved preferably from the senses and reason, using monistic philosophical assumptions. If the researcher assumes that reality is a single whole, then he will consider that in order to construct his object of study he will first have to draw general conclusions from premises containing particular data and then draw particular conclusions from general laws. It is granted, from the senses and reason, that the cognising subject can explore, describe, explain, interpret, understand, etc., reality in a monistic way.

In the *inductive-deductive* method, the problem about the classification of knowledge is solved preferably from the senses and reason; using mixed philosophical assumptions (intuitive-rational or rational-intuitive). Only from the senses and reason can the cognising subject assume that the objects of study are so complex that, in order to give an opinion on them, it is necessary to use both qualities of the researcher. It is considered that in order to know reality it is first necessary to induce it and then to deduce it.

In the *inductive-deductive* method, the problem about the concepts and criteria of truth of knowledge is solved, preferably, from the senses and reason; using mixed philosophical assumptions (transcendent-immanent and immanent-transcendent).

Only from the senses and reason can the cognising subject assume that truth is both the concordance of thought with the object thought, and the correspondence of thought with its own rules of creation. From the senses and reason it is considered that phenomena can be known *inductively-deductively*. The concept of truth of the definition being used is transcendent and immanent, because it is conceded that reality exists independently of thought and, furthermore, that each subject constructs it differently. It is presumed, from the senses, that the truth criteria of the *inductive-deductive* method are transcendent-immanent; because the cognising subject relates to real objects to be known, which have their own existence in reality, independently of thought, but that, also, each and every one of the different subjects who pretend to know reality will think about it differently, because they feel and think differently from the other subjects.

2.6.5.3.2 The analytical-synthetic method.

The *analytical-synthetic* method is an intellectual operation or methodological procedure to generate new knowledge from both qualities of the cognising subject: reason and the senses, which consists of breaking down the reality being investigated into the parts that form it and, once analysed, reconstructing them, integrating the parts back into the whole.

For I. Blauberg et al. (1983:12) *analysis* and *synthesis* (from the Greek analysis: decomposition, division, and *synthesis*: composition, union), are "...*processes of practical or mental division of the whole into parts, and the reunification of the whole on the basis of its parts (parts and whole)...*". The decomposition (analysis) is done from the senses and the composition (synthesis) is done from reason. As processes of practical or mental division they can be used to generate new knowledge both in the formal sciences (logic and mathematics) and in the factual sciences (natural and social).

It can be observed, as shown by the aforementioned authors when they state that both *analysis* and *synthesis* are "processes of practical or mental division of the whole into parts and the reunification of the whole on the basis of its parts", that one can *analyse* from the senses (processes of practical division) and *synthesise* from reason (processes of mental division). *Analysis* is an intellectual operation or methodological procedure (method) that the cognising subject can carry out with his object of study from the senses in order to generate new knowledge about it. On the other hand, *synthesis* is an intellectual operation or methodological procedure (method) that the cognising subject can carry out with his reason to generate new knowledge about his object of study.

Together these two methods (or methodological procedures or intellectual operations to generate new knowledge) constitute a new method: the *analytic-synthetic* method.

To paraphrase I. Blauberg et al. (1983:12), objects of study are complex, their apprehension cannot be limited to the sum of their parts (synthesis); for their reunification in thought (synthesis), with all the richness of their mutual relations, it is necessary to apply another methodological procedure or intellectual operation (method) to generate new knowledge: *synthesis*. By means of this intellectual operation or methodological procedure for generating new knowledge it is possible to reunify the whole in thought as a "*rich whole with numerous definitions and links*" (Marx, quoted by I. Blauberg et al. (1983:12), as a concrete whole.

The cited authors consider that knowledge of the objects of study is neither simple nor schematic, but complex. They state that *analysis* and *synthesis* are not isolated stages of knowledge, that they only complement and follow each other. They say that at each stage *analysis* and *synthesis* are inextricably linked; that *analysis* is not understood without *synthesis*, nor *synthesis* without *analysis*. They say that through *analysis* we separate in the object the properties that make it part of the whole, on the basis of a synthetic representation, even if it is the most general (prior) representation of the whole, while through *synthesis* we recognise the whole as composed of parts, related to each other in a certain way.

In the process of knowledge, *synthesis* is realised through *analysis* and *analysis* through *synthesis*. *<thought is composed both of the dismemberment of objects, by consciousness, into their elements, and of the reunification of the linked elements into a whole. Without analysis there is no synthesis >* (Engels, quoted by I. Blauberg et al. (1983:12).

The definition, characteristics, function, purpose, classification, etc., of the *analytic-synthetic* method is constructed from both qualities of the cognising subject: the senses and reason. The philosophical assumptions of the concept of the analytic-synthetic method are critical (possibility of knowing), intellectualist or apriorist (origin of knowledge), dialectical, phenomenological and monistic (pre-metaphysical, metaphysical and theological solutions, respectively, to the problem of the essence of knowledge), mixed <intuitive-rational or rational-intuitive> (classification of knowledge) and mixed <transcendent-immanent or immanent-transcendent> (concept and criterion of truth of knowledge).

In the *analytic-synthetic* method, the problem of the possibility of knowing is solved preferably from the senses and reason, using critical philosophical assumptions. If the cognising subject assumes that it is possible to know (dogmatism), but not in essence (scepticism), because each and every one of the cognising subjects thinks and feels differently (subjectivism), because truth changes in time, space and circumstances (relativism) and because, furthermore, all knowledge must have a certain utility for the subject who constructs it; He will try to use his senses and his reason to decompose, divide his object of study into its constituent parts and then integrate them, unite them, back into the whole and, if necessary for a better exploration, description, explanation, interpretation, understanding, etc., of his object of study, he will carry out this procedure every time he considers that reality (the whole) has already changed, moved and, therefore, is no longer the same.

In the *analytic-synthetic* method, the problem of the origin of knowledge is resolved, preferably, from both qualities of the cognising subject: the senses and reason; using intellectualist or apriorist philosophical assumptions (depending on whether he uses his senses first and then his reason or vice versa, respectively). If the cognising subject assumes that the origin of knowledge is to be found both in the senses and in reason, he will try to use the *analytical-synthetic* method to generate new knowledge about his object of study by breaking it down into its constituent parts (analysis) and then putting it back together again (synthesis) and, in a second moment, dividing it again and then putting it back together again (synthesis), with the idea of having a better understanding of the phenomenon.

In the *synthetic analytical* method, the pre-metaphysical problem about the essence of knowledge is solved preferably from the senses and reason, using dialectical philosophical assumptions. If the cognising subject assumes that in a relation of knowledge the two elements of knowledge (subject-object) determine each other in a never-ending dialectical relation (because we never finish knowing objects), then he can estimate that reality, the whole, must be *analysed* and *synthesised* as many times as necessary due to the constant change in which it finds itself. In the relationship between the cognising subject and the object to be known, it is estimated, from the senses and reason, that the cognising subject and the object to be known determine each other mutually and endlessly.

In the *analytic-synthetic* method, the metaphysical problem about the essence of knowledge is solved preferably from the senses and reason; using phenomenological philosophical assumptions. If the educational researcher assumes that reality exists, independently of the cognising subject, but that each subject knows it differently and only in appearance, never in an essential way, but only as a phenomenon located in time and space, then he/she will consider that it can be separated into its constituent parts and put together again, in order to know it better.

In the *analytic-synthetic* method, the theological problem about the essence of knowledge is solved preferably from the senses and reason, using monistic philosophical assumptions. If the researcher assumes that reality is a single whole, then he will consider that the object of study is only broken down into two or more parts (which may be similar or different from each other) for the purpose of observing certain relations between them and, once this is done, re-uniting these parts into the whole. It is granted, from the senses and reason, that the cognising subject can explore, describe, explain, interpret, understand, etc., reality in a monistic way.

In the *analytic-synthetic* method, the problem of the classification of knowledge is solved preferably from the senses and reason, using mixed philosophical assumptions (intuitive-rational or rational-intuitive). Only from the senses and reason can the cognising subject assume that the objects of study are so complex that, in order to give an opinion about them, it is necessary to use both qualities of the researcher. It is believed that reality can be divided into two or more parts for the purpose of comparing them with each other and discovering their similarities and differences (analysis); and, subsequently, to put these parts together again, in order to better understand the whole (reality).

In the *analytic-synthetic* method, the problem about the concepts and criteria of truth of knowledge is solved, preferably, from the senses and reason; using mixed philosophical assumptions (transcendent-immanent and immanent-transcendent). Only from the senses and reason can the cognising subject assume that truth is both the concordance of thought with the object thought, and the correspondence of thought with its own rules of creation. From the senses and reason, it is considered that relations of similarity and/or difference between the parts of phenomena can be discovered by *analysing* and *synthesising them* anew. The concept of truth of the definition being used is transcendent and immanent, because it is conceded that reality exists independently of thought and, furthermore, that each subject constructs it differently. It is presumed, from the senses, that the criteria of truth of the *analytic-synthetic* method are transcendent-immanent; because the cognising subject relates to real objects to be known, which have their own existence in reality, independently of thought, but that, also, each and every one of the different subjects who pretend to know reality will think about it differently, because they feel and think differently from the other subjects.

Up to this point, the analysis of the intellectual operations or methodological procedures that the cognising subject can carry out (from reason, from the senses or from both qualities of the researcher) to generate new knowledge about reality (third level and element of an epistemological orientation).

2.7 THE RELATIONSHIP BETWEEN THEORY AND METHOD.

Each of the five elements of an *epistemological orientation* fulfils different functions in the process of knowledge: the philosophical *assumptions*, to analyse reality, allow us to solve each and every one of the five main problems of knowledge from reason, from the senses or from both; the *theoretical* foundations, to problematise the objects of study, provide the epistemological elements to build the research; the *methodological* procedures or intellectual operations, to generate new knowledge, provide us with the method; the *technical strategies* to know reality, serve to explore, describe, explain, interpret, understand, etc. reality; and the *instruments* are used to gather information about the object of study.

Just as *theory* depends on *philosophy*, the *method* for generating new knowledge will depend on *the theories* with which the object of study is being problematised. For example, the *deductive* method; its opposite in philosophical and theoretical terms, the *inductive* method; and the intellectual operation or methodological procedure that aims, also in philosophical and theoretical terms, to reconcile both methods: the *inductive-deductive* or *deductive-inductive* method:

If the object of study is problematised with *general theories of objective knowledge* (such as mathematicism, mechanicism, etc.),

organicism, etc.), *particular to the objective social sciences* (such as positivism, functionalism, structuralism, systems theory, etc.) and *specific to the objective sciences of education* (such as behaviourism) the way to answer the research question, the path to the goal, will necessarily have to be *deductive*.

In the aforementioned theories, each of the five main problems of knowledge is solved by *reason*, using *dogmatic* (possibility of knowledge), *rationalist* (origin of knowledge), *objectivist, idealist* and *dualist* (pre-metaphysical, metaphysical and theological solutions, respectively, to the problem of the essence of knowledge), *rational* (classification of knowledge) and *immanent* (concept and criterion of truth of knowledge) philosophical assumptions.

The *method* used to generate new knowledge about any object of study that is intended to be constructed by problematising reality with the aforementioned theories is the *deductive* method.

In order to move from the research question to its solution using the intellectual operation or *deductive* methodological procedure, each and every one of the five main *problems of knowledge* is solved, as in the theories mentioned above, from *reason*. The *deductive method* is *dogmatic* (possibility of knowledge), *rationalist* (origin of knowledge), *objectivist, idealist* and *dualist* (pre-metaphysical, metaphysical and theological solutions, respectively, to the problem of the essence of knowledge), *rational* (classification of knowledge) and *immanent* (concept and criterion of truth of knowledge).

On the other hand, if the object of study is problematised with *general theories of subjective knowledge* (such as chaos, conflict, etc.), *particular to the subjective social sciences* (such as historicism, dialectical historical materialism, etc.) and *specific to the subjective sciences of education* (such as psychoanalysis, humanism, cognitivism, etc.) the way to answer the research question, the path to the goal, will necessarily have to be *inductive*.

In the aforementioned theories, each of the five main *problems of knowledge* is solved from the *senses*, using *sceptical, subjectivist, relativist, pragmatic* (possibility of knowledge), *empiricist* (origin of knowledge), *subjectivist, realist* and *dualist* (pre-metaphysical, metaphysical and theological solutions, respectively, to the problem of the essence of knowledge), *intuitive* (classification of knowledge) and *transcendental* (concept and criterion of truth of knowledge) philosophical assumptions.

The *method* used to generate new knowledge about any object of study that is intended to be constructed by problematising reality with the aforementioned theories is the *inductive* method.

In order to move from the research question to its solution using the intellectual operation or *inductive* methodological procedure, each and every one of the five main *problems of knowledge* is solved, as in the theories mentioned above, from the *senses*. The *inductive* method is *sceptical, subjective, relative* and *pragmatic* (possibility of knowledge), *empirical* (origin of knowledge), *subjectivist, realist* and *dualist* (pre-metaphysical, metaphysical and theological solutions, respectively, to the problem of the essence of knowledge), *intuitive* (classification of knowledge) and *transcendent* (concept and criterion of truth of knowledge).

Finally, if the object of study is problematised with *general theories of dialectical knowledge* (such as analogy, complexity, etc.), *particular to the dialectical social sciences* (such as phenomenology, critical hermeneutics, etc.) and *specific to the dialectical sciences of education* (such as genetic theory <Piaget>, sociocultural theory <Vigotsky>, etc.) the way to answer the research question, the path to the goal, will necessarily have to be *inductive-deductive*.

In the aforementioned theories, each and every one of the five main *problems of knowledge* are solved from the *senses* and *reason*, using *critical* (possibility of knowledge), *intellectualist* and/or *apriorist* (origin of knowledge), *dialectical, phenomenological* and *monistic* philosophical assumptions (pre-metaphysical, metaphysical and theological solutions, respectively, to the problem of the essence of knowledge), mixed <rational-intuitive> (classification of knowledge) and mixed <immanent-transcendent> (concept and criterion of truth of knowledge).

The *method* used to generate new knowledge about any object of study that is intended to be constructed by problematising reality with the aforementioned theories is the *inductive-deductive* method.

In order to move from the research question to its solution using the intellectual operation or *inductive-deductive* methodological procedure, each and every one of the five main *problems of knowledge* are solved, as in the theories mentioned above, from the *senses* and *reason*. The *inductive-deductive* method is critical (possibility of knowledge), *intellectualist* and/or *apriorist* (origin of knowledge), *dialectical*, *phenomenalist* and *monistic* (pre-metaphysical, metaphysical and theological solutions, respectively, to the problem of the essence of knowledge), mixed *<intuitive-rational>* (classification of knowledge) and mixed *<transcendent-immanent<* (concept and criterion of truth of knowledge).

In the same sense, the general *theories* of knowledge, particular theories of social sciences and specific theories of educational sciences mentioned above could be compared with the other *intellectual operations or methodological procedures* to generate new knowledge, also indicated in this work, such as addition, subtraction, multiplication, division, analysis, synthesis, classification, comparison and definition. As has been observed, the relationship between *theory* and *method*, as well as the relationship between *philosophy* and *theory*, is one of dependence of the latter on the former: just as *theory* depends on *philosophy*, method depends on *theory* and, therefore, on the *philosophy* on which the *theory* with which reality is being problematised depends in order to construct new knowledge. If an educational researcher does not realise this, he or she will construct an epistemologically incongruent object of study.

The following table summarises the relationship between theory and method:

THEORIES			METHODS		
GENERAL KNOWLEDGE	OBJECTIVES	MATHEMATICISM MECHANISM ORGANISM	**ADDITION MULTIPLICATION DEDUCTION SYNTHESIS CLASSIFICATION DEFINITION**	REASON	DOGMATISM, RATIONALISM OBJECTIVISM, IDEALISM DUALISM, RATIONAL IMMANENT
	SUBJECTIVES	CHAOS CONFLICT	**SUBTRACTION DIVISION INDUCTION ANALYSIS COMPARISON**	FEELINGS	SCEPTICISM, SUBJECTIVISM RELATIVISM, PRAGMATISM EMPIRICISM, EPISTEMOLOGICAL SUBJECTIVISM, IDEALISM DUALISM, TRANSCENDENT INTUITIVE
	DIALECTICS	ANALOGY COMPLEXITY	**INDUCTIVE - DEDUCTIVE ANALYTICAL - SYNTHETIC**	BOTH	CRITICISM, INTELLECTUALISM AND/OR APRIORISM, DIALECTIC-PHENOMENOLOGY, INTUITIVE-RATIONAL, TRANSCENDENT-IMMANENT
PARTICLE-SOCIAL SCIENCES	OBJECTIVES	POSITIVISM FUNCTIONALISM STRUCTURALISM SYSTEMS	**ADDITION MULTIPLICATION DEDUCTION SYNTHESIS SYNTHESIS CLASSIFICATION DEFINITION**	REASON	DOGMATISM, RATIONALISM OBJECTIVISM, IDEALISM DUALISM, RATIONAL IMMANENT

	SUBJECTIVES	HISTORICISM HISTORICO-DIALECTICAL MATERIALISM	**SUBTRACTION DIVISION INDUCTION ANALYSIS COMPARISON**	FEELINGS	SCEPTICISM, SUBJECTIVISM RELATIVISM, PRAGMATISM EMPIRICISM, EPISTEMOLOGICAL SUBJECTIVISM, IDEALISM DUALISM, TRANSCENDENT INTUITIVE
	DIALECTICS	PHENOMENOL GIA HERMENEUTICS CRITICS	**INDUCTIVE - DEDUCTIVE ANALYTICAL - SYNTHETIC**	BOTH	CRITICISM, INTELLECTUALISM O AND/OR APRIORISM, DIALECTICS PHENOMENOL GIA, INTUITIVE-RATIONAL, TRANSCENDENT IMMANENT
SPECIFIC TO EDUCATIONAL SCIENCES	OBJECTIVES	CONDUCTISM	**ADDITION MULTIPLICATIO N DEDUCTION SYNTHESIS CLASSIFICATION CLASSIFICATION DEFINITION**	REASON	DOGMATISM, RATIONALISM OBJECTIVISM, IDEALISM DUALISM, RATIONAL IMMANENT
	SUBJECTIVES	PSYCHOANALYSIS HUMANISM COGNOSCITIVISM	**SUBTRACTION DIVISION INDUCTION ANALYSIS COMPARISON**	FEELINGS	SCEPTICISM, SUBJECTIVISM, RELATIVISM, PRAGMATISM, EMPIRICISM, EPISTEMOLOGICAL SUBJECTIVISM, IDEALISM, DUALISM, TRANSCENDENTAL INTUITIONISM
	DIALECTICS	GENETICS SOCIOCULTURAL	**INDUCTIVE - DEDUCTIVE ANALYTICAL - SYNTHETIC**	BOTH	CRITICISM, INTELLECTUALISM AND/OR APRIORISM, PHENOMENOLOGICA L DIALECTICS, AND GIA, INTUITIVORATIONAL , TRANSCENDENTAL-IMMANENT

2.8 SUMMARY OF THE SUB-CHAPTER.

Up to this point we have studied the eleven most important *intellectual operations* or *methodological procedures* that the cognising subject can carry out with his object of study in order to generate new knowledge about it from reason, from the senses or from both qualities of the cognising subject. Possibly there are more. In this research only the eleven mentioned were analysed because we have not found more. It can even be affirmed that any other that can be handled falls within one or some of the intellectual operations or methodological procedures mentioned. For example: discriminating. On the one hand, by discriminating we are already focusing our attention on two or more objects in order to discover their relations or estimate their differences or similarities, and we fall into the comparative method. On the other hand, we also fall into the classification method, since we are grouping the elements of a set into subsets, classes or classificatory concepts that divide it in a disjunctive or exhaustive way. Finally, we also fall into division, because we are dividing the wholes into their constituent parts.

In the following table it is possible to appreciate, in a very summarised way, the *definitions* of the eleven *methodological procedures* or *intellectual operations* that the cognising subject can carry out with his object of study in order to generate new knowledge from reason, from the senses or from both qualities of the educational researcher:

METHODS FOR GENERATING NEW KNOWLEDGE FROM REASON (OBJECTIVES)	SUMA	Combining or adding two numbers to obtain a final amount or total. The process of putting two collections of objects together, in order to obtain a single collection.
	MULTIPLICATION	Abbreviated addition. Arithmetic decomposition operation consisting of repeatedly adding the first quantity as many times as indicated by the second quantity.
	DEDUCTION	Drawing particular conclusions from general laws.
	SUMMARY	Rebuilding, reintegrating the parts into the whole.
	CLASSIFICATION	Grouping of the elements of a set into subsets, classes or classificatory concepts that divide it disjunctively or exhaustively.
	DEFINITION	To set limits. Proposition or set of things that brings together the general and differentiating properties of something material or immaterial. Relationship between the genus and the specific difference.
METHODS FOR GENERATING NEW KNOWLEDGE FROM THE (SUBJECTIVE) SENSES	RESTA	Decomposition operation, which consists of, given a certain quantity, eliminating a part of it and the result is known as the difference. Inverse operation to addition.
	DIVISION	The operation of dividing a whole into its parts.
	INDUCTION	Drawing general conclusions from premises containing particular data.
	ANALYSIS	To break down a whole into its constituent parts.
	COMPARISON	To fix attention on two or more objects in order to discover their relationships or to estimate their differences or similarities.
METHODS FOR GENERATING NEW KNOWLEDGE FROM REASON AND THE SENSES (DIALECTICAL)	INDUCTIVE-DEDUCTIVE	Drawing general conclusions from premises containing particular data and then drawing particular conclusions from these general laws.
	ANALYTICAL-SYNTHETIC	Breaking down a whole into its constituent parts and then integrating the parts back into the whole, reconstructing it.

A detailed analysis of the main *intellectual operations*, or *methodological procedures*, that human beings perform to generate new knowledge is beyond the scope of the present work. For example: deduction and induction are dealt with by countless thinkers, among them Aristotle (in *the organon*) and Bacon (in *the new organon*); works that were constructed from reason and from the senses, respectively; so the philosophical assumptions are totally different and contrary. For this reason, in the present work only the epistemological aspect of these works was analysed, leaving a deeper analysis of each and every one of the aforementioned methods for future works.

2.9 TECHNICAL STRATEGIES, IN ORDER TO LEARN ABOUT THE EDUCATIONAL REALITY.

The fourth step of a knowledge process is the *technical* strategy that the educational researcher must choose to learn about the reality under study. Just as the theory or theories with which the cognising subject problematises his/her object of study, in order to construct it, depends on the assumptions from which each and every one of the five main *philosophical* problems of knowledge are solved (with reason; with the senses; with both, first reason and then the senses; or with both, first the senses and then the senses), so too, the method used to generate new knowledge depends on the assumptions from which each and every one of the five main *philosophical* problems of knowledge are solved; or with both, first the senses and then reason), and also, the *method* used to generate new knowledge about it will depend on the theory or theories on which the research work has been based; and, as a consequence, the *technique* with which the aim is to know reality will depend on the *method* with which the new knowledge is going to be generated.

2.9.1 *Definition of a technical strategy to get to know the reality.*

Traditionally, the Greek term *tekhné* was also translated by the Latin term *ars* (art) (from the Greek "to know how to do"). In its first meaning, as a noun, this term designates a set of skills and procedures that follow certain established and more or less codified rules in order to do something for a certain purpose. In this sense, it is the set of procedures used in a trade or art. As an adjective, it refers to everything that is relative to the activities of these trades or arts; as opposed to the theoretical knowledge on which they are based (Gutiérrez, 2007).

Technique is an art, a know-how. In the case of research carried out in the educational sciences, technique is a knowledge of how to know the educational reality; and it is linked, in an essential way, with the other epistemological levels of all research: philosophical (first), theoretical (second), methodological (third) and instrumental (fifth), the technical strategy constitutes the fourth epistemological level of all research.

Technique is a set of skills and procedures that follow certain rules for knowing reality, in accordance with methodological procedures or intellectual operations (methods) that are intended to generate new knowledge. This new knowledge about the object of study that is intended to be achieved through the methods is obtained with the use of certain technical strategies. The technique is at the service of the method.

According to Ander (1995) "*...the method is not enough, nor is it everything; procedures and means are needed to make the methods operational. Techniques are at this level. These, like methods, are answers to the 'how to do' in order to achieve a proposed end or result, but they are situated at the level of the facts or practical stages which, as auxiliary devices, allow the application of the method by means of practical, concrete elements adapted to a well-defined object...*".

Techniques are the operational agents of the methods, because through them, reality is known, the research question that the method suggests in order to arrive at the answer is answered.

Rojas (1987-2003) is of a similar opinion when he says that "*... in research practice, methodological guidelines are insufficient to reach scientific truth. It is* *necessary to resort to specific methods, to adequate and precise techniques and instruments to resolve and analyse that empirical information that the theory used and the hypotheses put forward indicate as relevant to formulate scientific knowledge...*". The only inaccuracy of the author in question is that he confuses the *method* for generating new knowledge with the *technique* for knowing reality. But it is important to consider what he says about *method* being insufficient to construct the object of study, that one must resort to *technical* strategies and *instruments* (fourth and fifth levels, respectively, of an epistemological orientation) to adequately relate theory to *method* and construct knowledge.

Due to the use and abuse that has been made of the concept of *technique*, it has generally been understood as a *method*.

Dieterich (2003: 100) relates the *theoretical* and *methodological* levels of a research very well when he states that "*.with the selection of the scientific disciplines that are needed for the description, explanation and prediction of the properties and behaviour of the object of research -* theory *- the researcher has also implicitly selected the methods - methodology -, concepts and knowledge that will be used during the work, since they form an integral part of a theory*". The scientific disciplines contain *the theories* with which reality was problematised and constructed and, implicitly, also the *methods* with which new knowledge about these disciplines was generated.

In the text under discussion, *method* is confused with *technique*, when it is stated that "*...all of them (techniques) can be subsumed under four (particular) methods or procedures, which are the only ones available to test a hypothesis and, therefore, to know whether it is true or not*" (Dieterich 2003: 101).

We believe, on the other hand, that *method* is the intellectual operation or methodological procedure carried out by the cognising subject in order to generate new knowledge about his or her object of knowledge.

study. The *technique*, on the other hand, is a different procedure that is carried out for the purpose of getting to know the reality that is being investigated. The *technique* depends on the *method*. *Method* is at the third level of knowledge and *technique* at the fourth. *Method* comes first and then *technique* in every process of knowledge.

By way of a partial conclusion on the *definition* of *technical* strategy, it can be stated that it consists of the procedures, operations or strategies that, in order to move from the research question to its answer, the *method* proposes. *Technical strategies* allow the educational researcher to know his or her object of study, the educational reality he or she wants to know. Technical strategies operationalise the method.

For example: if the intellectual operation or methodological procedure to generate new knowledge that is being used in a research is the comparative method, to answer the following research question: what are the similarities and differences between smokers and non-smokers with respect to cancer, one will have to use the *technique* to know the reality called *survey*; which consists of selecting two groups (one of smokers and one of non-smokers) and asking them whether or not they contracted the disease and all the other questions that lead to the answer of the formulated research question.

2.9.2 *Characteristics of the technical strategies to get to know the reality.*

The first important characteristic of any *technical* strategy for knowing reality is precisely that: it serves to know the phenomena.

The second characteristic that jumps out, following on from the previous one, is that any *technical* strategy for knowing reality is a knowing how to do, a knowing how to know that reality. The only problem that can be observed here is that this "knowing how to know reality" depends on the way in which each and every one of the five main philosophical problems of knowledge (possibility, origin, essence, classification and concepts and criteria of truth) are resolved. We already know that they can be solved from reason, from the senses, or from both; which brings us back to the epistemological problem of philosophical assumptions. We also know that the way in which the aforementioned problems are solved refers the researcher to certain theories that he will necessarily have to take into account in order to construct his object of study. We also know that the theories that the cognitive subject considers in order to problematise the investigated reality will determine the method or methods with which he will have to generate his new knowledge about the phenomena he is investigating. And, finally, the method or methods with which the educational researcher intends to generate new knowledge about the educational phenomena he/she is investigating will determine the technical strategies to get to know these realities.

The third characteristic of any *technical* strategy for knowing reality is that it involves certain procedures, skills or strategies that the cognising subject carries out in order to know his object of study.

The fourth characteristic of the *technical* strategy for knowing reality can be stated in the sense that it is not alone in the process of knowledge, but is totally related, in an indissoluble way, with the other levels of an epistemological orientation: philosophical, theoretical, methodological, and instrumental. Therefore, in order to know reality by means of a certain technical strategy, certain rules, mainly of an epistemological nature, must be respected in order to achieve certain ends.

The fifth characteristic of a *technical* strategy is that its realisation is implemented in every kind of art, craft or science, in order to know reality (in the latter).

The sixth characteristic of any *technical* strategy to learn about reality is that it is a means, used by the *method*, to move from the research question to its answer, generating new knowledge.

The seventh characteristic of the *technical* strategies for knowing reality that can be mentioned is that it is implicit in the *method*, it is the realisation of the intellectual operation or methodological procedure that the cognising subject carries out in order to know his object of study.

2.9.3 *The role of technical strategies to get to know reality.*

It is already known that the function of an entity consists in the need it satisfies in relation to a whole.

The function of any *technical* strategy to learn about reality is to serve as a procedure, skill, strategy, etc., for the method to generate new knowledge.

2.9.4 *Purpose of the technical strategies to get to know the reality.*

The purpose of any *technical* strategy for knowing reality, as its name indicates, is precisely that: to know reality.

2.9.5 *Classification of the technical strategies for learning about reality.*
There are only four known *technical strategies* to learn about any reality, concrete
or abstract: observation, experimentation, survey and documentation.

The *technical strategies* for knowing reality constitute, as mentioned above, the
fourth level of knowledge of an epistemological orientation. The first, second and
third levels are, respectively, the *philosophical* assumptions from which each and
every one of the five main problems of knowledge are solved, the *theoretical*
foundations with which the construction of the object of study is problematised
and founded, and the *methodological* procedures or intellectual operations with
which new knowledge about the objects of study is constructed.

The classification of technical strategies to know the reality is due to Dieterich
(2003: 102) when he states that the "*... methods of contrasting are: 1) systematic
documentation; 2) systematic observation; 3) the representative survey or census;
4) the systematic experiment*".

Note, again, that methodological procedure or intellectual operation to generate
new knowledge (method) is being confused with technical strategy to know reality
(technique). Observation, experimentation, survey and documentary are *technical*
strategies that the educational researcher can use to learn about reality. Any reality,
depending on the *method* used to generate new knowledge about it, can be known
either by observing, experimenting, surveying and/or documenting it.

Finally, for Dieterich (2003: 103) "*.the ultimate test of the veracity of a hypothesis
will always consist of its contrast with the real phenomenon to which it refers.* "

The idea of *technique* as a unique procedure available to contrast hypotheses with
reality seems to us to be correct, but not understood as a *method*, but as a *technique*;
that is, as a procedure to approach reality and contrast it with the hypothesis that
was proposed to explore it, describe it, explain it, interpret it, understand it, etc.

The philosophical, theoretical, methodological, technical and instrumental
elements of the epistemological orientations are only separated for the purposes of
study, anthologically they are inseparable, they constitute the gear of the discourse,
exploratory, descriptive, explanatory, interpretative, comprehensive, etc. of the
reality being studied.

According to the above, the four technical strategies for knowing reality can be
grouped, following the epistemological logic of this research, into objective,
subjective and dialectical, depending on whether reality is known with reason, with
the senses or with both characteristics of the cognising subject.

2.9.5.1 *Technical strategies to get to know the reality in an objective way.*
The *technical strategies* for knowing reality objectively are derived from the
intellectual operations or methodological procedures that the cognising subject
carries out with his object of knowledge from reason, i.e. objectively: addition,
multiplication, deduction, synthesis, classification and definition.

The *technical* strategies for learning about reality in an *objective* way are
experimentation and *documentary*.

2.9.5.1.1 Experimentation.

Experimentation is a technical strategy to learn about reality, from reason, in an
objective way, which consists of finding the behaviour of a variable from different

combinations of factors or input variables of a process that, by changing, affect the response.

Some authors consider the technical strategy to know the reality as a type of research, Tamayo (1982: 32-38), for example, thinks that experimentation is a type of research; he considers experiment, together with historical and descriptive research, as a type of research. Historical research and descriptive research could be classified as types of research, depending on whether they deal with past or present experiences, the former, or the scope of the enquiry (exploratory, descriptive, explanatory, interpretative, comprehensive, etc.), the latter.

On the other hand, the *experiment* cannot be considered as a type of research, because it is, according to Tamayo (1982: 36), "*...a situation provoked by the researcher to introduce certain study variables manipulated by him to control the increase or decrease of these variables and their effect on the observed behaviours*".

When an untested experimental variable is manipulated, "*.under rigorously controlled conditions, in order to discover in what way or by what cause a particular situation or event occurs*. (Tamayo: 1982: 36), the aim is to know reality from reason, i.e. objectively. The educational researcher who uses the experiment as a technical strategy to learn about reality, whether he knows it or not, is using the intellectual operation or *deductive* methodological procedure to generate new knowledge, because he is trying to learn about relationships of cause (independent variable) and effect (dependent variable).

Also for Ortiz (2003: 63), *experimentation* is "*.the classical method of the scientific laboratory where the elements manipulated and the effects observed can be controlled. It is the most accurate and powerful method for discovering and developing an organised body of knowledge*". In *experimentation*, elements are manipulated and effects are observed in order to learn about their relationships, i.e. it is a *technique* for learning about reality. We think that the research *method* is understood as the intellectual operation or methodological procedure carried out by the cognitive subject to generate new knowledge about the object of study and that the research *technique* is a strategy, procedure, etc., that makes possible the construction of the knowledge that is intended with the *method*.

In an attempt to clarify the position, we will now place the *technical* strategy for knowing reality called *experimentation* in its proper place in the process of knowledge, i.e. within an epistemological orientation.

In *experimentation*, each and every one of the five main philosophical problems of knowledge is solved by reason.

In *experimentation*, the philosophical problem about the possibility of knowledge is solved from dogmatic assumptions (first level or element of an epistemological orientation). It can be affirmed, according to Olea (1980: 33-34) that "*... the experimental method* (note that he also calls the technique in analysis a method) *does not start from given situations, but creates them to establish scientific principles by means of verification...*". It is assumed, from reason, that it is possible to know reality, because relationships between phenomena are being "invented" in order to establish principles about the form of these relationships, which are considered universally valid and logically necessary; therefore, they only require verification. It is presumed that reality does not move, that the relations between phenomena obey universal, eternal and immutable principles that exist on a metaphysical plane and that human reason can discover them through the elaboration of hypotheses, i.e. *deductively* (method).

In *experimentation*, the problem of the origin of knowledge is solved on the basis of rationalist philosophical assumptions. Experimentation "starts from existing theory and descends to empirical reality" (Sierra, 1983: 93). (Sierra, 1983: 93). This is done *deductively* (method: third element or level of an epistemological orientation). *Deduction* is the intellectual operation or methodological procedure carried out by the cognising subject to generate new knowledge from reason.

We have already seen that a *deduction* consists of a "*.movement of knowledge from the general to the particular.* (Blauberg, I., 1983:42), because it starts from knowledge previously established as true, logically necessary and universally valid. Knowledge that our reason judges that it must be so, that it has to be that way always and everywhere. For example: "if metals are good conductors of heat and steel is a metal, then steel is a good conductor of heat".

In *experimentation*, the problem of the essence of knowledge is resolved on the basis of objectivist philosophical assumptions. *Experimentation* is a technical strategy for getting to know reality, which consists, as we have already seen, in the demonstration of a hypothesis (deductive method). *Experimentation* assumes that the relationships between phenomena are in terms of cause-effect. *Experimentation* assumes that there is a universally valid and logically necessary order, which is the cause of all effects. In *experimentation* it is a matter of demonstrating *objective* truths (universally valid and logically necessary), applied to particular cases, which consist of contents of human knowledge that "*...do not depend on the subject, they depend neither on man nor on mankind.by knowing the world, the properties of things, man understands their essence. This means that in his consciousness things and their properties are reproduced as they are in reality, independently of man...*" (Blauberg, I., 1983:185). This would be a pre-metaphysical solution to the philosophical problem of the essence of knowledge, because it does not refer to reality itself, but to the relation of knowledge that is established between the cognising subject and the object to be known.

In *experimentation*, the problem about the essence of knowledge can also be posed in metaphysical terms and solved from idealistic philosophical assumptions. It is presumed that "*.the first basis of the existent (substance) is the objectively existing impersonal consciousness (absolute spirit, universal reason, universal will, etc.)* (Blauberg, I., 1983:185). The material world is considered to be the product of this superhuman consciousness, of the other being of the spirit (objective idealism). It is also conjectured that without subject there is no object (subjective idealism). This would be a metaphysical solution to the problem of the essence of knowledge, because it refers to the existence or non-existence of reality.

In *experimentation*, the problem of the essence of knowledge can also be posed in theological terms and resolved on the basis of dualistic philosophical assumptions. The technical strategy for knowing reality called *experimentation* consists of demonstration. Demonstration is a '*... substantiation of the truthfulness (or falsity) of an isolated judgment (of an opinion), of a part of a theory or of a whole theory... the substantiation of the authenticity of any judgment which rests, not only on logical reflection, but also on the testimony of the organs of sense, experience. ...*"

(Blauberg, I., 1983:44). A demonstration is supposed to be true or false, right or wrong. The *experiment* is the procedure to demonstrate the hypothesis, i.e. the technical strategy to know the reality. *Experimentation* is a technical strategy for knowing reality in which "*.the material and the psychic, the corporeal and the spiritual, validity and invalidity, constitute two principles independent of each other and not mutually conditional*" (*Blauberg, I.,* "The *material and the psychic, the corporeal and the spiritual, validity and invalidity, constitute two principles independent of each other and not mutually conditional*". (Blauberg, I., 1983:51). In experimentation reality is divided into two for study: truth-falsity. This would be a theological solution to the problem of the essence of knowledge, because, in philosophical terms, the knowledge one has about reality can be true or false (dualism).

In *experimentation*, the problem of the classification of knowledge is solved on the basis of rational philosophical assumptions. The technical strategy for knowing reality called *experimentation* provides a rational type of knowledge, because it is a demonstration, a syllogism emanating from reason, in which reality has nothing to do with it and, nevertheless, it is applied to reality in order to order it. In experimentation, as already observed, it is assumed that "*.only reason, the intellect, is capable of providing reliable knowledge of a general, necessary and not possible (casual) nature*". (Blauberg, I., 1983:154).

In *experimentation*, the philosophical problem about the concepts and criteria of truth of knowledge are resolved on the basis of immanent assumptions. In the technical strategy to know the reality called experimentation, it is considered that truth must be objective, absolute, not relative; that is to say, that the content of human knowledge "*...does not depend on the subject, it does not depend neither on man nor on mankind...*" (Blauberg, I., 1983:154). It is considered that truth must be absolute, an assumption that can only be achieved through reason. That is why truth is conceived as the concordance of thought with its own rules of creation and the criterion of truth is based on the fact that the cognising subject is confronted with ideal objects, which do not have their own existence in reality, which only exist in thought.

On the level or element of theory, which occupies the second place in an epistemological orientation, the general theories of objective knowledge (mathematicism, mechanicism and organicism), particular to the objective social sciences (positivism, functionalism, structuralism and systems) and specific to the objective sciences of education (behaviourism) are those which, more than the other theories (subjective and dialectical), can use *experimentation* as a technical strategy for knowing reality. This is because the explorations, descriptions, explanations, interpretations and understandings of reality in the aforementioned theories are based on reason.

At the level or element of method, which occupies the third place in an epistemological orientation, *experimentation* is a technical strategy for knowing reality that is derived mainly from intellectual operations or methodological procedures for generating new knowledge from reason (objectively), such as: addition, multiplication, deduction, synthesis, classification and definition.

It can be assumed that *experimentation* is a technical strategy for getting to know reality that derives from philosophical assumptions, theoretical foundations and methodological procedures that are born in the
reason, i.e. they are objective (in the terms agreed throughout this paper).

2.9.5.1.2 The documentary.

The *documentary* is a technical strategy to get to know reality that consists of all types of recording. *Documentary* is a technical strategy used to learn about objects that are not present in reality. *The documentary* is a technical strategy that consists of discourses that other cognitive subjects, before the educational researcher, have elaborated on the objects of knowledge and that are recorded. The *documentary* is a technical strategy for learning about reality in which a theoretician tells us something about an object of study.

Something similar to the epistemological analysis that we carried out with *experimentation*, we will do the same with the *documentary*, placing it in the place that corresponds to it in the process of knowledge, that is to say, within an epistemological orientation.

In the documentary, each and every one of the five main philosophical problems of knowledge is solved by reason.

In the *documentary*, the philosophical problem about the possibility of knowledge is solved from dogmatic assumptions (first level or element of an epistemological orientation). It can be affirmed, according to Ortiz (3003: 49-50), that the document is "... *all knowledge fixed materially on a support, which can be used for consultation, study or work, as an indispensable tool to transmit knowledge, ideas and give testimony of the facts, allowing communication, training and teaching...*". It is assumed, from reason, that it is possible to know reality, because the discourse that explores, describes, explains, interprets, understands, etc., is materially fixed on a support that can be used for consultation. It is assumed that reality does not move, that ideas can be transmitted just as they were elaborated by someone.

In the *documentary*, the problem of the origin of knowledge is resolved on the basis of rationalist philosophical assumptions. According to Ortiz (3003: 49), the documentary is a technical strategy for knowing reality that consists of a "...*filmed testimony of the facts; it is a form of direct communication to approach reality and attest to it as accurately as possible; the documentary is an instrument for gathering information that allows us to describe the meaning of a cut of reality, factual, temporal, contextual, to later make a reconstruction or concatenation with other facts*". The technical strategy to know the reality of the documentary can be derived from intellectual operations or methodological procedures to generate new knowledge from reason (addition, multiplication, deduction, synthesis, classification, definition).

In *documentaries*, the problem of the essence of knowledge is resolved on the basis of objectivist philosophical assumptions. The *documentary* is a technical strategy for knowing reality, which deals, as we have already seen, "...*with all the achievements that give an account of social events and human ideas or are the product of social life and, therefore, insofar as they record or reflect it, they can be used to study it indirectly...*" (Sierra, 2001: 284). The aforementioned author assumes that engravings record and reflect reality. In the *documentary* it is considered that the object to be known determines the cognising subject, because the recorded discourse on reality remains fixed and can influence whoever assimilates it. This would be a pre-metaphysical solution to the problem of the essence of knowledge, regarding the relation of knowledge that can be established between the cognising subject and the object to be known.

In *documentary*, the problem of the essence of knowledge can also be posed in metaphysical terms and resolved on the basis of idealistic philosophical assumptions. Etymologically, the term documentary is derived from the Latin "*documentum*", which is supposed to mean "*...teaching, model, proof and this from <docere>, to teach...documents are all the achievements of man, insofar as they are an indication of his action and can reveal to us his ideas, opinions and ways of acting and living...*" (Sierra, 2001: 284). In documentaries we are not dealing with reality, but with a discourse elaborated by one or more subjects who came before us. In the documentary it is considered that each subject constructs reality in a different way (subjective idealism).

In *documentary film*, the problem of the essence of knowledge can also be posed in theological terms and resolved on the basis of dualistic philosophical assumptions. In the documentary, as a technical strategy to know reality, those who elaborate it "*.do not offer the social phenomena themselves that have taken place, but the result of the perception and interpretation of them by the writer, which is always partial and incomplete*". (Sierra, 2001: 285). In the documentary it can be considered that an engraving can be true or false, original or altered. This would be a theological solution to the problem of the essence of knowledge as to whether reality is single, double or multiple.

In *documentary film*, the problem of classifying knowledge is solved on the basis of rational philosophical assumptions. In the application of the technical strategy to know the so-called *documentary* reality, it is assumed that the knowledge obtained is rational. The cognizing subject elaborates concepts about the engravings trying to describe their definitions, explore their classifications, explain their elements, interpret their causes, understand their purposes, etc., in order to put order in reality. In the documentary, as a technical strategy to know reality, the cognitive subject must carry out a content analysis, which consists of ".a research technique for the objective, systematic and quantitative description of the manifest content of communications, with the aim of interpreting them. (Sierra, 2001: 287).

In *documentary film*, the philosophical problem of the concepts and criteria of the truth of knowledge is resolved on the basis of immanent assumptions. In the technical strategy for knowing the so-called *documentary* reality, it is considered that truth must be objective, absolute, not relative; that is, that the content of human knowledge can be analysed. It is assumed that content analysis "... *is a technique for quantifying secondary data: it basically consists of isolating and counting units and indicators of the phenomena in which we are interested...*" (Sierra, 2001: 287). It is considered that truth must be absolute, a presumption that can only be achieved through reason. That is why truth is conceived as the concordance of thought with its own rules of creation and the criterion of truth is based on the fact that the cognising subject is confronted with ideal objects, which do not have their own existence in reality, which only exist in thought.

The same as we think about the technical strategy for knowing reality called *experimentation*, applies to the technical strategy for knowing reality called *documentary*; in both, as already mentioned in the respective section, at the level or element of theory, which occupies the second place in an epistemological orientation, the general theories of objective knowledge (mathematics, mechanicism and organicism), particular to the objective social sciences (positivism, functionalism, structuralism and systems) and specific to the objective sciences of education (behaviourism) are those which, more than the other theories (subjective and dialectical), can use the *documentary* as a technical strategy to know reality. This is because the explorations, descriptions, explanations, interpretations and understandings of reality in the aforementioned theories are made from reason.

The same thing we think about the technical strategy to know reality called *experimentation*, applies to the technical strategy to know reality called *documentary*; in both, as already mentioned in the respective section, at the level or element of method, which occupies the third place in an epistemological orientation, *experimentation* is a technical strategy to know reality that is derived mainly from intellectual operations or methodological procedures to generate new knowledge from reason (in an objective way), such as: addition, multiplication, deduction, synthesis, classification and definition.

It can be assumed that *documentary*, like *experimentation*, is a technical strategy for learning about reality that is derived from philosophical assumptions, theoretical foundations and methodological procedures that are born in reason, i.e., that are objective (in the terms agreed upon throughout this paper).

2.9.5.2 *Technical strategies for subjective knowledge of the educational reality.*

The *technical strategies* for knowing reality subjectively are derived from the intellectual operations or methodological procedures that the cognising subject carries out with his object of knowledge from the senses, i.e. subjectively: subtraction, division, analysis, induction and comparison.

The *technical* strategies for *subjective* knowledge of reality are observation and survey.

2.9.5.2.1 The observation.

Observation is a *technical* strategy for getting to know reality subjectively (from the senses) that consists of the deliberate and systematic use of the *senses* to perceive reality and obtain data that have previously been defined as being of interest. It is an act of conscious will that selects an area of reality to see something. Ortiz (2003: 120) agrees with us that *observation* is a research *technique*. The *technical* strategy for learning about reality, called *observation*, consists of a *"...procedure for collecting data and information that consists of using the senses to observe facts and social realities present and people in the real context in which they carry out their activities..."*. Facts, phenomena, etc., that occur in reality can be observed and perceived with the senses. Observation is a technical strategy to get to know reality with the senses, i.e. subjectively. The will of the subject counts a lot, that is why it is subjective. The subject, as the saying goes, sees what he wants to see. The problem is that no human being feels and thinks in the same way.

In direct contact with the reality under investigation, or fieldwork, *observation* ".*encompasses all the procedures used in the social sciences - also* in the natural sciences - *not only to examine the sources where the facts and data under study are to be found, but also to obtain and record them*". Sierra (2001: 240). *Observation* is a procedure for examining facts and data.

In the text commented on, the *technical* strategy for learning about reality called *observation* is confused with the others (experimentation, survey and documentary), when it is classified as direct (simple or *experimental*), documentary and *survey* (by questionnaire, interview or attitude scale) (Sierra: 2001: 241). In order to *observe*, the senses are used, in the *experiment* the phenomenon is produced artificially, in the survey "the person who knows is asked" and in the documentary, all types of recordings are studied. For this reason, they should not be considered as part of observation (which is a technical strategy to get to know reality) but as technical strategies independent of it, in which the aim is also to get to know the reality under study.

Observation is a technical strategy that the cognising subject carries out from the senses (subjectively) in order to know his object of study, which consists, as we have already seen, in the deliberate and systematic use of the senses to perceive reality and obtain data that have previously been defined as being of interest. It is an act of will from which an area of reality is selected in order to see something.

The definition, characteristics, function, purpose, classification, etc. of *observation* can be constructed from the senses (subjective).

The concept of *observation* depends on the way in which the five main philosophical problems of knowledge are solved, the theories with which the reality under study is to be problematised and the methods chosen to generate new knowledge.

Just as the method depends on the *theory*, the technical strategy for learning about reality will depend on the methods used to generate new knowledge.

Just as we have done with the other technical strategies for knowing reality in order to define the epistemological position, we will now place the *technical* strategy for knowing reality called observation in its proper place in the process of knowledge, i.e. within an epistemological orientation.

In *observation*, each and every one of the five main philosophical problems of knowledge is solved from the senses.

In *observation*, the philosophical problem about the possibility of knowledge is resolved from sceptical, subjectivist, relativist and pragmatic assumptions (first level or element of an epistemological orientation). It can be stated, according to Tamayo (1982: 99), that observation explicitly refers "...*to visual perception and is used to indicate all forms of perception used for the registration of responses as they are presented to our senses...*". In *observation* it is assumed, from the senses, that it is indeed possible to know reality, but not in essence, but only in a sceptical (doubting), subjective (from the senses of the cognising subject), relative (because it changes in time, space and circumstances) and pragmatic (because all knowledge must be useful to humanity) way. It is assumed that reality moves, that the relationships between phenomena obey the changes that reality undergoes and that they can be registered, through the senses, i.e. inductively (method).

In *observation*, the problem of the origin of knowledge is resolved on the basis of empiricist philosophical assumptions. Observation "...*is the basic way in which we obtain information about the world around us...*" (Pick, 2007: 57). This is done inductively (method: third element or level of an epistemological orientation). Induction is the intellectual operation or methodological procedure carried out by the cognising subject to generate new knowledge from the senses. Observation is a technique for knowing reality that makes possible the materialisation, instrumentation, implementation, realisation, etc., of the methodological procedure or intellectual operation to generate new knowledge called *induction*.

We have already seen that an *induction* consists of *a* ".*movement of knowledge from isolated statements to general conclusions*" (*Blauberg, I.*, 1983:100). (Blauberg, I., 1983:100), because it starts from facts, from phenomena, to conceptualisations of them.

In *observation*, the problem about the essence of knowledge is solved from subjectivist philosophical assumptions. *Observation* is a technical strategy to know reality, which has been defined as ".*a procedure of data and information gathering that consists of using the senses to observe facts and present social realities and people in the real context where they normally carry out their activities*" (Ortiz, 2003: 120). (Ortiz, 2003: 120). *Observation* can be considered as a technique to know reality in a subjective way, because, in the knowledge relationship, the subject determines the object. That the cognising subject determines the object to be known can be interpreted as meaning that no *observation* is neutral, innocent, etc.; rather, all *observation* will be partial and interested. The prejudices, life history, traditions, beliefs, myths, values, ambitions, etc. of the cognising subject contaminate the *observation* of facts, events or phenomena. This would be a pre-metaphysical solution to the philosophical problem of the essence of knowledge, because it refers to the relation of knowledge that is established between the cognising subject and the object to be known, not to the reality itself that is *observed*.

In the *observation*, the problem about the essence of knowledge can also be posed in metaphysical terms and solved from realist philosophical assumptions. It is presumed that "...*knowledge constitutes a complicated process of intermediations, composed of three elements: the subject, the object and the <given> (or essence), The latter expresses only the objects, indicates their presence, but is not identified with the psychic processes nor with the objects themselves...*" (Blauberg, I., 1983:157). The material world is considered to be independent of the spiritual world. *Observation* is a technical strategy to know the reality in which ".*it considers the phenomena as they are, without modifying them or acting on them*". (Bisquerra, S/F: 7), This would be a metaphysical solution to the problem of the essence of knowledge, because it refers to the existence or non-existence of reality.

In *observation*, the problem of the essence of knowledge can also be posed in theological terms and resolved on the basis of dualistic philosophical assumptions. The technical strategy for knowing reality called observation "...*is subject to verification and controls of validity and reliability*" (Bisquerra, S/F: 134). (Bisquerra, S/F: 134). Observation is a technical strategy for knowing reality that can accept criteria of validity and invalidity. Observation is a technical strategy for knowing reality in which ".*the material and the psychic, the corporal and the spiritual, validity and invalidity, constitute two principles independent of each other and which do not mutually condition each other"*. (Blauberg, I., 1983:51). In observation, reality is divided into two for study: truth-falsity. This would be a theological solution to the problem of the essence of knowledge, because, in philosophical terms, the knowledge one has about reality can be true or false (dualism).

In *observation*, the problem of classifying knowledge is solved on the basis of intuitive philosophical assumptions. The technical strategy for knowing reality called *observation* provides an intuitive type of knowledge, because "... *it consists of extracting from reality data that are standardised in such a way that they are comparable and correlating them...*" (Anguera, 1997: 21) The technique of *observation* is a strategy to materialise, to make real, the purpose of the *inductive* method: the generation of new knowledge. It has already been mentioned that induction is "*.the movement of knowledge from isolated statements to general conclusions*". (Blauberg, I., 1983:100). In observation, as already noted, it is assumed that the cognizing subject is able to directly contemplate his object of study; that he can achieve a visual representation of it (Blauberg, I., 1983:154).

In *observation*, the philosophical problem about the concepts and criteria of truth of knowledge are solved from transcendent assumptions. In the technical strategy for knowing reality called observation, truth is considered to be the concordance of thought with the object thought (transcendent concept of truth). Truth is considered to be subjective, relative and pragmatic; an assumption that is only achieved from the senses. The criterion for estimating the aforementioned transcendent concept of truth arises from conceding that the cognising subject is confronted with objects of knowledge that have real existence in the world (realism) independently of thought itself.

On the level or element of theory, which occupies the second place in an epistemological orientation, the general theories of subjective knowledge (chaos and conflict), particular to the subjective social sciences (historicism and dialectical historical materialism) and specific to the subjective sciences of education (psychoanalysis, humanism and cognoscitivism) are those which, more than the other theories (objective and dialectical), can use *observation* as a technical strategy for learning about reality. This is because the explorations, descriptions, explanations, interpretations and understandings of reality in the aforementioned theories are made from the senses.

At the level or element of method, which occupies the third place in an epistemological orientation, *observation* is a technical strategy for knowing reality that is derived mainly from intellectual operations or methodological procedures to generate new knowledge from the senses (subjectively), such as: subtraction, division, induction, analysis and comparison.

It can be assumed that *observation* is a technical strategy for getting to know reality that derives from philosophical assumptions, theoretical foundations and methodological procedures that are born in the senses, i.e. that are subjective (in the terms agreed upon throughout this paper).

The last of the four known technical strategies for ascertaining reality is the *survey*. In the following, we will try to construct the concept of the same, based on the theory of mental maps; and, subsequently, we will carry out the respective epistemological analysis; as is being done in the present research with each and every one of the elements of an epistemological orientation.

2.9.5.2.2.2The survey.

The *survey* is a *technical* strategy to know the reality that consists of a set of standardised questions addressed to a representative sample of the population or institutions, in order to know states of opinion. The *survey* is a *technical strategy* for ascertaining opinions by asking those who "know".

For Sierra (2001: 305), the *survey* "...*consists of obtaining data of sociological interest by questioning members of society*". It is assumed that the most suitable subjects are asked, those who are knowledgeable about the issue to be addressed. Some characteristics of the *survey*, to paraphrase Sierra (2001: 305), are:

1. - It is a non-direct observation of the facts.
2. - It is a method of data collection.
3. - It can be applied on a massive scale.

With regard to the first of the characteristics of the *survey* indicated by the author mentioned above, it does not seem to us that the *survey* is a non-direct *observation* of facts or phenomena, since *to survey* means to ask those who "know" something about the reality being investigated; while to *observe* means, as we have already seen, to use the senses to perceive things or events and obtain data about them. The *survey* is carried out by means of questions that can be put together or gathered using two *instruments*: the questionnaire and the interview. *Observation*, on the other hand, is done through the researcher's senses and the information is gathered in an *instrument* called a register. Recording will be discussed in more depth in the sub-chapter on instruments for collecting existing information on the object of study.

It can be observed that if this criterion is followed, the technical *strategy* to know the reality would be duplicated because, on the one hand, trying to know the facts or phenomena by asking those who "know" is a technical *strategy* to know the reality that is being investigated, and *observing* the facts or phenomena is another technical *strategy* to know the reality. In the first technical *strategy* to know the reality, *questions* are used, which can be collected using instruments to collect information, such as questionnaires and/or interviews (which are, as will be seen later, the two *instruments* through which the *survey* is carried out); in the second, nothing is *asked*, only the reality is *observed* and collected in an *instrument* called a *register*. With the first technical *strategy*, opinions can be ascertained; with the second, characteristics of the facts or phenomena that are *observed*. Both are, as mentioned above, different technical *strategies* to learn about reality.

Regarding the second characteristic that the author mentions about the *survey*, it does not seem to us that it is a *method* either, because the *method*, for the purposes of research, as was observed in the corresponding subchapter, is understood as an intellectual operation or methodological procedure that the cognising subject carries out to generate new knowledge about the subjects under investigation, and not as a strategy to learn about reality.

As already mentioned in the respective sub-chapters of this research, each and every level or step of an *epistemological orientation* serves different purposes and determines each other (from higher to lower and vice versa): The purpose of the *philosophical assumptions* is to solve the problems of knowledge (from reason and/or from the senses) and to determine the theory or theories that can serve to construct the object of study; The *theoretical foundations* serve to problematise reality and arrange the methods to construct new knowledge; the *intellectual operations or methodological procedures* (methods) are used to generate new knowledge about the object of study and decide on the technical strategies to know the reality; the *technical strategies* allow to know the reality and prescribe the instruments with which the existing information about the object of study will be gathered; and the *instruments* serve to gather the information about the subject under investigation.

We are of the opinion that the *survey* is not a *method* of data collection, because in order to obtain data we have the respective *instruments* of each and every one of the technical *strategies* that, in order to know the reality, are known to this day: observation, experimentation, survey and documentary. In the sub-chapter corresponding to the *instruments* for collecting information (infra. 2.12), it can be seen that the *instrument* for collecting data in the *technical* strategy called *"observation"* is the register; the technical strategy of *experimentation* does not have *instruments*, to carry it out it is only necessary to gather the necessary elements; those of the technical strategy of the *survey*, the questionnaire and the interview; and that of the *documentary* technical strategy, the work sheet.

A first approximation to the definition of the *survey* would be the following: the *survey* is a *technical* strategy to know the reality, consisting of states of opinion or specific facts, by means of opinion questions that the cognising subject asks, based on the senses, with people who know and are aware of the properties of certain facts and/or phenomena, through the use of questionnaires and/or interviews.

The definition, characteristics, function, purpose, classification, etc. of the *survey* can be constructed from the senses (subjective).

The concept *of enquiry* depends on the way in which the cognitive subjects solve each and every one of the five problems of knowledge: with reason, with the senses or with both qualities of the researcher; the theories, with which it is intended to problematise the reality under study, and the methods that are chosen to generate new knowledge.

As has been constantly reiterated throughout this research, just as the *method* depends on the *theory*, the *technical* strategy for learning about reality will depend on the *methods* with which it is intended to generate new knowledge.

Just as we have done with the other *technical* strategies for knowing reality, in order to define the epistemological position, we will now place the *technical* strategy for knowing reality called *survey* in the place that corresponds to it in the process of knowledge, that is, within an epistemological orientation.

In the *survey*, each and every one of the five main philosophical problems of knowledge is solved from the senses.

In the *survey*, the philosophical problem about the possibility of knowledge is solved from sceptical, subjectivist, relativist and pragmatic assumptions (first level or element of an epistemological orientation). It can be stated, according to García (1986: 123), that the *survey* is *"...an investigation carried out on a sample of subjects representative of a wider collective, which is carried out in the context of everyday life, using standardised interrogation procedures in order to obtain quantitative measurements of a wide variety of objective and subjective characteristics of the population".* In the *survey* it is assumed, from the senses, that it is possible to know reality, but not in essence, but only in a sceptical (doubting), subjective (from the senses of the cognising subject), relative (because it changes in time, space and circumstances) and pragmatic (because all knowledge must be useful to humanity) way. It is assumed that reality moves, that the relationships between phenomena obey the changes that reality undergoes and that they can be registered, through the senses, i.e. inductively (method).

In the *survey*, the problem of the origin of knowledge is solved on the basis of empiricist philosophical assumptions. The survey is a technique that consists of *".collecting information about a part of the population called a sample, for example: general data, opinions, suggestions or answers that are provided to questions formulated about the various indicators that are to be explored"* (Rojas, 1985: 137). This is done inductively (method:

third element or level of an epistemological orientation). Induction is the intellectual operation or methodological procedure carried out by the cognising subject to generate new knowledge from the senses. The *survey* is a technique to know the reality that makes possible the materialisation, instrumentation, implementation, realisation, etc., of the methodological procedure or intellectual operation to generate new knowledge called *induction*.

We have already seen that an *induction* consists of *"...the movement of knowledge from isolated statements to general conclusions..."* (Blauberg, I., 1983:100), because it starts from the facts, from the phenomena, to their conceptualisations. The *survey* is the technical strategy to learn about reality, the procedure that allows the generation of new knowledge that is intended to be achieved through induction.

In the *survey*, the problem about the essence of knowledge is solved from subjectivist philosophical assumptions. The *survey* is a technical strategy to know the reality, which has been defined as *".an answer to a <how>. It is a means to an end, but it is situated at the level of facts or practical stages ...it represents the stages of limited operations, linked to practical, concrete elements, adapted to a defined end"*. (Grawitz, 1984: 291). It can be considered that the *survey* is a technical strategy to know the reality in a subjective way, because, it is the means that serves the method (in this case deductive) to achieve the end: the construction of new knowledge. In the knowledge relationship, the subject determines the object. That the cognising subject determines the object to be known can be interpreted as meaning that no *observation* is neutral, innocent, etc.; rather, *every enquiry* will be biased and self-interested. The prejudices, life history, traditions, beliefs, myths, values, ambitions, etc. of the cognising subject, contaminate *the enquiry* he makes about facts, events or phenomena. This would be a pre-metaphysical solution to the philosophical problem of the essence of knowledge, because it refers to the relation of knowledge that is established between the cognising subject and the object to be known, not to the reality itself that is *surveyed.*

In the *survey*, the problem about the essence of knowledge can also be posed in metaphysical terms and solved from realistic philosophical assumptions. The *survey "...is presumed to be a method of obtaining information by means of oral or written questions, posed to a universe or sample of people who have the characteristics required by the research problem.* (Briones, 2008: 99). Between the question and the answer to the research problem, there is an intellectual operation or methodological procedure that the cognising subject carries out, from the senses, to generate new knowledge. In order to know the reality, the cognising subject must ask those who have news of it. This is done by means of the survey. The *survey* is the technical strategy of the method to answer the research question. This would be a metaphysical solution to the problem of the essence of knowledge, because it refers to the existence or non-existence of reality.

In the *survey*, the problem of the essence of knowledge can also be posed in theological terms and solved from dualistic philosophical assumptions. The technical strategy to know the reality called *survey* is a *".research method capable of responding to problems both in descriptive terms and in terms of the relationship of variables, after the collection of systematic information, according to a previously established design that ensures the rigour of the information obtained"* (Ortiz, 2003: 52). (Ortiz, 2003: 52). The *survey* is a technical strategy for learning about reality that can accept criteria of validity and invalidity. In the *survey*, reality is divided in two for its study: truth-falsity. This would be a theological solution to the problem of the essence of knowledge, because, in philosophical terms, the knowledge one has about reality can be true or false (dualism).

In the *survey*, the problem of classifying knowledge is solved on the basis of intuitive philosophical assumptions. The technical strategy to know the reality called survey provides an intuitive type of knowledge, because *"... in the survey we proceed to the collection of individual data to obtain during the evaluation aggregated data..."* (Mayntz et al., 1980: 133) The survey technique is a strategy to materialise, to make real, the purpose of the *inductive* method: the generation of new knowledge. It has already been mentioned that induction is *".the movement of knowledge from isolated statements to general conclusions"*. (Blauberg, I., 1983:100). In the enquiry, as already observed, it is assumed that the cognizing subject is able to ask the knower about his object of study; that he can achieve a generalisation of the behaviour of the object of study.

In the *survey*, the philosophical problem about the concepts and criteria of truth of knowledge are solved from transcendent assumptions. In the technical strategy for knowing reality called *survey*, truth is considered to be the concordance of thought with the object thought (transcendent concept of truth). Truth is considered to be subjective, relative and pragmatic; an assumption that can only be achieved through the senses. In the *survey*, *".although individuals are questioned, what interests the social researcher is the joint consideration of the data, grouped according to classes, groups or types of individuals. The object of the evaluation is not only description, but also the discovery or verification of relationships"* (Mayntz et *al.*, 1980). (Mayntz et al., 1980: 133). The criterion for estimating the above-mentioned transcendent concept of truth arises from conceding that the cognising subject is confronted with objects of knowledge that have real existence in the world (realism) independently of thought itself.

On the level or element of theory, which occupies the second place in an epistemological orientation, the general theories of subjective knowledge (chaos and conflict), particular to the subjective social sciences (historicism and dialectical historical materialism) and specific to the subjective sciences of education (psychoanalysis, humanism and cognoscitivism) are those which, more than the other theories (objective and dialectical), can use the *survey* as a technical strategy to get to know reality. This is because the explorations, descriptions, explanations, interpretations and understandings of reality in the aforementioned theories are made from the senses.

On the level or element of method, which occupies the third place in an epistemological orientation, the *survey* is a technical strategy to learn about reality that derives mainly from intellectual operations or methodological procedures to generate new knowledge from the senses (subjectively), such as: subtraction, division, induction, analysis and comparison.

It can be assumed that the *survey* is a technical strategy for learning about reality that derives from philosophical assumptions, theoretical foundations and methodological procedures that are born in the senses, i.e. that are subjective (in the terms agreed upon throughout this paper).

Up to this point, the analysis of the technical strategies that the cognising subject can use to know reality in a process of knowledge (fourth level and element of an epistemological orientation).

2.10 THE METHOD-TECHNIQUE RELATIONSHIP.

We regret having to be so repetitive, but we consider it necessary to do so because of the complexity of the treatment of the issue. As has been emphasised throughout this paper, each of the five elements of an *epistemological orientation* fulfils different functions in the process of knowledge: the philosophical *assumptions*, to analyse reality, allow us to solve each and every one of the five main problems of knowledge from reason, from the senses or from both; the *theoretical* foundations, to problematise the objects of study, provide the epistemological elements to construct the investigation; the *methodological* procedures or intellectual operations, to generate new knowledge, provide us with the method; the *technical* strategies to know reality, serve to explore, describe, explain, interpret, understand, etc. reality; and the *instruments* are used to gather information about the object of study.

It has already been said that just as *theory* depends on *philosophy*, the *method* for generating new knowledge will depend on the *theories* with which the object of study is being problematised.

It has already been said that the *technical* strategy used in the construction of the object of study will depend on the intellectual operation or methodological procedure used to generate new knowledge about reality (*method*).

If we seek to know reality with *objective technical strategies* (experimentation, documentary, etc.), it will be because the intellectual operations or methodological procedures with which we want to generate new knowledge are also *objective* (addition, multiplication, deduction, synthesis, classification, definition, etc.).

If we use *intellectual operations or objective methodological procedures* (addition, multiplication, deduction, synthesis, classification, definition, etc.) to generate new knowledge about our object of study, it is because we are problematising reality with *general theories of objective knowledge* (mathematics, mechanicism, organicism, etc.), *particular to the objective social sciences* (positivism, functionalism, structuralism, systems, etc.), and *specific to the objective sciences of education* (behaviourism).

If we problematise reality with *general theories of objective knowledge* (mathematicism, mechanicism, organicism, etc.), *particular*
of the objective social sciences (positivism, functionalism, structuralism, systems, etc.), and *specific to the objective sciences of education* (behaviourism).), and *specific to the objective sciences of education* (behaviourism); it will be because we are solving each and every one of the five main problems of knowledge using *dogmatic* (possibility of knowledge), *rationalist* (origin of knowledge), *objectivist, idealist* and *dualist* (pre-metaphysical, metaphysical and theological solutions, respectively, to the problem of the essence of knowledge), *rational* (classification of knowledge) and *immanent* (concept and criterion of truth of knowledge) philosophical assumptions.

Finally, if we are solving each and every one of the five main problems of knowledge using *dogmatic* (possibility of knowledge), *rationalist* (origin of knowledge), *objectivist, idealist* and *dualist* (pre-metaphysical, metaphysical and theological solutions, respectively, to the problem of the essence of knowledge), *rational* (classification of knowledge) and *immanent* (concept and criterion of truth of knowledge) philosophical assumptions, it will be because we are analysing reality from reason.

If we seek to know reality with *subjective technical strategies* (observation, survey, etc.), it will be because the intellectual operations or methodological procedures with which we want to generate new knowledge are also *subjective* (subtraction, division, induction, analysis, comparison, etc.).

If we use *intellectual operations or subjective methodological procedures* (subtraction, division, induction, analysis, comparison, etc.) to generate new knowledge about our object of study, it is because we are problematising reality with *general theories of subjective knowledge* (chaos, conflict, etc.), *particular to the subjective social sciences* (historicism, dialectical historical materialism, etc.), and *specific to the subjective sciences of education* (psychoanalysis, humanism, cognoscitivism, etc.).

If we problematise reality with *general theories of subjective knowledge* (chaos, conflict, etc.), *particular to the subjective social sciences* (historicism, dialectical historical materialism, etc.), and *specific to the subjective sciences of education* (psychoanalysis, humanism, cognoscitivism, etc.); it will be because we are solving each and every one of the five main problems of knowledge using sceptical, subjectivist, relativist and pragmatic (possibility of knowledge), empiricist (origin of knowledge), subjectivist, realist and phenomenalist (pre-metaphysical, metaphysical and theological solutions, respectively, to the problem of the essence of knowledge), intuitive (classification of knowledge) and transcendental (concept and criterion of truth of knowledge) philosophical assumptions.

Finally, if we are solving each and every one of the five main problems of knowledge using sceptical, subjectivist, relativist and pragmatic (possibility of knowledge), empiricist (origin of knowledge), subjectivist, realist and phenomenalist (pre-metaphysical, metaphysical and theological solutions, respectively, to the problem of the essence of knowledge), intuitive (classification of knowledge) and transcendental (concept and criterion of truth of knowledge) *philosophical assumptions*; it will be because we are analysing reality from the senses.

As has been well observed, the relationship between method and technique, like the relationship between *theory* and *method* and like the relationship between *philosophy* and *theory*, is one of dependence of the latter on the former: just as *theory* depends on *philosophy*, method depends on *theory* and technique on method and, therefore, on the *philosophy* on which the *theory* with which reality is being problematised depends in order to construct new knowledge. If an educational researcher does not realise this, he or she will construct an epistemologically incongruent object of study.

The following table shows the method-technique relationship:

METHODS			TECHNIQUES		
OBJECTIVES	SUMA MULTIPLICA CION	REASON	OBJECTIVES	EXPERIMENTATION DOCUMENTARY	REASON
OBJECTIVES	RESTA DIVISION	FEELINGS	SUBJECTIVES	OBSERVATION SURVEY	FEELINGS
DIALECTIVES	INDUCTIVE-DEDUCTIVE ANALITICOSYNTHETIC	BOTH	DIALECTICS	ALL	BOTH

2.11 SUMMARY OF THE SUB-CHAPTER.

By way of summary, the following table shows the main technical strategies to get to know the reality:

TECHNICAL STRATEGIES	**OBJECTIVES**	**EXPERIMENTATION:** A technical strategy used to find the behaviour of a variable from different combinations of factors or input variables of a process, which, when changed, affect the response.
		DOCUMENTATION: All types of engraving. It is not the object, it is the discourse, it is what a theoretician tells us, it is the object that is talked about.
	SUBJECTIVES	**OBSERVATION:** Deliberate and systematic use of the senses to perceive reality and obtain data that have previously been defined as being of interest. Act of conscious will that selects an area of reality in order to see something.
		SURVEY: A set of standardised questions addressed to a representative sample of the population or institutions, with the aim of ascertaining states of opinion or specific facts.
	DIALECTICS	ALL

2.12 INSTRUMENTS, IN ORDER TO RETRIEVE INFORMATION ON EDUCATIONAL ISSUES.

The fifth element of an epistemological orientation is the *instrument* or instruments that the educational researcher must choose to retrieve information about his or her object of study. Just as the theory or theories with which the cognising subject problematises his object of study, in order to construct it, depends on the assumptions from which each and every one of the five main *philosophical* problems of knowledge are solved (with reason; with the senses; with both, first reason and then the senses; or with both, first the senses and then the senses; or with both, first the senses and then reason); likewise, the *method* used to generate new knowledge about it will depend on the theory or theories on which the research work is based; and, as a consequence, the *technique* with which the aim is to know reality will depend on the *method* with which the new knowledge is to be generated; and, finally, the instruments with which the aim is to recover information about the object of study will depend on the technical strategy used to know reality.

The *instruments* of the epistemological orientations, with which data are recovered from reality to explore it, describe it, explain it, interpret it, understand it, etc., depend on the *technical* strategy with which we intend to know reality. If the *technical* strategy used is *observation*, the most suitable *instrument* to recover the data will be the *register*; if we use the *experiment* as a *technique*, the *tools* we use to carry out the *experiment* will be the respective *instruments* that allow us to recover the data we need; if we use the *survey* as a *technical* strategy, the appropriate *instruments* will be the *questionnaire* and/or the *interview*, and finally, if we use the *documentary technique*, the *instrument* that will allow us to collect the data we need will be the *work sheet*.

The following table shows the different *instruments* that can be used to collect information and the technical strategy to learn about the reality from which they are derived.

INSTRUMENT	TECHNICAL STRATEGY
REGISTRY	OBSERVATION
ELEMENTS	EXPERIMENTATION
QUESTIONNAIRE	SURVEY
INTERVIEW	
WORKSHEET	DOCUMENTATION

2.12.1 *The definition of an instrument to collect information on educational problems*.

For Ortiz (2003), an *instrument* "...*refers to the means that allow the researcher to obtain the central data...*". It is important to note, for the purposes of this study, that the *instruments* we are talking about are those that allow us, as researchers, to retrieve existing data (information) about the reality under investigation.

Research *instruments* are means, ways, procedures or forms of obtaining data for the construction of the object of study.

An instrument, in this case, is like an utensil (basket, basket), tool, apparatus, appliance, device, etc., by means of which data can be collected.

Data can be defined as the "*.systematised and objective product of some kind of facts: events, processes, phenomena, entities, physical things or concrete systems*" (Ortiz, *2003: 39*). (Ortiz, 2003: 39). A datum can be a note, a detail, an antecedent, a piece of news, etc. about the object of study.

A first approach to the definition of an instrument for collecting information on educational problems is as follows:

A research *instrument* is the means, manner, procedure or form; which may consist of a tool, implement, apparatus or artefact; that the educational researcher may use to collect notes, details, background, news, etc., about his/her object of study.

Instruments for retrieving information about the object of study are to data what a basket can be to its contents.

2.12.2 *Characteristics of the instruments for collecting information on educational problems*:

- The main characteristic of an *instrument* for collecting information on educational problems is that it is the means by which the reality is known with the respective technical strategy that is being used. If the reality is to be known by observing it, the instrument in which the notes about it should be collected will have to be the register; if by experiencing it, with the elements; if by documenting it, with the work sheets; and, finally, if by surveying it, by means of the questionnaire and/or the interview.

- It is a means, way, procedure or form of gathering information about the reality under investigation.

- They consist of utensils, tools, devices or artefacts for storing data, notes, details, background information, news, etc., related to the object of research.

- Only four *instruments* are known to retrieve research data: the *work sheet* (to learn about reality with the documentary technique); the *register* (to learn about reality by observing it); and the *questionnaire* and the *interview* (to learn about reality by surveying it). The experiment (the fourth and last technical strategy to learn about reality) does not have instruments; it is only necessary to gather the elements, resources or means necessary to carry it out.

- It is the fifth and final element, component, piece, part, etc., of an epistemological orientation, in the terms agreed upon throughout this research.

- The *instrument*(s) chosen by any educational researcher to retrieve existing information on the object of study will depend on the technical strategy(ies) with which the researcher intends to learn about the reality under investigation.

1.12.3 *The role of instruments for collecting information on educational issues*.

The main function of the *instruments* for collecting information on educational problems, the need they satisfy, is precisely that: the collection, ordering and systematisation of the information available on the object of study.

By satisfying the need to gather, order, organise, prepare and systematise the information available on the reality under investigation, the *instrument* is making it possible for the *technical* strategy to fulfil its proper function: to allow the researcher to gain knowledge of reality, in accordance with the method or methods with which it is intended to generate new knowledge.

1.12.4 *Purpose of the instruments for collecting information on educational issues*.

The purpose of any instrument for collecting data on the object of study is precisely that: to gather information on the reality under investigation.

2.12.5 *Classification of instruments for collecting information on educational problems*.

Following the same criteria used to classify philosophical assumptions, theoretical foundations, methodological procedures and technical strategies, *instruments* can be classified as objective, subjective and dialectical.

2.12.5.1 *The objective instruments for collecting information on educational problems.*

We consider that the objective instruments for gathering information on educational problems that best fit the model proposed in this research are the elements (from the experimentation) and the worksheets (from the documentary).

2.12.5.1.1 The elements.

From the Latin *elementum*, it is understood as "*...principle that enters into the composition of bodies...foundation, mobile or integral part of a thing...*" (Diccionario léxico hispano, 1983: 532). The technical strategy of experimentation does not require *instruments* to retrieve information about the object of study, instead we can speak of *elements*: that is, to know reality through experimentation, we only need to gather the elements, components, pieces, parts, principles, etc., that are needed to carry it out.

2.12.5.1.2 The worksheets.

For Ortiz (2003: 68), the work sheet "*.is the main instrument for recording documentary or field information. In this card, the relevant information can have different treatments (summary, commentary, analysis, textual quotation, etc.); they are basic for organising all the information that will make up the final report*". The work sheet is like the basket in which we gather the data required to know the reality with the technical strategy known as documentary.

For Tamayo (1982: 98), the *worksheet* is "*.of great value for documentary research. It is the instrument that allows us to order and classify the data consulted, including our observations and criticisms, thus facilitating the writing of the document...*". The work sheet allows us to order and classify the information with which we will learn about the reality being investigated, using the documentary as a technical strategy.

The *work sheet* allows "*... to collect information from books, magazines, newspapers, personal and public documents and any historical testimony...*" (Rojas, 1985: 69). The only source of the *work sheet* is the document. A document is any kind of engraving in which the object of study is not present, but in which a specialist talks about it. The most important documents in educational research are books, journal articles and bachelor's, master's and doctoral theses.

The *work sheet* is the means, way, procedure or form that the educational researcher can use to collect notes, details, background information, news, etc., which allow him/her to learn about the reality through documentation.

2.12.5.2 *Subjective instruments for gathering information on educational problems.*

2.12.5.2.1 Registration.

For Ortiz (2003: 141), the *register* is a "*.set of elements of information related to each other, which are treated as a unit, and whose main characteristic is a systematic order. Recording consists of taking notes, pointing out, inscribing, etc.* objective facts that can be observed), personal attitudes, opinions, etc.

For Munch (2003: 55), the *register* serves to "*.record objective facts, attitudes and opinions*". *Recording* is the *instrument* of *observation* to get to know realities that are present before the cognising subject, that exist independently of him.

Recording is the means, manner, procedure or form that the educational researcher can use to collect notes, details, background information, news, etc., that allow him/her to learn about reality through *observation*.

2.12.5.2.2 The questionnaire.

For Bisquerra (2000: 88), *questionnaires* are "... *a more or less extensive set of questions or issues that are considered relevant to the trait, characteristics or variables that are the object of study...*". The *questionnaire* is questioned because the technical strategy to know the reality that gives meaning to it is the *survey*, which means, broadly speaking, "asking those who know". It is, therefore, about questions, about questions that must be answered by the subjects surveyed.

For Ortiz (2003: 37), the questionnaire is ".*a data collection instrument, composed of a set of questions regarding one or several variables subject to measurement*". The questionnaire is applied to real people who have or may have different opinions about a certain reality.

For Munch (2003: 55), the *questionnaire* is ".*a format written in the form of an interrogation in which information is obtained about the variables to be investigated*".

Pick (2007: 61), defines a *questionnaire* as ".a method for obtaining information in a clear and precise manner, where there is a standardised format of questions and where the informant reports his or her answers". The *questionnaire* is not a method, because it is not an intellectual operation or a methodological procedure to generate new knowledge, it is an instrument to collect information about the object of study.

For Hernández et al., 1991: 276) the *questionnaire* is "... *a set of questions regarding one or more variables to be measured...*". The *questionnaire* obeys to the technical strategy to know the reality called, in this study, *survey*; and the *survey* can be due to the *inductive* or *deductive* method, that is why the questions respond to certain variables that have to be measured, with a view to establishing generalisations (*induction*) or *deductions* about the relationship between one or more phenomena.

For Sierra (1994: 306) the *questionnaire* is ".*a set of questions, carefully prepared, on the facts and aspects that are of interest in a sociological investigation, to be answered by the population or its sample to which the study undertaken extends...*". The *questionnaire* is generally applied to a representative sample of the population under study.

The *questionnaire* is one of the two means (the other is the interview), ways, procedures or forms that the educational researcher can use to collect the notes, details, background, news, etc., that allow him/her to know the reality through the *survey*.

2.12.5.2.3 The interview.

For Tamayo (1982: 100), the *interview* is ".*the direct relationship established between the researcher and his object of study through individuals or groups in order to obtain oral testimonies*". *To interview* is to ask the one who "knows" about the object of study.

For Bisquerra (2000: 88), the *interview* is ".*an intentional dialogue oriented towards certain objectives. The interview can fulfil different functions: diagnostic, orientative, therapeutic and investigative*". The *interview* is a personal, face-to-face situation where one person (the interviewer) asks another person (the interviewee) questions designed to elicit answers relevant to the research problem. The research *interview* "...is a conversation between two people initiated by the interviewer for the purpose of obtaining information relevant to an investigation". In the *interview*, the object of study is not present, but some people have an opinion about it. This is why this instrument is used to find out opinions about different phenomena.

For Munch (2003: 55), the *survey* "*is a technique that consists of obtaining information about a part of the population or sample through the use of a questionnaire or interview*". We agree with her that the *interview*, together with the *questionnaire*, are the two instruments that allow the technical strategy of the survey to obtain the necessary information about the object of study in order to know the reality.

But later on, Munch (2003: 62), believes that the *interview* is a technique, "*...by means of which one person (the interviewer) requests information from another (interviewee)*". We do not share this idea because, as we have already clarified at the time, the *technique* is a strategy to know the reality and, in this case, the *interview* is *an instrument* used by the *technical* strategy of the survey to gather the information that allows it to know the reality that is being investigated.

For Ortiz (2003: 37), the *interview* is the "*...personal interaction of a communicative type whose central objective is to obtain basic information to carry out an investigation*". The interview allows both quantitative and qualitative data to be obtained, which is why it is very important that it is face-to-face, in order to observe attitudes.

For Pick (2007: 66), the *interview* is the personal relationship between one or more subjects, in which one of them, the interviewee, has certain information to provide to another subject, the interviewer". Care must be taken in the use of the interview, because interviewees do not always tell the truth.

The interview is one of the two means (the other is the questionnaire, already mentioned), ways, procedures or forms that the educational researcher can use to collect the notes, details, background, news, etc., that allow him/her to know the reality through the *survey*.

Up to this point, the instruments used to collect information on the object of study have been described.

2.13 THE TECHNICAL-INSTRUMENT RELATIONSHIP.

It has already been said that the *technical* strategy used in the construction of the object of study will depend on the intellectual operation or methodological procedure used to generate new knowledge about reality (*method*).

Similarly, the instrument(s) that the educational researcher chooses to collect data on his or her object of study will depend on the technical strategy(ies) with which he or she intends to learn about reality.

The following table shows the relationship between technique and instrument:

TECHNIQUES			INSTRUMENTS		
OBJECTIVES	EXPERIMENTACION	REASON	OBJECTIVES	ELEMENTS	REASON
	DOCUMENTARY			WORK SHEETS	

SUBJECTIVES	OBSERVATION SURVEY	FEELINGS	SUBJECTIVES	REGISTRY QUESTIONNAIRE	FEELINGS
DIALECTICS	ALL	BOTH	DIALECTICS	ALL	BOTH

2.14 SUMMARY OF THE SUB-CHAPTER.

By way of summary, the following table shows the main data collection instruments:

INSTRUMENTS	**OBJECTIVES**	**ELEMENTS**: Grouping of factors that are part of a component.
		WORKING SHEETS: Instrument that allows us to order and classify the data consulted.
	OBJECTIVES	**REGISTRATION:** To note, mark, inscribe.
		QUESTIONNAIRE: A system of rational, ordered questions. coherently. **INTERVIEW**: An interpersonal, face-to-face situation where one person (the interviewer) asks another person (the interviewee) questions designed to elicit answers relevant to the research problem.
	DIALECTIVES	ALL

2.15 SUMMARY OF THE CHAPTER.

As has been demonstrated throughout this research, the philosophical, theoretical, methodological, technical and instrumental dimensions are determined reciprocally, in a descending manner; that is to say, the *philosophical* assumptions, from which reality is going to be studied, determine the *theoretical* foundations; the theoretical foundations, from which the object of study is going to be problematised, define the *methodological* procedures; the methodological procedures, to generate new knowledge, define the *technical* strategies; and finally, the technical strategies with which the phenomenon is going to be known, guide the *instruments*, with which it is intended to collect the information needed to know the reality.

When there is no congruence between these five dimensions of research, the study is said to lack methodological rigidity, I would call it epistemological lack of congruence.

In the following table it is possible to appreciate, in a general way, the philosophical assumptions, from which each and every one of the main problems of knowledge can be resolved, from the educational sciences; the theoretical foundations (general of the

The five stages of research are: the methodological procedures that can be used to generate new knowledge; the technical strategies that can be used to learn about reality; and the instruments that can be considered to collect the information needed to construct an object of study. The five stages of research mentioned above make up what I usually call: the epistemological orientation of educational science research:

EPISTEMOLOGICAL	1.PROBLEM OF	1.1 POSSIBILITY OF KNOWLEDGE	IS SOLVED FROM REASON, FROM THE SENSES OR FROM BOTH QUALITIES OF	DOGAMATISM: **Reason**
			SKEPTICISM: Senses
			RELATIVISM: **Senses**
			SUBJECTIVISM: **Senses**

THE COGNISING SUBJECT.		PRAGMATISM: **Senses**	
		CRITICISM: **Sense and reason or vice versa**	
1.2 ORIGIN OF KNOWLEDGE	IS SOLVED FROM **REASON, FROM THE SENSES OR FROM BOTH QUALITIES OF THE COGNISING SUBJECT.**	RATIONALISM: **Reason**	
		EMPIRISM: **Senses**	
		INTELLECTUALISM: **Senses and reason**	
		APRIORISM: **Reason and the Senses**	
1.3 ESSENCE OF KNOWLEDGE	IS SOLVED FROM **REASON, FROM THE SENSES OR FROM BOTH QUALITIES OF THE COGNISING SUBJECT.**	SOLUTIONS PRE-METAPHYSICS	**OBJECTIVISM:** Reason
			SUBJECTIVISM: Senses
		METAPHYSICAL SOLUTIONS	**REALISM**: Senses
			IDEALISM: Reason
			PHENOMENALISM: Reason and senses and vice versa
		SOLUTIONS THEOLOGICAL	**DUALISMAND THEISM**: Reason
			MONISMOY PANTHEISM: Reason and the senses or vice versa
1.4 TYPES OF KNOWLEDGE	IS SOLVED FROM **REASON, FROM THE SENSES OR FROM BOTH QUALITIES OF THE COGNISING SUBJECT**	RATIONAL: **Reason**	
		INTUITIVE: **Senses**	
1.5. CRITERIA FOR TRUTH	IS SOLVED FROM **REASON, FROM THE SENSES OR FROM BOTH QUALITIES OF THE SUBJECT COGNOSCENT**	TRASCENDENT: **Senses**	
		IMMANENT: **Reason**	
II. THEORETICAL UNDERPINNINGS	EXPLORATIONS, DESCRIPTIONS, EXPLANATIONS, INTERPRETATIONS, UNDERSTANDINGS, ETC., OF REALITY ARE CONSTRUCTED FROM REASON, FROM THE SENSES OR FROM BOTH QUALITIES OF THE COGNISING SUBJECT. OF REALITY ARE CONSTRUCTED FROM REASON, FROM THE	2.1 GENERAL THEORIES OF KNOWLEDGE: **Mathematicism, Mechanism, Organicism, Chaos, Conflict, Complexity, etc.**	
		2.2 PARTICULAR THEORIES OF SOCIAL SCIENCES: **Positivism, Functionalism, Structuralism, Marxism, Systems Theory, Historicism, Phenomenology, Hermeneutics,** etc.	
		2.3 SPECIFIC THEORIES OF EDUCATIONAL SCIENCES: Behaviourism, Psychoanalysis, Humanism, Cognoscitivism, Psychogenetics, Sociocultural, etc.	

	SENSES OR FROM BOTH QUALITIES OF THE COGNIZING SUBJECT.	
III. METHODOLOGICAL PROCEDURES OR INTELLECTUAL OPERATIONS TO GENERATE NEW KNOWLEDGE	Addition, Subtraction, Multiplication, Division, Analysis, Synthesis, Induction, Deduction, Abduction, Definition, Classification, Intuition
IV. **TECHNICAL STRATEGIES**	REALITY IS KNOWN FROM REASON, FROM THE SENSES, OR FROM BOTH QUALITIES OF THE COGNISING SUBJECT.	4.1 **OBSERVATION**: Senses 4.2**EXPERIMENTATION**: Rationale 4.3 **DOCUMENTARY**: Reason 4.4 **SURVEY: Senses**
V. INSTRUMENTS	INFORMATION IS GATHERED FROM REASON, FROM THE SENSES OR FROM BOTH QUALITIES OF THE COGNISING SUBJECT	5.1 **REGISTER: Senses** 5.2 **ELEMENTS**: Reason 5.3 **WORKING SHEETS**: Reason 5.4 **INTERVIEW**: Sentiments 5.5 **QUESTIONNAIRE**: Senses

CHAPTER 3

CHARACTERISTICS OF AN EPISTEMOLOGICAL ORIENTATION. The different possibilities of positioning the researcher with respect to the problem of knowledge.

III. CHARACTERISTICS OF AN EPISTEMOLOGICAL ORIENTATION. The different possibilities of positioning the researcher with respect to the problem of knowledge.

Scientific communities or research traditions construct their objects of study on the basis of certain perspectives, paradigms or epistemological orientations, depending on the programme or mode of knowledge production they adopt.

Epistemological perspectives, paradigms or *orientations* guide scientific communities or research traditions in the construction of their objects of study on the basis of certain programmes or ways of producing knowledge.

The programmes or ways of producing knowledge depend on the perspective, paradigm or *epistemological orientation* adopted by the scientific communities or research traditions that use them.

The *epistemological orientations* are positions on the problem of knowledge. They privilege different ontological and epistemological interests.

Because knowledge is not neutral, the researcher who constructs his objects of study from a certain epistemological orientation implicitly accepts the theoretical and practical consequences of his work.

All knowledge construction is self-interested, there is no science that is neutral; *knowledge* is *power* and power is the possibility of *domination*, both epistemologically and ontologically.

The elements of the *epistemological orientations* differ in meaning and scope, with respect to the problems of knowledge.

The *philosophical assumptions* from which each and every one of the five philosophical problems are solved from a certain epistemological orientation depend on the quality(ies) that the cognising subject uses to study reality and provide the "lenses" to see reality.

The cognising subject can use his reason, his senses or both qualities (reason first and then the senses or vice versa) to explore, describe, explain, interpret, understand, etc. reality.

The *theoretical foundations* with which reality is problematised from a certain epistemological orientation depend on the philosophical assumptions with which each and every one of the five main philosophical problems of knowledge are solved and serve to problematise the objects of study.

The *methodological procedures* or intellectual operations used to generate new knowledge from a certain epistemological orientation depend on the theoretical foundations with which reality is problematised and serve to generate new knowledge.

The *technical strategies* with which one intends to know reality on the basis of a certain epistemological orientation depend on the methodological procedures or intellectual operations with which one intends to generate new knowledge and serve to know reality.

The *instruments* used to collect information from a given epistemological orientation depend on the technical strategies used to learn about reality and serve to collect information about the objects of study.
The main characteristic of an epistemological orientation is that it is a stance on the problem of knowledge.

CHAPTER 4

**FUNCTIONS OF
EPISTEMOLOGICAL ORIENTATIONS**
. The educational researcher's guide in
the construction of his or her object of study.

IV. **FUNCTIONS OF EPISTEMOLOGICAL ORIENTATIONS.**
The educational researcher's guide in the construction of his or her object of study.

The fundamental function of any *epistemological orientation* is to provide the scientific community with the different philosophical assumptions, from which it can solve each and every one of the five main philosophical problems of knowledge; the theoretical foundations, to problematise the objects of study; the methodological procedures or intellectual operations, to generate new knowledge; the technical strategies, to learn about reality; and the instruments, to gather existing information about the object of study.

All educational researchers, whether they know it or not, when they try to construct an object of study, they leave the ontological sphere and place themselves in the psychological world: they transform themselves from an entity into a cognising subject.

The reality that the educational researcher intends to know, by the mere fact that he has fixed his senses and/or his reason on it, is also transformed from an entity into an object to be known; however, its sphere, world, reality, etc. remains unchanged on the ontological plane.

It is very important that the educational researcher reflects that, in order to establish a knowledge relationship with his object of study, he has only his reason and his senses and that, depending on the quality or qualities mentioned above, he will "know" reality in one way or another.

The need that an epistemological orientation satisfies is precisely that: to guide the cognising subject on the arduous path of constructing his object of study, giving him a choice between several alternatives, different solutions to each and every one of the five general problems of knowledge: philosophical, theoretical, methodological, technical and instrumental.

CHAPTER 5

PURPOSE OF AN EPISTEMOLOGICAL ORIENTATION.
The determination of the validity, scope and limits of
human knowledge, its nature and its truth in the field of
education.

V. PURPOSE OF AN EPISTEMOLOGICAL ORIENTATION.

The determination of the validity, scope and limits of human knowledge, its nature and its truth in the field of education.

The most important aims of *epistemological orientations* are to determine the validity, scope and limits of human knowledge; the nature and truth of human knowledge.

An *epistemological orientation* is a proposed solution to the five main general problems of human knowledge: philosophical, theoretical, methodological, technical and instrumental.

The main aim of any *epistemological orientation* is to solve each and every one of the five problems mentioned above in order to know any reality.

Knowledge is a problem that is solved from different *epistemological orientations*, as will be seen in the respective chapter.

There is no innocent knowledge, every construction of an object of study is intentional and, behind it, there are both ontological and epistemological interests at work.

The different *epistemological orientations* that we will analyse in the following chapter solve each and every one of the problems of knowledge in different ways and, for this reason, it is necessary for the educational researcher to know them and, in this way, be able to choose freely the *epistemological orientation* that best suits his or her ontological and epistemological interests.

Any epistemological orientation is a guide for the researcher not to get lost in the difficult process of knowledge.

CHAPTER 6

CLASSIFICATION OF
EPISTEMOLOGICAL ORIENTATIONS. The three ways in which
the educational researcher orients himself/herself and takes a
position on the problem of
knowledge.

VI. **CLASSIFICATION OF EPISTEMOLOGICAL ORIENTATIONS.** The three ways in which the educational researcher orients himself/herself and takes a position on the problem of knowledge.

For the purposes of this paper, *epistemological orientations* can be classified as objective, subjective and dialogical.

The classification criterion was taken from the pre-metaphysical solution (without referring to the ontological character of the cognising subject and the object to be known, but only to its epistemological character, i.e. the problem of knowledge, not the problem of being) of the problem of the essence of knowledge, i.e. the problem of the relation of knowledge between the subject and the object.

As already mentioned in previous chapters, the above-mentioned solution to the problem of the relation of knowledge between the cognising subject and the object to be known can be established in three senses:

OBJECTIVISM: The object determines the subject.

SUBJECTIVISM: The subject determines the object.

DIALECTICS: Subject and object determine each other through dialogue.

Considering the above criteria, *epistemological orientations* can be classified as objective, subjective and dialogical.

Recall that this is due to the quality that the cognising subject can use to solve the above-mentioned problem of the essence of knowledge: his reason, his senses or both (it can be reason first and then the senses or vice versa).

6.1 THE OBJECTIVIST EPISTEMOLOGICAL ORIENTATION. The quantitative aspect of educational research.

An action is *objectively* just if it is what the agent really ought to do (objectivism) and not simply what he thinks he ought to do (subjectivism), i.e. *epistemologically*, it is held that everything learned is independent of the learning subject. A reference to the *objective* is the self-transcendence of an immediately given content, whereby it is directed towards an *object*. In logic, aesthetics and ethics it is understood as a doctrine that holds that the mind possesses universally valid *objects*, norms or meanings. The opposite is subjectivism. An ethical *objectivist* will hold that ethical truths are not relative, that there are certain acts that are right or certain *objects* that are good in the same way for all individuals. The *objective* is something that has the characteristic of being an *object* that exists independently of the mind that knows it. It is understood that both subject and *object* are real in the same way and that both are equally manifestations of an absolute or idea. The world is supposed to consist of concretisations of universals that have their being independent of the mind (Runes, 1998:273).

For the purposes of this classification, it is necessary to characterise the *objective*, as an *epistemological orientation*, on the basis of the elements that make it up; that

263

is, the philosophical assumptions, from which each and every one of the five main problems of knowledge are resolved; the theoretical foundations, with which the objects of study are problematised; the methodological procedures, with which new knowledge is generated; the technical strategies, which are used to learn about reality; and the instruments, with which the information is collected.

6.1.1 *The philosophical assumptions of the objectivist epistemological orientation.*

In order to know reality, an objectivist epistemological orientation is based mainly on seven *philosophical assumptions* which, respectively, refer to the possibility, origin, essence, classification and truth criteria of knowledge.

Each and every one of the five main philosophical problems of knowledge is solved by reason.

The *first philosophical assumption* from which one starts, from an *objectivist* epistemological orientation to know reality, consists of conceding that the subject really apprehends the object, that knowledge is not a problem, that real contact between the subject and the object is possible and real, that knowledge is not a relation, that the objects of knowledge are absolutely given to us, etc.; that is, that it is possible to know in a *dogmatic* way, without asking reason for an account.

As far *as the possibility of knowing* is concerned, *dogmatism* predominates over *scepticism* in this epistemological orientation. This is because the philosophical problem of the possibility of knowing is resolved by reason.

The *second philosophical assumption* from which one starts, from an *objectivist* epistemological orientation in order to know reality, refers to the fact that the main source of human knowledge is considered to be in reason, in thought. It is conceded that knowledge only deserves this name when it is logically necessary and universally valid, when our reason judges that something has to be like this and cannot be otherwise, that it has to be like this always and everywhere.

On the *origin of knowledge, rationalism* predominates over empiricism in this epistemological orientation. This is because the philosophical problem of the origin of knowledge is resolved by reason.

The *third philosophical assumption* from which one starts, from an *objectivist* epistemological orientation to know reality, refers to the fact of conjecturing that, in the relation of knowledge (independently of the ontological character of the subject and the object, in pre-metaphysical terms) that is, in the relation between the apprehending subject and the object to be known, the object determines the subject. Objects are said to be something given, something that presents a structure that is reconstructed by the cognising consciousness, like a photograph of reality.

On the *essence of knowledge*, in *pre-metaphysical* terms, i.e. without saying anything about the ontological character of the subject and the object, in the *objectivist* epistemological orientation, *objectivism* predominates over subjectivism. This is because the pre-metaphysical problem of the essence of knowledge is solved by reason.

The *fourth philosophical assumption* of an *objectivist* epistemological approach to knowing reality is the view that, with respect to the ontological character of subject and object, i.e. in metaphysical terms, this epistemological approach also assumes that reality exists, in itself, independently of thought.

In *metaphysical* terms, that is, by referring to the ontological character of the subject and the object, this epistemological orientation is dominated by *realism* over idealism. This is because the metaphysical problem of the essence of knowledge is resolved by reason.

The *fifth philosophical assumption* from which one starts, from an *objectivist* epistemological orientation, to explain phenomena, consists in conceding that, in theological terms, for example, good and evil coexist in an eternal confrontation, until the former triumphs over the latter; that is, God and man are separated, because (in the case of Christianity) our first parents (Adam and Eve) were expelled from paradise; to which we will return by means of religion (religifying the unlinked).

In the problem of the relation of knowledge, in the objectivist epistemological orientation, the *dualistic and theistic theological solution* predominates over monism and pantheism. This is because the theological problem of the essence of knowledge is solved by reason.

The *sixth philosophical assumption* from which one starts, from an *objectivist* epistemological orientation to know reality, as far as the types of knowledge are concerned, consists in assuming that knowledge is the spiritual apprehension of an object; that is, it is a rational, mediate, discursive knowledge.

In the objectivist epistemological orientation, with respect to the types of knowledge, *rational* knowledge predominates over intuitive knowledge. This is because the problem of classifying knowledge is solved by reason.

The *seventh philosophical assumption* from which we start, from an *objectivist* epistemological orientation to know reality, consists in the opinion that thought must agree with itself in order to be true. A judgement is true when it is formed in accordance with the laws and rules of thought. Truth is something formal, it coincides with correctness (idealism).

In the objectivist epistemological orientation, the *immanent criterion of truth* predominates over the transcendent. This is because the philosophical problem of the concept and criterion of truth of knowledge is solved by reason.

6.1.2 *The theoretical foundations of the objectivist epistemological orientation*.

The objectivist epistemological orientation, by the fact of solving each and every one of the five main philosophical problems of knowledge from reason, only allows the construction of dogmatic (possibility of knowing), rational (origin of knowledge), objective, idealistic and dualistic (pre-metaphysical, metaphysical and theological solutions, respectively, to the problem of the essence of knowledge), rational (classification of knowledge) and immanent (concept and criterion of truth of knowledge) theories.

6.1.2.1 *General theories of knowledge of the objectivist epistemological orientation*.

The *objectivist* epistemological orientation is of *mathematical* origin (phenomena are thought of in terms of diversity, contraposition, or, relation), *mechanistic* (events are thought of in terms of laws of mechanics) and organicist (evolution).

For the purposes of the present research, for the reasons expressed in previous chapters, we call mathematicism, mechanicism and organicism *general theories of knowledge*. These theories originate in the mathematical, physical, chemical, biological, etc. sciences.

The *mathematical, mechanistic and organicist* foundations of the objectivist epistemological orientation allow theories to be generated from mathematics, physics, chemistry and biology, i.e. from the *formal or ideal sciences* and from the *natural* (factual) *sciences*. This explains its *objectivist* epistemological orientation, with roots in the Platonic school, which, forgetting the subject, concentrates all its attention on the object; that is, neglecting the being, it concentrates on the ought to be.

6.1.2.2 *The particular social science theories of the objectivist epistemological orientation.*

Taken to the level of the factual or material sciences, the general theories of knowledge (mathematicism, mechanicism and organicism) allow the emergence of *particular theories of the social sciences*, such as positivism, functionalism, structuralism, general systems theory, etc.

In all these theories, the common denominator is that society is compared to a machine (mechanicism), an animal (organicism) or a logical-mathematical ideal (mathematicism).

6.1.2.3 *Specific educational science theories of the objectivist epistemological orientation.*

The epistemological consequences of problematising reality in this way are obvious. In the field of education, *specific theories* appear that relate very well to the above assumptions. For example, *behaviourism* and its derivations.

6.1.3 **The methodological procedures of the objectivist epistemological orientation.**

In order to construct new knowledge, the *objectivist* mainly performs the following intellectual operations: addition, multiplication, synthesis, deduction, definition, classification, etc.

6.1.4 **The technical strategies of the objectivist epistemological orientation.**

The *technical strategies* that an objectivist uses to get to know reality are mainly experimentation and documentation.

6.1.5 **The instruments of the objectivist epistemological orientation.**

The *instruments* to collect data from reality depend on the *technique* with which the phenomenon under study is contrasted. If the *technique* used is *observation*, the most suitable *instrument* to recover the data will be the *register*; if we use the *experiment*, the *instruments* we use to carry out the *experiment* will be the respective *elements* that will allow us to recover the data we need; if we use the *survey*, the appropriate *instruments* will be the *questionnaire* and/or the *interview*, and finally, if we use the *documentary technique*, the *instrument* that will allow us to collect the data we need will be the *work sheet*.

It can be stated that the main instruments that an objectivist can use to collect existing information on his object of study are the following: the elements and the worksheets.

It can be inferred that this type of research is what other authors call quantitative.

6.2 THE SUBJECTIVIST EPISTEMOLOGICAL ORIENTATION. The qualitative aspect in the reconstruction of educational reality.

An action is *subjectively* just if it is carried out in the conviction that it *is objectively* just. Knowledge is restricted to the *cognising subject* (to his sensory, affective and volitional states) and to external realities that can be inferred from *the subjective* states of the spirit. In axiological terms, moral and aesthetic values reflect the *subjective* feelings and reactions of the spirits, and do not have a character independent of these reactions; that is, moral judgements only reflect the emotions of approval or disapproval. In *epistemological* terms, this is a doctrine according to which every apprehended object is created, constructed by the *subject*. Sometimes also called *psychological idealism*, it is a *theory of knowledge* according to which the world exists only for the spirit. The only world that exists is the world we know, enclosed in the domain of ideas. To be is to perceive (Runes1998:353).

For the purposes of this research, it is necessary to characterise the *subjective* as an *epistemological orientation*, based on the elements that make it up; that is, the philosophical assumptions, from which each and every one of the main problems of knowledge are resolved; the theoretical foundations, with which the objects of study are problematised; the methodological procedures, with which new knowledge is generated; the technical strategies, with which reality is known; and the instruments, with which the information is collected.

6.2.1 *The philosophical assumptions of the subjectivist epistemological orientation*.

In order to know reality, from a *subjectivist* epistemological orientation, we mainly start from seven *philosophical assumptions* which, respectively, refer to the possibility, origin, essence, classification and truth criteria of knowledge.

Each and every one of the five main philosophical problems of knowledge is solved from the senses.

The *first philosophical assumption* from which one starts, from a *subjectivist* epistemological orientation, to know reality, consists in admitting that the subject cannot really apprehend the object, that knowledge is a problem because real contact between the subject and the object is not possible. It is claimed that there are no universally valid truths, that truth is limited to the subject who knows and judges; that a judgement is valid only for the individual subject who formulates it; and that, ultimately, man is the measure of all things. In this sense, it is conceded that there are truths only in relation to a given humanity; and that the circle of validity of truths coincides with the cultural and temporal circle from which their advocates come.

With regard to the *possibility of knowing*, in this epistemological orientation, *scepticism, subjectivism, relativism* and *pragmatism* predominate over dogmatism and criticism. This is because the philosophical problem of the possibility of knowing is solved from the senses.

The *second philosophical assumption* from which one starts, from the *subjectivist* epistemological orientation, in order to know the phenomena, refers to the fact of conceding that the main source of knowledge is in experience. It is admitted that the cognising consciousness draws its contents from experience; that the human spirit is by nature empty, a blank slate, a sheet of paper to be written and on which experience writes; that the soul experiences only sensations; and that ideas are copies of impressions derived from sensations.

As far as the problem of the *origin of knowledge is* concerned, the *subjectivist* epistemological orientation favours *empiricism* over rationalism. This is because the philosophical problem of the origin of knowledge is solved from the senses.

The *third philosophical assumption* from which one starts, from a *subjectivist* epistemological orientation, to know the facts, refers to the fact of considering that, in the relation of knowledge (independently of the ontological character of the subject and the object), the *subject* determines the object. The world of ideas, the set of principles of knowledge, is placed in the subject.

In relation to the *essence of knowledge*, in *pre-metaphysical* terms, in the *subjectivist* epistemological orientation, the *subject* predominates over the object. This is because the pre-metaphysical problem about the essence of knowledge is solved from the senses.

The *fourth philosophical assumption* from which the *subjectivist* epistemological orientation starts in order to carry out research concerns the circumstance that - when considering the ontological character of subject and object in the knowledge relationship - all objects are assumed to possess an ideal, i.e. mental, being.

In *metaphysical* terms, in the problem of the *essence of knowledge*, the *subjectivist* epistemological orientation privileges *idealism* over realism. This is because the metaphysical problem about the essence of knowledge is solved from the senses.

The *fifth philosophical assumption* from which we start, from a *subjectivist* epistemological orientation, to explain the phenomena, consists in that, in theological terms, for example, to consider that good and evil coexist in an eternal confrontation, until the first triumphs over the second; that is, God and man are separated, thanks to the fact that (in the case of Christianity) our first parents (Adam and Eve) were expelled from paradise; to which we will return by means of religion (to reconnect the disconnected).

In the problem of the *essence of knowledge*, in *theological solutions*, the *subjectivist* epistemological orientation favours the *dualistic and theistic* solution over the monistic and pantheistic one. This is because the theological problem of the essence of knowledge is solved from the senses.

The *sixth philosophical assumption* from which we start, from a *subjectivist* epistemological orientation, to analyse reality, is that we apprehend in an immediate way all that is given in external or internal experience; that is, in a sensible and spiritual way. It is said that we apprehend in an immediate, intuitive way, both what is immediately given, as well as the ultimate principles.

In the *types of knowledge*, the *subjectivist* epistemological orientation privileges *intuitive knowledge* over rational knowledge. This is because the problem about the classification of knowledge is solved from the senses.

The *seventh philosophical assumption* from which the *subjectivist* epistemological orientation starts, in order to explore reality, is that it is based on transcendent concepts and criteria of truth; that is, truth is understood as the concordance of thought with the object. It is thought that all judgements are true that rest on an immediate presence or reality of the object thought of (realism) and that, with respect to real objects, in the data of consciousness we possess an immediate certainty, an immediate presence or reality of an object.

In the problem of the *criteria of truth of knowledge*, the subjectivist epistemological orientation favours *transcendent concepts and criteria of truth*. This is because the problem about the concept and criteria of truth of knowledge is solved from the senses.

6.2.2 *The theoretical foundations of the subjectivist epistemological orientation*.

The *subjectivist* epistemological orientation is of historicist, evolutionist, phenomenological, hermeneutic, linguistic, etc. origin.

Its *precursors* are Aristotle and Hegel, among others.

The *sciences* that stand out in this *subjectivist* epistemological orientation are mainly anthropology, historiography and linguistics.

The *subjectivist* epistemological orientation is opposed to the objectivist one in its claim to consider *scientific* only those explanations that fit the model of formal (mathematical) and factual (natural, such as physics, biology, chemistry, etc.) sciences.

The most representative *theorists* of this subjectivist epistemological orientation are: Husserl, Weber, Dilthey, Alfred Schutz, G. Gadamer, P. Winch, G. W. Wrigth, etc.

Theoretically, the existence of the *human sciences* or *sciences of the spirit* is justified. In these sciences, the object of study is the human world, a product of the human spirit, something historically created by man. It is not possible to dissociate the researcher and the reality under investigation in the social sciences. A subject-object identity is observed, and the most appropriate level of knowledge to know is *understanding*, which allows us to grasp a meaningful, intentional world.

6.2.2.1 *General theories of knowledge of the subjectivist epistemological orientation*.

The *general theories of knowledge* that serve to problematise the objects of study, from a *subjectivist* epistemological orientation, are those of chaos and conflict; that is, the focus is on the subject, neglecting the object.

Chaos theory constructs its objects of study on the basis of categories such as turbulence, disorganisation, the unexpected, chance, chaos, disorder, crisis, mobility, myth, ritual, change, etc.

According to *chaos theory*, reality is turbulent, disorganised, unexpected. It is dominated by disorder, related, in a complex and mysterious way, to order, both of which are an enigma in all times and cultures.

Origin myths are said to express and ritualise a primordial order out of chaos. In traditional societies the masks of disorder are witchcraft, symbolisations and rituals, as well as political power strategies to convert dispersed forces into collective energy.

In the current era, Balandier (2003) points out that the most characteristic figures of disorder are phenomena such as stock market crises, epidemic diseases such as AIDS, the violence of terrorism and the weakness of political discourse that creates uncertainty and disorientation.

However, the social disorder that occurs in any time of crisis has a positive aspect, because it implies mobility and a change of models. This is why Georges Balandier pays special tribute to the movement, both energising and appeasing, in order to allay fears and warn against attempts to succumb to the confusing fear it generates. A basic philosophical principle of chaos theory is that of *generation* (subjectivism) not *creation* (objectivism). That is, "*...chaos is the enigma that comes from very distant times, when myths tried to show how all things come from and are the result of successive genesis...*" (Balandier, 2003: 9).

It is said that in nature nothing is linear (objective) or simple (naive). Order (objective) is hidden behind disorder (subjective), the random (relative) is always at work, the unpredictable (relative) must be understood. This is a different description of the world, in which the consideration of movement (relativism) and its fluctuations predominates over structures (dogma), organisations (objective), belongings, etc.

The great myths (dogmas) of the societies of tradition (modernity) give a total explanation (dogma), they affirm, they say what is and what must be (Manichaeism). Today's science no longer attempts to arrive at a fully explanatory (objective) view of the world, the view it produces is partial and provisional (subjective). It is confronted with an uncertain reality (relativism), with imprecise or mobile frontiers (subjectivism), it studies the play of the possible (relativism), it explores the complex, the unpredictable, the unprecedented. It no longer has the obsession of harmony (order), it gives great place to entropy (indifference) and disorder (chaos), and its argumentation progressively discovers its limitations.

6.2.2.2 *The particular social science theories of the subjectivist epistemological orientation.*

Two of the *particular theories of social science* that emerge from general theories of knowledge such as chaos, conflict and uncertainty are *historicism* (looking at reality in terms of movement, change, etc.) and dialectical historical materialism (looking at reality in terms of conflict, struggle, etc.).

6.2.2.3 *Specific educational science theories of the subjectivist epistemological orientation.*

The *specific theories of educational sciences*, which are developed from the general theories of knowledge and particular theories of the social sciences mentioned above, are mainly cognoscitivism (promoting socio-cultural and holistic development), psychogenetics (enhancing development and promoting moral and intellectual autonomy) and humanism.

6.2.3 *The methodological procedures of the subjectivist epistemological orientation.*

In order to generate new knowledge, from the *subjectivist* epistemological orientation, the following *methodological procedures* or intellectual operations are mainly carried out: subtraction, division, analysis, induction, comparison, etc.

6.2.4 *The technical strategies of the subjectivist epistemological orientation.*

The technical strategies most likely to be used by a subjectivist to learn about reality are observation and survey.

6.2.5 *The Instruments of the Subjectivist Epistemological Orientation*.

The instruments most likely to be used by a subjectivist to retrieve information about his or her object of study are: the register, questionnaire and interview.

It can be inferred that this type of research is what other authors call qualitative.

6.3 DIALECTICAL EPISTEMOLOGICAL ORIENTATION. The quantitative-qualitative in the construction of educational reality.

In epistemological terms, according to Gutiérrez (2000:9) there is an attempt to overcome the univocism (objectivism) and equivocism (subjectivism) in which today's thinking is stranded. On the one hand, the univocity (objectivism) in the positivism and scientism of modernity; on the other hand, the equivocity (subjectivism) in many areas of so-called postmodern thinking.

It is said that, to overcome this impasse, Beauchot proposed a way out: neither univocity (objectivism) nor equivocity (subjectivism), but *analogy* (objectivism-subjectivism or dialogue). A tradition that dates back to the Greeks and was picked up in the Middle Ages, and which was not well understood either by modernity (univocity) or by post-modernity (equivocality).

It is a question of balancing, of mediating, between univocity (objectivism) and equivocity (subjectivism), although the latter, the difference, predominates.

According to Beauchot (Gutiérrez, 2000:12-18) *analogy* is understood as a mode of predication and signification between univocal terms (those which are attributed to their inferiors or signifies them, in a completely equal way, e.g. "man", predicated of all human individuals) (objectivism) and equivocal (they are attributed to their inferiors in a completely different way, e.g. "bear", which can be predicated of the animal and of the constellation) (subjective); on the other hand, an analogical term is attributed to its inferiors in partly the same and partly different ways, e.g. "healthy" can be predicated of the organism, of food, of medicine and of urine, since it is predicated of the organism primarily as of the subject of health, of food as of that which preserves it, of medicine as of that which restores it and of urine as of that which is its effect or manifests it (dialogue).

It is a matter of uniting the finite (dogmatism) and the infinite (scepticism), the union of opposites, a fundamental hermeneutic principle. In this way it is possible to reduce the dichotomies of the religious and the secular, the sacred and the profane, the symbolic and the literal, reality and ideality, etc.

The intervention of *analogy*, which is proportional, requires *dialogical* intervention, which is intersubjective; but it also involves the subject. Within the dialogue there is individual reflection, which makes the dialogue itself possible; seen as a sharing of what each one reflects from himself and in contact with others; thus, the reflection that is influenced by the dialogue also influences it. This reflection leads to abstraction, to universalisation, and leads to what is presented dialogically as a hypothesis to be tested in the inter-subjective debate.

According to Beauchot (2000), it is a matter of finding what is similar in things (objectivism), without forgetting that what is different, diversity, predominates (subjectivism); respecting differences without renouncing the similarity that makes it possible to achieve some universalisation (dialogue between the subject and the object).

In this sense, an action is objectively and subjectively just if, on the one hand, it is what the agent must (objectively) do and really wants (subjectively) to do, with wanting (subjective) predominating over duty (objective), but without neglecting a certain degree of universality (objective) with respect to what the majority understands as just (dialogic).

6.3.1 *The philosophical assumptions of the dialectical epistemological orientation.*

In order to know reality, from the *dialectical* epistemological orientation, we mainly start from seven *philosophical assumptions* that, respectively, refer to the possibility, origin, essence, classification and truth criteria of knowledge.

Each and every one of the five main philosophical problems of knowledge is solved from the senses and reason; privileging the former over the latter or vice versa.

The *first philosophical assumption* from which we start from a *dialectical* epistemological orientation to know reality, refers to the fact that the subject knows what he wants to know about the object, but according to the consensus with the other subjects; that is to say, in a *dialogical* way.

In the *dialectical* epistemological orientation, dogma is combined with the exception, privileging the exception, which leads us to a certain subjectivism, relativism, pragmatism and criticism, on the *possibility of knowledge*. This is because the problem about the possibility of knowledge is solved from the senses and reason or vice versa (criticism).

The *second philosophical assumption* from which one starts, from a *dialectical* epistemological orientation, to carry out research, consists of the opinion that, in order to know phenomena, both reason (rationalism) and experience (empiricism) are used, privileging experience over reason (*intellectualism*) or reason over experience (apriorism).

In the *dialectical* epistemological orientation, intellectualism or apriorism is privileged with respect to the *origin of knowledge*. This is because the problem of the origin of knowledge is solved from the senses and reason or vice versa (intellectualism or apriorism).

The *third philosophical assumption* from which one starts from a *dialectical* epistemological orientation, in order to know reality, consists in conceding that, in the relation of knowledge, the subject and the object mutually determine each other, with the subject prevailing over the object or vice versa.

In the *dialectical* epistemological orientation - *with respect* to the *pre-metaphysical solution to the problem of the essence of knowledge* - the dialogue between subject and object is privileged, with the former taking precedence over the latter or vice versa. This is because the pre-metaphysical problem of the essence of knowledge is solved from the senses and reason or vice versa (dialectic).

The *fourth philosophical assumption* from which one starts from a *dialectical* epistemological orientation, in order to know reality, consists in conceding that reality exists by itself, independently of thought; but that, nevertheless, objects possess a mental ideal being, which can be apprehended by subjects; this in a phenomenological way, that is, a certain universality (objectivism) can be reached in the subjective apprehension of reality.

In the *dialectical* epistemological orientation - *in* relation to the *metaphysical solution to the problem of the essence of knowledge* - the dialogue between reality and thought is privileged, privileging the former over the latter or vice versa. This is because the metaphysical problem of the essence of knowledge is solved from the senses and reason or vice versa (dialectic).

The *fifth philosophical assumption* from which one starts from a *dialectical* epistemological orientation, in order to know reality, consists in presuming that the divinity is the common source of thought and being, of the transcendent absolute, however, subject and object, thought and being, consciousness and things, are absorbed in a unity, in an immanent absolute.

In the *dialectical* epistemological orientation - *in* the *theological solution to the problem of the essence of knowledge* - monism and pantheism *are* privileged. This is because the theological problem of the essence of knowledge is solved from the senses and reason or vice versa (dialectic).

The *sixth philosophical assumption* from which one starts, from a *dialectical* epistemological orientation, to know reality, consists in conceding that knowledge is understood in terms of a spiritual apprehension of an object that is given in an immediate and discursive way; that is, everything given in internal or external experience is apprehended in an immediate way, in a sensible and spiritual way, in an intuitive way, both what is immediately given and the last principles, as well as in a rational, mediate and discursive way.

In the *dialectical* epistemological orientation, both intuitive and rational knowledge are privileged in the problem of the *types of knowledge*. This is because the problem about the classification of knowledge is solved from the senses and reason or vice versa (dialectic).

The *seventh philosophical assumption* from which one starts from a *dialectical* epistemological orientation, in order to know reality, consists in conjecturing that a judgement is true both when the thought agrees with itself and when it agrees with the object thought of; That is to say, all judgements are true both when they rest on an immediate presence or reality of the object thought (realism) and when they are formed in accordance with the laws and norms of thought (idealism); that is to say, with respect to real objects, in the data of consciousness we possess an immediate certainty of the objects and, with respect to mental objects, truth is something formal, which coincides with the correctness of thought.

In the *dialectical* epistemological orientation, both *concepts* and *transcendent* and *immanent criteria of truth* are privileged. This is because the problem about the concept and criteria of truth of knowledge is solved from the senses and reason or vice versa (dialectic).

6.3.2 *The theoretical foundations of the dialectical epistemological orientation*.

The dialectical epistemological orientation of *multidisciplinary* origin. It shifts from physics to life sciences and society.

6.3.2.1 *General theories of knowledge of the dialectical epistemological orientation.*

The main general theories of knowledge, from which objects of study can be problematised from a dialectical epistemological orientation, are analogy and complexity. These were mentioned in previous chapters.

6.3.2.2 *The particular social science theories of the dialectical epistemological orientation.*

The main particular theories of the social sciences, from which objects of study can be problematised from a dialectical epistemological orientation, are phenomenology and critical hermeneutics. These were mentioned in previous chapters.

6.3.2.3 *The specific theories of educational sciences of the dialectical epistemological orientation.*

The main theories specific to the educational sciences, from which objects of study can be problematised from a dialectical epistemological orientation, are genetic theory (Piaget) and socio-cultural theory (Vigotsky). These were mentioned in previous chapters.

6.3.3 *The methodological procedures of the dialectical epistemological orientation.*

In order to generate new knowledge, from the *dialectical* epistemological orientation, we induce-deduce, analyse-synthesise, etc.

6.3.4 The *technical strategies of the dialectical epistemological orientation.*

The *technical strategies* that, from the *dialectical* epistemological orientation, can be used to learn about reality are mainly observation, experimentation, survey and documentation. Here, the difference with the objectivist and subjectivist epistemological orientations is one of degree; that is to say, it depends on the explanatory, interpretative or explanatory-interpretative-comprehensive scope that, respectively, one wishes to give to the selected technique.

6.3.5The *instruments of the dialectical epistemological orientation.*

The instruments that, from the *dialectical* epistemological orientation, can be used to gather data are mainly the elements, the work sheet, the register, the interview and the survey. Here, the difference with the objectivist and subjectivist epistemological orientations is one of degree, i.e. it depends on the explanatory, interpretative or explanatory-interpretative-comprehensive scope that, respectively, the selected instrument is intended to have.

The difference with the objectivist and subjectivist epistemological orientations in terms of techniques - and their respective *instruments* - depends on the scope of the research. The subjectivist's observation is *qualitative,* the objectivist's is quantitative (qualities and data are recorded, respectively) and the dialectician's is *quantitative-qualitative.*

Finally, it can be inferred that this type of research is what other authors call mixed (quantitative-qualitative).

6.4 SUMMARY OF THE CHAPTER.

By way of summary, the following table shows graphically the philosophical assumptions, theoretical foundations, methodological procedures, technical strategies and instruments used to carry out research from each and every one of the epistemological orientations analysed in this chapter:

<table>
<tr><td rowspan="21" style="writing-mode:vertical-lr">EPISTEMOLOGICAL ORIENTATIONS</td><td rowspan="21" style="writing-mode:vertical-lr">I OBJECTIVE</td><td rowspan="10">1.1 PROBLEMS FROM KNOWLEDGE TO</td><td colspan="2">POSSIBILITY</td><td></td><td>DOGMATISM</td></tr>
<tr><td colspan="2">ORIGIN</td><td></td><td>RATIONALISM</td></tr>
<tr><td rowspan="4" style="writing-mode:vertical-lr">ESSENCE</td><td>SOLUTION PRE METAPHYSICS</td><td></td><td>OBJECTIVISM</td></tr>
<tr><td>SOLUTION META-PHYSICS</td><td></td><td>IDEALISM</td></tr>
<tr><td>SOLUTION THEOLOGICAL</td><td></td><td>DUALISM</td></tr>
<tr><td colspan="2">CLASSIFICATION</td><td rowspan="2" style="writing-mode:vertical-lr">SOLUTIONS</td><td>RATIONAL</td></tr>
<tr><td colspan="2">CONCEPT AND CRITERION OF TRUTH</td><td>IMMANENT</td></tr>
<tr><td rowspan="3">1.2 FUNDAMENTOS THEORISTS</td><td colspan="2">GENERAL THEORIES OF KNOWLEDGE</td><td>MATHEMATICISM, MECHANICISM AND ORGANICISM</td></tr>
<tr><td colspan="2">PARTICULAR THEORIES OF LAS C. S.</td><td>POSITIVISM, FUNCTIONALISM, STRUCTURALISM AND SYSTEMS</td></tr>
<tr><td colspan="2">SPECIFIC THEORIES OF EDUCATION SCIENCE.</td><td>CONDUCTISM</td></tr>
<tr><td colspan="3">1.3 PROCEDURES METHODOLOGICAL</td><td>ADDITION, MULTIPLICATION, DEDUCTION, SYNTHESIS, CLASSIFICATION, DEFINITION</td></tr>
<tr><td colspan="3">1.4 TECHNICAL STRATEGIES</td><td>EXPERIMENTATION, DOCUMENTARY</td></tr>
<tr><td colspan="3">1.5 INSTRUMENTS</td><td>ELEMENTS, WORKSHEETS</td></tr>
</table>

	2.1 PROBLEMS OF KNOWLEDGE TO	POSSIBILITY			SCEPTICISM, SUBJECTIVISM, RELATIVISM, PREGMATISM
II SUBOBJECTIVE		ORIGIN			EMPIRISM
		ESSENCE	SOLUTION PREMETAPHYSICS		SUBJECTIVISM
			SOLUTION METAPHYSICS		REALISM
			SOLUTION THEOLOGICAL		DUALISM
		CLASSIFICATION		**SOLUTIONS**	INTUITIVE
		CONCEPT AND CRITERION OF TRUTH			TRASCENDENT
	2.2 FUNDAMENTOS THEORISTS	**GENERAL THEORIES OF KNOWLEDGE**			CHAOS, CONFLICT
		PARTICULAR THEORIES OF LAS C. S.			HISTORICISM, MATERIALISM HISTORICAL-DIALECTICAL
		SPECIFIC THEORIES OF EDUCATION SCIENCE.			PSYCHOANALYSIS, HUMANISM, COGNOSCITIVISM
	2. 3PROCEDURES METHODOLOGICAL				**SUBTRACTION, DIVISION, INDUCTION, ANALYSIS, COMPARISON**
	2.4 TECHNICAL STRATEGIES				**OBSERVATION, SURVEY**
	2.5 INSTRUMENTS				**REGISTRATION, QUESTIONNAIRE, INTERVIEW**
III. DIALECTICS	3.1 KNOWLEDGE PROBLEMS	POSSIBILITY			CRITICISM
		ORIGIN			INTELLECTUALISM, APRIORISM
		ESSENCE	SOLUTION PREMETAPHYSICS		DIALECTICS
			SOLUTION METAPHYSICS		PHENOMENOLOGY
			SOLUTION THEOLOGICAL		MONISM AND PANTHEISM
		CLASSIFICATION		**SOLUTIONS**	MIXED (INTUITIVE-RATIONAL)
		CONCEPT AND CRITERION OF TRUTH			MIXED (TRANSCENDENT-IMMANENT

3.2 FUNDAMENT OS THEORISTS	GENERAL THEORIES OF KNOWLEDGE	ANALOGY, COMPLEXITY
	PARTICULAR THEORIES OF LAS C. S.	PHENOMENOLOGY, HERMENEUTICS CRITICS
	SPECIFIC THEORIES OF EDUCATION SCIENCES.	GENETIC THEORY (PIAGET), SOCIO-CULTURAL THEORY (VOGOTSKY)
3.3 PROCEDURES METHODOLOGICAL		INDUCTIVE-DEDUCTIVE, ANALYTICAL-SYNTHETIC
3.4 TECHNICAL STRATEGIES		ALL
3.5 INSTRUMENTS		ALL

CONCLUSIONS
GENERAL CONCLUSIONS

Epistemology is a branch of philosophy that deals with the problem of knowledge; the knowledge of knowledge.

Knowledge, understood as a process, is a problem because when human beings seek to know reality, they leave the ontological sphere and move into the psychological sphere, in relation to the object they seek to know; and, in doing so, they are separated from the object.

It is impossible for the cognising subject to penetrate the sphere of the object to be known. It is impossible to know reality in essence, what reality is. The educational researcher will have to be content with *assuming* the definition, characteristics, elements, function, purpose, classification, etc., of his research problem.

The main *problems* of knowledge, understood as a process, are philosophical, theoretical, methodological, technical and instrumental.

Each and every one of the five problems of knowledge mentioned above is solved by the cognising subject with his reason, his senses or both qualities.

An epistemological orientation consists of the way in which the researcher orients himself/herself in the knowledge process.

The *elements* of an epistemological orientation are the philosophical assumptions, from which each and every one of the five philosophical problems of knowledge are resolved; the theoretical foundations, with which reality is problematised; the methodological procedures, to generate new knowledge; the technical strategies, to learn about reality; and the instruments, to gather information.

In any educational research process, the above dimensions are determined reciprocally, in a top-down and bottom-up manner: the *philosophical* assumptions determine the *theoretical* foundations; the theoretical foundations define the *methodological* procedures; the methodological procedures decide the *technical* strategies; and the technical strategies determine the *instruments*; and vice versa.

When there is no congruence between these five dimensions of research, the study is said to lack methodological rigidity; it seems more correct to say that it lacks epistemological coherence.

An epistemological orientation is mainly *characterised* by the fact that the researcher takes a stance on the problem of knowledge; he (the researcher) will have to decide from which philosophical assumptions he intends to observe reality, with which theories he will problematise his object of study, which methodological procedure he will use to generate the new knowledge, with which technical strategy he will learn about reality and, finally, which instrument or instruments he will use to gather the information he needs to construct his object of study.

The choice of the above elements allows the educational researcher to place himself in any of the three epistemological possibilities to carry out his work; he can choose between the objectivist, subjectivist or dialectical epistemological orientations.

Since the aforementioned elements are of different natures and constitute a position on the problem of knowledge, it is not possible to define a single epistemological orientation for conducting research in the educational sciences; everything will depend on the object of study and the epistemological and ontological inclinations of the researcher.

BIBLIOGRAPHY

1. Abruch Linder, Miguel (S/F). *Metodología de las ciencias sociales*. UNAM. Mexico.

2. Anguera, María Teresa (1997). *Metodología de la observación en las ciencias humanas*. Cátedra. Spain.

3. Aristotle (A) (1992). *Metaphysics*. Porrúa (Col. "Sepan Cuántos...", no. 120), Mexico.

4. Aristotle (B) (1993). *Treatises on Logic*. Porrúa (Col. "Sepan Cuántos...", no. 124), Mexico.

5. Arntz, William et al. (2003): *What about you?* Kiev. Argentina.

6. Bacon, Francis (1991). *NovumOrganum*. Porrúa (Col. "Sepan cuantos...", núm.293). Mexico.

7. Balandier, Georges (2003). *El desorden*. Gedisa. Barcelona.

8. Beauchot, Mauricio (2000). *Treatise on analogical hermeneutics*. Itaca. México.

9. Bisquerra, Rafael (2000). *Métodos de investigación educativa*. Ediciones ceac. Spain.

10. Blauberg I, P. Kopnin and I. Pantin (1983). *Brief philosophical dictionary*. Carthage. Mexico.

11. Bosch García, Carlos (1982) *La técnica de investigación documental*. UNAM. México.

12. Briones, Guillermo (2008). *Métodos y técnicas de investigación para las ciencias sociales*. Trillas. Mexico.

13. Brom, Juan (1975). *To understand history*. Nuestro tiempo. México.

14. Bunge, Mario (1970). *La ciencia, su método y su filosofía*. Ediciones Quinto Sol. México.

15. Bunge, Mario (1992). *La investigación científica*. Ariel. México.

16. Cásares Hernández, Laura and others (2008). *Técnicas actuales de investigación documental*. Trillas. México.

17. Cicero (1993). *Los Oficios y los Deberes*. Porrúa (Col. "Sepan Cuántos...", no. 230). Mexico.

18. Chalmers F. Alan (1999), *What is this thing called science?* Siglo XXI. Mexico.

19. Comte, Auguste (1997). *La Filosofía Positiva*. Porrúa (Col. "Sepan Cuántos...", no. 340). Mexico.

20. Descartes (A) (1981). *Discurso del método*. Porrúa (Col. "Sepan Cuántos...", núm. 177), Mexico.

21. Descartes (B) (1981). *Meditaciones Metafísicas*. Porrúa (Col. "Sepan Cuántos...", no. 177). Mexico.

22. Dieterich Steffan, Heinz (2003). *New guide to scientific research*. Ariel. Mexico.

23. Dilthey, Wilhelm (1978). *Introduction to the sciences of the spirit*. F. C. E. Mexico.

24. Durkheim, Emile (2000). *The rules of sociological method*. Ediciones Coyoacán. Mexico.

25. Durkheim, Emile (2000). *Education and sociology*. Colofón. Mexico.
26. Duverger, Maurice (1999). *Métodos de las ciencias sociales*. Ariel. Mexico.
27. Freire, Pablo (1982). *La educación como práctica de la libertad*. Siglo XXI. Mexico.
28. Gaarder, Jostein (2001). *Sophie's World*. A Novel about the History of Philosophy. Patria / Siruela. Mexico.
29. Gadamer, Hans-Georg (1977). *Truth and Method I*. Sígueme. Spain.
30. Galindo Cásares, Luis Jesús (1998) *Técnicas de investigación en sociedad, cultura y comunicación*. Pearson. México.
31. García Ferrando, Manuel, Jesús Ibañez and Francisco Alvira (1986). *El análisis de la realidad social. Métodos y técnicas de investigación*. Alianza Universidad Textos. Madrid.
32. García, Rolando (2000). *El conocimiento en construcción*. Gedisa. Spain.
33. G. W. F., Hegel (A) (1997). *Encyclopaedia of Philosophical Sciences*. Porrúa (Col. "Sepan Cuántos...", no. 187). Mexico.
34. G. W., F. Hegel (1993). *Phenomenology of Spirit*. F. C. E. Mexico.
35. Gibsons et al (1997). *La nueva producción del conocimiento*. Pomares. Barcelona.
36. Grawitz, Madeleine (1984). *Methods and techniques in the social sciences*. Mexico.
37. Gutiérrez Pantoja, Gabriel (A) (1984). *Metodología de las Ciencias Sociales I*. Harla. Mexico.
38. Gutiérrez Pantoja, Gabriel (B) (2007). "*Course on Law and Methodology of the Social Sciences*". 26 May to 1 June 2007. UAEM. Faculty of Law. Toluca.
39. Gutiérrez Robles, Alejandro (2000). *Analogical hermeneutics: towards a new order of rationality*. Universidad Intercontinental. Mexico.
40. Gutiérrez Saenz,Raúl (1987). *Historia de las Doctrinas Filosóficas*. Esfinge. Mexico.
41. Gutiérrez Saenz,Raúl (2005). *Introducción a la lógica*. Esfinge. Mexico.
42. Heidegger, Martín (1993). *Being and Time*. F. C. E. Mexico.
43. Hessen, Juan (1999). *Theory of Knowledge*. Porrúa (Col. "SepanCuantos ...", num. 351). Mexico.
44. Hobbes, Thomas (2003). *Leviathan*. F. C. E. Mexico.
45. Hume, David (1992). *Treatise on Human Nature*. Porrúa (Col. " Sepan Cuántos...", no. 326). Mexico.
46. Husserl, Edmund (1995). *Ideas relative a una fenomenología pura y una filosofía fenomenológica*. F. C. E. Mexico
47. Imre, Lakatos (2001). *History of science*. Techno. Spain.
48. Imre, Lakatos (2002). *Philosophical writings*. Alianza. Spain.
49. Johann Gottlieb, Fichte (1994). *The Destiny of Man*. Porrúa (Col. "Sepan Cuántos...", no. 641). Mexico.
50. Kant (1996). *Critique of Pure Reason*. Porrúa (Col. "Sepan Cuántos...", no. 203). Mexico.
51. Kant (1994. *Philosophy of history*. FCE. Mexico.
52. Kart R., Popper (1999). *La lógica de la investigación científica*. Tecnos. Spain.

53. Kuhn T., S (1999). *The Structure of Scientific Revolutions*. F. C. E. (Breviarios). Mexico.

54. Larroyo, Francisco (1978). *Historia y Sistema de las Doctrinas Filosóficas*. Porrúa. Mexico.

55. Leibniz (A) (1991). *New Treatise on Human Understanding*. Porrúa (Col. "Sepan Cuántos...", núm. 321). Mexico.

56. Leibniz (B) (1991). *Monadología*. Porrúa (Col. "Sepan Cuántos...", núm. 321). Mexico.

57. Locke, John (1994). *Essay on Human Understanding* (volume I) Gernika. Mexico.

58. Magee, Bryan (1994). *Popper*. Colofón. Mexico.

59. Mayntz Renate, Kurt Holm and Peter Hubner (1980). *Introduction to the methods of empirical sociology. Alianza Editorial. Spain.*

60. Mardones José, M. (2003).*Filosofía de las ciencias humanas y sociales*. Anthropos. España.

61. Melich, Joan-Charles (1961). *Antropología simbólica y acción educativa*. Paidós. Barcelona.

62. Mendoza Navarro, Alfonso (1997). *Filosofía Jurídica*. Notas del Curso impartido en el Primer Semestre de la Maestría en Derecho, Grupo Piloto. Faculty of Law. UAEM. Toluca.

63. Mercado Maldonado, Asael (1997). *Sociología norteamericana: Un diagnóstico de nuestro tiempo*. U. A. E. M. Research Centre in Social Sciences and Humanities. Toluca.

64. Messer, Augusto (1999). *El Realismo Crítico*. Porrúa (Col. "Sepan Cuántos...", no. 351). Mexico.

65. Migueles, Roberto (1977). *Epistemología y ciencias sociales y humanas*. UNAM. México.

66. Montesquieu (1997). *The spirit of the laws*. Porrúa (Col. "Sepan Cuántos...", no. 191). Mexico.

67. Morín, Edgar (A) (2001). *Los siete saberes necesarios para la educación del futuro*. UNESCO. Mexico.

68. Morín, Edgar (B) (2001).*Introducción al pensamiento complejo*. Gedisa. Spain.

69. Munch, Lourdes and Ernesto Ángeles (2003). *Métodos y técnicas de investigación*. Trillas. Mexico.

70. Muñoz, Jacobo and Julián Velarde (2000). *Compendium of epistemology*. Trota. Madrid.

71. Nietzsche, Frederick (1976). *Beyond Good and Evil*. Editores Unidos Mexicanos, S. A., (Col. Obras de Federico Nietzsche). Mexico.

72. UN. WORLD DECLARATION ON HIGHER EDUCATION IN THE 21ST CENTURY. VISION AND ACTION.

73. Ortiz Uribe, Frida Gisela (2003). Mexico. *Diccionario de metodología de la investigación científica*. Limusa.

74. Pick, Susan and Ana Luisa López Velasco de Faubert (2007). *Cómo investigar en ciencias sociales*. Trillas. Mexico.

75. Plato (A) (1998). *Dialogues*. Porrúa (Col. "Sepan Cuantos...", núm. 13). Mexico.

76. Plato (B) (1991).*The Laws*. Porrúa (Col. "Sepan Cuántos...", núm. 139). Mexico.

77. Ponce, Anibal (1993). *Educación y lucha de clases*. Editores unidos mexicanos. Mexico.

78. Reyes Parra, Juvencio (1983). *Matemática explicada*. Ediciones Mucar. Mexico.

79. Rojas Soriano, Raúl (1985). *Guía para realizar investigaciones sociales*. UNAM. Mexico.

80. Runes, Dagoberto D. (1998). *Diccionario de filosofía*. Grijalbo. Mexico.

81. Saint Augustine (1994). *The City of God*. Porrúa (Col. "Sepan Cuántos...", núm. 59). Mexico.

82. Sandoval, Edgar (2006). *Semiotics, logic and knowledge. Homage to Charles Sanders Peirce*. UACM. México.

83. Schopenhauer, Arthur (1997). *The World as Will and Representation*. Porrúa (Col. "Sepan Cuántos...", no. 419). Mexico.

84. Schutz, Alfred (1974). *The problem of social reality*. Amorrortu. Argentina.

85. Schutz, Alfred (1977). *The structures of the lifeworld*. Amorrortu. Argentina.

86. Schwarts, Howard and Jerry Jacobs (1996). *Qualitative Sociology. Method for the reconstruction of reality*. Trillas. Mexico.

87. Seneca (1999). *Philosophical Treatises*. Porrúa (Col. "Sepan Cuántos...", no. 281). Mexico.

88. Sierra Bravo, Restituto (2001). *Técnicas de investigación social*. Paraninfo. Spain.

89. Sierra Bravo, Restituto (1984). *Ciencias sociales. Epistemología, lógica y metodología*. Paraninfo. Spain.

90. Spinoza (1990). *Ética*. Porrúa (Col. "Sepan Cuántos...", no. 319), Mexico.

91. Tamayo y Tamayo, Mario (1982). *El proceso de la investigación científica*. Limusa. Mexico.

92. Thomas Aquinas (1991). *Summa Contra los Gentiles*. Porrúa (Col. "Sepan Cuántos...", no. 317). Mexico.

93. UAEM (1999). *Interdisciplinary University*. Editorial Emahaia. Toluca, Mexico.

94. Von Wriht, G. H. (1979). *Explanation and understanding*. Alianza. Madrid.

95. Weber, M. (A) (1969). *Economy and society*. F. C. E. Mexico.

96. Weber, M. (B) (1971). *On the theory of social science*. Península. Spain.

97. Wilhelm, Dilthey (1978) *Introducción a las ciencias del espíritu*. F. C. E. Mexico.

98. Winch, P. (1972). *Social science and philosophy*. Amorrortu. Argentina.

99. W. M. Jackson, Inc. publishers (1983). *Hispanic lexical dictionary*. Mexico.

Buy your books fast and straightforward online - at one of world's fastest growing online book stores! Environmentally sound due to Print-on-Demand technologies.

Buy your books online at
www.morebooks.shop

Kaufen Sie Ihre Bücher schnell und unkompliziert online – auf einer der am schnellsten wachsenden Buchhandelsplattformen weltweit! Dank Print-On-Demand umwelt- und ressourcenschonend produzi ert.

Bücher schneller online kaufen
www.morebooks.shop